THE PEOPLE OF QUITO, 1690–1810

Dellplain Latin American Studies

No. 10 *Tierra Adentro: Settlement and Society in Colonial Durango*, Michael M. Swann

No. 11 *Andean Reflections: Letters from Carl O. Sauer While on a South American Trip Under a Grant from the Rockefeller Foundation, 1942*, edited by Robert C. West

No. 12 *Credit and Socioeconomic Change in Colonial Mexico: Loans and Mortgages in Guadalajara, 1720–1820*, Linda Greenow

No. 13 *Once Beneath the Forest: Prehistoric Terracing in the Río Bec Region of the Maya Lowlands*, B. L. Turner, II

No. 14 *Marriage and Fertility in Chile: Demographic Turning Points in the Petorca Valley, 1840–1976*, Robert McCaa

No. 15 *The Spatial Organization of New Land Settlement in Latin America*, Jacob O. Maos

No. 16 *The Anglo-Argentine Connection, 1900–1939*, Roger Gravil

No. 17 *Costa Rica: A Geographical Interpretation in Historical Perspective*, Carolyn Hall

No. 18 *Household Economy and Urban Development: São Paulo, 1765–1836*, Elizabeth Anne Kuznesof

No. 19 *Irrigation in the Bajío Region of Colonial Mexico*, Michael E. Murphy

No. 20 *The Cost of Conquest: Indian Decline in Honduras Under Spanish Rule*, Linda Newson

No. 21 *Petty Capitalism in Spanish America: The Pulperos of Puebla, Mexico City, Caracas, and Buenos Aires*, Jay Kinsbruner

No. 22 *British Merchants and Chilean Development, 1851–1886*, John Mayo

No. 23 *Hispanic Lands and Peoples: Selected Writings of James J. Parsons*, edited by William M. Denevan

No. 24 *Migrants in the Mexican North: Mobility, Economy, and Society in a Colonial World*, Michael M. Swann

No. 25 *Puebla de los Angeles, Industry and Society in a Mexican City, 1700–1850*, Guy P. C. Thomson

No. 26 *Generations of Settlers: Rural Households and Markets on the Costa Rican Frontier, 1850–1935*, Mario Samper

No. 27 *Andean Ecology: Adaptive Dynamics in Ecuador*, Gregory Knapp

No. 28 *Disease and Death in Early Colonial Mexico: Simulating Amerindian Depopulation*, Thomas Whitmore

No. 29 *Veracruz Merchants, 1770–1829: A Mercantile Elite in Late Bourbon and Early Independent Mexico*, Jackie R. Booker

No. 30 *Laricollaguas: Ecology, Economy, and Demography in a Seventeenth-Century Peruvian Village*, David J. Robinson

No. 31 *Encomienda Politics in Early Colonial Guatemala, 1524–1544: Dividing the Spoils*, Wendy Kramer

Dellplain Latin American Studies

PUBLISHED IN COOPERATION WITH
THE DEPARTMENT OF GEOGRAPHY
SYRACUSE UNIVERSITY

Editor

David J. Robinson

Editorial Advisory Committee

John K. Chance
Arizona State University

William M. Denevan
University of Wisconsin

John E. Kicza
Washington State University

Asunción Lavrin
Howard University

W. George Lovell
Queen's University

Publication Design and Cartography

Marcia J. Harrington
Syracuse University

THE PEOPLE OF QUITO, 1690–1810
CHANGE AND UNREST IN THE UNDERCLASS

Martin Minchom

Dellplain Latin American Studies, No. 32

Westview Press
BOULDER • SAN FRANCISCO • OXFORD

Dellplain Latin American Studies

This Westview softcover edition is printed on acid-free paper and bound in library-quality, coated covers that carry the highest rating of the National Association of State Textbook Administrators, in consultation with the Association of American Publishers and the Book Manufacturers' Institute.

All rights reserved. No part of this publication may be reproduced or transmitted in any form or by any means, electronic or mechanical, including photocopy, recording, or any information storage and retrieval system, without permission in writing from the publisher.

Copyright © 1994 by the Department of Geography, Syracuse University

Published in the United States of America by Westview Press, Inc., 5500 Central Avenue, Boulder, Colorado 80301-2877, and in the United Kingdom by Westview Press, 36 Lonsdale Road, Summertown, Oxford OX2 7EW

A CIP catalog record for this book is available from the Library of Congress.
ISBN 0-8133-8831-7

Printed and bound in the United States of America

∞ The paper used in this publication meets the requirements of the American National Standard for Permanence of Paper for Printed Library Materials Z39.48-1984.

10   9   8   7   6   5   4   3   2   1

Contents

List of Tables ix
List of Figures xi
List of Abbreviations xiii
Preface and Acknowledgments xv

1 Introduction 1

PART I: STRUCTURES AND CONTINUITIES

2 The Organization of Urban Space 17
   The Urban Environment 17
   The Commons, the Corregimiento and Rural Hinterland 33

3 The Social Formation of Colonial Quito, 1534–1720 49
   The Socio-racial Matrix, 1534–1600 51
   Quito and the Textile Economy, 1600–1800 64
   Economic Readjustment, 1690–1720 68

4 Artisan and Confraternity: The Socio-economic Role of the Church 75
   The Socio-economic Role of the Church 75
   Annual Communion and Religious Compliance 79
   Religious and Artisanal Forms of Association:
      The Smiths, Barbers, and Weavers 82
   Conclusion: The Church and Social Hierarchy 94

PART II: THE POPULAR DIMENSION OF EIGHTEENTH-CENTURY FISCAL REFORM AND ECONOMIC CHANGE

5 The Informal Economy: The Urban Marketplace and the
   Petty Traders 101
   The Dual Economy: Preliminary Considerations 101
   The *Pulperías,* the Petty Traders and the Urban Market
      (Sixteenth and Seventeenth Centuries) 103
   Urban Commercial Activity and Economic Change in the Eighteenth Century 109

6 Demographic Change and Social Structure 117
   The Sources 117
   Parish Demographics to 1780 125
   Demographic Change After 1780 129
   Urban Decline and Urban-Rural Contrasts 137

7 Socio-racial Status and Mobility: The Declarations of Mestizo 153
   Sources and Possibilities of the Declarations of Mestizo 153
   Declarations of Mestizo Sought in Quito and the Audiencia of Quito,
      1686–1800 158
   The Language of Race: A Discussion of Socio-racial Terminology 170
   "Vile and Mechanical Offices" 183
   "Indians Dressed as Spaniards": The Urban Center as an Agent of Acculturation 189

    A Parallel Life: The Ethnic Background of Eugenio de Santa Cruz y Espejo 191
    Conclusion: The Indian/White Dichotomy in Ethnic Classification 198

8 Religious Riots and Civil Disturbances 201
    Traditions of Popular Protest 203
    The Barrios and Social Order: The Franciscan Disturbances and the Parish of
       San Roque, 1719–1765 210
    The Impact of the Bourbon Reforms and the 1765 Rebellion 222
    The Political Landscape After 1765: Reaction and Conspiracies 233
    The Quito Revolts of 1809–1810 241
    Conclusion 253

9 Conclusions 257

Glossary 265
Bibliography 271
Index 295

Tables

2.1	Urban-Rural Characteristics of the Parishes of Quito in the Early Nineteenth Century	32
3.1	Baptisms of Children of Indian Artisans, 1596	54
3.2	Place of Origin of Indian Parents, 1596, 1612	57
4.1	Sixteenth-Century Confraternities in Quito	84
5.1	Composiciones of Pulperos of Quito, 1642	106
5.2	Alcabala Income in the Royal Treasury of Quito, 1751–1800	115
6.1	Major Epidemics: The City of Quito, 1690–1820	130
6.2	Deaths in El Sagrario in the Epidemic of 1785	132
6.3	The Population of the City of Quito, 1670–1814	135
6.4	Quito and the Corregimiento: Population Estimates Provided by Official Census Data, 1781–1825	140
6.5	Ethnic Classification of the Population of Quito and Its Corregimiento, c. 1780	143
6.6	Ethnic Classification of the Population of Quito and Its Corregimiento, 1781	144
6.7	Sex Ratio in Quito, 1781–1825 (Men per 100 Women)	145
6.8	Number of Persons per Household, Santa Bárbara, 1768	151
6.9	The Social Composition of Four Quito Parishes, 1797	152
7.1	Occupational and Socio-racial Classification: the Parish of Santa Bárbara, Quito, 1768	184
8.1	Social Tensions, 1700–1780	204

Figures

Map of Quito by Dionisio Alsedo y Herrera, 1732		15
2.1	Eighteenth-Century Quito	22
2.2	The Corregimiento of Quito	38
2.3	The Urban Settlements of the Audiencia of Quito	43
6.1	Annual Baptisms in El Sagrario and Santa Bárbara Parishes, Quito, 1690–1780	121
6.2	Indian and Mixed Burials in Urban and Rural Parishes, 1693–1793	122
6.3	Annual White/Mestizo and Indian Baptisms in Santa Bárbara Parish, 1646–1825	128
6.4	Indian Deaths and Foundlings (*Expósitos*) Among Spanish Baptisms in Santa Bárbara, 1741–1800	136
6.5	Annual Baptisms of the "*Gente Decente*" of Central Quito: El Sagrario, Santa Bárbara and San Marcos, 1793–1825	138
6.6	Indian Tributaries of Quito and Its Corregimiento, 1779–1802	139
6.7	Annual Indian Baptisms in Three Rural Parishes, 1737–1825	142

Abbreviations

AA/C	Archivo Arzobispal, Cuenca
AA/L	Archivo Arzobispal, Lima
ACM/Q	Archivo de la Curia Metropolitana, Quito
AF/Q	Archivo Franciscano, Quito
AGI	Archivo General de Indias, Seville
Quito	Section Audiencia de Quito
AGN/L	Archivo General de la Nación, Lima
AHBC/I	Archivo Histórico del Banco Central, Ibarra
AHBC/Q	Archivo Histórico del Banco Central, Quito
AHN/M	Archivo Histórico Nacional, Madrid
AM/Q	Archivo Municipal, Quito
LCQ	Libros de Cabildo
ANC/B	Archivo Nacional de Colombia, Bogotá
ANH/Q	Archivo Nacional de Historia, Quito
Carn. y Pulp.	Section Carnicerías y Pulperías
Ind.	Section Indígenas
Mz.	Section Mestizos
Not.	Notarial Register
Pres.	Section Presidencia de Quito
Reb.	Section Rebeliones
ANH/C	Archivo Nacional de Historia, Azuay (Cuenca)
AP/Q	Parish Archives, Quito
BL	British Library, Department of Manuscripts, London
BN/Bogotá	Biblioteca Nacional de Colombia, Santafé de Bogotá
BN/M	Biblioteca Nacional, Madrid
BNP/L	Biblioteca Nacional del Perú, Lima
GS	F. González Suárez, *Historia General de la República del Ecuador* 3 vols., Quito, 1969–70
HAHR	*Hispanic American Historical Review*
LCQ	*Libro de cabildo,* published by the Municipality of Quito
RGI	*Relaciones Geográficas de Indias: Perú,* (ed.) M. Jiménez de la Espada, 3 vols., Madrid, 1965

Preface and Acknowledgments

In writing *The People of Quito* I wished to break away from the established pattern of regional studies of colonial Spanish America (still largely polarized between White elites and the Indian peasantry) with a study of the social history of colonial Quito rooted in the experience of its lower strata. Although my use of the term "people" (perhaps influenced by European studies such as Daniel Roche's *Le Peuple de Paris*) was therefore primarily intended to evoke non-elite social groups, the book was given a broadly based form so as to be able to contribute to our understanding of Quiteño society as a whole.

Its geographical scope is that of urban Quito, a vertical terrain hemmed in by mountains and divided by ravines, which proved to have played its own hidden role in shaping the city's social geography. I have tried to take account of the urban center's close interaction with its rural hinterland, and place this evidence in the broader context of the Audiencia of Quito (the administrative forerunner of the modern Republic of Ecuador). One of the corollaries of my use of "Braudelian time" (combining the study of geographical factors, long-term structural change and *évènementielle* history) is that the dates in the title are essentially there as a flag of convenience; the continuities and structural features of Quito society call, I think, for long-term comparative analysis. As for the subtitle "Change and Unrest in the Underclass," this was not intended to provide an exhaustive description of the contents, but rather to highlight the dynamic dimension of the tensions generated by economic change and Bourbon fiscal reform in the late-colonial period.

This book began life as a dissertation for a doctoral degree, completed in 1984, and it is appropriate to comment on the relationship between the two pieces of work. Although *The People of Quito* retains the general structure of the dissertation, most chapters have been substantially rewritten, and there are new sections such as the discussion of the life of Eugenio Espejo, the examination of the rebellions of 1765 and 1809, and the modified conclusions. There has also been added a considerable amount of new source material which includes the demographic data on the parishes of Santa Bárbara, San Marcos, El Quinche, Cayambe and Tabacundo. In relation to the economic background, I have tried to go beyond terms such as "crisis" to develop my argument that commercial indices begin to lose their value once the commercial activity of a stagnant economy falls below a certain level. In those few cases where streamlining of the text has led to an author's disappearance from the footnotes, I have kept his or her work in the bibliography by way of acknowledgment.

The incomplete nature of the historical literature on colonial Ecuador has only reinforced my indebtedness to the handful of historians who followed along the path opened up by John Leddy Phelan in the 1960s: of those whose work was available to me when I began my research, I am conscious of a particular debt to Rosemary Bromley, Michael Hamerly and

R. B. Tyrer for locating census data and establishing the demographic framework. New research which became available when this book was in its final stages (specifically that which is now appearing on the wider demographic background of the Audiencia) was taken account of, but less extensively than if it had been available earlier. The work of Kenneth Andrien and Anthony McFarlane on the 1765 rebellion, however, relates directly to the theme of popular organization and mobilization which is at the heart of this study and has been fully incorporated into the discussion of social unrest in Chapter 8.

I wish to thank the directors and staff of the national, municipal, ecclesiastical and Banco Central archives in Quito; of the regional, notarial and ecclesiastical archives in other parts of Ecuador, especially Guayaquil, Cuenca and Loja; of the National Archives of Colombia and Peru; of the Archive of the Indies in Seville, the National Archives in Madrid, the National Library in Paris; and of the (I hope eternal) reading room of the British Library in London. My particular thanks go to the parish priests in the provinces of Pichincha and Loja in Ecuador who went out of their way to help me. Financial assistance from the British Department of Education and Science, the University of Liverpool and the British Academy is also gratefully acknowledged.

Of my personal debts, in first place I want to mention my parents who offered practical assistance, interested themselves in my research, enthusiastically tracked down nineteenth-century traveller's accounts for me and proofread parts of this book. I also wish to recall the early help of my history teachers (and archaeology organizer) at school; my tutors, especially Cliff Davies, at Wadham College, Oxford; and my teachers and fellow research students, especially Tim Sedgewick-Jell, at the Center (now Institute) of Latin-American Studies in Liverpool. My thesis director Professor John Fisher provided orientations and support at key stages of my research; Professor John Lynch, who was on my thesis jury, also offered stimulating criticism of my work. The editor of the Dellplain Series, Dr. David J. Robinson, improved the book manuscript with his detailed and helpful comments. I also want to mention Linda Newson, Javier Ortiz de la Tabla, and Tom and Louisette Zuidema.

In Ecuador, the late Prof. Dr. Udo Oberem was courteous and helpful to a generation of students of Ecuadorian ethnohistory. The late Sr. José Miguel Vacacela, of Lagunas, Saraguro, inspired great affection and respect in all who knew him. I also have fond memories of Presley Norton's generous and engaging personality. Among many others, I wish to express my gratitude to Monseñor Cadena, Arq. Hernán Crespo, Dr. Juan Freile-Granizo, Dr. Julio Estrada Ycaza, Monseñor Luna, Dra. María del Carmen Molestina, Dr. Diego Mora, Doña Grecia Vasco de Escudero and the late Fray José María Vargas O.P.; to all those who collaborated with the Loja program of the Institut Français d'Etudes Andines under its then directors, Jean-Paul Deler and Yves Saint-Geours, as well as to Mathias Abram, Juan Castro y Velázquez, Nadia Flores, the late Enrique Grosse, John and Jennifer Isaacson, Carlos Marchán, Manuel Miño, Jorge Moreno Egas,

Carmen Rosa Ponce and her family, Fernando Rosero and Martha Moscoso, Lucía Suárez and Anne Christine Taylor-Descola.

For the warmth of their friendship and hospitality in Colombia *un abrazo muy fuerte* for Carlos Eduardo Jaramillo and Ximena Pachón, Ricardo Avila and Magdalena Cabrera and to all the Cabrera family in Santafé de Bogotá and Ubaté; and in Seville, to Aurelio Tejera and Silvia Padilla. Finally, my deepest thanks go to Chantal Caillavet who saw *The People of Quito* through from archival project to book manuscript, and contributed greatly to it at each stage.

These people, and many more, helped me to complete this book; any errors, needless to say, are my own.

Martin Minchom

Chapter 1

INTRODUCTION

"The colonial history of this favored spot is as lifeless as the history of Sahara ... Buried between treeless, somber sierras, and isolated from the rest of the world by impassable roads and gigantic cordilleras, Quito appears to us of the commercial nineteenth century as useless as the feudal towns perched on the mountains of Middle Europe."[1]

The People of Quito sets out to give life to what the nineteenth-century observer James Orton described as a colonial history "as lifeless as the history of Sahara." In a sense, Orton's comments anticipate, albeit in jaundiced form, the great divide of Ecuador's national history: the divergent path which its highland capital Quito—reputedly static, immobile and inward-looking, the "cloister in the Andes"—has taken from the more dynamic coastal port of Guayaquil.[2] Orton's categorization of Quito as

---

[1] J. Orton, *The Andes and the Amazon, or Across the Continent of South America*, London- New York, 1870, p 57, 59.

[2] M. L. Conniff, "Guayaquil through Independence: Urban development in a Colonial system," *The Americas*, (33) 3, (1977), 385–411, and 409 for the "openness" of Guayaquil. In contrast, note the title of R. Descalzi, *La Real Audiencia de Quito. Claustro en los Andes* (Barcelona, 1978). The regional history of Ecuador was developed by M. T. Hamerly, *Historia social y económica de la antigua Provincia de Guayaquil, 1763–1842*, (Guayaquil, 1973); and R. D. F. Bromley, *Urban Growth and Decline in the Central Sierra of Ecuador, 1698–1940*, doctoral dissertation, University of Wales, 1977. For another regional study see *Cultura, Revista del Banco Central del Ecuador*, (Edición monográfica dedicada a la Provincia de Loja), 15, (Quito, 1983). On Quito, detailed research is available for the prehispanic period: F. Salomon, *Ethnic Lords of Quito in the Age of the Incas: The Political Economy of North-Andean Chiefdoms*, doctoral dissertation, Cornell University, 1978, revised as: *Native lords of Quito in the age of the Incas. The political economy of north Andean chiefdoms*, (Cambridge, 1986). Segundo Moreno Yánez, (ed.) *Pichincha: Monografía histórica de la Región Nuclear Ecuatoriana*, (Quito, 1981), includes C. Borchart's Moreno's work on the mid-colonial rural history of the city's corregimiento. See also Szászdi's bibliographical essay, "The Economic

"isolated ... [and] useless" to "the commercial nineteenth century," advises us of the city's, and its region's, transformation since its heady moment of regional prosperity two centuries before. Although the Audiencia's mineral wealth had never been on a scale to rival that of the great mining centers of Mexico or Peru, its economic relations had stabilized in triangular form in the seventeenth century: cloth exports to other Spanish colonies, notably Peru, in return for specie; imports of luxury and other goods through the transatlantic trade. This triangular relationship of Quito–Spanish colonies–Metropolis, which underlay the mid-colonial economy, was progressively broken as English and French textiles began to flood the Spanish American market, and Quito's textiles, handicapped by high overland costs, were undercut on the Peruvian market.[3] In the eighteenth century both city and highlands entered a period of economic stagnation which outlasted the separation of colony and homeland.[4]

For the Spanish Crown this was, even in its heyday, an imperial backwater, and despite the juridical subordination of the early Presidency of Quito to the Viceroyalty of Peru, those examining social realities rather than legal principles have tended to see the gradual creation of a measure of de facto independence.[5] Geographical remoteness from the centers of Viceregal authority (Lima and later Bogotá), and from the great mining regions (Mexico and Potosí), facilitated this process and fostered the formation of that strong local identity which is a constant in Quito's colonial history from at least the 1590s onwards. How this peripheral, strongly localist, society responded both to difficult economic readjustments, and to the unwelcome fiscal pressures to which it was subjected by the reorganized Bourbon monarchy in the eighteenth century, is at the heart of this study.[6]

    History of the Diocese of Quito, 1616-1787," *Latin American Research Review*, vol. 21 (1986), 266-275.

3   R. B. Tyrer, *The Demographic and Economic History of the Audiencia of Quito: Indian Population and the Textile industry*, doctoral dissertation, Berkeley: University of California, 1976. J. Ortiz de la Tabla Ducasse, "El obraje ecuatoriano. Aproximación a su estudio," *Revista de Indias*, 149/50, (1977), 471–542. N. P. Cushner, *Farm and Factory: The Jesuits and the Development of Agrarian Capitalism in Colonial Quito*, (Albany, 1982).

4   Recent research has stressed Quito's economic difficulties in the mid-eighteenth century; K. J. Andrien, "Economic Crisis, Taxes and the Quito Insurrection of 1765," *Past and Present*, 129, (1990), 104–131. The problem of decline figures in the Ecuadorian historiography: Carlos Marchán Romero, "Economía y Sociedad durante el siglo XVIII," *Cultura, Revista del Banco Central del Ecuador*, 24, (Quito) (1986), 55–76.

5   I. Sánchez Bella, *Quito, audiencia subordinada*, (Quito, 1980) for a legalistic approach, but J. L. Phelan, *The Kingdom of Quito in the seventeenth century: Bureaucratic Politics in the Spanish Empire*, (Madison, 1967), for local realities.

6   K. J. Andrien, "Economic crisis, Taxes and the Quito insurrection," for the link between economic change, political reform and the Quito rebellion of 1765; A. McFarlane, "The 'Rebellion of the Barrios': Urban insurrection in Bourbon Quito,"

I have attempted to trace the impact on settled artisans and vagrants, poor Spaniards, Mestizos (mixed-blood) and acculturated urban Indians, that heterogeneous lower strata which was collectively dismissed as the *plebe* by colonial administrators or socially conscious creoles. One of my aims was to put into effect my conviction that at least part of the tale is in the telling, and that a fresh perspective on such notably complex issues as socio-racial status could be gained by approaching the subject "from within" and supplying the material in which the voices of the plebe could be directly heard, allowing them to provide their own answer to Orton's comments.

This study is divided into two parts. Part One reviews the urban environment, and then examines certain continuities in social organization which appear to invite long-term structural analysis. In Part Two, a micro-level analysis of those caught up in an imperial program of socio-racial classification, along with a discussion of demographic change and social unrest, brings out some of the more dynamic features of eighteenth century Quito society. This framework broadly follows the great French historian Fernand Braudel's distinction between the *longue durée,* long- and medium-term analysis of structural change, in contrast to short-term *évènementielle* history. The potential applicability of this approach to Latin American social history was pointed out by Mörner in his 1983 overview of research on "Economic factors and stratification."[7] It is particularly appropriate in the case of Quito because it enables me to strike a balance between the elements of continuity and change, and take account of slow-moving rhythms of change which might have been otherwise imperceptible. Apparent structural immobility is always, in part, a matter of perspective and degree: whether the sea is motionless depends, after all, on whether you are a swimmer or an airplane pilot, and even the most characteristically "static" Asian (and for all I know Saharan) societies have proved to be less rigid than once thought.[8] The choice of the dates 1690-1810 to accompany the title—taking the subject from the epidemics of the 1690s through to the beginnings of Quito's Independence movement—is essentially a

---

HAHR, 69 (1989), 283–330. For the Bourbon reforms, Montserrat Fernández Martínez, *La Alcabala en la Audiencia de Quito, 1765–1810* (Cuenca, 1984); D. A. Washburn, *The Bourbon Reforms: A Social and Economic History of the Audiencia of Quito, 1760–1810*, doctoral dissertation, University of Texas at Austin, 1984.

[7] M. Mörner, "Economic Factors and Stratification in Colonial Spanish America with special Regard to Elites," HAHR, 63 (1983), 335–369. The classic use of this approach was in F. Braudel, *The Mediterranean and the Mediterranean World in the Age of Philip II* (1949), Eng. trans., 2 vols., (New York and London, 1972–73).

[8] For a discussion of "... concepts of continuity and change in history," see P. Burke's introduction in P. Burke. (ed.), *The New Cambridge Modern History*, vol. XIII, (Cambridge, 1979). For limited social mobility within nominally rigid caste societies see for example, E. Leach (ed.), *Aspects of Caste in South India, Ceylon and North-West Pakistan* (Cambridge, 1971), 8–9 and passim.

compromise between the wider canvas of the early chapters and the narrower focus of the second part.[9]

My focus is on non-elite urban groups. The historiography of Latin America, and specifically the Andean countries, has traditionally been polarized between the dominant Spanish elite and the rural Indian peasantry, with an informal division of labor allocating the former to the historians and the latter mainly, although not exclusively, to the anthropologists. A vast terrain lies beyond these two groups composed not only of the Mestizos, but also of the urban Indians, the artisans or the vagrants—all products of a new society, belonging definitively to neither the Spanish nor Indian worlds. The first overview of this question for the whole of Latin America has described work on these groups as "fragmentary and scattered," although in a few areas work has begun to appear.[10] We are beginning to understand more, for example, about the activities of artisans in colonial Spanish America through their role in the guilds which regulated their economic activity, and the lay brotherhoods or *cofradías* which were their social and religious form of expression.[11] Detailed demographic studies have correlated socio-racial and occupational status, and provided a wealth of statistical information.[12] On the "underclass" of Latin American cities, two parallel lines of enquiry have emerged; one concerned with official measures to maintain public order, control vagrancy or develop philanthropic institutions; the other approaching criminality through judicial

---

[9] For the importance of the 1690s as a watershed, see Susan A. Alchon, "The effects of Epidemic Disease in Colonial Ecuador: the Epidemics of 1692 to 1695." Paper presented at the 1982 Annual Meeting of the American Historical Association, Washington, D.C.; see also her fuller study, *Native Society and Disease in Colonial Ecuador* (Cambridge, 1991).

[10] L. S. Hoberman, and S. M. Socolow, *Cities and Society in Colonial Latin America* (Albuquerque, 1986), 280, and the bibliographical discussions on pp. 248–50; 279–83; and 309–312.

[11] L. J. Johnson, "The Silversmiths of Buenos Aires: A Case Study in the Failure of Corporate Social Organisation" *Journal of Latin American Studies*, 8 (1976), 181–213; and the same author's wider synthesis in L. S. Hoberman, and S. M. Socolow, *Cities and Society*, 227–250. See also, for example, Jay Kinsbruner, *Petty Capitalism in Spanish America: The Pulperos of Puebla, Mexico City, Caracas, and Buenos Aires* (Boulder, 1987).

[12] Considerable research on Mexico has included: J. K. Chance, *Race and Class in Colonial Oaxaca* (Stanford, 1978); J. K. Chance and W. B. Taylor, "Estate and Class in a Colonial City: Oaxaca in 1792," *Comparative Studies in Society and History*, 19 (1977), 454–487. For a summary of the controversy which their approach generated see F. Bronner, "Urban Society in Colonial Spanish America: Research Trends," *Latin American Research Review*, 21 (1986); R. D. Anderson, "Race and Social Stratification: A Comparison of Working-Class Spaniards, Indians, and Castas in Guadalajara, Mexico in 1821," *HAHR*, 68 (1988), 209–243; and Michael M. Swann, *Tierra Adentro: Settlement and Society in Colonial Durango* (Boulder, 1982).

documents. The geographical framework for this research, however, has been Argentina or the larger urban centers like Mexico City or Lima.[13]

Studies which have included material on the popular strata in their analyses of regional societies have been noticeably influenced by the importance they have attached to one kind of source. One of the pioneering studies of colonial Spanish American society, James Lockart's *Spanish Peru,* built up a picture of sixteenth-century Peruvian society by the use of notarial records of day-to-day economic activity, and a school of historians has continued this approach by making "total" studies of cities' notarial records over roughly thirty-year periods.[14] This approach has provided very valuable economic evidence, but has tended to project an extremely static image of colonial society because the thirty-year "slice" of notarial records can take no account of either long-term structural change or specific "conjunctures." More recent, essentially demographic, studies, notably on Mexico, have provided a more dynamic picture of social change at the lower levels of society.[15] The broader-based regional study combining different varieties of source material has also existed, but has generally been oriented towards local elites with a strong political dimension either at the local *cabildo* or at the imperial level. Phelan's study of seventeenth Quito, which remains a landmark in the Ecuadorian historiography, was explicitly a study of the functioning of the imperial bureaucracy.[16]

To the best of my knowledge, this is the first time a wide variety of sources—official reports, litigation records, parish and notarial data—have been assembled for a broad monograph-length examination of the plebe of any Spanish colonial city. Many interconnections emerged in the course of my research to justify the premise that urban popular society was indeed a natural and autonomous subject of investigation. One of the clearest examples of this is the way the social geography and demographic characteristics of the popular districts combine with information on the

---

[13] A. Flores-Galindo, "Los Rostros de la Plebe," *Revista Andina,* (Cuzco), 1 (1983), 315–352; S. M. Socolow, "Women and Crime: Buenos Aires, 1757–97," *Journal of Latin American Studies,* 12 (1980), 39–54; M. C. Scardaville, "Alcohol Abuse and Tavern Reform in Late Colonial Mexico City," *HAHR,* 60 (1980), 643–671; and his doctoral dissertation, *Crime and the Urban Poor: Mexico City in the Late Colonial Period,* University of Florida, 1977; Kicza, J. A. "Life Patterns and Social Differentiation among Common People in Late Colonial Mexico City," *Estudios de Historia Novohispana,* 11 (1991), 183-200. Although non-urban, see also W. B. Taylor, *Drinking, Homicide and Rebellion in Colonial Mexican Villages* (Stanford, 1979).

[14] The classic for this approach is J. Lockhart, *Spanish Peru, 1532–1560: A Colonial Society* (Madison, 1968). D. Gibbs, *Cuzco, 1680–1710: An Andean city seen through its economic activities,* doctoral dissertation, University of Texas at Austin, 1979.

[15] See note 11 above.

[16] J. L. Phelan, *The Kingdom of Quito*; see also Peter Marzahl, *Town in the Empire: Government, Politics and Society in Seventeenth-Century Popayán* (Austin, 1978).

organization of festivals to show the very different roles which the *barrios* played in social unrest. On the other hand, I should stress that the orientation of my research was towards specific themes within my overall framework: namely, socio-demographic change, mobility and social unrest; these were three areas in which the popular dimension of economic and political pressures could be measured.

Although conditions are now slowly improving in Ecuadorian archives, in the 1980s these were poorly organized and frequently difficult of access. I would have liked to have located more data on artisanal occupations in the notarial registers I consulted (which had become more socially exclusive during the seventeenth century), and I was also unable to locate apparently extant material on guilds and lay-brotherhoods in Quito's National Archives.[17] Records relating to criminal activities constitute a particularly attractive means of access to the underclass, because it involves those least likely to pass before notaries to have their daily transactions recorded for posterity. Practical considerations, however, intervened: the "Criminales" section in the National Archives is both voluminous and unclassified. Some gaps in the research were involuntary, while others were a matter of priorities, and specifically my conviction that the social history of the city and its region would only begin to be intelligible once its demographic history had been put on a sounder footing.

The material I located led me towards a relatively structured society, organized into different forms of association, and divided into relatively well-defined communities: the Quito of the more stable artisanal and service populations. Vagrancy was a major feature of the society, both urban and rural, of late-colonial Quito as a result of the extreme mobility of the Indian population, but officials tended to identify as vagrant anybody who moved, and measures to incorporate these groups into the more fixed structure of urban society continued throughout the late-colonial period. The demographic evidence can at least suggest the scale of this phenomenon, while the problem of the cultural absorption of Indian migrants into urban society may be considered another aspect of the same process.[18]

---

[17] This material is mentioned in J. Freile-Granizo, *Guía del Archivo Nacional de Historia* (Guayaquil, 1974), but could not be found in the reclassified archives using the up-dated *Guía del Archivo Nacional de Historia* (1981).

[18] The place of the *forasteros*, or migrants/outsiders, whether displaced into the Spanish sector or incorporated into the structure of Indian society, provides the rural counterpart to urban social transformations, and has attracted growing attention. For the interaction of *forasteros* with host Indian communities, see T. Platt in D. Lehmann (ed.), *Ecology and Exchange in the Andes* (Cambridge, 1981); also B. Larson; "Caciques, Class Structure and the Colonial State in Bolivia," *Nova Americana*, 2 (1979), 197–235; and Ann Wightman, *Indigenous migration and social change: the forasteros of Cuzco, 1570–1720* (Durham, 1990). Also important is the recent study of Karen Powers, "Indian migrations in the Audiencia of Quito: Crown manipulation and local co-option," in David J. Robinson (ed.), *Migration in Colonial Spanish America* (Cambridge, 1991), 313–323.

The theme of European popular history has attracted growing attention during recent years, but defining the same subject in Andean terms runs up against barriers of ethnicity: who are the people, if not the Indians? Although Andean popular society gains in richness from the contributions of quite distinct civilizations, the absence of a common culture running through the different social strata deprives us of one means of access.The degree to which the elite participated in the same culture, notably at festivals, provides a common thread through the European evidence, at least at certain periods[19]; in other words, if we wish to understand the European lower strata, we can sometimes reach them heuristically through the elite groups. In colonial Quito, as in many parts of Latin America, one section of the Spanish conquerors quickly constituted an elite which continually absorbed newcomers from Spain, and whose cultural values were essentially those of the metropolis. It participated in a common culture with the lower strata, only in the nominal sense that the Church embraced all elements in society. In Quito (the opposite has been claimed for other areas) the hierarchical framework of society does not seem to have been broken or inverted during religious or civic festivals, while many forms of religious association seem to have reinforced rather than diminished class distinctions.[20] The spread of literacy, and more particularly of the printing-press, in Europe, often permits a direct testimony on what the common people of Europe seem to have thought, or at any rate, read or sung. In Quito, however, even more than other parts of Latin America, the printing-press was restricted to very limited official and ecclesiastical use; those Mestizos who painted or sculpted, did so for the Church, although their work did sometimes take on its own local flavor.[21] Official culture was therefore entirely divorced from that of the mass of the Indian population, although that of the latter was subject to innumerable modifying religious, linguistic and social pressures. The intention here is not to exaggerate the degree of cultural fusion or the importance of the social groups under review; the highlands of Ecuador were still 70 percent Indian and almost 90

---

[19] P. Burke, *Popular Culture in Early Modern Europe*, (London, 1978, repr. 1983), 23–9, 270–281.

[20] See Chapters 4 and 8.

[21] A. Stols, *Historia de la imprenta en el Ecuador de 1755 a 1830* (Quito, 1953), lists the publications which came out in late-colonial Ecuador. E. Keeding, *Das Zeitalter der Aufklärung in der Provinz Quito* (Köln-Wien, 1983) examines the intellectual impact of the Enlightenment, making use notably of private late-colonial libraries. The late Fray J. M. Vargas O. P. published several dozen works on the religious and cultural history of the country; see, for example, *Historia de la Cultura Ecuatoriana* (Quito, 1965) in which culture is defined somewhat narrowly. The fine colonial painting of the Last Supper in the Convent of San Diego, Quito, which includes the Andean dish of guinea-pig, suggests that it is not entirely impossible to look for local adaptation within "official" culture. For an interpretation along these lines, but based on Peruvian materials, see P. Macera, *Pintores Populares Andinos* (Lima, 1979).

percent rural in the 1780s.[22] This theme may cover only a relatively small section of late-colonial society, but it is one full of significance for the future, even if the nationalist dreams of an earlier generation of a linear advance towards a uniform Mestizo culture now seem exaggerated.

To what extent did an intermediate urban popular culture exist between the dominant Spanish and subordinate Indian cultures; and if it did exist, did it evolve as a distinctively Mestizo culture, or was it continually pulled towards one or other of its parent cultures? Although the social organization of the urban population, its spatial distribution, or behavior in riots, enables us to see how the plebe functions as a community, it is much more difficult to define the lower strata in cultural terms, and not only because of its lack of homogeneity. Direct evidence of what was believed and felt is not lacking, but tends to be fragmentary and difficult to interpret; even when the documents speak directly to us, it is in the "Sunday best" language prepared for the law-courts, rather than as an expression of unconscious beliefs.[23] Other major cities of the Andean region had significant Black slave populations, which later merged with Spanish and Indian elements to reinforce the diversity of a quite distinctive urban culture. The racial mix in Quito, however, was mainly Indian-White, a reflection of the stable or growing Indian population in the mid-colonial period, which obviated the need for the mass importation of slaves. In Quito we find the presence of Spanish and Indian influences, but not the evolution of a complex and quite distinctive urban popular culture to the extent which may have happened elsewhere; the cultural syncretism of the mixed Black, Indian and White populations of Lima or Mexico, for example, was a fertile terrain for the type of popular beliefs which attracted Inquisitorial interest.[24] It may be, therefore, that an examination of the external features of popular society is a more appropriate avenue of enquiry for the late-colonial city of Quito, than it would be for other urban centers.

---

[22] See Chapter 6.

[23] For an incursion into the field of mentalities, using an Ecuadorian case, see Frank Salomon, "Shamanism and politics in late-colonial Ecuador," *American Ethnologist,* 90-3, (1983), 413-428. The "Sunday best" language of the Declarations of Mestizo in Chapter 7, is still roughly hewn and provides a direct and interesting testimony; but it cannot be compared with say the dreams recorded by K. Thomas, *Religion and the Decline of Magic* (London, 1971, repr. 1973), 151–153. The confessions of the population of Quito in 1797 provides a guide to religious practice, if not belief (see Chapter 4).

[24] The interesting section of documents on "idolatrías" in the Archivo Arzobispal of Lima, used by P. Duviols in his study: *La lutte contre les religions autochtones dans le Pérou colonial* (Paris-Lima, 1971) includes a number of examples of interethnic magical practice for Peru, but not for the Quito region. The Inquisition tribunals were located in Lima and Cartagena, far from Quito, and there appears to be relatively little material on Quito among the Inquisition documents in the National Archives in Madrid.

Race and class are the instruments with which historians and sociologists have constructed their models of social stratification for colonial society, and the relative weight attached to ethnicity and economic factors in imposing constraints on vertical social mobility has been a matter of debate.[25] A full study of social stratification, correlating occupational and socio-racial categories, hinges on more complete census data than it was possible to locate for Quito; although a range of data was uncovered, it appears possible that an official house-to-house census for the 1780s may have disappeared from the archives.[26] Furthermore, the parish records consulted in Quito did not include in the late-colonial period the occupational data which would permit us to study the role of matrimonial alliances in fostering social mobility. Without occupational data and the detailed use of notarial evidence to confirm its socio-economic significance, the mere fact of inter-ethnic marriages has to be treated with some caution. The "Declarations of Mestizo"[27] include the offspring of Indian *cacicas* who had married Spanish men in what may have been a trade-off of equals (for land or prestige); but the question remains—who was moving "up" and who "down"?[28]

Some of these deficiencies in the economic and social data are not insuperable, but impose the adoption of fairly flexible class categories, the justification of which is the peculiar difficulty social scientists from Marx onwards have always experienced in classifying the peripheral groups who constitute neither a rural peasantry nor an urban proletariat, often displaying a signal lack of class unity or consciousness. Where do we place, for example, the market-women, mini-capitalists, yet who form a part of the lower plebe? The inclusion of wealthier artisans such as the silversmiths in this study is not intended to force them into any unnatural class unity with the lower plebe; on the contrary, they are of interest precisely because of the contrast they offer. It would be unwise, *a priori*, to exclude them from the scope of this study, insofar as smiths (like *pulperos*) ranged from rich to relatively marginal individuals. Although the formal categorization of colonial society by social classes is considered somewhat arbitrary and

---

[25] A summary is M. Mörner; "Economic Factors." For an article on New Granada in the late eighteenth century, see J. Jaramillo Uribe, "Mestizaje y Diferenciación Social en el Nuevo Reino de Granada en la segunda mitad del Siglo XVIII," *Anuario Colombiano de Historia Social y de la Cultura*, 2:3 (1965), 21–48. Especially noteworthy is the interesting discussion of the title "Don" in this article.

[26] ANB, Censos Varios departamentos, Tomo 8; Tomo 327, Quito, 3 de Marzo de 1783; "El Presidente remite el Padrón General de Habitantes de aquella Capital y Corregimiento del Distrito, correspondiente al año de 1782 ...." Folios 307–326 are missing, and there is the annotation that these had disappeared before December, 1971.

[27] This litigation to establish non-Indian tributary status is examined in Chapter 7.

[28] See, for example, the qualifications about Chance's work noted in: G. Thomson "Local History in the Colonial Era," *Latin American Research Review*, vol. XVIII, (1983), 265–6; J. K. Chance, *Race and Class*.

premature, the role of class and economic factors in underpinning social stratification is nevertheless not neglected. Where direct evidence is missing, a strong indirect light can be shed from other types of data: are the riots of the eighteenth century the product of class alliances, for example, or can they be better understood in terms of class conflict? However inchoate the formation of class structure in colonial Quito—or most pre-industrial societies—it will be argued that it takes us closer to an acceptable model of social tensions than do alternative approaches.

Economic data has been increasingly incorporated into the study of Spanish colonial social stratification, but to what extent do ethnic criteria provide a guide to status or prestige, or the alternative model of a caste society? If caste is taken as one of the most inflexible models of a closed society, the fluidity of ethnic categories in colonial Quito suggests that it had broken down as a rigid system well before the 1770s. On the other hand, it is possible to document many features of a closed society for colonial Quito, including the values of a caste society, as well as (within the limitations of the demographic evidence noted above) a high correlation between ethnic status and certain occupational categories. The major series of petitions of Mestizos to avoid tribute payment on the grounds that they were not Indian constitutes one means of examining mobility across ethnic boundaries. The examination of ethnic categories, notably with regard to the Mestizos and the urban Indians, forms a key part of the study which follows. Although the data cited hereinafter question the meaningfulness of the Mestizo as an independent socio-racial category by the late-colonial period, its examination can still have heuristic value in advancing our understanding of the workings of class and ethnicity.[29]

The themes of ethnic and cultural interaction, and urban popular society have been taken as closely inter-related subjects. Colonial cities have been recognized as artificial "implantations," centers of domination from which Spanish influence radiated outwards.[30] As such they constituted a highly

---

[29] The process of race mixture in Latin America, and the legal position of the Mestizos, were examined by A. Rosenblatt, M. Mörner and R. Konetzke, although research interest has waned; a synthesis of the state of research as it existed in 1967 may be found in M. Mörner, *Race Mixture in the History of Latin America* (Boston, 1967); also relevant is the same author's "Economic factors."

[30] The literature on Spanish colonial urbanization has been summarized and related to the central Ecuadorian highlands by R. D. F. Bromley in: "Urban-rural interrelationships in colonial Hispanic America: A case study of three Andean towns" *Swansea Geographer*, 12 (1974); and "Disasters and Population Change in Central Highland Ecuador, 1778–1825," in David J. Robinson (ed.), *Social Fabric and Spatial Structure in Colonial Latin America* (Ann Arbor, 1979), 85–115. Richard Morse, "Some Characteristics of Latin American Urban History," *American Historical Review*, 67 (1962), 317–338. The interrelationship of urban centers and their rural hinterlands is stressed in a series of studies collected in J. E. Hardoy and R. P. Schaedel (eds.), *Las ciudades de América Latina y sus áreas de influencia a través de la historia* (Buenos Aires, 1975). Nearly all detailed economic studies emphasize this interaction; see, for example, E. Van Young, "Urban Market and

important focus of Spanish-Indian contact; they absorbed Indians as specialist artisans, or servants catering for the needs of the urban population, as well as, in the case of Quito, a labor force for the textile work-shops, or *obrajes*. They were not the only social arena. The original Spanish ideal of distinct and parallel polities, "the Republic of the Spaniards" and "the Republic of the Indians," separated from each other on the basis of a strict socio-racial segregation, broke down early in rural areas, and Indian villages faced White and Mestizo penetration which had partly transformed their demographic structure by the late-colonial period. This penetration often had cultural implications beyond the numbers of those involved, as the Whites and Mestizos were often able to employ a variety of stratagems (intermarriage, alliances with the priests, or brute force), to take over the *cacicazgo,* the position of Indian leader, and integrate themselves in the structure of Indian society.[31] Similarly, the biological process of race mixture was the unique preserve of neither country nor city. Nevertheless, when the imperial censuses were carried out in the late eighteenth century, the pattern they revealed for the region of Quito was of a largely White or Mestizo capital within an administrative district (its *corregimiento* of villages) that was overwhelmingly Indian.[32]

It has long been recognized that racial categories should be used in a socio-cultural rather than biological sense, and it is clear that the urban centers had (and have) a role as transforming agents. The occupational diversity of the urban centers provided several avenues of social mobility. The evasion of tribute to which Indians were liable was notably easier in the relative anonymity of the cities, in a cultural context in which an Indian became virtually indistinguishable from a Mestizo through an act as simple (albeit symbolically charged) as changing his clothes. Nevertheless, this process requires elucidation. Is there nothing more to the urban Indian than

---

Hinterland: Guadalajara and its Region in the Eighteenth Century," *HAHR*, 61 (1981), 593–635; and his critical commentary on historical regional analyses in Eric Van Young (ed.), *Mexico's Regions: Comparative History and Development* (San Diego, 1992), 1–38. A work on urbanization which includes a contribution from R. D. F. Bromley on Ecuadorian material, is W. Borah, J. Hardoy, G. A. Stelter (eds.), *Urbanization in the Americas: The background in Comparative Perspective* (Ottawa, 1980).

[31] Numerous examples of this process are preserved in the ANH/Q, for example ANH/Q Indígenas 26, doc. 1701–IX–17, Indígenas 70, doc. 1756–29–VII and notably in the section Cacicazgos. M. Mörner has given examples in "Aspectos socio-raciales del proceso de poblamiento en la Audiencia de Quito durante los siglos XVI y XVII," in *Homenaje a don José María de la Peña y Cámara* (Madrid, 1969). See also the same author's *La corona española y los foráneos en los pueblos de indios de América* (Stocholm, 1970).

[32] The Indian population of Quito and the corregimiento was 43,535 out of 65,935 in the census summary of 1781; see Chapter 6 for the demographic sources. The Indian dominance of the countryside is of course far more marked if we leave the city out of the calculations; the censuses are contradictory with regard to the Indian population of the capital.

a transitional anachronism on his way into white society, or does he manage to recreate and preserve certain Indian social traits in an urban setting? How does the Indian *cholo* succeed in incorporating himself into Mestizo society and what kind of tensions, if any, does this generate within urban society? There appears to have been no systematic attempt to answer these questions for any Andean city in the colonial period, a fact that is all the more surprising in view of the wide recognition of their continued urgency today.[33]

---

[33] Lockhart included data on the urban Indian in his study of *Spanish Peru*. Gibbs includes a chapter in his *Cuzco, 1680–1710*, 14–53, revealing some of their economic activities from the evidence of the notarial records. As the former Inca capital, the Indian population of that city had certain distinctive features to its social organisation. See also Moscoso, M. C., "Indígenas y ciudades en el siglo XVI," in E. Kingman (ed.), *La Ciudad en la Historia* (Quito, 1989), 343-356. K. Spalding has pointed out this lack of attention in *De indio a Campesino* (Lima, 1974), 245–247. Some of the ramifications of the modern debate are examined in Chapter 5.

PART I

✜ ✜ ✜

STRUCTURES AND CONTINUITIES

✜ ✜ ✜

Map of Quito by Dionisio Alsedo y Herrera, 1732

(Source: AGI, Panamá, 134. Reproduced with permission.)

Chapter 2

THE ORGANIZATION OF URBAN SPACE[1]

The Urban Environment

Quito lies at over 9,200 feet (2,810 meters), almost exactly on the equator, where the flat plain of the inter-Andean basin which runs through the Ecuadorian Sierra, narrows to form a kind of bottleneck—"una especie de garganta" as the eighteenth century Spanish observers Jorge Juan and Antonio de Ulloa put it.[2] The city was founded—or more exactly, refounded—by its Spanish conquerors in 1534 as a "natural fortress" in hostile Indian countryside, on an inaccessible site bounded by ravines which had served the same function under the Incas who had conquered the

---

[1] For the eighteenth century, the map of Quito by Alsedo is preserved in AGI Mapas y Planos, Panamá 134. The Franco-Spanish expedition of the late 1730s carried out the surveying which led to the maps of Jorge Juan and Antonio de Ulloa, and of La Condamine. For a manuscript copy based on these observations, see BL, Additional, 15,331; "Quito, capitale de la Province du même nom ... levé en 1736." For the copy of Juan and Ulloa; *Relación Histórica del Viage a la América Meridional,* (Madrid 1748; facsimile edn., 2 vols., Madrid, 1978), 362-3. Both the map of Alsedo and the maps which resulted from the Franco-Spanish expedition have been widely reproduced. A more general eighteenth century map of the Audiencia by Maldonado has been often republished. I have consulted some of the nineteenth-century maps for comparative data, although some of these are still based on the evidence of the 1730s and 1740s, for example, the map of Salazza (1846), a copy of which is in the BN, Paris, Cartes et Plans, C 3593; E. Whymper's *Travels amongst the great Andes of the Equator,* (London, 1892), 167, is based on J. B. Menten. Other maps from this period are available in E. Enríquez B., *Quito a través de los Siglos,* (Quito, 1938). The nineteenth-century boundaries given by Salazza (1846) are consistent with the characteristics of the parishes as they emerge from the colonial documentation.

[2] Juan and Ulloa, *Relación Histórica*, 350.

region a generation earlier.³ From the sixteenth century onwards, observers noted that its position, squeezed between mountain and ravine, would render its subsequent expansion difficult, and the main residential concentration of white Quito society remained largely enclosed in the original Spanish city until only a few years ago.⁴ Far more than most major Andean cities such as Lima or Bogotá, Quito's location left its mark in a distinctive urban geography—river gullies running through the city, houses built on arches over ravines, streets on an irregular terrain forced into the colonial grid pattern. Nineteenth century visitors could till observe ravines, which when they were not covered by arches on which the houses rested "disclose to the eye hideous abysses, the sides of which are overgrown with rank weeds,"⁵ and many of these ravines or *quebradas* were only ironed out by industrial development in the early twentieth century.

In this chapter, an attempt will be made to underline the constants in Quito's pre-industrial urban morphology, and to relate these natural constraints to the lines of social demarcation within the city, and to the relationship of the urban center to its rural—and semi-rural—periphery.⁶ Dionisio de Alsedo y Herrera's letter, preserved in the Archive of the Indies, may serve as an introduction to the two recurring themes in descriptions of the city: its difficult geography, and the contrast between present and past splendors, an early hint (in 1732) of what was to become a

---

[3] For the defensive function of the city (as well as climatic considerations), Salazar de Villasante, "Relación general de las Poblaciones Españolas del Perú," *RGI*, I, 132; Pedro Rodríguez de Aguayo, "Descripción ... de Quito" *RGI*, II, 221; (see also *RGI*, II, 232; and *RGI*, III, 6). Rodríguez de Aguayo, mentions the *quebradas*, and emphasizes the continuity with the prehispanic site, 201. For the military function of Incaic Quito, see F. Salomon, *Ethnic Lords of Quito in the age of the Incas: The Political Economy of North-Andean Chiefdoms*, doctoral dissertation, Cornell University, 1978, 209–214.

[4] This point was already made by the perceptive Pedro Cieza de León in *La Crónica del Perú*, published in the 1550s; BAE, T. 26, Atlas, Madrid; American edition, V.W. von Hagen, *The Incas*, Oklahoma, 4th repr., 1976, 42. Juan and Ulloa, *Relación Histórica*, 350, make the same point.

[5] F. Hassaurek, *Four years Among the Ecuadorians* [1867] (C. H. Gardiner (ed.), Urbana, 1967, 49. For Quito's "vertical" geography, Holinski's observation is still true enough today: "monter et descendre, descendre et monter; tel est le sort des habitants de Quito," A. Holinski, *L'Équateur: scènes de la vie sud-américaine*, (Paris, 1861), 142.

[6] "Quito" is here defined as the cathedral parish of El Sagrario, and five ancillary parishes, although parts of the latter were not as fully urbanized as the nuclear center. See Frontispiece.

near torrent of reports and projects towards the end of the colonial period:

> The capital is this city of Quito, ancient Court with that of Cuzco of its first Barbarian Princes, situated ... on an uneven terrain, and divided by five rivers or gullies [quebradas] which descend from the summit of the volcano (Pichincha) ... (These) confuse the order of the city with such unevenness, that its population circulates by means of sixteen bridges which facilitate the circulation of the residents in those periods when abundant rainfall raises the level of the rivers. Among these bridges is the Bridge of the Barrio of La Merced, constructed by the first conquerors on the principal ravine which divides the community at four blocks from the main square ... [This bridge] had its foundations weakened by the injury of time, continual flooding, and the neglect of the residents, and since its repair was very difficult it was allowed to deteriorate until its final ruin, when it collapsed into the depths of the ravine and was carried away by the currents ... Being grieved that a city so extensive and populated, seat of an Archbishopric which is first after the two Metropolis (Lima and Mexico), and of a Royal Audiencia, and the other tribunals which compose a Republic governed by the Catholic and Sovereign dominion of His Majesty should have such a nefarious progenitor, occasion of so many misfortunes and ruin of a population which had so much splendor and opulence from the time of its ancient Pagan rulers ... I proposed its reconstruction.[7]

Here we have a rare opportunity to use documentary and cartographic evidence in association with each other. Although Alsedo's letter concerned the reconstruction of the bridge of the Barrio of La Merced, it also constitutes a geographical description of the city, and a copy of the map accompanied the letter to Spain (see Frontispiece).[8] In order to ascribe capital importance to his bridge-building endeavors, it was no doubt in Alsedo's interest to depict a city unhappily divided by river-gullies, subject to periodic flooding, its roads and bridges in ill repair, and incapable by virtue of its poverty of carrying out the necessary repairs. Nevertheless, these difficulties were certainly real, and there is other evidence that as both city and region moved into economic difficulties in the late-colonial period, there were problems of municipal funding which restricted the possibility of human works—bridge-building and the like—controlling the urban environment.[9] Disasters reinforced the difficulties of the natural

---

[7] Letter of Dionisio de Alsedo y Herrera, President of the Royal Audiencia of Quito, June 18, 1732. AGI Quito 132, fols. 5-7

[8] Alsedo's letter is conserved in AGI Quito 132, the accompanying map being transferred to AGI Mapas y Planos Panama 134. The map has often been reproduced, but without reference to the letter and with varying dates ascribed to it; the letter permits us to date it to 1732. For a later account by the same author which includes much less detail, see his *Descripción geográfica de la Real Audiencia de Quito* [1766], (Madrid, 1915).

[9] For the problem of municipal funding of the bridge of La Merced see Alcedo's letter, AGI Quito 132, fols. 8–10; P. Herrera, *Apunte Cronológico de las Obras y Trabajos del Cabildo o Municipalidad de Quito, desde 1534 hasta 1714; Desde 1715*

environment, although their importance should not be exaggerated. Major earthquakes hit Quito twice in the late-colonial period, in 1755 and 1797, but they do not seem to have caused the immense damage which the 1797 earthquake caused in the Central Sierra. Nevertheless, they exposed the physical vulnerability of the city: in 1797, a decree called for experts to inspect the damage to arches and ravines.[10] Although urban growth had involved the partial filling-in of some ravines during the mid-colonial period, the difficulties of Quito's natural environment were largely unchanged by the late eighteenth century, and it is therefore possible to examine certain continuities in the organization of the urban space.

Of the "five rivers or quebradas" cutting through the city—and this passage shows in contra-distinction to general usage the root sense of quebrada was closer to "river" than "ravine" in colonial Ecuador—three defined the city. Like a medieval city with its population spilling beyond the city walls, these quebradas did not enclose the urban population. But as the cartographic evidence indicates, all major Spanish buildings were located within these river-gullies; and all the ancillary parishes, which initially provided a supporting Indian population, lay beyond them. Although the unevenness of the terrain meant that blocks were slightly smaller than in certain urban centers, the city was as far as possible based on the rectilinear grid pattern which was the norm in early Spanish colonial urbanization.[11] The location of the main official and ecclesiastical buildings did not change significantly after their establishment during the sixteenth century. The Audiencia (and prison), cathedral, Archbishop's palace and municipality were all grouped around the main square, the locus of authority, as well as an important zone of economic activity, although the square of San Francisco inherited the principal pre-Hispanic market-

---

hasta 1733 (Quito, 1916), 377–8. For Quito's ongoing crisis of municipal funding, see the "decadencia total de los Propios y Rentas de este Cabildo" (1766), AM/Q, vol. 54, fols. 11–12, (although at a time when Quito was subject to increased fiscal pressures, and the cabildo therefore doubly likely to plead poverty).

[10] AGI Quito 188, for the earthquake of 1755. One of the mestizo petitioners in Chapter 7 (case 196) claims he was baptised in a hut serving as a chapel in the main square three years later. The cabildo buildings were also destroyed; AM/Q vol 54, fol. 11. Despite the earthquake, the city was probably expanding in the period 1750–60 (see Chapter 6), so it is probably misleading to cite the 1755 earthquake as a background factor in relation to the 1765 rebellion. AGI Quito 403, fol. 4, for the inspection of the quebradas; according to the same testimony there was damage to almost all the houses, but no major loss of life, and little evidence of the disruption caused in the central highlands.

[11] See the sixteenth century map of the city published in *RGI*, II, 231. and especially the marginal annotation (p. 232), with regard to the size of the *cuadras,* which were smaller than in the coastal cities Lima and Trujillo. Also, "La cibdad de ... Quito, 1573," *RGI*, II, 222. For an account of the foundation of the city see J. W. Schotellius, "Die Gründung Quitos," *Ibero-Amerikanisches Archiv*, IX, (1936/7), 276–294; X, (1936/37), 55–77.

place.[12] The extreme concentration of religious functions in the city of Quito can be measured by the space occupied by the churches and convents within the city (Figure 2.1).[13] The slaughterhouse was located to the north, on the edge of the Spanish city, with a supply of water from the quebrada, and out of contact with the residential areas; the Barrio de la Carnicería, the "area of the slaughterhouse" was later to straddle the boundary between the parishes of San Blas and Santa Bárbara. Beyond the ravines lay the Indian parishes of San Sebastián and San Blas to the north and south of the city. This dichotomy of Spanish urban center, and Indian satellite parishes was common to many early colonial cities, and reflected their essential role in the process of colonization. The dominance of the White city over the Indian countryside was the spatial expression of conquest and the role of the urban center as an enclave of White residential concentration and official and ecclesiastical authority in an Indian countryside which it controlled and whose economic activity it directed.[14]

Although two ravines marked off the Spanish city, one great quebrada ran directly through the heart of the Spanish city. This ravine separated the main square from a "principal" part of the city, the Convent of San Francisco and the parish of San Roque, as well as the monastery of Santa Clara and the retreat of San Diego which dates from the beginning of the eighteenth century.[15] The "new bridge" ("puentenuevo" in the key to Alsedo's map) is strikingly illustrated on the map as a testimony of Alsedo's labors. Although traffic continued by the damaged bridge because of the "long detour by other streets" which was necessary to avoid it, the four blocks of urban construction which had emerged over the central ravine in the neighborhood of the cathedral are clearly shown. During the seventeenth century, a process of land reclamation involved the filling-in of ravines;[16] but this process was in part a haphazard one as a law-suit brought by Joseph Jaime Ortiz, the architect of a chapel in the cathedral in the 1690s demonstrates.[17] According to the architect, the central ravine had been filled in simply because it had been used for waste disposal. When he attempted to lay the foundation of the chapel, he had to continue to depths of fifteen and even fifty feet to find firm ground: "it was shifting earth and since the foundation of this city, rubbish had been thrown into it." Only when he had begun work did he find that similar problems had beset

---

[12] Salomon, *Ethnic Lords of Quito*, 146.
[13] See also Chapter 4.
[14] See Introduction, note 30.
[15] Alsedo, AGI, Quito 132, fol. 6.
[16] P. Herrera and A. Enríquez; *Apunte Cronológico*, 153, based on the LCQ for April 1668.
[17] ACM/Q Cofradía (1655–1762), "Civiles ... de la Catedral" (1699) fols. 1, 4.

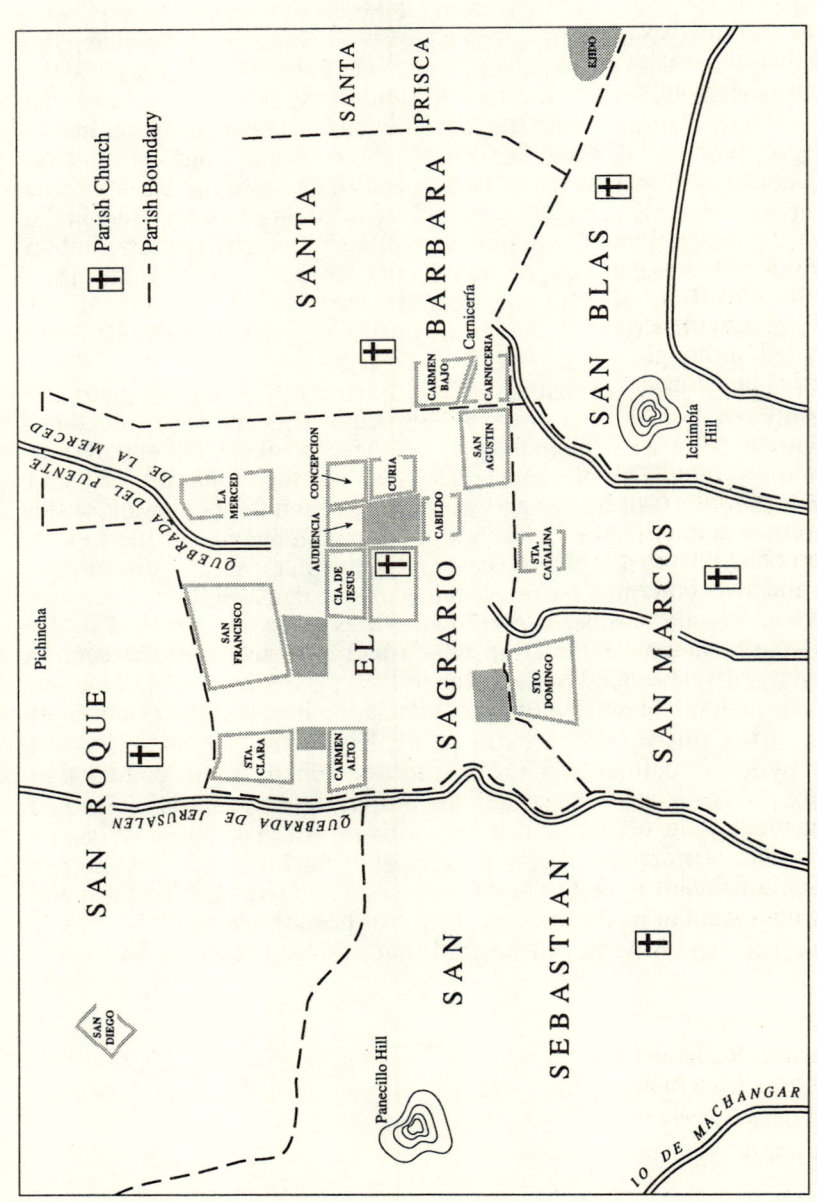

Figure 2.1 Eighteenth-Century Quito

the Jesuits just opposite the cathedral (and on the other side of the original ravine).[18] If the central area of Quito had therefore achieved a degree of integration by the eighteenth century, this was clearly only relative, and the city was still difficult to circulate and build in. It is therefore unsurprising to find that this was even more true when we turn to the ancillary parishes, and their relationship with the urban center.

PAROCHIAL ORGANIZATION AND THE RITUAL DIVISION OF THE CITY

Robinson has stressed that it is still unclear whether the "institutional framework"—parish and confraternity—promoted or merely reflected social cohesion, and that we know little of socio-spatial organization at this level.[19] The evidence on Quito's natural boundaries—the ravines which constituted, although progressively less so, major barriers beyond which the barrios developed their distinctive identities—will here be collated with the overall character of parochial organization which gave institutional shape to the urban communities. I have little evidence for the role of the confraternities in this respect, but a ritual pre-Hispanic division of the city may have played a considerable unseen role in shaping the patterns of social cohesiveness at inter-parochial level.[20]

Parochial history can be briefly noted. The Sagrario was the cathedral parish and was coterminous with the original Spanish city. The parish structure of the city took shape in the sixteenth century, and notably in the period of reorganization of the Indian communities common to the Viceroyalty of Peru in the 1560s and 1570s; in particular a very early Indian parish on the river Machángara disappeared, perhaps being absorbed into San Sebastián.[21] After the parishes of San Blas and San Sebastián, which were in existence before 1573, the parish of Santa Bárbara was created by the 1580s. When Diego Rodríguez Docampo wrote his description of the ecclesiastical state of Quito in the 1650s, all six urban parishes—the Sagrario, the cathedral-parish and its ancillary parishes, San Sebastián, San Blas, Santa Bárbara, San Roque and San Marcos—were in existence and no new ones were to be created in the period dealt with here.[22]

---

18 *Ibid.*

19 David J. Robinson (ed.), *Social Fabric and Spatial Structure in Colonial Latin America,* (Ann Arbor, 1979), 13–15.

20 For some evidence on the confraternities see Chapter 4.

21 Salazar de Villasante, "Relación general ...," 134–135, for the two parishes of Villasante and Velasco (probably San Sebastián and San Blas), and a good description of the process of "reducing" "indios derramados" into concentrated settlements.

22 Diego Rodríguez Docampo, "Descripción y Relación del Estado Eclesiástico del Obispado de San Francisco de Quito" (1650), *RGI,* III, 5, but especially 24–25.

It has been argued that the orientation of Quito's churches and parochial administration may correspond to pre-Hispanic ritual divisions of the city;[23] although little evidence has yet been located for this hypothesis, the Spanish Church certainly evangelized indigenous peoples by channeling their existing forms of worship into acceptable forms, and this included building chapels on sites of local worship. The ritual division of pre-Hispanic Quito into the Andean moieties of Hanan/Hurin ("upper/lower") is better documented, corresponding to an Incaic imposition of the sacred geography of the Inca capital of Cuzco. In a mirror reversal of Cuzco's social organization, Hanan or Upper Quito was the southern half of the city as well as the countryside lying to the south, and the Incaic aristocracy of Quito was concentrated in this part of the city.[24] In order to exert control over a numerically dominant Indian population, Spanish colonial society—like many other colonial societies—manipulated existing social structures rather than attempting to create a *tabula rasa*. Pre-Hispanic elements were co-opted into the new social order, notably the Indian leaders, curacas or *caciques*, who were used as intermediaries with the Indian population. Spanish colonial society sometimes found it convenient not merely to perpetuate but even to "improve" on pre-Hispanic institutions, one example of which was the propagation of Quichua. The autochthonous inhabitants of the Equatorial Andes spoke non-Quichua languages, and Quichua must therefore have been spread in the colonial period by the Church, or even paradoxically by the urban centers where Indians of different kinship groups had contact. Quichua continued to be spoken in the city of Quito in the eighteenth century, and parish priests continued to require—if we believe the official documentation—proficiency in Quichua.[25]

In this tradition, the colonial municipality continued throughout the colonial period the practice of electing—or more exactly, designating—*alcaldes mayores* of Indians who represented the communities to the north (hurin) and south (hanan) of the city. This division cut the city in half, the

---

[23] H. Burgos-Guevara, *El Guaman, El Puma y el Amaru: Formación Estructural del Gobierno Indígena en Ecuador*, doctoral dissertation, University of Illinois at Urbana-Champaign, 1975, 244–257.

[24] Burgos-Guevara, *El Guaman*, 244–257, 264–266; and Salomon, *Ethnic Lords of Quito*, 248–258. For the importance of dualist systems in Andean society, see M. Rostworowski de Diez Canseco, *Estructuras Andinas del poder. Ideología religiosa y política*, Lima, 1983. This feature has also been found in the Latin American lowlands: C. Lévi-Strauss, *Anthropologie Structurale*, (Paris, 2nd edn. 1978), 147–180.

[25] Cieza de León, *La Crónica*, 54 for autochthonous languages, and ANH/Q, Pres. 60, doc. 2673, fols. 79–80, for the election of the parish priest of San Blas, Nov. 22, 1766. B. Recio mentions dispensations from speaking Quichua in his *Compendiosa relación de la cristiandad de Quito* [1773] (Madrid, 1947), 256. (See Chapter 4 for the claimed low standards of parish priests). Salomon mentions a number of "retroactive Inca-izations," such as the colonial utilization of the term "ayllu," which nevertheless fitted the pre-Hispanic type of communal structure.

parishes of Santa Bárbara and San Blas lying in Hurin Quito.[26] The alcaldes were given a judicial role in mediating disputes, and in the administration of the *mita* system of forced rotating labor; in the sixteenth century, they also played an important role in the *reducciones,* the program of Indian resettlement.[27] The Indian alcaldes appear to have continued exercising a role in mediating disputes, but to judge from the reluctance of caciques to accept the post, and the explicit commentary of Juan and Ulloa, the post supplied few major powers in the eighteenth century.[28] Furthermore, the Indian population of the city was undergoing an absolute and relative decline in the eighteenth century. It cannot therefore be argued that the Hanan/Hurin moieties had major political significance by the eighteenth century even in their Spanish colonial dress.[29]

On the other hand, secular rituals may have a shaping influence on the social order. Although no colonial description of the election of the alcalde is known, the nineteenth century description of Kolberg suggests that the ceremony was a key one. After the election, the alcalde paraded through the streets with a ceremonial hat which served as a helmet. Indians who had been allowed to go onto the balconies of the second floor (i.e. the upper class level) threw fruit at him—fruit subsequently collected and received as tribute by the newly elected alcalde. The fruit listed by Kolberg (lemons, oranges, papaya, pumpkins) includes luxury produce grown in hot lands. These were prestige items either brought into the city by Indians from outlying areas or exchanged by those living near the city, but not food grown on agricultural plots in the city. The throwing of the fruit took on the traditional Spanish form of a regicide, a ritualized aggression, which marked the transition into the office of alcalde. In analogous ceremonies

---

[26] Salomon's *Ethnic Lords of Quito,* 250–253 is more reliable for the pre-Hispanic period than Burgos' *El Guaman,* 264, who uses mid-colonial documentation (dated 1695). On the other hand, colonial deformations are precisely what interests us here, so the confirmation that in 1695, Santa Bárbara and San Blas were Hurin and San Sebastián and San Roque, Hanan, is of great interest.

[27] For the *alcalde mayor* see W. Espinoza Soriano, "El alcalde mayor en el Virreinato del Perú," *Anuario de Estudios Americanos,* XVII (1960), 183–300. For an example from this region, F. Salomon, "Don Pedro de Zámbiza, un Varayuj del Siglo XVI," *Cuadernos de Historia y Arqueología,* (Guayaquil), 42 (1975), 285–315.

[28] Juan and Ulloa, *Relación Histórica,* 360.

[29] In 1712, for example, the *cabildo* issued threats against the *cacique* of Machache that he should come to Quito on his election as *alcalde mayor* of the Hanansayas, or risk suspension of his *cacicazgo*; AM/Q, LCQ, 1712, fol. 94. Elections took place each year, and can be found at the beginning of the municipal records for the relevant year. In the eighteenth century, elections followed the north/south divide between the two moieties. The kind of distinction that this made can be seen by the way the cabildo mobilized Indian labor for the repairs of the bridge over the Pisque in 1692, calling on the caciques of the "Unansayas" to co-operate with Indians; AM/Q, LCQ, May 6, 1692, fol. 54.

marking present-day rites of passage in Ecuador, sweets and fruit are thrown until the face bleeds. The participation, albeit passive, of the elite who allowed access to their balconies, emphasizes the importance of the ceremony.[30]

Consequently, the fact that both for the authorities and for at least its Indian population, Quito was divided into two parts is of considerable interest for the social geography of the city. In effect, the jurisdiction of the Sagrario stretched up to the Sugarloaf Hill *(panecillo)* and formed a type of wedge between San Roque/San Sebastián to the south and Santa Bárbara/San Blas in the north. It can therefore be said that the organizational division of the city (parish and moiety) both reflected and reinforced a genuine geographical separation. During the 1765 rebellion, the first riot was the result of the combined action of the parishes of San Roque and San Sebastián, while a later outbreak was a result of the combined action of San Blas and Santa Bárbara. These were not Indian rebellions, but genuine popular outbursts by the racially mixed plebe of the city; however, they certainly provide additional confirmation of the compartmentalization of the city. The distinctiveness of the Sagrario, both as the place of residence of much of the Creole elite as well as of the location of the main official and ecclesiastical buildings, is reinforced by this evidence of barrio separation during the 1765 rebellion, which suggests an extension of its fortress role of the early sixteenth century.

The cartographic evidence provides the best indices of the physical separation of the outlying parishes. According to Juan and Ulloa's map (although less clearly shown on Alsedo's), the continuous-block residential organization largely gave way to disorganized clusters of houses in the parishes beyond the quebradas. In the north of the city, the quebrada which marked off San Blas and Santa Bárbara had been partly filled in by the late-colonial period, notably between the Sagrario and Santa Bárbara, although the latter parish was on a steep slope leading out of the center. In the south, running west-east off the volcano Pichincha was the quebrada Jerusalén, a ravine which was only filled in at the beginning of the twentieth century, as early photographs indicate.[31] The eighteenth century maps testify that this remained one of the best preserved quebradas, still providing a form of boundary to the south. Beyond it lay the parish of San Sebastián, and a semi-rural part of San Roque in the east. Although in the sixteenth century, the parish of San Sebastián disputed with San Francisco the jurisdiction of the south-east of the city, the heart of Incaic Quito and the place of residence of the Inca aristocracy[32] the orientation of the church, well beyond the

---

30 Kolberg, *Hacia el Ecuador,* (Quito, 1977), 189.

31 J. E. Enríquez B., *Quito a través de los Siglos* (Quito, 1938, n. p.) reproduces a number of old photographs of the city including one of the quebrada Jerusalén, subsequently transformed into the Avenue 24 de Mayo.

32 F. Salomon, *Ethnic Lords of Quito,* 155–6; 238–241; 245; 251–3, citing AF/Q legajo 8 (1), "Padrón de los yndios de San Sebastián." U. Oberem has examined the fortunes of the Incaic aristocracy, and specifically the Emperor Atahualpa's

ravine and at some distance from the city, is suggestive of its original function. According to the anonymous description of 1573, the churches of San Sebastián and San Blas, both rudimentary adobe huts at that date, served to administer the sacraments to the Indians settled outside the city.[33] The barrios began as quasi-rural aggregations to organize the Indian population of the immediate district, and it would be an anachronism to identify them as specifically urban *reducciones,* even if their proximity to an urban center meant that they developed in close symbiosis with it. It may be appropriate to note that the term *barrio* connoted a semi-rural entity, rather than carrying its modern urban associations.[34] Although directly interrelated with the city, parishes which were villages in the sixteenth century had not been fully subsumed into the city by the late-colonial period, or may even have been partly rerural ized if the decline of certain forms of economic activity placed an additional importance on the agricultural plots.

THE BARRIOS: HIERARCHIES OF URBANITY

How do we measure the urban traits of the late-colonial barrios of the city, and to what extent can we establish a hierarchy of urbanization between the different parishes? Can patterns of concentrated urban residence be placed on a sliding-scale alongside social hierarchy, and distance from the urban center identified with a weakening of urban traits and a descent down the social hierarchy? Four criteria have been used to permit the correlation of urban traits with the social composition of the parishes:

- Urban/rural jurisdictions.[35]

- Urban morphology: agricultural plots, the density of settlement, and types of residential structure.

- Occupational data: although weaving, for example, should be best viewed as a quasi-rural activity even when carried out within the technical jurisdiction of the city.

---

descendents, under Spanish rule; c. f. "Ein Beispiel für die Soziale Selbsteinschätzung des Indianischen Hochadels im Kolonialzeitlichen Quito," *Ibero-Amerikanisches Archiv,* 15 (3) (1979), 215–225.

[33] "A los naturales que estan poblados fuera de la ciudad." "La cibdad de ... Quito, 1573," *RGI,* II, 223.

[34] See the definition in *Diccionario de Autoridades* [1726] (Madrid, repr. 1976), 567. The role of the *barrios* in providing the artisanal and service populations hardly needs stressing, whereas their rural dimension is easily overlooked. For the formation of quasi-rural parishes the account of Salazar de Villasante is most explicit, "diles estos dos sitios y repartíles unas tierras valdías en que siembren su maíz y hiciesen huertas," "Relación general," 134.

[35] For boundaries, see footnote 1 regarding the cartographic evidence.

- The quebradas: the existence of ravines between certain parishes and the center may have reinforced the abruptness of the transition between urban center and periphery, and reinforced the village character of the barrios.

These points (and most notably the third) will be partly clarified by the demographic and economic evidence given in later chapters.

The cartographic evidence diverges with regard to the rurality of the ancillary parishes. The maps of Juan and Ulloa, and La Condamine, both based on the observations of the Franco-Spanish scientific expedition of a decade or so later, show a less dense and more dispersed pattern of settlement beyond the quebrada Jerusalén than Alsedo's map of 1732—this semi-rural aspect applies, although in lesser degree, to the other peripheral districts. Alsedo's map not only shows much denser occupation, but suggests extensive urban development up to and around the Panecillo. Despite the difference in date between the two maps, it would be unwise to interpret the differing representation of the parishes as cartographic evidence of the urban recession which cannot have entailed an immediate physical transformation on such a scale. The cartographers were not perhaps greatly interested in the peripheral areas of the city, and we do therefore not have to attach equal validity to both maps. Although later maps were often copied in part from those of the Franco-Spanish expedition, few show a pattern of settlement in the peripheral parishes even remotely compatible with Alsedo's, even when we have allowed for a degree of urban decline. Recalling the purpose of Alsedo's map—which relates to building improvements in the urban nucleus—may reinforce the impression that his map was totally stylized in its representation of the popular parishes, and that the maps of La Condamine and Juan and Ulloa were in this respect more accurate. Confirmation of this point comes from an early nineteenth century painting which shows irregular occupation on and beneath the lower slopes of the Panecillo.

This point can be confirmed by the property transactions preserved in the notarial records. At least in the seventeenth century, plots of land without houses were being sold in San Roque, which does not suggest intensive urban settlement at that date.[36] For San Sebastián, the notarial records confirm the semi-rural character of the parish suggested by Juan and Ulloa—they reveal an extensive but diversified pattern of settlement,

---

[36] ANH/Q 1 Not. Fernando Zurita, Tomo 54, fols. 106–107; Oct. 1, 1623, Don Carlos Atabalipa Ynga, *vecino* of Quito sold a plot of land in San Roque for 60 *patacones*. (He was son of don Alonso Auqui and doña Beatriz Ango, i. e. a grandson of the Inca Emperor Atahualpa, and it is interesting that a descendant of the pre-Hispanic aristocracy still had interests in the south of the city, where they had formerly been resident.) Another example of January 24, 1624 is found at fol. 123.

broken by plots of land, and textile workshops.[37] It is of interest that research on the epidemics of the 1690s has found a higher rate of mortality in urban parishes than in rural areas: in the case of Quito, Santa Bárbara had a higher mortality rate than San Sebastián, which may suggest that the former was a more crowded urban parish than the latter.[38] When property was sold in the peripheral areas of the city, it was nearly always with a small *huerta,* or fruit and vegetable garden attached, sometimes with additional plots as well; the urban plots were often small. In a transaction dated April 29, 1720, for example, houses were sold with their patios and huertas in the parish of San Blas, along with a plot of land measuring only forty yards by thirteen.[39] We find the same formula ("con su patio y huertesita") for the "Barrio de Hichimbia," in the same parish, a district shown on La Condamine's map with the agricultural plots clearly indicated.[40] Moving away from the center, property being transferred in the parish of Santa Prisca, is clearly surrounded by agricultural land.[41] These examples could be multiplied; the urban agricultural plot was virtually a standard feature of property transactions in the barrios of the city.

In property sales, the distinction is made between "alto" and "bajo," that is one and two story houses. In the sale of property mentioned above, for example, (April 29, 1720), one of the houses is "alto" while the rest are "bajos." This distinction is an essential one with regard to the social interaction of the different urban social strata. Visiting the city in 1805, the scientist, Caldas made the perceptive comment: "The nobility and middle class always occupies the upper floor; the downstairs rooms are for the plebeians. Each family rents one of these, and *each household comes to be a small village* ("pueblo" my italics).[42] Fortunately, the demographic data enable us to quantify household size, and can therefore confirm statistically the cartographic and notarial evidence. Continuous block (i.e. two story)

---

[37] Multiple transactions; see, for example, ANH/Q 1 Not. Diego de Ocampo, Tomo 276, fols. 661–663, 7 Aug. 1755; ANH/Q 1 Not. 246, fol. 378 (año 1729). For an earlier example, ANH/Q 1 Not. Diego Rodríguez de Urbán (1621–40), fol. 48.

[38] Sixty-three percent in Santa Bárbara and 52 percent in San Sebastián with much lower rates, but certain undercounting in rural areas. Calculations of S. A. Alchon in "The effects of epidemic disease in colonial Ecuador," Paper presented at the American Historical Association Annual Meeting, 1982, based on ANH/Q Pres. vol. 13, 1696.

[39] ANH/Q 1 Not. vol. 246, Don Diego de Ocampo, fol. 53, April 29, 1720 ("44 varas de largo y 14 de ancho").

[40] *Ibid.*, vol. 1728–31, fol. 77.

[41] *Ibid.*, fols. 443–445, October 2, 1730.

[42] F. J. de Caldas, "Viaje de Quito a Popayan," *Semanario de la Nueva Granada* (Paris, 1849), 505–506; "La nobleza y el estado medio ocupan siempre el alto: las piezas bajas estan destinadas a la plebe. Cada familia alquila una de estas, y una casa viene a ser un pequeño pueblo." See also the description of the election of the alcaldes by Kolberg, *Hacia el Ecuador,* 189.

residential structure characterized the Sagrario, most of Santa Bárbara, but only those parts of the other parishes contiguous with the urban center. Although the pattern of settlement was varied in the peripheral parishes, low household size in single tier residences—and this particularly characterized San Roque—indicates a popular district in which the level of social interaction between upper and lower strata was extremely small, and the degree of social control exerted by the upper classes was correspondingly diminished. When the evidence on popular unrest is examined in Chapter 8, this point will help to explain why the parish of San Roque rioted so often in the eighteenth century.

The existence of "urban" economic activity does not necessarily contradict the evidence of the rurality of a parish and in particular it may be somewhat misleading to classify the obrajes as urban textile factories: the maps show that the River Machángara was, although within the legal limits of the city, at some distance from the main urban settlement and most of the urban obrajes appear to have been located along this river, requiring large amounts of water.[43] The mills were located along the river Machángara for the same reason, although there were also some using the water of the upper reaches of the quebrada Jerusalén.[44] None of the urban centers of the Audiencia of Quito seem to have had a major industrial function with the exception of the gunpowder factory in Latacunga.

The semi-rural character of much of the outlying peripheral area of the city, has to be balanced against the distinguishing "urban" traits—ethnic, occupational—of Quito's plebe, which are equally clear. In order to synthesize the two types of evidence, it is necessary to identify in more detail the social characteristics of the parishes. This is a problem for which a full eighteenth century house-to-house census, complete with occupational data, would provide the clearest answer. Taking up the points made above and anticipating the detailed demographic evidence, a brief preliminary sketch of the distinguishing characteristics of the parishes will be given, to introduce, as it were, the *dramatis personae*.

EL SAGRARIO: The nuclear center of the city, and the largest parish, including its principal administrative and ecclesiastical buildings, and the focus of economic activity, including the markets which took place in its principal squares. El Sagrario parish was the original Spanish city, and was still the place of residence for much of the creole elite in the eighteenth

---

[43] The location of many late-colonial workshops in San Sebastián supports this point (see Chapter 5), which is also suggested by a reading of the maps listed in note 1. The *obraje* of don Joaquín Fuentes in San Sebastián (first reference in note 37) was at the foot of the *panecillo*. In line with Juan and Ulloa, Salazar's much later map indicates several "molinos" on the river Machángara well away from urban settlement.

[44] In addition to the maps cited in note 1, see also the account of P. Rodríguez de Aguayo, "Descripción de ... Quito," *RGI*, II, 201.

century. By that period, it also had a major "popular" presence, although part of this was its considerable servant population.

SANTA BÁRBARA: This parish was close to El Sagrario (i.e. not separated by *quebradas*) and has many of the same characteristics. It had a socially mixed composition, as the *padrón* of 1768 would reveal, including some of the households of the creole elite. It was an essentially urban parish but an examination of its parish records revealed that a number of infants were being brought in for baptism from rural areas.

SAN MARCOS: The comments on Santa Bárbara seem generally applicable to San Marcos.

SAN SEBASTIÁN: A dispersed semi-urban parish, mainly divided by a ravine from El Sagrario, with a low level of upper-class residence. The jurisdiction extended to a rural area in the south.[45]

SAN BLAS: A semi-urban parish and like San Sebastián a popular parish, although a demographically unimportant one in the late-colonial period. It included marginal hillside land with dispersed settlements and its jurisdiction extended into the rural areas north of the city.

SAN ROQUE: This was a large parish divided into an important urban popular sector giving directly on to El Sagrario as well as a less settled semi-rural part across the *quebrada* Jerusalén. It appears to have been divided into San Roque Alto (upper) and San Roque Bajo (lower), but it is difficult to prove that this corresponds to dualist Andean categorization when referring to a parish which stretched up the lower slopes of the volcano Pichincha.[46]

SANTA PRISCA: This extramural rural parish, to the north of the city, was sometimes included in lists of the urban parishes, but was entirely rural and is not considered here part of the urban center.[47]

The later evidence of the circa 1830 census suggests that these characterizations continued to be substantially accurate into the nineteenth century, and perhaps beyond. Although in general the extrapolation of later data to correct *lacunae* in the colonial period poses obvious problems, Quito, was not expanding demographically and economically during this

---

[45] There were eight haciendas in the parish according to the church padrón of 1797; ACM/Q, "Visita Pastoral, Ilmo. Pérez de Calama (1790)."

[46] ANH/Q Reb. doc. 1748–1–1, fol. 2.

[47] See, for example, Juan de Velasco, *Historia del Reino de Quito en la América meridional,* [1789] (Quito, 1977–78), 113.

period. In view of the decline of the textile industry, sheep grazing near the capital may have been less intensive than in the eighteenth century.

TABLE 2.1 URBAN-RURAL CHARACTERISTICS OF THE PARISHES OF QUITO IN THE EARLY NINETEENTH CENTURY

Parish	Tiled Houses	Thatched Houses	Cattle	Sheep	Goats	Horses, Mules, Donkeys
El Sagrario	400	—	—	—	—	—
Santa Bárbara	—	—	—	—	—	—
San Blas	115	39	91	898	83	30
San Roque	191	—	50	150	—	19
San Sebastián	—	71	423	103	22	—
San Marcos	104	—	—	—	—	—
Santa Prisca	48	211	370	2,030	30	22

Source: AM/Q vol. 64, fols. 1-3; "Padrón de Quito ..." (1830-31) One may note that San Blas and Santa Prisca also had a small production of wheat and barley, and San Blas also produced maize, hides, cacao, salt, and sugar.

The urban characteristics of El Sagrario and Santa Bárbara were clearly demonstrated, while, on this evidence, San Marcos was also an unambiguously urban parish at that date. Santa Prisca was clearly rural, while the other parishes exhibited more mixed characteristics. Most houses in the city had tiled roofs. If we include Santa Prisca in the corregimiento rather than with the city of Quito, only 4.6 percent of recorded "urban" houses were thatched. This proportion reflects the demographic dominance of El Sagrario and it is probable that San Sebastián for which no data is given, would have had some thatched houses. On the other hand, even in the parish of San Blas the proportion of thatched houses was only 27.3 percent. Wealthier rural residents also lived in houses with tiled roofs, but in general the rural district of the capital presented quite a different picture. In the corregimiento there were 1,057 recorded tiled houses, although data was not given on some villages. This can be compared to a total of 5,656 thatched houses. In other words, 84.3 percent of recorded houses in the rural district were thatched, and only 15.7 percent tiled. The survey of livestock in contrast emphasizes the semi-rural dimension of the popular parishes. The agricultural production of San Blas included products (salt, sugar) which may have been processed there for the urban market, while its leather production can be explained by the proximity of the municipal slaughterhouse. Clearly, the "rural" activity of the peripheral districts was directly related to the capital.

The Commons, the Corregimiento and Rural Hinterland

Beyond its immediate jurisdiction, Quito exerted an influence on a wider area which both supplied the city, and produced the textiles and agricultural products which determined the degree of vitality of the regional economy. Within its legally defined jurisdiction, there was no abrupt transition between the city and its rural hinterland, except in the sense which was discussed above, where it was suggested that the ravines marked off the nuclear center from its ancillary parishes *within* what would normally be considered the city. In this section, I discuss the immediate rural hinterland of the common lands and the city's administrative district (Five Leagues), while the wider region of the Ecuadorian Highlands is also briefly introduced; in accordance with the larger theme of this study, the discussion is progressively less detailed as the focus shifts away from the city. Within these general contours, some of the implications of one genuine urban-rural dichotomy—the demographic contrast between the Indian countryside and the non-Indian city—will be stressed.

THE COMMON LAND

In the previous section several aspects of Quito's vertical urban geography were noted, along with its function as the locus of Spanish authority radiating outwards. The role of the city as a concentrated form of settlement which organized and exploited the open space of the countryside around it is exemplified in its administration of its common lands. Quito's difficult location contrasted with the flat lands which lay beyond it, and preserving this land for agricultural purposes may have been an additional reason for founding the city over the ravines. The commons (*ejidos*) of the city were Turubamba in the south, and Añaquito in the north. In the latter area lay a lake which was being dried out during the colonial period to gain land for grazing, but was still in existence in the eighteenth century.[48] Controlled by the municipality, the common lands were a direct extension of the urban space, and their utilization would reflect the requirements of wealthy urban White residents through the cabildo which was the expression of their interests.

At least in origin, however, the common lands allowed the Indian communities—and all animal-owners—to have access to grazing land, at a time when land was being distributed among the Spanish conquerors. According to a sixteenth century description, the ejidos were mainly for

---

[48] P. Rodríguez de Aguayo, "Descripción de ... Quito," *RGI,* II, 201; "La cibdad de ... Quito, 1573," *RGI,* II, 210. This lake was described by Montúfar, "Razón ... [acerca] del estado de la Real Audiencia de Quito," (1754), *Revista del Archivo Nacional de Historia, Sección del Azuay* (Cuenca, Ecuador), 3 (1981), 102, and appears on the eighteenth-century maps. The area was still marshy in the early years of this century.

cattle, sheep and horse grazing, but even at that period their extreme fertility had already resulted in the diversion of part of the best land into wheat, barley and maize production.[49] This process continued in the early seventeenth century with the sale of some of the land for the sake of municipal funding, and perhaps also in the interest of cabildo members.[50] The cabildo was responsible for the administration of the common lands, and periodic municipal inspections were carried out throughout the colonial period. The open nature of the common grazing land made it vulnerable to irregular Indian occupation which was summarily dealt with by officials appointed by the cabildo, through measures which included the burning of huts and houses, and the uprooting of crops.[51]

By the late-colonial period, there was therefore nothing new in the cycle of land occupation and violent dispossession, encroachment on grazing rights, or the use of the cabildo as a tool for the interests of the local elite. During the second half of the eighteenth century, however, the pressure on the common lands increased, as the municipality rented out land from the ejidos, mainly to the leading landowners of the district. The earliest of these rents of ejido land listed in the municipal accounts of 1795 dates back to only 1763, whereas many of the other forms of obligation listed on the same occasion dated back to the mid-colonial period.[52] This acceleration of the erosion of the common lands from their original function as grazing pasture can be attributed to a number of factors. Among these, no doubt, was the municipality's shortage of funds and its quest for new sources of revenue; the cabildo, however, was dominated by a creole elite for its own economic ends, and an intensification of arable agriculture was probably one of the readjustments which that elite made to the decline of its textile manufacturing/sheep grazing base.[53]

In any case, some major landowners acted without waiting for formal rights, and counted on tacit cabildo acceptance of their illegal enclosures.[54] The Indian communities, as so often in Spanish America, were the prime victims of this hacienda expansion. Who were they? The fact that a lawsuit relating to the villages of San Juan Evangelista de Chimbacalle, Santa

---

[49] "La cibdad de Quito ... 1573," 212.

[50] *LCQ*, Sept. 28, 1604, 159.

[51] *LCQ;* Nov. 27, 1602, 361; *LCQ;* May 2, 1650, 42. Regulation of the *ejidos* continued throughout the colonial period, for example, AM/Q, LCQ, vol. 1664–65, 28, and many other examples.

[52] AHBC/Q 1a Colección. Ms. Azules, vol. 7, "Hijuela de Rentas de propios de Quito" (1795), 293–294.

[53] The complicity of the authorities is suggested by the documents cited below: the cabildo participation of leading *obrajero* and land-owning families has been mapped in the genealogical tables of J. Ortiz de la Tabla Ducasse: "El obraje colonial ecuatoriano. Aproximación a su estudio," *Revista de Indias,* 149–150 (1977), opposite page 536.

[54] See ANH/Q Ind. 83 doc. 29–VII–1767.

María Magdalena and Chillogallo mentions mules among the animals which they grazed suggests that proximity to the capital and access to grazing lands provided work as mule breeders and *arrieros* for inter-regional transport. If so, this was certainly combined with other forms of agricultural activity.[55] Independent evidence confirms that the village of Chillogallo had a tradition of mule grazing.[56] Around 1831, for all the erosion of grazing rights, there were still 175 recorded mules in the village, the highest number in the corregimiento of the city, (followed by Amaguaña with 125 and Yaruquí with 77).[57] We can broadly distinguish between three types of Indian land use. Along with the tradition of sporadic squatter invasions of the common lands, there were neighboring Indian communities with marginal lands bordering on the ejidos, who relied on them for communal pasture rights, as well as a small number of communities whose occupation of small plots of ejido land was formalized in a rent paid to the cabildo. In 1795, the municipal accounts listed the holdings of 75 Indians (probably male tributaries) in Guajaló, 20 in Casapamba, ejido of Turubamba, 34 in the site of Batán in Añaquito, and 37 in the site of Chaupi-Cruz, also Añaquito.[58] A fifth property listed in the 1795 accounts was held by a white of land "desocupado" by an Indian, a small example of the larger process of the transfer of Indian land into Spanish hands. Some of this land alienation was through sales by caciques.[59]

The enforced contraction of Indian grazing rights was a brutal process, ineffectively resisted by the only available form of action, namely the traditional Indian recourse to the Spanish system of justice. In 1768, the Indian communities of San Juan Evangelista de Chimbacalle, Sta. María Magdalena and Chillogallo complained of the encroachments on the ejido of Turubamba by the hacienda of the Marquis of Villaorellana in the site of El Calsado, complaining that part of this land had been illegally enclosed.[60] The response was the burning down of seventy-one houses, with all their tools and agricultural produce, for having had the temerity to bring the Marquis before the law-courts. This was with the collaboration of the cabildo, and was actually carried out by officials of the city, a connivance

---

[55] ANH/Q Ind. doc. 16–IX–1768.

[56] For earlier data, ANH/Q Ind. 28–IV–1703 for a case of damage to land in Chillogallo by mules. AGI Quito, 254 "Relación de las causas criminales" (1804) includes the theft of a mule in the same village, and the census in AM/Q, "Padrón de Quito ..." (c. 1831), vol. 64, fol. 2, reveals the continuity of the tradition of mule rearing.

[57] AM/Q, "Padrón de Quito ..." (c. 1831), vol. 64, fol. 2. Magdalena and Chimbacalle were mainly sheep-grazing at that date, but Chillogallo had the greatest concentration of cattle (7,096), sheep (5,418) and horses (1,852, including 1,531 mare) because of Spanish-owned livestock and horses grazing on the common lands.

[58] "Hijuela de Rentas," 294.

[59] ANH/Q Ind. 29–VII–1767.

[60] ANH/Q Ind. doc. 1768–V–18.

which need not surprise us in view of the eight haciendas which the Marquis owned in the corregimiento, and his close ties with other leading property-owners.[61] In the face of illegal Spanish innovation, and in a mirror reversal of traditional land invasions, we find the Indian peasantry cast in the role of defenders of traditional rights. If such an apparently uneven legal battle seems surprising, this may suggest the importance attached to grazing rights, and a degree of desperation on the part of the Indian communities. From the point of view of Indian communities, it may be that Royal justice, however ineffective and improbable a solution, was the only straw to grasp at in the face of oppression by the local elite. The litigiousness of the Indian population, with varying degrees of success, has been emphasized in studies of other regions, and Quito does not appear to be an exception.[62]

"Nature abhors a vacuum," but nowhere more than on highly fertile land near dense concentrations of population. We have pointed out the continual colonial encroachments on the open grazing land near the city, culminating in the consolidation of the hacienda system at its expense. This process took virtually the same form as the enclosures in the English countryside at the same period—not least in the somewhat summary form of legal confirmation—and the consequences must have been largely similar in both cases: disruption of the peasant economy, enforced mobility, the absorption of an excess population by the cities insofar as they were able to sustain immigration, and the incorporation of part of the peasant labor force into the farms. The relationship between the expansion of the hacienda and the disappearance of Indian communities in the Andes has long been recognized, and perhaps somewhat exaggerated.[63] In the disappearance of Indian communities in the neighborhood of the capital, the factors discussed above played some role. The proximity and economic dominance of the

---

[61] ANH/Q Ind. doc. 16–IX–1768. See: J. Ortiz de la Tabla Ducasse, "Panorama económico y social del Corregimiento de Quito," *Revista de Indias,* (1976), 83–98.

[62] See, for example, Steve Stern, *Peru's Indian Peoples and the Challenge of Spanish Conquest: Huamanga to 1640,* (Madison, 1982). His material on litigation has also been published separately in G. A. Collier et al., *The Inca and Aztec States, 1400–1800,* (New York, 1982), 288–320.

[63] The hacienda was clearly an influence, but only one among many. The impact of the hacienda on indigenous communities as stressed by J. Lockhart in "Encomienda and Hacienda: The Evolution of the Great Estate in the Spanish West Indies," *HAHR,* 49 (1969), 425,427, has been subject to reservations by E. Grieshaber, "Survival of Indian Communities in Nineteenth Century Bolivia: A Regional Comparison," *Journal of Latin American Studies,* 12 (1980), 223–269. For a later description of the *ejidos,* confirming the retreat of grazing at the expense of intensive agriculture, see *Colombia, Relación Geográfica, Topográfica, Agrícola, Comercial y Política de este País,* (London, 1822), 213; the "two plains of Turubamba and Inna Quito were covered with small farms (*quintas*) and well cultivated."

capital, and later industrial growth must have completed a process of which one phase can be observed in the late-colonial period.

THE CORREGIMIENTO

The city of Quito with its rural district formed a single unit for administrative purposes, the *corregimiento* of Quito, comprising the city and its "five leagues," a little under thirty villages listed with slight variations on several occasions in the eighteenth century: San Juan Evangelista de Chimbacalle, María Magdalena, Chillogallo, Aloac, Aloasí, Machachi, Perucho, San Antonio de Lulumbamba, Pomasque, Calacalí, Cotocollao, Guayllabamba, Zámbiza, el Quinche, Yaruquí, Puembo y Pifo, Tumbaco, Cumbayá, Guápulo, Alangasí, Conocotoc, Pintag, Sangolquí, Amaguaña, Uyumbicho (Figure 2.2).[64]

Most essential agricultural products could be supplied from within a relatively narrow radius of the city, as the different ecological levels, providing complementary types of produce, are situated close together in the Ecuadorian Highlands.[65] One of the colonial descriptions summarized the broad distinction between these different altitudinal levels; at the higher altitudes, the "haciendas de Páramos" produced wheat, barley and potatoes; on the plains, maize production predominated; and at the lower levels, sugar cane etc.[66] For the mid-seventeenth century, the description of Diego Rodríguez Docampo fills out these general ecological imperatives with a detailed picture of the rural district of the capital.[67] Certain of the villages in the rural district were satellites of the city at that date, carrying out economic

---

[64] This paragraph summarises the lists of Juan and Ulloa, Alsedo, Montúfar, and the Anonymous of 1755. These lists have already been compared, see Don Dionisio de Alsedo y Herrera, *Descripción geográfica de la Real Audiencia de Quito,* [1766], (Madrid, 1915), note, p. 75; J. Ortiz de la Tabla Ducasse, "Panorama," 90; but for the reasons discussed in the text, it is not felt that these differences are a real problem.

[65] Oberem's concept of "micro-verticality" is an adaptation of the central Andean model of the "vertical archipelago," i. e. Indian "colonies" located at different ecological levels, to the ecological distinctiveness of the northern Andes. Indian groups, like the colonial city of Quito, did not have to look far afield for the produce of different ecological levels; U. Oberem, "El acceso a recursos naturales de diferentes ecologías en la sierra ecuatoriana. Siglo XVI," in: *Actes du XLII Congrès International des Américanistes,* (Paris, 1976) vol. IV, 51–64. J.V. Murra, *Formaciones económicas y políticas del Mundo Andino,* (Lima,1975), 59–115. Salomon, *Ethnic Lords of Quito,* 32–70, includes a discussion of ecology, partly following the geographer Acosta-Solís.

[66] Juan and Ulloa, *Relación Histórica,* 417–419.

[67] Diego Rodríguez Docampo, "Descripción y relación del estado eclesiástico ... de Quito" [1650], *RGI,* 3, 5–77.

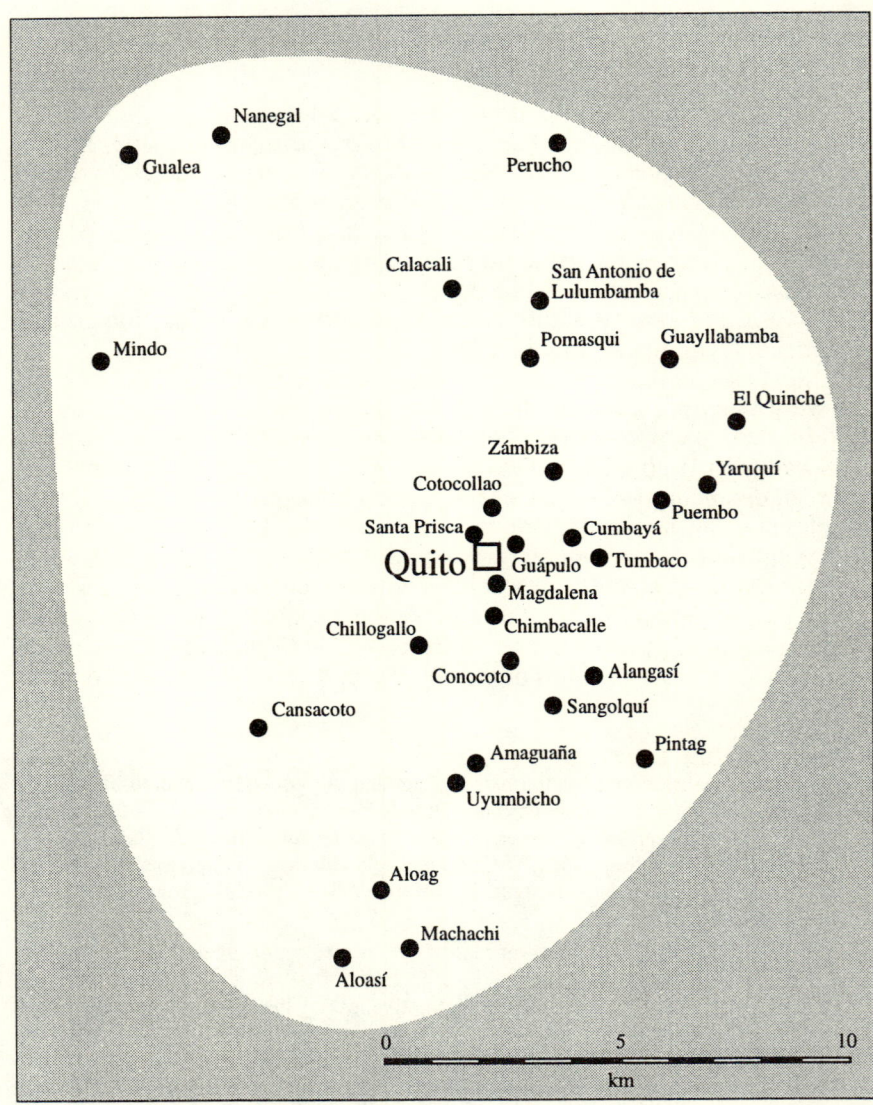

Figure 2.2 The *Corregimiento* of Quito

activities which directly served urban needs. The clearest example of this was the village of Uyumbicho, a community which had fled into the forest refuge to avoid the Spaniards, and had then been resettled in their modern location during the reducciones of the second half of the sixteenth century.[68] In 1650, the forest of Uyumbicho still supplied "wood, timber, panels, coach-straps, planks, door-posts, beams, rafters and a lot of firewood." If as this list implies, much of the wood was being prepared *in situ* for urban use, this suggests a local craft specialization in carpentry for the urban market.[69] The early seventeenth century action brought by an Indian carpenter from Uyumbicho, resident in Cuenca, but who carried out a contract for the construction of a mill in Latacunga, confirms this craft specialization as well as showing in striking fashion the mobility of skilled labor, a phenomenon which has been almost entirely hidden by more visible Indian migrations.[70] Another source of material for the city were the limestone quarries which provided lime for urban construction, and were located near Machachi further south.

With regard to the different ecological levels, only the "Provincia de Panzaleo," (Machachi) could be described as the place of "haciendas de Páramos" in Diego Rodríguez Docampo's account—described as "flat and cold," potatoes and barley were grown there, along with the grazing of animals. The rich agricultural land of the Chillos, at a slightly lower altitude than Quito, supplied wheat, maize and barley; this valley had been one of the most highly prized in the sixteenth century, as indeed it still is today.[71] Also at a lower altitude than the city, was the valley of Pomasque, described as the "principal gift of this city, for the orchards it contains."[72] For mid-

---

[68] Salomon, *Ethnic Lords of Quito,* 75–79. The carpenters are mentioned in: C. Caillavet, "Una 'Relación geografica' inédita de 1582 sobre Ecuador: Oyumbicho y Amaguaña del valle de los chillos," *Revista Andina*, Año 6, no. 2 (Dec. 1988), 525–536.

[69] Diego Rodríguez Docampo, "Descripción y relación del estado eclesiástico ... de Quito," 62–63.

[70] ANH/C 499, Not. I, July 22, 1612, fol. 240–241, Joan Pacha, Indian "carpintero" of Uyumbicho.

[71] For the Chillos see N. Cushner, *Farm and Factory: The Jesuits and the Development of Agrarian Capitalism,* (New York, 1982); C. Borchart de Moreno, "Composiciones de tierras en el valle de los Chillos a finales del siglo XVII: una contribución a la Historia Agraria de la Audiencia de Quito," *Cultura, Revista del Banco Central del Ecuador,* (Quito) 5 (1980), 257–281; F. Salomon, "Seis comunidades indígenas en las cercanías de Quito, 1559: la visita de Gaspar de San Martín y Juan Mosquera," *Boletín de la Academia Nacional de Historia,* (Quito), LIX (1977), 139–190; C. Caillavet, "Una Relación geografica inédita." By the mid-nineteenth century, the valley was already serving its present-day function of providing weekend villas for the richer residents of Quito; see Onffroy de Thoron, *L'Amérique* ... [1866], 268.

[72] Diego Rodríguez Docampo, "Descripción y relación del estado eclesiástico ... de Quito," 62: "es el principal regalo de esta ciudad, por las huertas que en sí tiene." I

colonial Cuzco, Gibbs found artisans investing in rural property, and a degree of diversification seems to have characterized Quito society at many different social levels.[73] For almost the same date as Diego Rodríguez Docampo's description, we find Francisco Hernández, master tailor of Quito, with a business in the main square—clearly dealing directly with affluent White society—purchasing an orchard of limes, oranges and other fruits in Pomasque, a hot valley north of Quito irrigated since Inca times.[74] Descending to a lower and therefore hotter ecological level, the valley of Guayllabamba supplied sugar as well as wheat and maize, and—like the hot cotton producing western slopes of the Andes—also produced tropical fruit.[75] Although the corregimiento produced a wide variety of agricultural products, the city also participated in a more long-range circuit of supply.[76]

When Juan and Ulloa visited the region in the late 1730s and early 1740s, they commented on the density of haciendas in the rural hinterland.[77] According to Alsedo, writing in the 1760s, although resident much earlier, the space between the villages in the neighborhood of Quito were so filled with "farms, animal-pens, country residences, fields and orchards ... that it could be said of Quito without exaggeration that it is a city so populous that it has for its suburbs the five leagues of the district of its corregimiento."[78] The type of production does not seem to have changed since the mid-seventeenth century—wheat, maize, barley, sugar from the hot valleys, and cattle grazing, with a production specifically geared to local urban consumption.[79] As elsewhere in the Audiencia, textile production was closely linked to the haciendas.[80] Although the thirty or so

---

know of a rich present-day Quiteño who offers himself the similar "treat" of properties at all the different ecological levels down to the tropical coast.

[73] Gibbs, *Cuzco, 1680–1710*, 126–7. See also Chapter 5 below.

[74] ANH/Q, 3 Not. Tomo I, Francisco Diaz de Asteiza, June 24, 1658, fol. 232; "una huerta de legumbres limas y naranjas y otros arboles frutales en el valle de Pomasque."

[75] Diego Rodríguez Docampo, "Descripción y relación del estado eclesiástico ... de Quito," 62; ANH/Q, 3 Not. Tomo I, Francisco Diaz de Asteiza Sept. 12, 1653, fol. 37, for the sale of "una estancia de cañaberales de castilla y mais y huerta ... en el valle de Guayllabamba."

[76] Marzahl, *Town in the Empire,* 27–31. For the later export of bread from Ambato to Quito, see Juan and Ulloa, *Relación Histórica,* 428; R. D. F. Bromley, *Urban Growth and Decline,* 128.

[77] Juan and Ulloa, *Relación Histórica*, 417.

[78] Don Dionisio de Alsedo y Herrera, *Descripción geográfica de la Real Audiencia de Quito,* [1766], (Madrid, 1915), 7.

[79] Montúfar, "Razón ...," 99. Juan and Ulloa, *Relación Histórica*, 402–403, also make the general point that the "Frutas de la Tierra" were mainly consumed locally in the Audiencia, in part because of high transport costs.

[80] See J. Ortiz de la Tabla, "Panorama," 94 for a list of *obrajes* (summarizing the *padrón* of *alcabalas,* 1768–1775).

villages of the Five Leagues represented the post-reducción ideal of nucleated centers through which the autocthonous population could be more easily controlled, Juan and Ulloa's comments show a relatively dispersed pattern of settlement. Apart from the church and the clergyman's house, "the rest can be reduced to mud huts covered with straw scattered in the fields, where each one has his *chacarita* or plot of land to sow."[81] The predominance of thatched roofs over tiled roofs in the rural district of the capital was noted above.

The broad demographic contrast between a mainly Indian countryside and a more racially mixed capital was strikingly demonstrated by the official censuses, which for all their defects, were unambiguous on this point. Mestizo penetration had affected some villages, but not to the extent of undermining this Indian predominance.[82] In what ways can we see the influence of the city on the Indian population of the corregimiento; and to reverse the question, how did the Indians of the rural zone contribute to urban society? Undoubtedly, the proximity of a major urban center stimulated particular forms of economic activity among the Indian population. Above we noted the Indian communities grazing mules on the common lands, and therefore almost certainly participating in mule-driving for inter-regional commerce. Within the corregimiento there was the domestic weaving of cotton cloth for consumption by the lower strata.[83] The peasant economy of the Indian communities surrounding the city interrelated directly with the hidden economy of the city, supplying agricultural produce which was often marketed independently of official controls.[84] Urban supply presupposed the physical presence of Indians from the corregimiento, and outlying regions who served as carriers, and were often depicted in later paintings of the city.[85]

The Indian population of the rural corregimiento formed a pool of labor on which the city could draw, both on a continuous small-scale level, and in a wider sense. Although the urban *mita,* the system of forced rotating Indian labor, had been technically abolished in the early seventeenth century,[86] the city often continued to require the mobilization of labor on a scale which the free market was unable to provide. A notable example of this was the rebuilding of the bridge of La Merced to which reference was made in the first part of this chapter. The Church played an indispensable role in mobilizing Indian labor for this work. In view of the cost and labor

---

[81] Juan and Ulloa, *Relación Histórica,* 419.
[82] See Chapter 5, below.
[83] Montúfar, "Razón ...," 100.
[84] See Chapter 5, below.
[85] The *costumbrista* painters of the nineteenth century include Juan Agustín Guerrero, *Imágenes del Ecuador del siglo XIX,* W. Hallo (ed.) Quito, 1981; Joaquín Pinto, *Ecuador Pintoresco,* Quito, 1977, and the anonymous painter of the collection Castro y Velázquez, Guayaquil.
[86] Cushner, *Farm and Factory,* 119.

requirements, Alsedo convoked "all the pueblos of the jurisdiction of the corregimiento, sending instructions to the priests and coadjutors so that they should come with all the people of their pueblos" to carry out the work which—for two months and twenty days, and between 5 o'clock in the morning and mid-day—they did.[87] This type of mass convergence of the Indian population on the city, albeit mobilized by the Church in the interests of the community, may shed an indirect light on the tensions between the urban plebe and the rural Indian population which will be examined below.[88] The centripetal role of the capital within its corregimiento—the Indians also came into the city for religious festivals—helps explain the plausibility of a mass Indian invasion of the city in 1765.[89] The close relationship of the rural zone with the capital must have reinforced the identification of Indians with forced—or semi-forced—manual labor. Although the city was mainly non-Indian by the second half of the eighteenth century, it had frequent contact with the rural Indian population, and its population had in some cases only recently left it. The white and mixed-blood city and the Indian countryside were in no sense isolated from each other.

THE ECUADORIAN HIGHLANDS

Quito was the capital of the Audiencia of the same name, but that entity consisted of a network of distinct jurisdictions, some of which lay beyond its effective authority.[90] In administrative terms, a limited field of direct Audiencia influence can be identified, consisting of the northern and central Ecuadorian Highlands—the city of Quito, the *villas* of Ibarra, Ambato, and Riobamba, and *asiento* of Latacunga along with associated villages and smaller centers (Figure 2.3). The northern and central highlands can be

---

[87] Alsedo, letter, June 18, 1732, AGI Quito 132, fol. 9.
[88] See Chapter 8 below on the "scare" of 1762.
[89] See details of the 1765 rebellion in Chapter 8 below.
[90] A. Pareja Diezcanseco, *Las Instituciones y la Administración de la Real Audiencia De Quito* (Quito, 1975), 224-227, for the different jurisdictions. The *corregimiento* of Guayaquil was promoted into a semi-autonomous *gobernación* in 1763, as was that of Cuenca after 1770, Cuenca later being the scene of the only attempt to introduce the Intendant system into the Audiencia. Along with Quito both Cuenca and Guayaquil housed Royal Treasuries. Although administrative control can be measured by different indices, one of the best ways of measuring it is through the Audiencia's exercise of its judicial authority, in principle, its highest function. After the 1770s nearly all the cases heard before the Audiencia with regard to tribute exemption on the grounds of being Mestizo came from the area mentioned above (see Chapter 7). Marzahl's examination of Popayán shows the way different jurisdictions overlapped in what was also technically part of the Audiencia of Quito: Marzahl, *Town in the Empire,* 9.

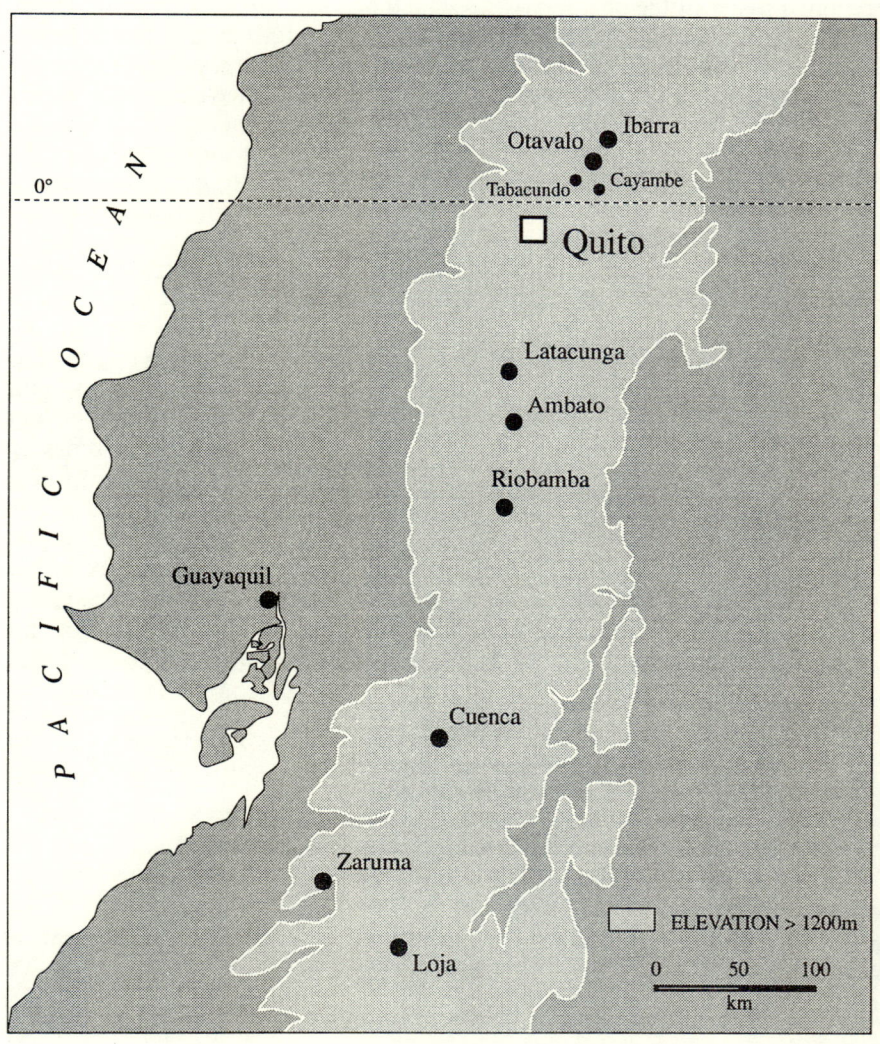

Figure 2.3 The Urban Settlements of the Audiencia of Quito

considered together for other than purely administrative reasons. In the seventeenth century, this area had been the center of the textile industry, and retained many of the characteristics which had sustained its growth—major self-sufficient estates oriented around textile and agricultural production, a substantial rural Indian population to provide them with a stable labor force, and considerable grazing lands for the sheep which provided wool for the obrajes. A series of urban centers—Ibarra, Quito, Latacunga, Ambato and Riobamba—formed economic, administrative and ecclesiastical centers which commercialized rural products, and directed the local economy, as well as serving as centers of cultural diffusion in a predominantly Indian countryside. The different socio-economic roles of city and countryside were reflected in their distinctive demographic characteristics. The urban centers were predominantly white and Mestizo, while the region as a whole was 70.7 percent Indian.[91]

It is not within the scope of this study to examine this wider area in detail, but it is appropriate to stress the difficulties of communications in the Audiencia which were certainly no better than in the early colonial or Inca periods.[92] Roads within the corregimiento of Quito were liable to break up into ravines in the rainy season.[93] The fiscal accounts of Indian prisoners in 1778, being escorted from Quito to imprisonment in the textile factories of the Central Sierra, may be taken as illustrative of the conditions of transport within the Audiencia, the journey between Quito and Ambato taking six days.[94] More typical traffic using horses and mules was, however, quicker, according to a description of the distances between Quito and its principal port of Guayaquil written at the beginning of the nineteenth century.[95] This

---

[91] Calculation based on R. B. Tyrer, *The Demographic and Economic History of the Audiencia of Quito: Indian Population and the Textile Industry*, doctoral dissertation (Berkeley, 1976), 51, from the censuses for 1779, now in the section reclassified "Empadronamientos" of the ANH/Q. The Whites and Mestizos were 26.3 percent, the (small) difference being made up of free coloreds and slaves. Chapter 6 demonstrates the White and Mestizo dominance of Quito; for the Central Sierra, see R. D. F. Bromley, *Urban Growth and Decline*.

[92] J. C. Super, "Partnership and Profit in the Early Andean Trade: The Experience of Quito merchants, 1580–1610," *Journal of Latin American Studies*, 11 (1979), 265–267.

[93] The *libros de cabildo* in the AM/Q include constant references to this problem throughout the colonial period.

[94] ANH/Q Pres. 112, doc. 3930, fol. 4.

[95] BL Add. 17,588, fol. 67: "Razon de las leguas y jornadas que hay desde Guayaquil a Quito" (26 Nov.1812). The fact that the Indian prisoners (fol. note 96) stopped at Mulalo, Machachi and Tambillo confirms their role as staging posts, otherwise indicated in the case of Tambillo by its name which is from the Quechua term for inn. For a traveller who left Quito on July 28, 1766, and arrived in Lima, November 21, 1766, see. "Cuaderno de Guachucal en la Provincia de los Pastos ..." Ny kgl. Samling 568 (4), manuscript of the Royal Library, Copenhagen, consulted in the transcription of Juan Castro y Velázquez. For a traveller of the 1740s who

long thirteen-day journey to the principal port of Guayaquil involved a difficult descent of the Andes, and was notorious for "the roughness of the journey."[96]

Trading links followed essentially the north-south axis of the Equatorial Andes, along which the main population centers of the Audiencia were located, together with lateral links to the coast, notably Guayaquil. The three main routes were either south to Lima via Guayaquil, or the alternative overland route of Cuenca-Loja-Piura, and—increasingly after the failure of the Quito textiles to maintain their competitiveness on the Lima market in the early eighteenth century—north to the markets of Popayán and New Granada.[97] Contemporaries recognized that high overland costs were reducing the competitiveness of the region's exports. The project to open up the shorter east-west route to Esmeraldas which would reduce the isolation of the Audiencia and stimulate its economy was seen as the *deus ex machina* which could save the Audiencia.[98] Nevertheless, although some improvements were made to the Lima-Quito road by intendants in the north of Peru,[99] it is clear that communications with other areas were essentially unimproved prior to the second half of the nineteenth century. According to Tyrer, transport costs for Quito's textiles were rising at the time when prices were falling on the Lima market in the eighteenth century, and it is

---

also passed through Machachi and Tambillo see David J. Robinson, *Mil leguas por América, de Lima a Caracas, 1740–1741: Diario de don Miguel de Santisteban* (Bogotá, 1992), 75, 108–109.

[96] AGN/L Superior Gobierno, Leg. 15. Cuad. 400, 1776: "Autos promovidos ante el Superior Gobierno el Dr. don Luis de Santa Cruz, Oidor de la Real Audiencia de Quito, que fuera nombrado para igual cargo en la de la Plata, solicitando se le permitiese permanecer en Lima, pues el largo viaje de Quito a Guayaquil lo habia imposibilitado para continuar [el] viaje al lugar de su destino," fol. 1. He set off for Lima despite "... lo aspero de la Montaña de Guaiaquil, fragosidad de caminos, y notorios quebrantos de salud."

[97] For these three routes, D. Alsedo y Herrera, *Descripción*, 8–11. For the textile industry's decline, R. B. Tyrer, *The demographic and economic history*.

[98] For early attempts to open up a route to the coast, J. L. Phelan, *The Kingdom of Quito*, 3; for the late-colonial period, abundant documentation has been published by José Rumazo González: *Documentos para la historia de la Audiencia de Quito*, (Madrid, 1948–1950). See, for example, vol. 5, 115, the "Edicto del Obispo de Quito Don José Pérez Calama sobre el proyecto de apertura del camino de Malbucho"; "... las Provincias de Ibarra y Octabalo formen pacto social, o Hermandad Mercantil con las de Isquandé, Chocó, Barbacoas, y la Plaza de Panamá. Con esto tendremos Oro y Plata; las Manos muertas resucitarán, y se convertirán en Avejas Industriosas. Y en una palabra: habremos encontrado, y poseeremos el arte de *hazer Oro.*" In the early nineteenth century, Bolívar offered tax exemptions for settling on the route Quito-Esmeraldas; David Bushnell, *The Santander Régime* (Westport, 2nd edn. 1970), 140. A railway was built earlier this century.

[99] J. R. Fisher, *Government and Society in Colonial Peru: The Intendant System, 1784–1814,* (London, 1970), 147, 170.

clear that Quito's distance from its market severely handicapped its competitiveness.[100]

The consequences of Quito's geographical isolation from the main centers of the Indies were therefore economically significant as well as psychologically so. Isolation, marginality, economic stagnation: Quito was clearly one of the backwaters of the Spanish Empire. As symptomatic of the way social evolution interacted with these geographical imperatives to create an inward-looking hierarchical society, we may note the extensive use of Indians as carriers, in part to offset the difficulties of transport. This early colonial practice was still firmly entrenched when the Austrian-born North American Hassaurek visited Quito in the mid-nineteenth century, and his comments clarify the deep-rooted nature of colonial attitudes which certainly did not end with formal independence from Spain:

> "... while horses and mules are called bagajes mayores, asses and Indians are called bagajes menores; that is to say, as a beast of burden, the Indian is considered below the horse and the mule, and on a level with the donkey."[101]

Unlike coastal ports, and to a lesser extent than the Viceregal capitals, Quito had little direct contact with the outside world—its peninsular Spanish presence was extremely reduced[102]—and the society discussed hereinafter is certainly one which looked inwards rather than out.

Conclusion

Alsedo's identification of the whole of the corregimiento as a kind of suburb is a valuable reminder of the determining influence of the city on its rural vicinity. The extent to which an urban-rural continuum has been recognized within urban societies has varied considerably in analyses of modern Latin-American cities. It is argued here, that the geographical particularity of colonial Quito—combined with its lack of dynamic growth and size as a medium-sized city in the late-colonial period—make this emphasis particularly appropriate.

In the sixteenth century, the Spanish city was founded across ravines for strategic reasons, as a protective measure in hostile Indian countryside.

---

[100] Tyrer, *The Demographic and Economic History,* 210.

[101] Hassaurek, *Four years Among the Ecuadorians,* 105; Super noted the use of Indian carriers in the early colonial period; "Partnership and Profit ...," 266. For illustrations see the genre painters, cited above.

[102] Fewer than 100 Spaniards lived in Quito; ANC/B, Colonia-Aguardientes del Ecuador, Tomo II, fols. 436–459 (census 1765); 37 Europeans married in the Sagrario, Quito, 1764–1805; J. Moreno Egas, "Resumen alfabético del segundo libro de matrimonios de españoles ..." *Revista del Centro Nacional de Investigaciones Genealógicas* 1 (Quito) 1981, 195.

If we follow Alsedo's definition of the quebradas as rivers, or river-gullies, we are less likely to miss a dimension which was equally present in early-modern Europe, such cities as Seville and its more popular district of Triana, or the more and less fashionable parts of London, also being separated by rivers. The physical separation of one part of Quito from one another can only have reinforced the village character of the barrios. If we see the barrios acting as cohesive communities, not least when they riot, this may be precisely because they are—or have been—villages, in a literal rather than a metaphorical sense: separate communities with their own territory, marked off by ravines, giving radially onto a nuclear center which retained its residential prestige.

The parish has necessarily been accepted as an essential unit of study. Nevertheless, there are several hints in the documentation of what might be called sub-barrios, more restricted neighborhoods which may lie within, or even overlap the parishes. Does the phrase "el barrio de ... X" simply mean "near X," or does it denote a locality with a substantive existence?[103] It is difficult to go beyond noting their existence, for that would be to enter the substratum of Quito society beneath—or more exactly between—the levels (family and parish) which the historian can reach. A society functions at many levels, and many threads bind communities together: in emphasizing the territoriality and cohesiveness of certain of these, and the frontiers which reinforce their coherence and identity, it is not necessarily intended to identify the neighborhood as coterminous with the parish in a legalistic sense. Nevertheless, it is striking to see the extent to which the riots appear to involve either the mobilization of a particular parish, or the association of one or more different parishes in collaboration with each other.

A corollary of an emphasis on the quasi-rural characteristics of the barrios, (villages separated by ravines/rivers from the center of the city, and in some cases semi-agricultural) is that urban society can only be understood through a careful sensitivity to urban-rural contrasts. The extramural parish of Santa Prisca or villages like Guápulo lay directly within the sphere of influence of the city, while some of those baptized in the urban parishes were brought in from rural obrajes. The cultivation of small agricultural plots within the city, or such examples as the attempts recorded in the municipal records to control pigs running through the streets,[104] are a continuous reminder of the proximity of city and countryside. The size of a city certainly plays a role and we may expect different characteristics in a city with a recorded population of around 25,000 inhabitants in 1780, than in Lima or Mexico City which may have been two to four times as large.

---

[103] See for example ANH/Q, 1 Not., Diego de Ocampo, Tomo 246 (1728-1731), fols. 77, 79, 81, 254, 337, which mention "el barrio de Ichimbía" and "el barrio de la Carnicería," etc.

[104] AM/Q Cartas de Cabildo, (vol. 54), 7 Jan. 1772, fol. 24, and other examples in the libros de cabildo from the sixteenth century onwards.

The city of Quito provides the urban setting of the rest of this study, while its rural hinterland, and to a lesser extent the Andean region as a whole, provide the larger framework within which the evidence can be examined. When data are introduced relating to rural areas, they are identified as such, and used to establish to what extent, if at all, it is possible to separate "urban" and "rural" in the social history of colonial Quito. The division of the city into six parishes, cannot be taken as an exact definition of its urban space. This legal ambiguity in the separation of city and countryside is, however, common to many Spanish-American and indeed European cities.[105] Specific to Quito is the extent to which its social geography was shaped and reinforced by a difficult and distinctive urban environment.

---

[105] See, for example, Antonio Domínguez Ortiz, *Sociedad y Estado en el siglo XVIII español,* (Madrid-Barcelona, 2nd edn. 1981), 385.

Chapter 3

THE SOCIAL FORMATION OF COLONIAL QUITO, 1534–1720

The second chapter presented a social geography of colonial Quito, stressing continuities in the utilization of the urban space. Here that spatial overview is complemented by a diachronic analysis which underlines those themes from the sixteenth and seventeenth centuries which reappear in the late-colonial period. To hold the threads together over such a varied terrain, a considerable sharpening of focus has been necessary. In assimilating the treatment of the relevant themes to specific phases in the city's growth, it is intended to supply the essential early and mid-colonial background. The three themes examined here are:

- The character and consequences of Spanish-Indian culture contact, and the early formation of the Mestizo class (to c. 1600/1620)
- The economic organization of the capital during the seventeenth century expansion of the textile economy
- A period of economic readjustment (1690–1720)

Although each period was defined in relation to the theme of this study, they correspond very loosely to a telescoped version of the familiar transition from a conquest society to a more stable, organized one; and from the mid-colonial period to one of difficult readjustments, economic decline and fiscal pressure which was to culminate in the "importation" from neighboring regions of political independence from Spain. The chronological separation of the first two themes is a reflection of the higher level of visibility which certain subjects possessed at specific periods. The term "Mestizo" had a real social (and biological) meaning in the sixteenth century, before the process of *mestizaje* blurred racial boundaries. During the seventeenth century, the category disappeared into the shadows out of which it would only be brought by a partial attempt by the Crown to revive caste for fiscal purposes in the late eighteenth century. Similarly, the particular interest of the sixteenth century evidence on Spanish-Indian interaction hardly needs stressing, but it may be noted that at that period, the

Crown was interested in familiarizing itself with its new subjects, and the early colonial ethnographic evidence is incomparably superior to that on the seventeenth century. For seventeenth-century Quito, discussion shifts therefore from social and racial interaction to an examination of the textile industry which had an important role in shaping the social structure which characterized late-colonial Quito.

The three groups whose interaction concerns us were Spaniards, Indians and Blacks, but the relatively small place occupied by the Black presence in the discussion which follows requires some explanation. In the early and mid-colonial period, highland Ecuador had a large and relatively stable Indian population and Black slaves were not required on a large scale except in coastal regions and the extreme north and south of the Audiencia where sugar plantations in the low, hot valleys were supplied with a Black labor force.[1] In Quito there was a nominal Black presence from its foundation, and a small-scale importation of slaves throughout the colonial period, but the urban Black population was still only 1,483 out of 25,325, (5.85 percent) according to the census summary of 1781.[2] This is a demographic fact of some significance for the examination of Quito's plebe, as it marks a real difference with nearly all other major Spanish American urban centers,[3] and constitutes an additional argument for examining Quito in close relationship with its rural hinterland. The city's racial mix was largely Indian-White, similar to that of the surrounding society.

Nevertheless, although small, Quito's urban Black population had a social importance somewhat beyond its numbers. As will be argued below, slaves had a key and by no means subordinate role to play in relation to the "free" urban lower strata. Although not dominating the lower artisanal and petty mercantile classes, free Blacks certainly occupied a small but significant place. In the padrón of Santa Bárbara in 1768, for example, there were *mulato* women working as *chagro,* that is selling items of prime

---

[1] L. B. Rout Jr., *The African Experience in Spanish America: 1502 to the Present Day,* (Cambridge, 1976), 226–235, summarizes the Ecuadorian evidence, but for the Independence period. For the "problem" of the Black population of the south of the Audiencia, see M. Minchom, "The making of a white province: demographic movement and ethnic transformation in the south of the Audiencia de Quito," *Bulletin de l'Institut Français d'Études Andines,* XII, 3–4 (1983), 23–39.

[2] For the Black presence at the foundation of Santiago de Quito (the foundation which preceded Quito's present site) see *LCQ* Libro Primero, Tomo I (1534), 35: "Anton de color negro"; See also p. 55, "Pedro de Salinas de color negro." "Bartolomé de color moreno" was named town crier (*pregonero*) in 1573; *LCQ,* July 3, 1573, 42–43. For slave sales see footnote 22. For the census of 1781 see Chapter 5, following the volume "Censos del Ecuador" in the ANC/B.

[3] For estimations of the Black population of Lima, see F. P. Bowser, *The African Slave in Colonial Peru,* (Stanford, 1974); Spanish edn. Siglo XXI, 407–411. Guayaquil had a more substantial Black presence than Quito: see Juan Antonio Zelaya, "Estado de la Provincia de Guayaquil, Agosto 17, 1765," *Revista del Archivo Histórico del Guayas,* (Dec. 1974), 98.

necessity to the lower strata. The tailor Parra, variously described as *sambo* and mulato, was the prisoner liberated by the "lads" of San Roque on December 31, 1747. Quito's Tom Paine, the Enlightenment propagandist, philosopher and rebel, Espejo, was also possibly of part-Black origin.[4] The difficulty of ascertaining the exact ethnic status of Parra or Espejo is symptomatic of the process of absorption of the free Black population into urban society, which made ethnic classification of urban groups in more racially diverse urban centers particularly hazardous.[5] In the ecclesiastical padrones of the 1790s which adopted "minimal" ethnic identification, we find almost no free Blacks. It may certainly be argued that late-colonial data on all free Black urban populations (including better-known cases like Buenos Aires) have to be treated with extreme caution. However, although its quantification may be suspect, there is little doubt that the Black presence in colonial Quito was indeed small, and that the process which essentially concerns us is the interaction of Spanish and Indian societies.

The Socio-racial Matrix, 1534–1600

The Spaniards who conquered the region of Quito in 1534, encountered a dispersed population divided into the numerous small chiefdoms which the Inca had harnessed to their Empire by a mixture of force and astute realpolitik.[6] Although from its foundation urban Quito had an autochthonous population directly alongside the Spanish settlement, the pre-Hispanic population of the city and its immediate vicinity was probably not dense; its colonial Indian population was essentially the product of reorganization into settled parochial structures in the 1560s and 1570s, and the subsequent expansion of the city.[7] The concentration of Spanish settlement into the quebradas of nuclear Quito was accompanied by the usual measures of conquerors in colonial Spanish America: the creation of a municipality, distribution of urban plots and rights to land.[8] Quito's urban morphology took on the shape discussed in the previous chapter.

For the sixteenth century, a series of descriptions compiled in the 1570s and 1580s may be used to provide an overview of Quito's crystallizing social structure before we turn to the parish records for more

---

[4] According to a contemporary, "su madre fue fulana Aldaz, aunque es dudosa su naturaleza, pero toda la duda recae en si es india o mulata," cited by P. Astuto, "Eugenio Espejo: A man of the enlightenment in Ecuador," *Revista de Historia de América,* 44 (1957), 371.

[5] M. Minchom, "The making of a white province," 29, 36–38.

[6] For pre-Hispanic Quito, F. Salomon, *Ethnic Lords of Quito*, 1978.

[7] *Ibid.*, 206, where Salomon argues that the pre-Hispanic settlement may not have been dense. For the parochial structure of the city, see Chapter 2.

[8] Compare, for example, J. W. Schotellius, "Die Gründung Quitos," *Ibero-Amerikanisches Archiv,* IX-X (1936–7), 276–294; 55–77.

detailed data on the lower strata. The *relaciones geográficas* show clearly that the main benefits of conquest went to a fairly restricted group of Spaniards, and by the 1570s, the city had a small élite of over thirty *encomenderos*.[9] These were joined, however, by half a dozen wealthy merchants involved in international commerce whose wealth—at a doubtless approximate figure of 15,000–20,000 pesos—surpassed that of all but four of the encomenderos.[10] More small-scale merchants selling through retail outlets were considerably less rich, as were a hundred or so land-holding *moradores* (residents holding an inferior statute to the *vecinos*), and diverse other residents.[11] According to the Anonymous account of 1573, there had been a shortage of artisanal skills in the earliest period of settlement, and the municipality was still badly built: the shortage of skilled labor had now been overcome.[12] There was a "good number" ("bastante número") of what was still a fairly narrow range of artisanal occupations, "tanners, shoemakers, saddlemakers, harnessmakers, blacksmiths, masons, carpenters, hosiers and silver-smiths."[13] The more specialist requirements of a settled urban population were soon being provided by *inter alia* a small number of foreigners, if the Portuguese can be described in these terms: in 1596 an apothecary and a hatmaker paid for their licenses in Quito.[14]

---

[9] The *relaciones geográficas* were published in the nineteenth century by Marcos Jiménez de la Espada, *Relaciones Geográficas de Indias: Perú*, 3 vols. (Madrid, 1965), cited hereafter as *RGI*. "Relación de las cibdades y villas que hay en el distrito de la Audiencia Real que reside en la cibdad de Quito," *RGI*, II, 183, mentions 48 for 1583. Pedro Rodríguez de Aguayo, "Descripción de la ciudad de Quito y vecindad de ella," *RGI*, II, 203, for 30 in the 1570s. Anónimo, "La cibdad de Sant Francisco de Quito, 1573," *RGI*, II, 215–6, lists 37 *encomiendas* including vacant ones.

[10] "La cibdad de Sant Francisco de Quito, 1573," 217–218. Furthermore, one of these *encomenderos* appears to have acquired his wealth in the same way; the two richest *encomenderos*, Rodrigo de Salazar and Francisco Ruiz, at 50,000 *pesos*, were exceptional in holding the major *encomiendas* of Otavalo and a number of Indian communities near Quito. The other *encomenderos* were 10,000 *pesos* or less, and some of them in debt. According to Pedro Rodríguez de Aguayo, "Descripción de la ciudad de Quito," 203, there were 14 merchants "de tiendas gruesas" as well as the small-scale retail *pulperos*. J. Super, on the other hand, argues that few merchants were able to "... accumulate the wealth needed for entry into ... the Andean elite"; "Partnership and profit in the early andean trade: experiences of Quito merchants, 1580–1610," *Journal of Latin American Studies*, 11 (1979), 279.

[11] "La cibdad de Sant Francisco de Quito, 1573," 216, 218; from 200 *pesos* up to 6,000.

[12] *Ibid.*, 222.

[13] *Ibid.*, 218.

[14] Javier Ortiz de la Tabla Ducasse, "Extranjeros en la Audiencia de Quito (1595–1603)," *América y la España del Siglo XVI* (Madrid, 1983), vol. II, 107–113

Super has noted that Quito merchants, unlike their English counterparts, did not make provision in their wills for the continuation of their enterprises.[15] Despite an "aggressive commercial outlook," profits were finally channeled into ecclesiastical bequests and commercial activity cannot therefore be said to have been translated into a mercantile mentality which undermined conservative social attitudes. At the lower level of the urban artisans of Quito, social values were characterized by the Anonymous account of 1573:

> Those who do not use their offices are Antón Prieto, mason, because he is rich, and a fellow called González because he is married to a woman who has Indians; he is a mason. None of the said officials (tanners, shoemakers ...) is rich.[16]

The artisans who arrived in the Indies did not do so in order to be artisans, but to take advantage of the possibilities of New World wealth and social mobility. If González has been able to make an advantageous marriage that is also because he is White, and social distinctions have not yet solidified into racial ones. The values of a non-mercantile conquest society, in which manual labor in particular was considered dishonorable, has often been considered a Medieval characteristic, albeit given a new expression in colonial society in which one of the initial sources of personal wealth and prestige was Indian tribute and labor.[17] Social barriers widened with the formation of an essentially Mestizo and Indian artisanal urban sector along with the parallel emergence of a Creole elite which, if it was still absorbing newcomers from the metropolis, formed a direct link with the *hacendado-obrajero* families of the eighteenth century.[18] In Spanish America, the category of Spaniard was assimilated into that of noble.[19]

---

publishes the *composiciones* found in AGI Contaduría 1537; "La cibdad de Sant Francisco de Quito, 1573," 224.

[15] Super, "Partnership and profit," 279–281.

[16] "La cibdad de Sant Francisco de Quito, 1573," 219; "Los que no usan sus oficios son Antón Prieto, albañil, por estar rico, y fulano González, por estar casado con muger que tiene indios; es albañir. Los dichos oficiales [c.f. footnote 13 above] no hay alguno de ellos que esté rico."

[17] See J. H. Parry, *The Spanish Seaborne Empire,* (London, 2nd edn. 1973), 1–13, for a brief summary of "the tradition of conquest." I do not feel that the essential point is undermined by A. Arriaza, "The Castilian Bourgeoisie and the Caballeros Villanos in the Concejo before 1300: A Revisionist View," *HAHR,* 63 (1983), 517–536, who upgrades the role of the Castilian bourgeoisie.

[18] See the work of Javier Ortiz de la Tabla, and especially the genealogical tables published in: "El obraje ecuatoriano. Aproximación a su estudio," *Revista de Indias,* 145/50, (1977), 471–542. This approach, however, is open to criticism for its misleading use of ascendant genealogy. The fact that the leading eighteenth-century families had *some* ancestors who were first generation *encomenderos,* does not disprove the existence of some measure of élite circulation; nearly all White

In the 1570s Spaniards and Indians could still be found in the same occupational categories; according to the Anonymous report of 1573, for example, both Spaniards and Indians were already engaged in saddle- and harness-making at that date.[20] The category of "poor Spaniard," however, would soon lose much of its precision, as many artisanal occupations were progressively subject to a socio-racial transformation exemplified in contracts between Spanish artisans and Indian apprentices.[21] The baptismal records of the El Sagrario parish, Quito, include occupational data for the late sixteenth century, and the births of the children of a number of artisans are recorded for this period of transition. In late 1596, the following entries appeared in the baptismal records largely reserved for the Indians and Blacks :

TABLE 3.1 BAPTISMS OF CHILDREN OF INDIAN ARTISANS, 1596

Date	Parents			Origin of Parents	Godparent
	FATHER	OCCUPATION	MOTHER		
8/11/1596	Domingo	sastre	Barbola (I)	Chillo	I
9/15/1596	Blas (I)	pintor	Catalina (I)	unknown	I
10/6/1596	Gaspar	pintor	Ynes Chubay	Quito	Congo S
10/21/1596	Joan	ollero	Beatris	Cotocolla	S
11/24/1596	Pedro	yndio sapatero	Joana	Quito	unknown

Note: I: Indian S: Slave

Source: APQ/ Sagrario, "Libro de Bautismos de Mestizos, Montaneses, Yndios" (1594–1605).

These artisans—a tailor, two painters, a saddlemaker, and a shoemaker respectively—have names which show they have lost all contact with autochthonous lineages; they are married to Indian women, but their occupation identifies the sense in which they are specifically urban rather

> Quiteños and many mixed-bloods and perhaps Indians too must also have been descended from *encomenderos* by the eighteenth century. To set the genealogical evidence against the data on a rapid turnover of property transactions in other regions, as Mörner does, is therefore to mix quite distinct forms of evidence. See Mörner "Economic Factors and Stratification in Colonial Spanish America with special regard to Elites," *HAHR,* 63 (1983), 351, note 39.

19 See the discussion in J. L. Phelan, *The Kingdom of Quito,* 234.
20 "La cibdad de Sant Francisco de Quito, 1573," 222.
21 This process was emphasized by J. Lockhart, *Spanish Peru.* Artisanal data are abundant in the early colonial records but progressively lose much of their detail. See, for example, ANH/Q Not. 1, vol. 2 (1588) fol. 238; Not. 6 vol. 2 (1583) fol. 1,154 for contracts of apprenticeship.

than part of traditionally structured rural Indian society. All have "low" ethnic status, in that they are Indian, married to Indians, and/or have ties of *compadrazgo* (compaternity) with Blacks. Other Indian baptisms between July and December 1596 include a high ratio of Blacks serving as godparents to Indians, constituting 19.3 percent of the total of godparents to non-Black children (18 out of 93), which can be compared with a total of only 6 Black baptisms out of 99.

The role of Blacks as godparents certainly provides an interesting clue to inter-ethnic relations in the lower urban strata. It is difficult to say how far compaternity really created ties of spiritual kinship (as well as economic links) at this level of society in early colonial Quito. In many of these cases, the common service role of both Indian and Black categories to the Spanish population explains this interaction without clarifying the workings of these ties within the household. Possibly the rarity of slaves in colonial Quito, who cost the very considerable sum of 400 pesos or so,[22] reinforced their position in the hierarchy of domestic service, and made them a power to be reckoned with for the Indian lower strata. Far more rapidly assimilated to Spanish culture than the Indians,[23] the Blacks must have mediated between the Spanish owners and Indian society, serving as the last step in the rung of Spanish society and taking on the ties of compaternity which were beneath the master's sphere of direct contact. That the role of the Blacks as *compadres* apparently extended beyond the Spanish household may suggest either that they were artisans themselves (not apparently so in this case) or that they were able to extend a measure of patronage by bringing artisans within the protection of a wealthy Spanish household. Independent confirmation of this hypothesis is given by a somewhat later law-suit from the seventeenth century, when it was claimed

---

22   Slave prices can be culled from the notarial records, and obviously depended on age, sex, physical fitness etc. The slave market in Quito was always a fairly small-scale affair. The largest consignment I noted was for 5 slaves in 1634, all African-born, for a total of 2,080 *patacones,* i.e. a little over 400 apiece (ANH/Q Not. Diego Rodríguez Urbán, Tomo 55, fols. 9–10). By the eighteenth century, the market was on an even smaller scale, and weighted towards female slaves, presumably for domestic service. When two slaves were sold it was usually because they belonged to the same family (e. g. ANH/Q 1 Not. Ambrosio del Capillo, Tomo 244, fols. 63–64, Aug. 14, 1728; ANH/Q 1 Not. Diego de Ocampo, Tomo 276, fols. 184–185, May 21, 1754). Slave prices stayed fairly high in the eighteenth century which, in view of the deflation of Quito's economy suggests they were becoming, if anything, an even more precious "commodity." Slaves were the auxiliaries of White society, and we will later note the hostility of the *plebe* to the black servant of a Court official Blacks were certainly often a force that were hated and feared. On the other hand, the data given in the text show that inter-ethnic relations in the lower strata should not be over-simplified. We may note the purchase of a young girl for 330 pesos by a wealthy cacique, don Justo Titusunta de Llamoca, of Angamarca and Saquisilí, but resident in Quito, on August 22, 1731. (ANH/Q 1 Not. Diego de Ocampo, fols. 643–4).

23   This is a point made repeatedly by Bowser, *The African Slave in Colonial Peru.*

that Black slaves were stealing food delicacies (*alfaxores, bocadillos, turrones*) from White households which were subsequently resold by Indian market-women in the market squares of the city.[24] The evidence of this small-scale independent economic activity and of separate ties with the non-servant population certainly shows that slavery was a far more flexible and permeable system than its stereotype allows.[25]

For the early colonial period, it is probably safest to stay with strictly racial categories rather than attempting to discuss the lower strata in terms of "popular society," a more diffuse concept which is probably best reserved for the more diverse society of the late-colonial period. The place of the Indians and Mestizos in Quito society may therefore be emphasized. The general demographic background for highland Ecuador was a relatively stable Indian population which may have been exempt from the worst demographic consequences of the Spanish conquest, or received a masked immigration in the form of "refugees" from the mita service of the Central Andes; the authors of the geographical descriptions of the 1570s concurred in ascribing an expanding Indian population to both the general district of Quito and the city itself.[26] The baptismal records reserved for the Indians, Blacks and Mestizos of the Cathedral parish of the Sagrario, Quito, were examined for the period July 14 to December 1, 1596, and during 1612. Since El Sagrario parish corresponded to the Spanish city, these groups can

---

[24] ANH/Q Carn. y Pulp. Doc, 7–VII–1642.

[25] See, for example, D. L. Chandler, "Slave over master in colonial Colombia and Ecuador," *The Americas,* 38 (1982), 315–326, for an interesting discussion of a number of ways slaves could "play the system." Despite its title, however, this article uses almost no Ecuadorian material.

[26] For the growth of the city, and Highlands, "Relación de las cibdades y villas," 183; Rodríguez de Aguayo,"Descripción de la ciudad de Quito," 203; "La cibdad de Sant Francisco de Quito, 1573," 221. The role of the Potosí *mita* in generating demographic movement over a vast region of the Andes including regions of refuge has been examined by N. Sánchez-Albornoz, *Indios y Tributos en el Alto Perú,* (Lima, 1978). For the possibility of the Audiencia of Quito as a "region of refuge," see "Relación del distrito del Cerro de Zaruma y distancias a la ciudad de Quito ..." (1592), *RGI,* II, 319; "Y el acudir tantos vagabundos a lo de Quito, lo causa ser la tierra fertilísima y de lindísimo temple y no les costar casi nada la comida, *y lo principal, no haber minas donde los puedan echar."* (My italics). Cook's study of Peru does not include Ecuadorian data; N. D. Cook, *Demographic Collapse, 1520–1620,* (Cambridge, 1981). For the population curve of the Indian population see the first chapter of R. B. Tyrer, *The demographic and Economic History of the Audiencia de Quito.* See now S. A. Alchon, *Native Society and Disease in Colonial Ecuador,* Cambridge, 1991. Also Linda Newson, "Old World epidemics in early colonial Ecuador," in N. D. Cook and W. G. Lovell (eds.) *'Secret Judgements of God': Old World Disease in Colonial Spanish America* (Norman, OK, 1992), 84–112.

be taken as the ones on which Spanish influence was most strongly exerted. Mestizos were often included in the book of Spanish baptisms, and this register was composed essentially of Indian baptisms, with a few slaves. There were 99 baptisms in the first period, and 651 during the second (including 248 during the comparable period of July 15 to December 2, 1612). Although this is only a narrow sample, the rise in annual baptisms corroborates the major demographic expansion of the city in the late sixteenth and early seventeenth centuries, a growth which was to be maintained until the second half of the seventeenth century.[27]

The extent to which the urban center acted as a pole of attraction for Indian immigration can also be examined by analyzing the parents' place of origin which is given for both dates. Between July 14 and December 1, 1596, in only 24 cases of the 99 baptisms (almost 24 percent) was either parent from Quito, if the 16 unspecified were Quiteño as is likely; in only two cases was one parent from Quito and the other from another region. The proportion falls even lower when the six slaves, either unspecified or from Quito, are subtracted from the total, falling to 19.3 percent. Between January 1 and February 5, 1612, five slaves of creole or African origin and two foundlings were baptized. Of the remaining 75 only six were unspecified or from the city of Quito. The origins of the parents of baptized infants are summarized in Table 3. 2.

TABLE 3.2 PLACE OF ORIGIN OF INDIAN PARENTS, 1596, 1612

	1596	1612
	(%)	(%)
Quito	19.3	8.0
Corregimiento	40.8	49.4
Highlands	41.9	42.7

Source: APQ/ Sagrario, "Libro de Bautismos de Mestizos, Montaneses, Yndios" (1594–1605), "Libro de Bautismos ... Mestisos, Yndios" (1606–). Note: samples from July 14 to Dec. 1 1596, and Jan. 1 to Feb. 5, 1612. Proportions do not sum to 100 percent because of two split marriages in 1596, and rounding for 1612.

Table 3.2 is based on too narrow a sample to be taken as an index of demographic change between the two dates. The high proportion of infants being baptized whose parents came from the corregimiento can be explained partly in terms of the role of El Sagrario parish as the cultural focus and place of residence of the Spanish elite, whose Indian servants were

---

[27] The estimate of 2,500 houses in Diego Rodríguez Docampo's (1650), *RGI,* III, 6, may be a more objective point of comparison with the 1570s and 1580s than the actual population estimates. According to the *relaciones* cited in footnote 26, there may have been 1,000 houses in the 1570s. Chapter 6 examines the demographic history of the city from the late seventeenth century onwards.

sometimes baptized in the capital, but may have later worked on their rural properties outside the city. For this reason, the annual baptismal rate at this early period, should not be taken as an indication of the total urban Indian population of El Sagrario. Some other Indians from more distant areas may also have belonged to the encomiendas of leading citizens of the city, and been baptized there for the same reasons. Even allowing for this factor, the proportion of parents born in Quito is extremely low, which may be attributed to the expansion of the city. The geographical spread of place of origin suggests that the city absorbed immigrants only from the Ecuadorian highlands, but with the caveat that in El Sagrario parish we are dealing with the Indian population directly linked to Spanish urban society; if there were immigrants from more distant regions of the Andes, it is perhaps not in El Sagrario that we should expect to find them.

Nevertheless, for the Ecuadorian highlands as a whole, there is certainly evidence of an extremely mobile Indian population, the *indios peinadillos,* considered vagabonds addicted to the vices of drunkenness and idleness, allegedly fleeing the mita of the great mining regions such as Potosí.[28] According to a relación dating from the early 1590s, it was specifically an attempt to fix migrants in the settled colonial order which motivated some early attempts at reducciones in the neighborhoods of Quito.[29] The extraordinary mobility of the Indian population in the late-colonial period clearly therefore had its roots at least as far back as the initial contact between Spanish and Indian societies, and owed much to the nature of colonial impositions as well as the possibility of minimizing their impact through devices such as migration. Some of the Mestizo petitions examined in Chapter 7 reveal an analogous process of adaptation to the possibilities left open by a colonial society through migration, ethnic change and tax evasion.

The early descriptions of the city emphasize the role of the Indians in supplying its service population, local Indian labor already having been mobilized in the construction of the Cathedral.[30] The mita, whereby Indian communities supplied one fifth of their labor force in rotation was the essential mechanism of labor supply.[31] The role of service as an agent of acculturation of the Indian population, and a means of entry into the White world may be noted in the practice of Indian parents sending their children as servants to Quito so that they learn "good customs" ("buenas costumbres").[32] At a higher social level, the fortunes of the Inca Atahualpa's descendants in Quito shows clearly the diversity of indigenous

---

[28] "Relación del distrito del Cerro de Zaruma y distancias a la ciudad de Quito...," 319.

[29] *Ibid.*, in the neighborhood of Añaquito.

[30] Pedro Rodríguez de Aguayo, "Descripción de la ciudad de Quito," 203.

[31] For good descriptions of the *mita,* see "La cibdad de Sant Francisco de Quito, 1573," 220, 226; "Relación del distrito del Cerro de Zaruma y distancias a la ciudad de Quito ...," 319.

[32] "Relación del distrito del Cerro de Zaruma y distancias a la ciudad de Quito...," 319.

responses to conquest.[33] To the highly acculturated former Inca elite which was sometimes absorbed into the higher reaches of colonial society, or the local Indian leaders co-opted into the Spanish colonial system as intermediaries, defeat offered different possibilities to those available to the indios peinadillos, and the rest.

As in other regions, the biological process of miscegenation between Spaniard and Indian began with conquest,[34] in part because of the absence of Spanish women, and little that is distinctive to Ecuador in this process can be emphasized, except to take note of Cieza de León's comment that the women in the region of Cuenca were attracted to Spanish men.[35] By the mid-1560s a small Mestizo presence was already being recorded in the earliest surviving baptismal records of El Sagrario, Quito.[36] If we believe the prejudiced comments of the *corregidor* of Quito, Don Sancho Díaz de Zurbano at the beginning of the seventeenth century, mestizaje was particularly advanced in the city by that date: "The Spaniards have mingled to such an extent with the Indians that there are more Mestizos in this city than in the rest of Peru."[37]

---

[33] U. Oberem, "La familia de Atahualpa bajo el dominio español," a study republished in the collection of essays, S. Moreno Yánez and U. Oberem (eds.), *Contribución a la Etnohistoria Ecuatoriana*, (Otavalo, 1981), 153–224. For an example of the acculturation of the upper Indian elite and privileges accorded by the Crown, see, for example, R. Konetzke, *Colección de Documentos para la Historia de la Formación social de Hispanoamérica, 1493–1810*, (Madrid, 1953) vol. 1, 580.

[34] The social history of the Mestizo class in colonial Quito falls into fairly clearly defined phases up to the early seventeenth century, a trajectory which was certainly also followed in many other regions of colonial Spanish America. The civil wars in sixteenth-century Peru certainly had an important Mestizo element at leadership level, while the process of exclusion of the Mestizos from office around 1600 was a general imperial phenomenon. Still the standard account, building on the work of scholars such as Konetzke and Rosenblatt, is M. Mörner, *Race Mixture in the History of Latin America*, (Boston, 1967). There is an abundant more specialized literature on the Mestizos, but generally from the juridicial or demographic perspective. For a study based on Ecuadorian material see C. Caillavet and M. Minchom, "Le Métis Imaginaire: idéaux classificatoires et stratégies socio-raciales en Amérique Latine (XVIe-XXe siècle)," *L'Homme*, 122-124, XXXII (1992), 115-132.

[35] *The Incas of Pedro Cieza de León*, (ed. V. W. von Hagen), (Norman, OK, 4 edn. 1976), 71. For the argument for a different region that *mestizaje* was perhaps less of an enforced process than is sometimes casually assumed, see Bernardino Cárdenas, O.F.M. "Memorial y Relación de cosas ... del Peru," (n. d. but probably early seventeenth century; Cardenas had lived in Charcas), BN/M ms. 3198, where he points out the advantages to Indian women of alliances with Spaniards (sons free of tribute etc.).

[36] J. Moreno Egas, "Apuntes para el estudio de la población del siglo XVI de la Real Audiencia de Quito," *Museo Histórico*, XXVIII (56), (1978), 73, 83–84.

[37] AGI Quito 28, Letter of Don Sancho Díaz de Zurbano, March 22, 1609.

The corregidor's comments may tell us as much about the attitudes of officials as about the actual process of race mixture. Those Spaniards attempting to come to terms with the new phenomenon of mestizaje nearly always emphasized the scale of its expansion, its sinful character as the product of irregular unions, as well as the sense in which it broke the established hierarchy by bringing a new element into the symmetrical order of the Republics of Indians and Spaniards.[38] The association of Mestizos with vagrancy, idleness, and a threat to the established order was present from the first generation onwards, and remained a constant in official and ecclesiastical attitudes, independent of the changing characteristics of the Mestizos themselves.[39] The absorption of many Mestizos into Creole society certainly reinforced the nascent conflicts between creoles and peninsular-born Spaniards by injected a quasi-racial element into their rivalries, notably in the religious orders.[40]

There was a sense in which officials were right in seeing this group as a seditious element, whatever the exaggeration in their idea that Mestizos were pulled between two cultures, and therefore innately constituted an unstable element in the body politic. In the disorders which marked the transition from a conquest society to a more organized "colonial" one, the kinship of many "upper" Mestizos to leading conquerors, often the offspring of their alliances with members of the indigenous elite, created a privileged but ambiguous social position, while conquest traditions must have left their own heritage of unruliness in sixteenth-century society. A Mestizo son of the conqueror of the Quito region, Benalcázar was involved in rebellion in the 1580s,[41] but the most important Mestizo rebellion came in the 1590s. The cabildo-led resistance to the colonial imposition of the

---

[38] See, for example, Bernardino Cárdenas, O.F.M. "Memorial y Relación de cosas ... del Peru," fol. 64; "mestiços se llaman en este reyno del Peru los hijos de españoles y de indias y de estos ay muchissimos, porque el pecado de mesclarse los españoles con las indias es generalissimo y muy frequentado, porque las indias son faciles y el avito que traen muy lacivo y desonesto ["descubiertos los braços y pies" crossed out] ... y que los hijos mestizos avidos en pecado tan grave tan escandoloso y aborrecido de Dios an de ser faborecidos, y libres de tributo y serviçio personal como lo son todos los mestizos que ni sirven a Dios ni al rey ... no solo porque es gente viciosa ... sino porque todo lo que se va multiplicando de mestizos inutiles ...."

[39] "Descripción de Quito en 1577," *Museo Histórico,* XXVIII, (1978), 63, "Habra en esta ciudad y distrito dos mil mestizos y mestizas ... Es gente belicosa, ligeros, fuertes e ingeniosos ..."; AGI Quito 27, Carta de Don Sancho Díaz de Zurbano, 13 Feb. 1609; "... que se ba aumentando cada dia mucho de gente perdida viciosa y holgazana que ay muchos mestizos, quarterones, cholos, que asi llaman a los que nascen de mestizos y indias ..." For a different late-colonial definition of *cholo,* see the discussion of socio-racial terminology in Chapter 7.

[40] See, for example, AGI Quito 32, Letter of Morga, April 20, 1631, "Estado actual del Catolicismo, Político y Económico de los Naturales del Peru," April 30, 1747, BNP/L , c 881, Cap 1:2a.

[41] AGI Quito 17, Cartas de cabildo, Letter of May 24, 1585.

traditional Spanish sales-tax or *alcabala,* in 1592–93 was a concerted act of defiance to Spanish authority in which the Mestizos of the city played a prominent role. In an action which the barrio of San Roque was to emulate a century and a half later, the prison was attacked and the dissident attorney *(procurador)* of the cabildo opposing the measures was released, the first major action in what became a major insurrection. In the resistance to fiscal measures, the alliance of Creole and Mestizo elements against Spanish authority, the attacks on the symbols of authority (prison or Audiencia), and the final military expedition from outside, the events of 1592–93 anticipate closely the rebellion of 1765. As in 1765, there was not one but a series of rebellions, in which initial divisions at elite level brought the urban crowd into play, and provoked generalized disorder. The ambiguity of the church's role, sections of which sided with the opposition to the fiscal measures of the 1590s, was present in both rebellions, while the way creole-peninsular tensions within the religious orders interacted with secular tensions also anticipates later disorders. As in the 1760s the ringing of church bells sounded the tocsin for revolt in a symbolic action which may have marked not only the organized collective dimension of revolt, but possible ecclesiastical involvement. The key role of the Church as intermediary with the plebe was clear in the 1590s when the intercession of the Image preserved in the church of Guápulo was used to calm spirits when popular enthusiasm had gone too far.[42]

Quito was a community evolving its own identity from the sixteenth century onwards, perceiving fiscal pressures and the officials who attempted to implement them as alien intruders in a local society far from the viceregal capitals. In this sense the "community cohesion" approach to social disorder has clear relevance to the outbreaks of both the sixteenth and eighteenth centuries. Nevertheless, in at least one key sense, Quito society had profoundly changed between its two great pre-Independence eruptions, namely in the width of the barriers which separated the elite from the plebe. In the 1590s the cabildo official released from prison during the first disturbance was himself a Mestizo, while royal officials were in no doubt that unrest had a specifically Mestizo origin: "The most guilty in these crimes have been the Mestizos of this city."[43] Thus there was a sense in which the poorer Mestizos of the city were rescuing one of their own "community" when they smashed the prison to rescue the procurador Bellido, who was known as the cacique because of his part-Indian origins. The endogamous wealthy creole elite which dominated the late-colonial

---

42   Diego Rodríguez Docampo, "Descripción y Relación ...," 10.

43   AGI Quito 8, fol. 807, Carta de Nov. 27, 1593: "Los mas culpados en estos delictos, an sido los mestiços de esta ciudad." For a short account of the rebellion, based on González Suárez, see A. Pareja Diezcanseco, *Las Instituciones y la Administración de la Real Audiencia de Quito,* (Quito, 1975), 144–147. See now, B. Lavallé *Quito et la crise de l'Alcabala (1580-1600),* (Paris, 1992). F. Hassaurek wrote a historical novel on the subject of the rebellion, *The Secret of the Andes,* (Cincinnati, 1879).

cabildo had virtually no direct ties with the urban plebe, and the leadership thrown up by the late-colonial barrios came from their own Mestizo or "poor White" artisanal ranks. Although officials saw an element of Creole complicity in the 1765 rebellion, it will be argued that a clear tradition of urban social disorder in the eighteenth century underlines the class and barrio origin of these outbreaks, and that the late-colonial plebe was a far more autonomous agent than may at first sight appear.

The widening of social barriers between elite and popular society took on a clear racial dimension. By the early seventeenth century, the better-placed Mestizos were being squeezed out of their ambiguous place alongside White society, in part as a result of official pressures.[44] Royal officials continued to see the Mestizos as a potential threat to the social order in the early seventeenth century, but the social context was changing, and with the advance of the process of mestizaje, Mestizos merged into either the creole elite, Indian society, or an indeterminate urban lower social strata. One of the best indices of this transformation is the gradual disappearance of the category Mestizo from the entries in the baptismal records of El Sagrario parish at the beginning of the seventeenth century.[45] The most logical interpretation is not that the number of biological Mestizos was declining, but that the category was beginning to lose its precision, and some Mestizos were henceforth being considered Spanish, while others were losing their place in recognized White society.

This process of racial and cultural mixing meant that by the late-colonial period, there was no clear borderline between "poor Whites" and Mestizos, while the separation of Indian and Mestizo, although given legal sanction through tribute obligations, was also problematic. In the Declarations of Mestizo examined in Chapter 7, we find only "Indians dressed as Spaniards" ("indios vestidos de españoles") for the eighteenth century city. On the other hand, those petitions also include Mestizos who have been partially reabsorbed—if they ever fully left—Indian culture in more isolated rural districts. Acculturation[46] was a process of complex

---

[44] *Colección de Documentos sobre el Obispado de Quito,* (Quito, 1946), Tomo 1, 543, 546, (Oct. 12, 1582), for protests against the Mestizo priest Diego Lobato; Tomo II, 46–47, for exclusion from office, (1602).

[45] The Mestizo "disappearance" from the register of Spanish births in El Sagrario dates from the period 1601–10, according to data compiled by Sr. Jorge Moreno Egas. These data are unpublished, but see his "Apuntes para el estudio de la población ..." and numerous transcriptions of births, marriages etc. in the ongoing *Revista del Centro Nacional de Investigaciones Genealógicas y Antropológicas* (Quito), of which he is the editor.

[46] For a discussion of different forms of acculturation, specifically adapted to Latin American materials, N. Wachtel, "L'Acculturation," in J. Le Goff and P. Nora, *Faire l'histoire,* (Paris, 1974), 24 *et seq.* F. Salomon sees the Indian women as outside the "rubric of acculturation," because their "strategy of innovation" was unlinked to European cultural competence, re-working relationships of "both native and colonial origin ... as entryways into a rapidly expanding market economy." in:

interaction rather than a linear movement towards the adoption of Spanish cultural norms, and for the early colonial period, there is certainly evidence that Indian culture initially exerted a strong influence on a substantial part of the Mestizo population. Clothing was (and still is) an essential element in the material culture which defines ethnic boundaries. For a relatively late date (1633), we find complaints that Mestizas in the city of Quito were obstinately clinging to Indian dress, in spite of official attempts to discourage this, and were spending a great deal on silk.[47] The notarial records confirm the existence of this category, again specifically feminine.[48]

Deep-rooted cultural factors can doubtless be invoked to explain this gender differentiation which may also have been reinforced by occupational differences; in Quito today, an Indian woman often continues with traditional clothing, while her more acculturated husband wears shirt and jeans. Nevertheless, there is little doubt that for the period in question, the main reason lay in the selective nature of colonial impositions, whereby tribute and mita service were adult male obligations, and the pressure on males not to be identifiable as culturally Indian were consequently far stronger. The existence which this presupposes of "split" couples—male Mestizo, female Mestiza but "dressed as Indian"—certainly shows that ethnicity was extremely loosely defined, and that many of the conventional criteria for defining race can be highly misleading. Along with clothing, language is often used as a key criterion of ethnicity, but at least in eighteenth-century Quito, Quichua was very much a day-to-day language. Even members of the elite spoke Quichua as well as Spanish as a consequence of their upbringing by Indian women.[49]

The Mestizo litigation of the 1770s will show the extreme socio-racial confusion of pre-Bourbon reform society. Many people in the lower strata did not belong definitively to Spanish or Indian society, and the official attempt to establish who the Indian population was for fiscal purposes underlined this previous lack of definition. That as late as the 1630s mixed-blood women in the capital were still "dressed as Indians" emphasizes the slowness rather than the rapidity of the city's acculturating influence. The tenuous and incomplete diffusion of Spanish culture can be further stressed by noting the ambiguity of colonial socio-racial categories in which an Indian silk dress might provide equivalent social prestige to more humble mixed-blood clothing. By the eighteenth century, there is no evidence of "Spaniards dressed as Indians" in the capital itself, and the Declarations of

---

F. Salomon, "Indian women of early Colonial Quito as seen through their testaments," *The Americas,* 40 (1988), 341.

[47] AGI Quito 32, Carta de Lucas Dorotines, April 28, 1633.
[48] ANH/Q 1 Not. vol. II, (1593), fol. 443; a debt to "Ysabel de Bustamante, mestiza en abitos de yndia que reside en esta ciudad."
[49] Juan y Ulloa, *Relación Histórica,* 377. On language adaptation and adoption see B. Mannheim, *The language of the Inca since the European invasion* (Austin, 1991).

Mestizo attest to the sense in which the urban Mestizo considered himself Spanish, or near-Spanish. Nevertheless, the ambiguity persisted, notably at the level of the cacique class, who considered Mestizos unfit for the "superior and honorific position of cacique."[50] In certain measure, the Bourbon reforms ironed out this ambiguity by making tribute payment so exacting that to be recognized as Mestizo by the authorities offered a far more marked advantage over Indian status than it had in the early colonial period.[51]

Quito and the Textile Economy, 1600–1800

The economic history of both the city and Audiencia of Quito in the mid-colonial period was closely inter-related with the growth and decline of its textile industry, a process which we now know in detail as a consequence of recent historical research. Great estates made full use of their Indian labor and saved cash expenditure in what was increasingly to become a demonetarized economy through vertically-organized enterprises which combined sheep-grazing with textile production. A stable or expanding Indian population supplied the labor force for these textile factories, (obrajes), through the mechanism of rotating labor service (mita), gradually replaced by a mixture of free (although indebted), and forced labor. Other forms of textile production existed, notably urban workshops, and the *obrajes de comunidad,* which were originally located in Indian villages as a means of guaranteeing tribute collection. During the seventeenth century, a steady labor supply and ample pasture for sheep-grazing laid the foundations for the expansion of a sector which exported woolen cloth to the mining economies of Peru and New Granada. When English and French textile imports began to undercut prices in Peru in the eighteenth century, the more distant suppliers of textiles from the Audiencia of Quito, handicapped by high overland costs, were the first to lose their profitability. Quito had few exportable commodities, and the export of textiles for this inter-provincial trade provided, as Tyrer has emphasized, virtually the only source of specie to participate in the transatlantic trade—the only barrier against a "life of complete provinciality, wealthy only in grain, livestock, and home-made commodities."[52]

Despite a body of valuable research on the obraje economy, our understanding of the organization of the textile mills in the vicinity of the

---

50   ANH/Q Ind. 80, doc., 13–II–1764, fol. 2; the said Mestizo has the "oficio de aferrador, y debe ocuparse en el, y no el Superior, y honorifico empleo de Governar dicho casicasgo."

51   See Chapter 7.

52   R.B. Tyrer, *The Demographic and Economic History,* 9. J. L. Phelan, *The Kingdom of Quito*; J. Ortiz de la Tabla, "El obraje ecuatoriano. Aproximación a su estudio," *Revista de Indias,* 149/150, (1977), 471–542; R. D. F. Bromley, *Urban Growth and Decline.*

capital is somewhat unclear because these were not usually the major licensed textile factories, but smaller-scale ones called *chorrillos*. This form of enterprise poses problems for a number of reasons. We are unlikely to find for these small-scale workshops the relatively complete series of accounts which would permit the equivalent of the full-scale reconstruction of the economy of a major rural obraje-hacienda complex which Cushner has been able to assemble from the Jesuit archives.[53] The coarse cloth produced in the chorrillos varied considerably in quality, and therefore pricing, and Tyrer's examination of the production costs and marketing of textiles concentrated in consequence on Quito's quality cloth (*paño azul*); production statistics for the urban textile economy are therefore lacking. Most important, the small urban workshops were often illegal, in the face of an official policy which controlled the issue of licenses for both venal and policy reasons, as a consequence of the selectively and intermittently applied economic theory that colonies should not compete with the production of the metropolis. Reports at both the beginning and end of the seventeenth century identified a considerable number of illegal obrajes in Quito. It was claimed that in 1603 that there were 60 illegal ones operating in the vicinity of the capital.[54] *Visitas* of the urban obrajes in the 1680s uncovered a number of small workshops, some of which were immediately destroyed, but the clamp-down was somewhat nominal; there were at least 37 illegal obrajes in the corregimiento of the capital around 1700.[55] As with all forms of illicit economic activity, we can assume that the real level of illegal textile activity was higher, and the quantification of any aspect of chorrillo activity must therefore be considered speculative.

The characteristics of the textile industry in and around the capital were different from those of the major rural obrajes. The small urban workshops, seldom employing more than twenty people, wove coarse cloth for consumption by the local population, and exported to the nearby markets of New Granada; they did not, however, participate in the export of quality cloth to the more distant Lima market. Except when both sectors were exposed to extortionate fiscal pressures from the Crown, they formed quite different interest groups, and in the 1660s and 1670s the licensed rural sector supported the royal officials in their attacks on the urban sector.[56] In 1680, President Munive defended the necessity of a legalized local production of coarse cloth, and requested (and was later granted) authority to grant licenses to obrajes which would make coarse cloth in rural areas and redirect Indian migration into rural areas.[57]

The role of the mid-colonial textile industry in making Quito a focus of

---

[53] N. P. Cushner, *Farm and Factory*.
[54] Phelan, *The Kingdom of Quito*, 69.
[55] Tyrer, *The Demographic and Economic History*, 157, 160–1.
[56] *Ibid.*, 155–158.
[57] *Ibid.*, 156–157.

Indian migration was denounced by the municipality in 1651:

> In this city there are many little textile workshops, established by different people in which they weave and make *jerguetas, bayetas* (dark, coarse cloth), and other cloths, and they have received many Indians, both from the villages of this district and the rest of this Province, leaving the said villages abandoned ... This has arrived at such an extreme that even the very Indians, in all the parishes, have set up the said workshops in their houses and have many retainers (*indios de servicio*) for their work-force. [58]

In 1660, the attorney (*procurador*) of the municipality returned to the theme, claiming that 20,000 Indians were around the city, either employed in Spanish obrajes or acting as independent agents in cloth production.[59] In Munive's letter of 1681, he claimed that 30,000 Indians were employed in the capital.[60] The accuracy of these figures may be debated: the degree of exaggeration in Munive's estimate may be taken to depend on the scope of his comments—whether he really meant the capital or was including unspecified nearby villages. Nevertheless, it is clear that urban textile production was attracting major immigration, and the extent of the city's growth is indicated in the difference between the descriptions of the 1580s and that of Diego Rodríguez Docampo in 1650.[61] The municipality's denunciation of the Indians for establishing their own enterprises shows that textile production was generalized throughout the city, and a similar small-scale Indian production continued for domestic consumption and urban needs, even when the city's textile industry was greatly reduced in the eighteenth century.

As was argued in the Chapter 2, however, considerable care should be used in defining textile production as an urban industry. It is obvious from the points noted above, that licensed workshops only constituted a part of the textile production of the city, but we may take note of Munive's list of obrajes for the corregimiento of the city in the late seventeenth century ; four obrajes to which *mitayos* were assigned were listed alongside eleven obrajes relying on free or semi-free labor, and four chorrillos. Production was mainly in the rural district of the capital, while perhaps more interestingly, the four chorrillos which we might expect to be more likely to be "urban" were in San Diego, San Sebastián, Recoleta and Loloncoto, that is away from the nuclear district of the city.[62] The mid-colonial evidence

---

58 *LCQ* January 9, 1651, p. 85.
59 Tyrer, AM/Q, 173.
60 AGI Quito 69, Carta de Munive, July 30, 1681, fol. 332, published by Landázuri.
61 See footnote 27; Diego Rodríguez Docampo, "Descripción y Relación ..."(1650), *RGI*, III, 6.
62 Munive's account in AGI Quito 69, lists the following for around 1680:
—*Obrajes* with *mitayos:* Yaruquí, Puembo, Pansaleo, Añaquito, Machángara.
—*Obrajes* with *voluntarios:* Cumbayá, Guahaló, Chillogallo, Cotocollo, Añaquito,

may be set against that for late-colonial Quito. According to a tribute document of 1804, there were 12 chorrillos in Quito, of which seven were in the parish of San Sebastián.[63]

This localization of textile activity in the parish of San Sebastián can be attributed to its location along the river Machángara which provided the necessary supplies of water for the fulling mills. In neither the eighteenth nor the nineteenth centuries, does urban growth seem to have spread effectively to this area according to the cartographic evidence, so the late-colonial "urban" workshops should therefore best be described as disguised rural ones. In view of the clear evidence for extensive and widespread textile activity in the mid-colonial city, the localization of the late-colonial workshops may be interpreted in two ways. First, it may be taken as confirmation of the decline of urban weaving, at least outside domestic artisanal Indian production; the fact that the nominally urban workshops were in fact located outside the city, can be taken as further evidence that the urban textile industry was unable to withstand competition from rural obrajes once the latter turned to lower quality cloth production for the New Granada market in the eighteenth century. The second interpretation is that the location of the seventeenth century workshops may also have been less urban than immediately apparent, a phenomenon partly disguised by the domestic or very small-scale Indian artisanal weaving which caught the attention of the municipality.

What is clear is that the scale and quality of seventeenth-century urban textile production was never such as to permanently deprive weaving of its associations as a fundamentally rural activity. In the late-colonial documentation, the weavers were exclusively Indian and despite the skills which some textile processes involved, the occupation continued to be a low status one. As a traditional rural activity, weaving was carried out by Indians, in a continuation of the pre-Hispanic tradition.[64] Confirmation that as an urban activity it stayed entirely in Indian hands, can be found in the padrón of Santa Bárbara in 1768.[65] In 1762, the Mestizos of San Roque emphasized that they "do not work in the fields or have other mechanical offices" like Indians.[66] This equation of Mestizos with urban residents and Indians with rural occupations is a suggestive one. The fundamental

---

San Blas, Puembo, Tumbaco, Oyambaro, Santa Bárbara
—*Chorrillos:* San Diego, Recoleta, San Sebastián, Loloncoto.

Most of these licensed workshops were no longer functioning by the 1760s; J. Ortiz de la Tabla, "Panorama económico y social del Corregimiento de Quito," *Revista de Indias*, 145/146 (1976), 96.

[63] Oberem, *Contribución,* 347.

[64] C. Caillavet, "Tribut textile et caciques dans le nord de l'Audiencia de Quito," *Mélanges de la Casa de Velázquez*, (Paris-Madrid), vol. XVI (1980), 179–201.

[65] For the *padrón* of Santa Bárbara, published in *Museo Histórico,* 56 (1978), 93–122, see Chapter 7. All eleven weavers in the parish were Indian.

[66] See Chapter 8 on the "scare" of 1762.

character of the hacienda-obraje complex was basically rural, the techniques of textile manufacturing being essentially non-industrial, and its production processes closely linked with sheep grazing and agricultural activity. In the eighteenth century, this form of textile production was the only major remaining one with the failure of the urban textile economy, and the community obrajes. When the Mestizos of San Roque compared Mestizo artisanal activities with those of the Indians in the 1760s, they were indirectly asserting the failure of the city's economy to sustain and integrate a dynamic urban weaving industry, which would transform its social structure.

Economic Readjustment, 1690–1720

Late eighteenth-century Quito witnessed a flood of reports on the decay of the Audiencia in which latter-day *arbitristas* amalgamated Enlightenment rationalism and the theme of decadence to which Hispanic thought was highly attuned, to attempt projects which would "reanimate the dying realm."[67] If we read these reports carefully, however, it is clear that they placed Quito's immediate difficulties within a long-term process of decline, while we can certainly find an anticipation of their themes in the letter of Alsedo in 1732,[68] or in the appeals of the cabildo for lower *censos* in the 1720s which we will examine in this section. How literally we have to take the late-colonial commentators is a moot point, and we should bear in mind that the volume of paperwork essentially monitors not one but two processes, namely Quito's actual decline, and the increased fiscal pressure to which it was subject, which stimulated both the complaints of the Quiteños, and the cautious assessments by officials of potential risks to the Crown's interests. In a study on the southern portion of the Audiencia, I

---

[67] R. J. Shafer, *The Economic Societies in the Spanish World (1763-1821)*, (Syracuse, 1958), 168-177, and here 169, citing the *Mercurio Peruano*, No. 103 (Dec. 29, 1791), 300-306. For the theme of decadence in seventeenth-century Spain, see J. H. Elliott, "Self-perception and decline in early seventeenth-century Spain," *Past and Present*, 74 (1977), repr. in: J. H. Elliott (ed.), *Poder y sociedad en la España de los Austrias*, (Barcelona, 1982), 198–223. The decadence of the Audiencia was examined by innumerable writers: "Representación hecha al Rey por Don Miguel de Uriarte y Herrera, natural de San Francisco de Quito," [1757], in Don Antonio Valladares, *Semanario erudito* .... vol. 24 (Madrid, 1788), 238, (get "minerals out of the veins of the earth and circulating in the veins of the monarchy"); "Defensa de los curas de Riobamba" [1786] in *Escritos del doctor Francisco Javier Eugenio Santa Cruz y Espejo*, vol. 3 (Quito, 1923), 172–3, for Espejo's laconic comment: "*Comercio:* ... En esta Provincia, no hay alguno que se puede llamar con este nombre." Carondelet, President of the Audiencia at the beginning of the nineteenth century, wrote some of the most frequently cited reports on the state of the Audiencia.

[68] Letter of Dionisio de Alsedo y Herrera, President of the Royal Audiencia of Quito, June 18, 1732. AGI Quito 132.

was struck by the contrast between observers' impression of decline, and the evidence of modest growth.[69]

The second part of the present study examines themes such as demographic change and social unrest, which shed a partial light on this process, but examining the chronology of crisis may clarify some of the problems which will be examined later. If we emphasize in this section, for example, the extremely early beginnings of Quito's economic difficulties, it will also be argued in Chapter 8 that those difficulties generated major social tensions well before the great Quito rebellion of 1765. Pushing Quito's decline back to the late seventeenth century will also force us to reconsider the nature of the city in the eighteenth century, asking whether it was really in "permanent decline" or enjoyed periods of recovery and intensified crisis. It has become clear that the restriction of trade between Guayaquil and Callao (Lima) after 1735, and the liberalizing of trade regulations in the last quarter of the eighteenth century were not the fundamental reason for Quito's decline, although the demographic evidence cited in Chapter 6 certainly suggests an intensifying of Quito's problems from the 1780s onwards. In general, the Ecuadorian historiography locates Quito's economic difficulties from the mid-eighteenth century onwards, but Tyrer's study has shown that prices of *paños* were falling on the Lima market well before that date, and therefore affecting the profitability of Quito cloth production.[70] In the 1690s major epidemics hit the region and high mortality rates provoked labor shortages which can only have reinforced the difficulties of the textile industry.[71]

Evidence from the 1710s and 1720s, specifically the documentation relating to the lowering of censos, enables one to synthesize the evidence of early decline for the period between 1690 and the 1720s, as well as place short-term cyclical down-turns alongside the evidence for major structural change.[72] Although there were different kinds of censo, these can be most widely defined as obligations assumed on property in return for services (spiritual or financial) rendered mainly by the Church.[73] Spiritual services

---

[69] M. Minchom, "Historia demográfica de Loja y su Provincia: Desde 1700 hasta fines de la Colonia," *Cultura, Revista del Banco Central del Ecuador,* (Quito) 15 (1983), 149–169.

[70] Tyrer, *The Demographic and Economic History*, 255 and 311 ff.

[71] See S. A. Alchon, "The effects of epidemic disease in colonial Ecuador: the epidemics of 1692 to 1695," Paper presented at the Annual Meeting of the American Historical Association, Washington D.C., 1982. From the evidence of Chapter 6 the population of the city may have peaked even before the epidemics of the 1690s.

[72] AGI Quito 181 "Autos por el procurador general de la ciudad de Quito sobre minoración de censos; año 1755." The document is classified under this date because of a subsequent appeal; the documentation is, in fact, from the 1710s and 1720s.

[73] This definition is based on the article by A. J. Bauer, "The Church in the Economy of Spanish America: Censos and Depósitos in the Eighteenth and Nineteenth

might include *capellanías* founded to perpetuate masses for the founder's soul, and which would support an ecclesiastical living. Financial services might involve a direct loan for the purchase of a house or a piece of land. In either case, the result was a permanent annuity which was owed to the institution in which the censo was vested. Although censos could also be held, for example, by secular institutions such as the municipality, the religious orders appear to have been the main beneficiaries of what seems to have turned into a major drain on the resources of property-owners. Bauer's warning against translating censo too freely as mortgage, and seeing it as a device which necessarily and primarily involved the actual circulation of capital, applies nowhere more exactly than for late-colonial Quito.[74]

Virtually every transaction which passed before a notary in eighteenth-century Quito involved property which was burdened with censos, and the repayment of annuities in cash became increasingly difficult: "... it is impossible to pay by virtue of the lack of money from which this province suffers."[75] Appealing for a diminution in the annual rate of repayment (normally fixed at five percent of the capital), the procurador for the city of Quito in 1714, cited both a series of climatic problems and poor harvests, as well as more deep-rooted problems which were to become the staple of late-colonial Quito; demonetarization, and the failure of the cloth exporting economy. According to the procurador, "in this district alone, the annual repayment amounted to 150,000 *pesos* on a total of three million pesos principal." A later witness in 1723 argued that only a dozen haciendas were exempt from censo, because they had been effectively established in entail; as he put it, those who received the censos could "freely be called the owners of all the Province."[76] Temporary reductions in the rate of payment at this period were followed by a reduction in 1755, and again under the Republic of Gran Colombia in the early nineteenth century.[77] These reductions were one admission of the onerousness of this system of obligations and the economic difficulties of the late colonial economy of Quito.

With regard to the specific data on the period up to the 1720s, it is clear that the region was undergoing a twenty-or-so year medium-term

---

Centuries," *HAHR*, 63 (1983), 707–733. For an examination of the functioning of censos in the south of the Audiencia, see C. Caillavet, "Les rouages économiques d'une société minière: échanges et crédit. Loja: 1550-1630," *Bulletin de l'Institut Français d'Etudes Andines,* (Paris-Lima), XIII (1984), 31-63.

[74] Bauer, *op. cit.*, 708–9, and passim; and *GS,* II, 967 ff., but González Suárez did not take much account of medium-term agricultural factors.

[75] AGI Quito 181, petition of the procurador, Sept. 26, 1714, fol. 1.

[76] *Ibid.*, fols. 57–58, (1723).

[77] For the later history of the censos, see D. Bushnell, *The Santander Régime,* 4.

agricultural cycle of bad harvests and possible land exhaustion.[78] Undoubtedly, existing labor shortages were reinforced by the difficulty of paying tribute at a time of agricultural depression which led to evasion, and allegedly, the virtual abandonment of villages and farms.[79] For the purposes of this study, the most interesting aspect of this body of documentation is the light it sheds on the forms in which economic crisis hit the urban popular sectors, a direct testimony which is often lacking in later periods. The interaction of agricultural crisis and the urban economy emerges clearly and supports the correlation of the rhythms of rural economic change and urban social unrest which is attempted below in Chapter 8. The quality of food consumption dropped with the fall in meat supply for the urban market, and was limited to vegetables and maize broth ("masamorras de mais"),[80] a factor to be kept in mind when we turn to the evidence on mortality rates in Chapter 6. Conspicuous consumption also declined in contrast to the references to the fine shirts, jewelry etc., which were formerly worn, notably in festivals.[81]

Worse, it was claimed that inhabitants of the barrios were compelled to leave their houses in order to "go and live in the city," sometimes breaking apart their houses to sell the materials or otherwise just leaving them deserted. In the city, they would rent rooms or "serve those who would keep them."[82] The notarial records partly bear out the picture of the decline of the barrios at this period. For the late 1720s we find the caciques of Guápulo buying two houses in San Blas, one of them unroofed.[83] Juan and Francisco Xavier Bustos, minors, sought permission to sell their house to feed themselves; they were not living in their house in the parish of San

---

[78] AGI Quito 181, for numerous witnesses on the agricultural depression, and fol. 58 (testimony of 1723), that tithe was down by a half in the last twelve years. The auction value of tithes was down at this period, Tyrer, *The Demographic and Economic History*, 62. R. D. F. Bromley noted low tithe levels for the Central Sierra, *Urban Growth and Decline*, 83–84.

[79] AGI Quito, 181, Leonardo Suares de Figueroa, testigo (1723) f 108; "se imposibilitan assi Amos como yndios de pagar tributos, y se ocultan y retiran a temples contrarios y montes donde paresen estar desiertos los mas Pueblos y hasiendas sin jente con que cultibarlas en tiempo que era necesarrio doblar el travajo." Several witnesses, some of them the members of the religious orders, who had an interest in keeping the *censo* rate high, argued that different ecological levels were less affected, such as the higher land in Cayambe, or sugar production in the lowlands.

[80] *Ibid*, Don Antonio Fernández de Obiedo, fol. 61.

[81] *Ibid*, Cap. Joseph de Sola, fol. 67.

[82] *Ibid*, fols. 56; 58, (just the walls of the houses left); 66–67, 72, ("arrendando quartos o sirviendo a quienes los mantengan"); 74; 80.

[83] ANH/Q 1 Not. Don Diego de Ocampo, vol. 246, fol. 81; May 29, 1728.

Sebastián, and robbers had stolen the doors.[84] In May 1729, another house which was falling apart, and from which the robbers were stealing the tiles and doors, was sold to an Indian, Felipe Casilema, who subsequently made it over to the Convent of La Merced on account of jewelry he owed them.[85] An explanation for why an Indian might owe jewelry to the church will be suggested in the next chapter: it is unsurprising to find property finally making its way into ecclesiastical hands, the only major group in society exempt from the burden of censos. Although low, the prices in these transactions—130, 72 and 45 pesos respectively, partly in cash—do not suggest that the property market had entirely collapsed.

The annual rhythm of baptisms, on the other hand, does not entirely bear out the theme of movement to the nuclear center of the city. The central district, the Sagrario, experienced a decline comparable to that of the parishes of San Blas and Santa Bárbara, although San Roque was probably declining more rapidly. The capacity of White society to absorb Indian and Mestizo immigrants at a time of economic depression was probably limited, and I suspect the witnesses gave prominence to a real but relatively small-scale if (for them) highly visible phenomenon. On the other hand, in calling attention to mobility as an imposed response to economic difficulties, they certainly emphasized a real feature of colonial society. Some of those who were not absorbed into "the city" (and the terminology is a revealing indication of the city-barrios dichotomy emphasized in the previous chapter) may well have been absorbed into the surrounding rural society.

Although the depression of the early eighteenth century clearly coincided with medium-term cyclical factors, when taken together with the epidemics of the 1690s and the decline of the cloth industry, it is clear that a major reorientation of Quito's economy was occurring during the period 1690–1720s. The textile economy which was labor—rather than capital—intensive had lost much of its abundant labor supply, at least on the scale which had permitted its expansion, and more particularly its place in the Lima market to which it exported its finished products. Many of the familiar themes of the late-colonial period (lack of specie etc.) were already commonplace in the early eighteenth century. Even in the 1720s the Peruvian market was virtually being described as a thing of the past, although those representing ecclesiastical interests tried to make the most of the New Granada trade which partially offset it.[86] Quito's transition from an outpost of the great "internal market" generated by the mining districts of Peru and Upper Peru to a supplier of the more isolated and much less important New Granada mining areas was confirmed by the transfer to the

---

[84] ANH/Q 1 Not. Don Diego de Ocampo, vol. 246, fol. 378, (1729); "porque estamos sumamente desnudos aun sin camisa."

[85] ANH/Q 1 Not. Don Diego de Ocampo, vol. 246, fol. 254 (May 21, 1729), and fol. 267 (June 9, 1729).

[86] AGI Quito 181, fol. 30; "El defecto no a sido total pues es constante aver entrado considerables cantidades de las Provincias de Popayán, Barbacoas, y Chocó."

Viceroyalty of New Granada. The reorientation of Quito towards New Granada was not a smooth readjustment, however. In Chapter 8, I will argue that economic crisis in the early eighteenth century interacted with political factors to create tensions which anticipated better-known late-colonial events. To judge from the demographic evidence, however, and to a lesser extent the economic indices, the worst effects of epidemics, agricultural crisis and the early weakening of the textile economy had already worked themselves out by the late 1720s. From this period onwards, Quito underwent a slow recuperation and relative stability which was to last until the downturn which preceded the 1765 rebellion.[87]

---

[87] See K. J. Andrien, "Economic crisis, Taxes and the Quito Insurrection of 1765," *Past and Present,* 129, (1990), 104–131 for economic change up to 1765, and Chapter 5 below for some economic data.

Chapter 4

ARTISAN AND CONFRATERNITY:
THE SOCIO-ECONOMIC ROLE OF THE CHURCH

The Socio-economic Role of the Church

This chapter focuses on the role of the church in relation to popular society, notably through the religious lay brotherhoods, but that role is perhaps best set within the larger framework of the place of the church in society. The sacramental function of the church, that of ordering the lives of the community through ritual, and channeling religious emotion into such organized manifestations as festivals, was common to all parts of the Christian world. More particularly, the church of colonial Ecuador was highly involved in the economy both as a major landowner, and as a drain on the finances of property-owners through the different annuities which it had progressively accumulated. In late-colonial Quito, the church was subject to widespread denunciations for its low standards, although it is hard to separate rhetoric from reality in these accusations. It is possible that economic difficulties hit the church as badly as other landowners, and forced it to seek out somewhat irregular sources of income, while the quality of ecclesiastical appointments does not seem to have been high.[1]

---

[1] For the church in general, see F. González Suárez, F. *Historia General de la República del Ecuador* [1890–], 3 vols. (Quito, 1969–70), and the numerous works of Fray José María Vargas. For the alleged low standards of the church in the Audiencia, see Cushner *Farm and Factory*, 23; "Cuaderno de Guachucal en la Provincia de los Pastos hasta la ciudad de Cuenca y Quito", (1766), The Royal Library, Copenhagen, Ny kgl. Samling 568(4) (Transcr. Juan Castro y Velázquez); and for one irregular source of income, the alleged bootleg production of *aguardiente* in the monasteries prior to the 1765 rebellion. Cushner has worked on the Jesuits in several other Spanish American regions, so his opinion that the church in Quito may indeed have been more unruly etc. has some authority. The church as a social institution can be considered virtually unexamined despite the considerable emphasis on ecclesiastical history in the traditional historiography. In addition to Cushner's

These problems merit some attention here. If many ecclesiastical institutions were in a state of some neglect in late-colonial Quito, that problem requires its own treatment, lying largely beyond the scope of the present study. Nevertheless, it is appropriate to emphasize the role of the church as a social institution, the ramifications of which were felt at many different levels of the social order. The extreme concentration of religious functions in Quito, the seat of an Archbishopric, can be measured by the space occupied by churches, convents and monasteries in the city (see Figure 2.1). If we believe the official censuses, the ecclesiastical population was over 1,000 around 1780.[2] Few if any colonial Spanish-American cities had a concentration of clergy and religious orders on this scale. Mexico City had 1,134 ecclesiastics around 1790, but for a population several times larger, while Lima, also a much larger city, had 1,306.[3] Quito's total was equivalent to 4.4 percent of the total population, some 6.3 percent of the White population, and perhaps an even higher proportion of the creole elite. According to the oidor don Gregirio Hurtado de Mendoza, in 1765 the "extinction" of noble families and the growth of the Mestizo class could be attributed to the influence of the church, as well as the absence of alternative careers.[4] The accusations which González Suárez, himself a distinguished Archbishop, leveled against the colonial religious orders ninety years ago, need not shock us today. The social history of the church in Quito has to be viewed as a close reflection of, as well as shaping influence on, the society around it. The fact that strains between Creoles and peninsular Spaniards appear to have started much earlier in the religious orders than elsewhere in the viceroyalty of Peru, reaching some intensity during the seventeenth century, is therefore a valuable indication of the maturing of a strong Quiteño creole consciousness.[5] The tensions within the religious orders merely reflected the wider growth of anti-Spanish sentiment which had already been expressed in the sales-tax riots of the 1590s, and was to reemerge during the Quito rebellion of 1765. Prior to the second of these major rebellions,

---

work on the Jesuits, also useful is E. Keeding, *Das Zeitalter der Aufklärung in der Provinz Quito,* (Köln-Wien, 1983), which clarifies the role of the church in the reception of Enlightenment culture.

[2] The figure was 1,112 according to the 1781 summary, for example. ANC/B Hacienda Real, Varios No. 2893, "Censos del Ecuador."

[3] B. Roberts, *Cities of Peasants* (London, 1978), 42, based on Brading for Mexico.

[4] AGI Quito 398, July 4, 1765, fol. 343.

[5] B. Lavallé, *Recherches sur l'apparition de la conscience créole dans la vice-royauté du Pérou: l'antagonisme hispano-créole dans les ordres religieux (XVI–XVII s.)* (Lille, 1978), 108, and passim. For another example of the early date of the creole "consciousness" of the Quiteños, see M. Góngora, *Studies in the Colonial History of Spanish America,* (Cambridge, 1975), 214–5, citing: Antonio Eguiluz, O. F. M., "Fray Gonzalo Tenorio y sus teorías ...", *Missionalia Hispánica,* 48 (1959). Tenorio attributed his failure to publish in Spain to anti-creole prejudice.

the close inter-relationship of secular creole society, and local elements of the church had already been clearly manifested in a number of major disturbances, while during the 1765 rebellion itself, the religious orders were closely allied to the creole elite during the early stages of the *cabildo abierto* which set out objections to royal policy. Far from the main foci of both viceregal and ecclesiastical authority the church developed in a close symbiotic relationship with the society around it. The Franciscan rejection of the Visitor from Lima in the 1740s, like the response to the royal introduction of fiscal reforms in the 1760s, demonstrate the extent to which external forms of authority could be conceived as foreign intrusions into an organically evolving community with its own strong sense of *de facto* local autonomy.[6]

The state of the secular clergy aroused as much criticism as that of the religious orders. During the judicial inspection of the retiring President of the Audiencia in February 1690, accusations were listed of his nomination of illegitimate, or illiterate parish priests, accused of varying forms of incapacity. One of these was Doctor Santa Cruz considered to be of "muy cortas letras" who was alleged to have purchased the post of parish priest of San Blas, Quito, for the considerable sum of 5,000 pesos; the appointment to the parish of San Blas in Cuenca was also simoniacal.[7] It may be no coincidence that both these appointments were to popular parishes which must have been lower level appointments than parishes such as El Sagrario; if the allegations are true, they suggest that no over-tight distinction can be drawn between appointments to rural and urban parishes, although many of the accusations against the rural parish priests were worse than this.[8] The financial records of a rural parish within the Corregimiento of the city reveal income from marriages and funerals (although not baptisms), and from masses, and festivals.[9] These sources of income have, of course, no rural particularity, but payment in agricultural produce may have lubricated the economic functioning of the rural parishes.[10] On the evidence of a late seventeenth-century law-suit, rural parish priests may have been involved in the mobilization of their Indian parishioners for agricultural work, as well

---

[6] This argument is not an explanation for why outbursts actually occurred. In the 1740s some Franciscans sided with the Visitor and others with local interests, while in the 1760s Quiteños had real economic reasons for rejecting the implementation of fiscal reform. But so many of the disputes in eighteenth-century Quito involved this element that I would argue that it forms a common thread, albeit sometimes partially hidden, which runs through many different types of disturbance.

[7] AGI Quito 72, "Residencia", February 11, 1690, fol. 9.

[8] *Ibid.*, fol. 8 ff.

[9] ACM/Q, "Visita Pastoral ... Ilmo. Pérez de Calama" (1790); "Relación jurada que yo el Doctor Don Nicolas Pastrana, cura de la Parroquia de San Pedro de Conocotoc ... (1788–1792)."

[10] *Ibid.*, fol. 3, for produce given by the parishioners, but not sold and given to friends.

as being engaged in illicit commerce.[11] Urban parish priests had more limited economic possibilities in this respect, so the economic importance of festivals, noted below, may have been reinforced as an important element in the parish economy. Unfortunately, no specific data was noted which could throw detailed light on the financial resources and other activities of urban parish priests. Lack of data does not mean lack of importance, however; it may be noted that during the period of unrest which separated the two rebellions of 1765, the parish of San Blas revolted to impose its own choice of parish priest, so the parish priest could clearly be a key figure within the urban parishes.[12] In general, the state of the parishes does not appear to have improved noticeably during the eighteenth century. In 1767, Don Serafín Veyan, oidor of Quito, alleged that many priests were absent from their parishes, sometimes appointing a replacement, but sometimes not;[13] in 1790, Bishop Calama claimed that many parishes had not seen a priest for fifty years.[14] The alleged ineffectiveness of the secular clergy permits us to ask to what extent the church, so often cited as a dominant influence in general terms, really did shape the daily life of its parishioners.

In order to do so, it is appropriate to stress not only the fact that the church was embodied in many different institutions, but also the diversity of its economic and social role at different levels of society. Given the probable bias of ecclesiastical recruitment towards the upper social strata, the demographic preponderance of ecclesiastics in Quito certainly suggests that there can have been few creole families which did not have kinship ties with members of the church. Links with the church were reinforced and perhaps complicated by relations of economic interdependence. For the property-owning classes, the closest economic nexus was probably with the religious orders, through the system of *censos*. Although these were also held, for example, in the municipality, the church was certainly the main beneficiary of what seems to have turned into a major drain on the resources

---

[11] HAA/L, Apelaciones de Quito, Leg 15 (1682–9), don Salvador Guerrero y don Felix de Luna contra don Juan Fermín de Aguirre (1689), fols. 11–13. See also the letter of Dionisio de Alsedo y Herrera, President of the Audiencia of Quito, June 18, 1732, AGI Quito 132.

[12] AHBC/Q, vol. 00010, "Diario de lo acaecido en San Francisco del Quito desde el día 22 de Mayo hasta 2 de Julio," (written by a peninsular Spaniard) fol. 1.

[13] AGI Quito 289, Letter of October 15, 1767.

[14] AGI Quito 223, for the "Humilde Memorial de Pérez de Calama" (1790). These parishes would not be urban ones, and many others had at least coadjutors, but Calama's polemic certainly suggests the general state of neglect of the church prior to his own efforts to reform it in the 1790s. These efforts ran up against the obdurate ecclesiastical resistance of the local church. Calama's role as a renovator is exemplified in his role as patron of the Patriotic Society whose activities are documented in the historiography on Espejo cited below.

of property-owners.[15] Censos affected all property-owners, and, as such, also affected more humble residents of the city, and it may be stressed that the economic interplay of religious orders and secular society ran deep into the lower strata of the city. In the 1740s, the split within the Franciscan order led to rioting in support of one faction in the neighboring parish of San Roque. The Franciscans appear to have been more heavily engaged in property transactions in the parish of San Roque than in other parishes of the city.[16] The riots had a ritual aspect, which defies too mechanistic an economic interpretation, but these economic links can scarcely be ignored. The most obvious interpretation of these economic links is that they created a measure of Franciscan control over the population of the parish.

Two aspects of the church's role will be given particular attention in the rest of this chapter. First, to what extent might ecclesiastical neglect be translated into a weakening hold on the population or even an active process of secularization? Second, the confraternities, or lay brotherhoods, constitute a particularly interesting form of religious association at all levels of society. The first of these themes will be dealt with relatively briefly; the second constitutes one of the key means of access into understanding the urban popular sectors.

Annual Communion and Religious Compliance

Whether the hold of the church on the population is directly related to such questions as the quality of its parish priests, can never be formally established, but the communion data provide some evidence of external observance. It is not intended here to attach any exaggerated importance to this kind of data. After all, if we chose to take baptism as the key

---

[15] AGI Quito 181, "Autos ... obre minoración de censos ... de la Ciudad de Quito" (1755); and the discussion on censos above. The reduction from 5 to 3 percent in 1755 did not eliminate the burden of censos, not least as it was not fully followed; see AGI Quito 289, "[Carta] sobre lo representado por el oydor de Quito Don Serafín Veyan acerca de no observarse en aquella Provincia puntualmente la cédula expedida en 3 de Septiembre 1755 rebajando los censos de ella de 5 al 3 porciento" (1768).

[16] These are listed in the *Catálogo del Archivo General de la Orden Franciscana del Ecuador*, A. Kennedy Troya (ed.) (Quito, 1980) entries 12–93; 12–107; 12–177; 12–179; 12–198. Other transactions in San Roque were 7–1iii; 12–165; 12–232ii; and 12–368. The next most related parish was San Sebastián, also in the south of the city and near San Francisco. The fact that the Order had less influence in San Blas, Santa Bárbara, and San Marcos is not surprising in view of the socio-geographical division of the city emphasized in Chapter 2. The problem with the riots stems from the fact that since the parish of San Roque came out in support of one faction of the Franciscan Order, and the Franciscan Order was itself divided, it is difficult to talk in terms of Franciscan dominance *tout court*.

sacramental test, virtually everybody could be included.[17] The church censuses which were carried out in the 1790s do nevertheless provide useful evidence; Jorge Moreno Egas kindly shared his calculations with me and these form the basis of this discussion.[18] As a comparison with the other demographic evidence suggests that the totals in this census are somewhat on the low side, the figures given here do not minimize and may slightly exaggerate communion compliance. As so often, the documentation essentially refers to fixed households rather than to the floating vagrant population, but evidence from an earlier period suggests that the church had some problem evangelizing these groups. In the 1720s, when economic depression must have swollen the ranks of the mendicants, González Suárez tells us that Bishop Romero questioned the beggars on religious matters and found, perhaps unsurprisingly, enormous ignorance. On asking the parish priests, he was told that beggars had no fixed home, and therefore belonged to no fixed parish.[19] In principle, special priests were established to minister to them, but if they were established no evidence of their existence was encountered in the late-colonial documentation.

As the proportions must therefore be considered minimum estimates, the total of only 36 percent of the eligible population of the city of Quito (i.e. excluding young children) attending annual communion in the year prior to the censuses in 1797 seems low. This proportion was slightly higher for women (39%), than it was for men (31%), which may suggest a domestic, familial role in communion observance. Perhaps the most interesting light the communion data shed is on the differential compliance within different parishes, providing an important clue to the nature of the barrios. The rate in three parishes (Santa Bárbara, San Marcos and San Sebastián) averaged 40 percent. Three parishes stood out, those of San Roque (26%), El Sagrario (34%) and San Blas (50%). The difference between the latter two figures could be that El Sagrario was ten times larger than San Blas, and that a greater measure of social control and parochial influence was possible in the smallest of all the parishes, the one indeed, which, as noted above, had already rioted to impose its own choice of parish priest. The relatively low total for El Sagrario also suggests that as the nuclear district of Quito it attracted a more floating population than some of the peripheral districts.

The extremely low rate of 26 percent in San Roque calls for particular attention, not least as this parish is the one which will be discussed in detail in Chapter 8. Two factors may be adduced as possible explanations. First,

---

17   Baptism was not normally a service for which a fee was paid, which is one of the reasons why it is usually a better index than recorded burials etc.

18   The censuses listing communion data are in the ACM/Q; "Visita Pastoral ... Ilmo. Pérez de Calama" (1790). They are for 1797 in all parishes except San Marcos which has an earlier (and complete) *padrón* of 1791. In addition to Sr. J. Moreno Egas, I wish to thank Monseñor Cadena for locating this document for me.

19   González Suárez, *Historia General de la República del Ecuador*, vol. 2, 953.

as San Roque was a popular parish, it can be argued that parochial church influence weakened in intensity, as it descended the social scale. That this was not the invariable rule is clear from the parish of San Blas, which was precisely the parish with the highest attendance. As San Roque was a highly popular district, the proportion there may also have been distorted by the absence of a significant servant population. It was not possible to identify servants as such, but the evidence of the free Blacks is probably analogous. Of 141 recorded free Blacks (132 being resident in El Sagrario), only eighteen complied (13%), compared with 25 out of 33 slaves. This evidence certainly suggests that religious practice was identified by many Blacks as an alien imposition to be shrugged off where possible. The high proportion of slaves receiving communion reflects their special legal position, but it seems likely that the social dominance exerted over Indian and Mestizo servants was cemented by religious pressures. Often whole households received communion in Quito in 1797, and in the later padrón of the village of Conocotoc (1816), this process could be seen more clearly in a rural setting, in that almost all the workforce had received it on the haciendas.[20] In this perspective, religious practice emerges as one of the key features of the social order, and its élite character is reinforced.

Perhaps, however, we should qualify this by specifying that communion data clarify the role of the secular clergy rather than that of the church as an all-embracing entity. Another factor which I would argue lowered the figures for San Roque was that some of the people of the barrio were probably receiving annual communion in the convent of San Francisco. Although the riots of the Franciscan Order date from the 1740s, they show unambiguously the close ties between San Francisco and San Roque (see Chapter 8). It is clear from other sources that there was considerable rivalry between the secular clergy and the religious orders, operating for example with regard to burials, many people taking their dead to the convents and monasteries and it was specifically high fees for burials which generated unrest in the barrio of San Roque in the early eighteenth century.[21] Although urban society was organized into a parochial structure, we should not forget the older and parallel tradition of the *doctrina* for evangelizing the indigenous population, an institution in which the religious orders, and especially the Franciscans, played a prominent role. When we find the Franciscans deeply involved in what had formerly been an Indian district near their convent such as San Roque, we may simply be seeing the

---

[20] After I consulted this *padrón* in the ACM/Q in December 1982, Monseñor Cadena placed it in the same box as the censuses of the 1790s.

[21] For the competitiveness of the secular clergy and the religious orders over burials, see AHBC/Q OOO29, Libros Verdes 1, "Lista de las personas ... que han fallecido ... desde 23 de Agosto de 1785" (Sagrario), fol. 256, September 4, 1785. Interestingly, the Franciscans are specifically identified: "... sin poderlo remediar los Curas se entierran clandestinamente en las Religiones y Monasterios especialmente en las de San Francisco, San Buenaventura y San Diego." The petition against high burial fees in the early eighteenth century is discussed in Chapter 8.

perpetuation of independent ties to the popular sectors within a long evangelizing tradition. I have not seen this hypothesis applied to any other urban center, but there were few Spanish American cities in which the religious orders occupied a position analogous to that which they held in Quito.

Religious and Artisanal Forms of Association: The Smiths, Barbers, and Weavers

Of all the different faces of the church, the lay brotherhoods, or confraternities (cofradías), constitute the one which most clearly illuminates an urban social order which was far from being unstructured in its lower rungs. Confraternities were an inheritance from Medieval Spain which existed throughout colonial Spanish America, founded by and for different social groups, in churches, monasteries or convents. Their function was to organize and direct communal religious activity, especially with regard to the worship of particular saints, and the festivals which punctuated the religious calendar formed the highlight and ultimate expression of that communal activity. From the sixteenth century onwards, they penetrated beyond the Spanish elite into the urban Indian and Mestizo sectors. The richer urban Indians were indeed quick to take to the confraternities to show their acceptance of the religious and cultural norms of the new society: the participation of the descendants of Atahualpa in lay brotherhoods may be cited as one example.[22] There also seems to have been a confraternity founded by the Mestizos in one of the convents of Quito, although this was not necessarily exclusively for Mestizo use.[23]

Throughout the colonial period, the lay brotherhoods formed a common theme in the social organization of different strata of society, and one of the best means of examining its lower and intermediate groups. The confraternities have only recently begun to attract attention, perhaps because it has been hard to gain access to the relevant ecclesiastical archives. It is difficult to talk, therefore, of an existing orthodoxy, but one possible approach to confraternities is to view them as institutions which drew together different social classes, uniting them in collective activity, and therefore reinforcing vertical bonds within society. From this perspective, the church would, through the confraternities, be serving a stabilizing role, cementing class alliances. With regard to the economic role of the lay brotherhoods, these have tended to be categorized as "mutual aid

---

22 See Oberem, "La familia del Inca Atahualpa," in S. Moreno and U. Oberem (eds.), *Contribución a la Etnohistoria Ecuatoriana*, (Otavalo, 1981), 182–184.

23 ANH/Q Not. 1 Diego Bravo de la Laguna. vol. 3, (1593–7), fol. 385, "hermanos montañeses." For the use of the term "montañés," see Chapter 7. For a *mestizo* confraternity, see also Table 4.1.

societies,"[24] holding considerable capital (jewelry, statues, and sometimes land), and serving as a source of revenue for parish priests. How far does the evidence from Quito clarify these questions? If the material examined here has suggested a somewhat different emphasis, it is worth establishing to what extent this may be the result of focusing on urban as opposed to rural society, of examining particular social groups, or especially of the particularity of Quiteño society. It is possible that the lay brotherhoods played a more "vertical" role in at least some rural communities, where society was less diversified and different social groups would collaborate in the same confraternity; the preponderance of the Indian population in the countryside must nevertheless have been reflected in the ethnic composition of these confraternities. Some urban confraternities in Quito do seem to have had membership which cut across socio-racial boundaries,[25] while multiple membership of confraternities may have created overlapping ties of spiritual kinship which transcended more immediate loyalties.

Nevertheless, the evidence collected here, which makes no pretense to be comprehensive, underlines much more strongly the way in which the confraternities reinforced horizontal bonds of cohesion within certain sectors, as well supporting wider class distinctions. A summary of what may have been the earliest organization of the lay brotherhoods in Quito, confirming the existence of a Mestizo confraternity, shows that they reflected a distinctive hierarchical structuring of the urban social order from the earliest colonial period (see Table 4.1)

For other areas, the hypothesis has been advanced that the confraternity may have served as a transposition of pre-Hispanic kinship groups or *ayllus,* which were recreated in the confraternity as a form of protective mechanism in a colonial environment.[26] If the lay brotherhoods enjoyed such a success in Spanish America, it is certainly possible that this was at least in part because they reflected existing types of social structure. However, at least in the urban setting of early colonial Quito, the cofradías reflect an extremely early model of socio-racial segregation which points to an ecclesiastical role in both responding to and helping to shape the new realities. The division into confraternities of Mestizos, acculturated Indians ("indios ladinos"), and "other Indians" in Table 4.1 may be noted, because at least one trace of this seems to have survived the whole colonial period,

---

[24] O. Celestino and A. Meyers, *Las cofradías en el Perú: región central,* (Frankfurt, 1981), for rural confraternities, and the review of their work by R. Keith in *HAHR,* 63 (1983), 171, "... confraternities ... which often served also as mutual aid societies." For a "vertical" interpretation of the confraternities, see G. Graff, *Cofradías in the New Kingdom of Granada: Lay Fraternities in a Spanish American Frontier Society, 1600–1755,* doctoral dissertation, University of Wisconsin, 1973, as used by A. McFarlane, "Civil Disorders and Popular Protests in Late Colonial New Granada", *HAHR,* 64 (1984), 50.

[25] See Rodríguez Docampo, "Descripción y relación del estado eclesiástico del Obispado de San Francisco de Quito "(1650), *RGI,* 3.

[26] Celestino and Meyers, *Las cofradías en el Perú,* have also argued along these lines.

an interesting testimony of cultural continuity. It is unsurprising that the formation of confraternities does not seem to have followed pre-Hispanic social structures in a city which did not have a dense pre-Hispanic population, and was soon attracting immigrants from rural areas.[27]

TABLE 4.1 SIXTEENTH-CENTURY CONFRATERNITIES IN QUITO

Congregación de clérigos y estudiantes (Jesuitas)	Dominica
Cofradía de seglares	?
Cofradía de mestizos	Nuestra Señora de los Reyes
Cofradía de indios ladinos	Nuestra Señora de la Presentación
Cofradía de El Salvador	Morenos y Pardos
Cofradía de el Niño Jesús	"El resto de los indios"

Source: "Cartas anuales jesuitas, 1600," but referring to divisions created "muchos años atrás"; cited by H. Burgos in *El Guaman, el Puma y el Amaru: Formación Estructural del Gobierno Indígena en Ecuador*, doctoral dissertation, University of Illinois at Urbana-Champaign, 1975: p 256. Note: The list is preceded by the following annotation:

"La ciudad sola [de Quito] se divide en tantas diferencias de gente que de muchos años atrás están divididas las congregaciones y cofradías, en proporción de sus condiciones porque se aplique a cada una la doctrina competente ... seis congregaciones según los barrios, estados y suertes que hay en la ciudad; que son ..."

Burgos advances the hypothesis that the six confraternities may correspond to the six barrios in a ritual socio-political structure, for which, however, he offers little evidence.[28] If such a ritual division did exist, it may be wrong to interpret it too literally in terms of the socio-racial segregation of the barrios, not least in view of the inclusion of categories such as "Morenos y Pardos," and "Mestizos." Whatever the initial parish-confraternity pattern, there was little evidence of this structure by the time Diego Rodríguez Docampo compiled his account of the ecclesiastical state of Quito in the mid-seventeenth century. By that date, confraternities had multiplied, and although the names of the confraternities in Docampo's account are not identical with those in the earlier list, they reveal the same socio-racial hierarchy. There is a confraternity for *morenos,* those of Black or part-Black origin,[29] and others reserved for the Indian population.[30] Some confraternities were racially mixed,[31] but Diego Rodríguez

---

[27] See Chapter 3.

[28] H. Burgos, *El Guaman, el Puma y el Amaru*, 257.

[29] Diego Rodríguez Docampo, "Descripción y relación del estado eclesiástico del Obispado de San Francisco de Quito." *RGI,* 3, 37.

[30] *Ibid.*, 37.

[31] *Ibid.*, 33, 37.

Docampo's own qualification for one of these makes it clear that their "vertical" nature by no means reached into the higher social strata: "it is a brotherhood for the natives and other people of the Republic, excluding the most important." [32]

The strengthening of horizontal loyalties through the lay brotherhoods was particularly true at certain levels of society, such as those of the urban merchants, craftsmen and artisans, and that is the aspect which the surviving documentation allows us to examine here. Docampo's mid-seventeenth century account recalled the founding in 1581 of a confraternity by the merchants in thanks for a miracle at sea.[33] The confraternities formed an accompaniment to, and expression of, guild organization; when the silversmiths act together, it is explicitly as "the guild and confraternity of St. Eloy."[34] As such, the data on the confraternities shed an interesting light on artisanal or craft association. The evidence of the way festivals in Quito were organized and financed also provides a perspective on the forms of social hierarchy, as well as showing the economic role of the confraternities.

Data were collected on three urban guild-confraternities, the silversmiths, the weavers and the barbers, illustrating quite distinct levels of prestige and economic activity. While the silversmiths were White or Mestizo, the documentation cited here identified the weavers and barbers as specifically Indian; they were the "Indian barbers" or the "Indian weavers of this city."[35] This is not of course to argue that the guild-confraternities did not have their own hierarchies of wealth and prestige. Like all institutions, the confraternities reflected the economic power and political possibilities of the society around it. The characteristics of social club-cum-religious association which we can find in the wealthier artisanal sector such as the silversmiths diminished in proportion as one descended the social scale.

THE SILVERSMITHS

The documentation relating to the silversmiths presents the fewest problems and may be introduced first; if such groups have little in common with the weavers or barbers, it is precisely the comparison which is instructive. The confraternity of St. Eloy was founded in the sixteenth century, in honor of the patron saint of this occupation, and the special provision was made that it should be reserved for Spaniards and exclude

---

[32] *Ibid.*, 37 "Es hermandad de los naturales y demás jente de la república, *fuera de la esencial,*" *(my italics).*

[33] *Ibid.*, 10.

[34] ACM/Q Cofradías (1655–1762), Cofradía de San Eloy (1754) fol. 1; "Gremio y confraternidad del Gloriosso Sto. Eloe", see also the elections of the weavers in 1785, cited below for the connection of guild and confraternity.

[35] ANH/Q Ind. 95 doc. 14–V–1778; Ind. 100 doc. 1780–IV–26.

Indians.[36] The notarial records demonstrate the social transformation of certain artisan and craft occupations in the late sixteenth and early seventeenth centuries measured, for example, by the contracts between Spanish artisans and Indian apprentices.[37] In contrast, Sebastián Gutiérrez, who makes his will is peninsular born and extremely rich, he owns land and slaves, and has left dowries worth 4,100 pesos. The contract he makes the same day for the transfer of his office in the mint is with another Spaniard, the *platero* Miguel de Rodríguez.[38]

This shortage of specie in the Audiencia of Quito may have encouraged fraudulent practice, but the eighteenth century municipal records suggest that the guild was well able to take care of itself by influencing the Council over the supervisory inspection of weights and measures.[39] The ability to influence the eighteenth century municipality is one measure of the collective influence of the guild; another is its capacity for religious action on behalf of its patron saint. In order to honor God and their patron saint in the 1750s they wish to establish "a chapel dedicated to His Image, in which there would be an Altar with a fine tabernacle, in which would be placed our glorious Patron."[40] It was expensive to build a chapel; another wealthy confraternity had commissioned a chapel for the impressive sum of 4,500 pesos at the end of the seventeenth century.[41] Although a simple enough action, the chapel-building is cited here to indicate one level of action of the confraternities, that of a group committing itself to costly works to express its religious faith and collective self-confidence.

THE BARBERS

The *barberos* were an Indian occupational group in eighteenth-century Quito, but this occupation was an intermediate one, which as in Europe, consisted both of barbering and minor surgery. In view of their role as phlebotomists, the barberos were obliged to pass an examination before they could practice, while the medical skills of the barberos were fully

---

36 The title of foundation is preserved in the AF/Q, Leg 2:9. L. J. Johnson has examined some of the difficulties this group had in forming a corporate structure in Buenos Aires, but it is clear that they still formed a highly elite artisanal group; "The Silversmiths of Buenos Aires: A Case Study in the Failure of Corporate Social Organization", *Journal of Latin American Studies,* 8 (1976), 181–213.

37 See Chapter 3.

38 ANH/Q 1 Not. (Diego Rodríguez Urban (1621–40), 9 Marzo 1634, fols. 44–53.

39 AMQ, LCQ, vol. 131, fol. 133, Feb. 1775.

40 ACM/Q Cofradías (1655–1762), Cofradía de San Eloy (1754).

41 ACM/Q Cofradías (1655–1762), "Cofradía (del Santissimo Sacramento) de la Catedral" (1699). Neither building program was successfully carried out, giving rise to ecclesiastical lawsuits.

mobilized during the 1785 epidemic.[42] In other major Andean cities, this kind of ancillary position was often held by Blacks; that the barbers were Indian in Quito is demonstrated both by the contemporary description, and by the evidence of the padrón of the parish of Santa Bárbara in 1768, when barbers were clearly identified as such.[43] Indian—but belonging to the Spanish world—barbers were, by definition, urban dwellers serving a bearded, and therefore white or mixed-blood population. In 1762, the notification to enumerate the cholos of the city, lists don Manuel Coronel, as Governor and Principal Master of the "guild of the barbers of the Cathedral [parish], their work is in the main Spanish city."[44] The Spanish travelers Jorge Juan and Antonio de Ulloa left an interesting description of the barbers which makes it clear that they belonged to an acculturated Indian elite. With their linen breeches, gold- or silver-buckled shoes, sleeveless shirt and Spanish cape, the barbers were specifically picked out by the Spanish travelers as a group which stood out within the Indian population.[45] The illustrations of Indian barbers (fortunately they were sufficiently colorful to attract the painters' attentions) confirm the sartorial elegance of an occupation which wore clothes at the limit of non-Spanish dress.[46]

Although classified as Indian (and it may be that "Indianness" formed part of the "tools of the trade," that is the cultural expectations of the customer), the barbers form an urban group which was virtually a distinct social category. During one of the Declarations of Mestizo law-suits examined in Chapter 7, Angelina Flores, a "White woman" gets exemption for her children, who are the sons of Diego de Alcocer, identified only as Master Barber; in other words, he may not be Spanish, but neither is he wholly Indian, as a barber who has married a Mestiza.[47] In the cold climate of the post-1776 fiscal changes, at least one barber was able to get fairly respectable citizens to testify that he was mixed blood, which seems to have

---

[42] AM/Q vol. 37, Demandas y Juicios (1642–1687), fol. 245. See the documentation from the AGI on the epidemic of 1785 cited in the list of epidemics in Chapter 6 which specifically mentions the mobilization of the barbers. AHBC/I (Juicios), 41, "Autos de Yndulto de Mariano Folleco" (1784), for the barber's role in stitching up wounds after a fight (an example from Ibarra).

[43] See the "Padrón de Santa Bárbara," *Museo Histórico,* 56, (1978), 93–122, a document further discussed in Chapter 6.

[44] ANH/Q Reb 1, doc. 1762–V–24.

[45] Juan and Ulloa, *Relación Histórica,* 367.

[46] *Ibid.*, 378. By the nineteenth century, the ruff round the neck had disappeared, and the barber wore long sleeves, but the "barbero antiguo" was recognizably the same elegant figure: see *Ecuador Pintoresco. Acuarelas de Joaquín Pinto,* (Barcelona-Quito, 1977), 28.

[47] ANH/Q Mz. 1, doc. 2–VI–1741.

been a testimony to his respectability rather than his technical ethnic status.[48]

Although it is possible to identify with some precision the cultural and social position of the barbers, it is much harder to say what their economic position was. The lawsuit examined here certainly suggests that it would be wrong to imagine that acculturated urban Indians can be automatically pushed into the socio-economic category of a prosperous petty bourgeoisie. It is difficult to say how much barbers were paid; it is extremely unlikely that barbers ever passed before notaries to make contractual work agreements, and even if they did, this would not tell us how many transactions they had each week. As property purchasers, however, the barbers did leave some evidence in the notarial registers. A rich master barber, Don Juan Paltan, could afford an extremely expensive 500 peso tiled house in the *calle* Ronda in 1729.[49] He clearly belonged to a different economic level than the two barbers of over a generation later discussed below. As the barbers belonged economically to the urban monetary economy, it is possible that their condition was more difficult in periods of urban recession. This may be one factor to consider in the case brought by two Indian barbers in 1778.[50]

The two barbers were called Diego Silva and Bartolomeo Dias (both Spanish names) who, forty-five and seventeen years ago respectively, had contracted debts with their confraternity. Why they had done so is not explicit in the documentation,[51] but it is claimed that the different confraternities of the city carried out the same practice, which suggests that the confraternities constituted one of the major agencies of credit circulation for the urban lower strata. Another document of the same period explicitly states that Indians frequently lost jewels belonging to the confraternities while drunk during festivals, and that the Indians in order to pay off their debts "remained enslaved all their lives."[52] There is the suggestion in this case, however, that the origin of the indebtedness may have been forced loans, and the application of repayment requirements was invidious in the extreme. The Indians received money, but were obliged to repay their loan at the rate of 2 pesos for each 10 received, an annual interest rate of 20 percent. On a debt of 42 pesos, one has paid a total of 94 pesos, the other

---

48   This is the case-study of Ortuño examined in detail in Chapter 7.

49   ANH/Q 1 Not. Diego de Ocampo, Feb. 7, 1729, fol. 215–7. This is one of the most expensive house purchases I have seen for this period. Another barber in the 1768 *padrón* cited above, was barber and *pulpero*, which suggests he had a rich enough clientele to acquire capital and diversify economically.

50   ANH/Q. Ind. 95, doc. 14–V–1778, "Autos de Diego Silva Bartholo Dias Yndios Barberos sobre que se quite el abuso de plata de aumento de las cofradias."

51   *Ibid.*, the document simply states: "se distribuye cierta porcion de dinero entre los yndios."

52   ANH/Q Ind. 100, doc. 1780–IV–26, fol. 2.

incurred a debt of 30 pesos 45 years earlier, and has repaid a total of 282 pesos!

These figures are so extreme that the superficial role of the confraternities in circulating credit has to be immediately qualified. This is closer to debt-peonage, paralleling the use of debt by rural landowners to control their labor force, a practice which has been shown to exist in the region of Quito, by Cushner's work on Jesuit haciendas.[53] The Indians are required to repay the annual 20 percent or cancel the entirety of their debt, a clearly impossible requirement. It is claimed that the officials of the confraternities, the *síndicos,* have enforced payment with "extraordinary violence."[54] The confraternities may be circulating credit, in other words, only in the same sense that *censos* are a credit system; the initial loan is quickly transformed into a virtually permanent repayment program which for the Indians might be termed a second tribute system. The figure of 6–8 pesos was a little higher than tribute, although as urban artisans, the barbers had access to the urban monetary economy. Unfortunately, as was stated above, it is not known how much a barber earned; in order to stress that this was a considerable sum, it may be noted that annual income in the textile industry was 20–30 pesos a year, while the urban worker may have gained half a *real* for a day's work.[55]

Little opposing evidence is offered, the suggestion merely being advanced that the guilty party may not be the priests, but that the problem might arise from the ignorance of the Indians concerning the crime of usury, from their "rustic nature," and their excess of religious devotion. Episcopal approval is granted to the Royal Provision ending the practice, with the proviso "if indeed it exists."[56] The attempt to shift the burden of guilt onto the Indians is interesting, even if we do not fully accept it. Who were the Indians responsible? Although the Indians were considered collectively responsible through their ignorance, the officials of the confraternity may also have served as the villains of the piece. If these were indeed often Indian in the Indian confraternities—and in the lawsuit cited below, the síndico was specifically identified as such—this may suggest a form of social mobility within the confraternity, an ability of some of its members to turn the institution to their advantage at the expense of the rest. The temporary dispensation to a barber in 1785 to open a shop while he qualified in phlebotomy, was accompanied by the specific injunction that the Master-barbers should not take action against him.[57] It may be,

---

[53] Cushner, *Farm and Factory,* 128–129.

[54] ANH/Q Ind. 95, doc. 14–V–1778, fol. 1, "extraordinaria violencia."

[55] This sentence is based on the general literature on *obrajes,* but a discussion of costs, including those of labor, is available in Tyrer, *The Demographic and Economic History,* 184–229.

[56] ANH/Q Ind. 95, doc. 14–V–1778 fol. 6, reply of the fiscal, May 1778; fols. 7–8, episcopal agreement, June 15, 1778.

[57] AM/Q Demandas y Juicios vol. 37, (1642–1687), fol. 245.

therefore, that the barbers Diego Silva and Bartolomeo Diaz were at the lower end of a somewhat closed guild-confraternity with its own hierarchies.

But the question of the role of the confraternities in fostering social mobility, in permitting Indians to develop positions of authority, is certainly a double-edged one. We may distinguish between different levels of authority within the confraternities. The *síndicos*, the officials considered implacable by our two barbers clearly do belong to the power structure of the organization, although there is no more evidence than the points noted here to say who exactly they were. On the other hand, certain positions, notably in the festivals, were much more ambiguous, conferring prestige, but involving (as they still do) a very high cost. Thus, paradoxically, the barbers Silva and Diaz complain that they were forced into fulfilling the role of "constable, mayor, *prioste* and other positions normal for officials of the guild." There is evidence from other areas of the reluctance with which Indians were sometimes forced into serving as priostes, a key figure in the festival, this leading on occasion to their total ruin.[58] In his accounts for San Pedro de Conocotoc, in the Corregimiento of the city, the parish priest notes the problem of securing priostes for the festivals, and says that sometimes the festival had to go ahead without them.[59] The weavers' petition of 1780, examined below, suggests that it may not be wise to force too far the dichotomy between social prestige and economic pressures, and apply our own forms of reason to a quite different society. An Indian may be forced into an economically catastrophic honorific position in a festival, which at a different level, brings him enormous prestige; many societies function through similar contradictions, and it is misleading to attempt to iron out these differences, and impose an alien form of logic.

The Weavers' Festival Petition of 1780

The evidence from the third confraternity (the petition of Quito's weaving officials dates from 1780) allows us to discern a wider setting of rivalry and social prestige. In underlining the financial burden of the festivals, it also suggests one of the ways in which the income of the confraternities was recycled. Up to a certain point, it provides the religious dimension which is missing in the economic evidence.

The background to the petition is a series of attempts in the late eighteenth century to eradicate the dancers (*dansantes*), the bejeweled

---

58 ANH/Q Ind. 83, doc. 2–VII–1767, for the town of Cusubamba (Latacunga). AGI Quito 248, "Relación jurada que forma el Sr. Juan Josef Villalengua y Márfil ... Yndice de los Autos Acordados" included the provision that *caciques* and other Indians should not be forced to serve as *priostes* (Feb. 23, 1776).

59 ACM/Q Ind. 83, doc. 2–VII–1767 "Relación jurada," fol. 7.

participants in the festival of Corpus Christi.[60] The Indians had enthusiastically adopted this Christian festival, perhaps because it coincided with an important pre-Hispanic harvest festival around May–June, and given it their own flavor, not the only example of religious syncretism and native cultural adaptation to the colonial environment.[61] So much so indeed, that the fiscal in this case even identifies this Spanish inheritance as specifically Indian and refers to the "ancient customs" of the Indians! The dancers are considered "grave irreverences and not at all appropriate for the Divine Cult," the loss of jewelry leads to the enslavement of the Indians, while there is also the problem of disorder.[62] The voice of the fiscal is also the voice of the state: the measures against the dancers form part of a larger series of late eighteenth-century attempts to control the excesses of popular enthusiasm.[63]

We may let the Indian weavers speak for themselves, the petition is short and direct:

> The weaving officials, Indians native to this city, with the most heartfelt submission appear before Your Excellency, and say that in Devotion at the Festival of Corpus Cristi we have showed our joy (*Alegria*) dancing in the procession with the usual costume, which is called dansantes ; and although this practice has been stopped in the interests of saving expenditure, yet since this devotion [corrected to: festivity] is voluntary, and moderate in expenditure according to our limited possibilities: We kneel to the piety of Your Excellency, according to his best desire. Quito, April 26, 1780."[64]

Who are these Indian weavers? Unfortunately, there is no evidence on whether they belong to textile obrajes or how the organization of the textile factories would inter-relate with the confraternities. Independent textile workers with a small-scale domestic production did exist in the city of Quito, and it is probable that the confraternity grouped together these artisans who worked outside control of the textile factories, since by that date there was little obraje activity in the city of Quito. Five years after this petition, the master weavers of the guild of elected their Principal Master, and the minutes of their meeting have survived.[65] The first to vote was the

---

[60] ANH/Q Ind: doc. 1780–IV–26. fol. 4.

[61] Salomon, *Ethnic Lords of Quito*, 113–114. Also R. T. Zuidema, "Batallas rituales en el Cuzco colonial," in *Cultures et Sociétés. Andes et Méso-Amériques. Mélanges en hommage à Pierre Duviols,* vol. 2 (Univ. de Provence, 1991), 811-834.

[62] ANH/Q Ind. doc. 1780–IV–26. fol. 4.

[63] There were various attempts to control festivals, but this was notably at periods when there was a major threat of rioting, see AGI Quito 289, "Yndice de las representaciones que Don Serafín Veyan," (6 de Junio, 1768); and ANC/B Misc. de la Colonia, Tomo 67, Letter of don Joseph de Cistue to don Pedro Mesía de la Zerda, June 6, 1766, fol. 641, following the rebellion of 1765.

[64] ANH/Q Ind. doc. 1780–IV–26, fol. 1.

[65] AM/Q vol. 37, fol. 323, for the election of the *texedores* in 1785.

síndico of the Confraternity of Nuestra Señora de la Presentación which confirms the inter-relationship of positions of authority within guild and confraternity. More interesting, however, is the fact that this confraternity, which two centuries earlier had been the confraternity of the acculturated Indians, was still serving precisely the same role. Of the twelve master weavers who vote, it is clear that all are Indian, either by their name, or the title don, which was only carried by important Whites or leading Indians. In this case, the acculturated Indians have remained precisely that: these weavers, like the barbers, have remained Indian despite all their cultural contact with the Spanish-Mestizo society of the capital. Unlike the barbers, their production of low-quality cloth for the poorer population of the city does not bring them into direct contact with Spanish society.

According to a group who oppose them only "two or three of them" are interested in reestablishing the dancers.[66] The counter-petition is led by Don Manuel Coronel, already encountered above as Governor of the barbers, Don Santiago Rodríguez, like him a principal master of the barbers, Don Simon Tipantalsi, formerly principal master and now síndico of the office of embroiderers, Mariano Cantos, weaver by office (who five years later would be don Mariano Cantos, and be voting as a master in the elections of the guild of weavers), Don Asencio Calivezerra, current mayor (alcalde) of the office of shoemakers; and other officials (*alguaciles,* alcaldes) of distinct unidentified offices.

The Indians opposing the reintroduction of dancers include important, acculturated Indians; several have Spanish surnames, and they are able in several instances to sign their own names, while the title don reflects their status. They represent, in other words, the cream of the urban Indian artisans and craftsmen, and a spectrum of artisanal or craft guilds (barbers, embroiderers, shoemakers) opposed to the reintroduction of the dancers. Why the weaving officials wished to reintroduce the dancers can only be guessed at, but the presence of a weaver on the list opposing the dancers may be noted. After several decades of recession in the textile industry, it is difficult to imagine that the weavers as a group were more capable than the rest of the artisan population of supporting the expense of the festival. We are left initially with two possibilities; the counter-petitioners' claim that they are a small minority, perhaps those officials who manage to play on the economic and social possibilities of the confraternities; and the petitioners' own claim that they wish to express their own devotion and "alegría."

The Indians opposed to the festival make it clear that the festival is an expensive business: the economic drawbacks of the festivals are graphically depicted. Each dancer will receive presents, perhaps a sucking-pig, mutton or poultry. On the other hand, he has to pay out roughly 36 pesos in renting jewelry, and has to spend generously on drink for those who come to celebrate in his house. The Indian officials tell a sad enough tale, of those who lost jewels and had to repay them slowly, of the length of time

---

[66] ANH/Q Ind. doc. 1780–IV–26, fols. 2–3.

involved in making clothes, that "we are miserable folk and God knows how we satisfy the tribute."[67]

So far, this is a familiar type of evidence, and supports the sense of the barbers' allegations cited above. But the Indian officials strike a new note: "... if today this festivity is claimed to be voluntary, next year we will have to participate," and if not, the other guilds will steal a step on us. The Protector is even more unambiguous: the prohibition should be against all, because if the weavers are allowed to dance, the other guilds will be forced to imitate them.[68] The festival is a high prestige game, and the barbers and the shoemakers cannot allow themselves to be out-maneuvered by the weavers. We are approaching perhaps another interpretation of the weavers' actions in these conflicting rivalries. The Protector's comments clarify this point as well as providing an excellent description of the festivals:

> In this capital [of Quito] the Indians of all the guilds are accustomed to go out in turn, dancing in the procession of Corpus of this Holy Cathedral, and successively in the other churches; for which in rivalry with one another, they dress up, and adorn themselves with many precious jewels, and in order to obtain these, they rent them at a not inconsiderable cost. For these dances, they prepare themselves and practice for many days in advance, and then continue celebrating them for various days. All these functions are accompanied by disorder with the drunkenness to which they blindly give themselves, either by their inclination to drink, or by the custom which the Indians have of carrying all their functions in abandonment to drunkenness and disorder.[69]

Perhaps the most interesting part of this valuable description is at the beginning: the Indians are accustomed to go out dancing in turn ("por turnos"). The description of the Protector shows clearly that the festival was, despite its accompanying drunkenness and disorder, a highly structured event in which the confraternities tended to reinforce the ties within the different Indian occupations. A weaver will not only work with other weavers, he will, prior to the festival, spend a considerable preliminary period practicing with them (and it may be noted that the weavers dated their petition the 26th of April, quite some time before the actual festival).[70] His dancing with them constitutes both an act of collective

---

67 *Ibid.*, "que somos unos micerables, que Dios save como satisfacemos el Real Tributo."
68 *Ibid.*, fol. 3.
69 *Ibid.*
70 Juan and Ulloa, *Relación Histórica*, 361, confirm that practice, for the festivals began well in advance, and continued afterwards. For the timing of the 1765 rebellion, this allows us to confirm the correlation of the May rebellion with Corpus Cristi, by showing that organized festivities were under way before the event itself.

affirmation, and a challenge to the rival guilds. We can only imagine the panic of the other leading Indians at the thought of the weavers coming out as dansantes, and themselves unadorned!

Conclusion: The Church and Social Hierarchy

In one sense, the exceptional place occupied by the church in Quito society is beyond question, and few observers, whether contemporaries or historians, have failed to comment on it. This emphasis can certainly be misleading, however, if it makes us approach the church as a monolithic institution, and one with a uniform degree of penetration into all sectors of Quito society. If the communion attendance figures are taken as one index, we could indeed argue for a relatively low level of penetration into Quito society, and one which appears to have diminished as it descended the "free" social order. Judging only from the slender data of the 1720s, noted above, this influence may well have virtually disappeared before it reached the floating, vagrant population. The sense in which the religious orders may partially have filled the vacuum left by the secular clergy only reinforces the importance of examining the church through the diverse agencies in which it was embodied if we are to do justice to the complex symbiosis of church and secular society.

Whatever the level of formal compliance and actual religious faith at the lower levels of society, it is clear that the church had a major role in shaping the social organization of the artisanal classes through the lay brotherhoods. There certainly seems a sense in which the confraternities were a microcosm of the society around it, recreating patterns of social, religious and occupational interaction which we find in the wider society. Although the confraternities reinforced horizontal ties at the artisanal level, they certainly had their own internal hierarchies which were probably most marked in an occupation such as the barbers, where some members of the occupation worked for the highest social strata and therefore had the capital to diversify economically, while others were dependent on business with the lower strata of the city, and were probably the first to suffer in periods of economic difficulty.

It is clear from the account of Jorge Juan and Antonio de Ulloa that the church had a high consumption (notably in festivals) which recycled much of its income,[71] while we argued above that the Indians who were bullied into serving as *prioste* may well have received social prestige from a position which practically ruined them. In addition to their role as "mutual aid societies," there was also a sense in which the confraternities had established a regularized mechanism for the extraction of surplus from the Indian population which was analogous to the tribute system. Some urban Indians were in effect paying tribute twice, both to the secular authorities and to the confraternities. Bauer, in his excellent survey of the role of the

---

71 Juan and Ulloa, *Relación Histórica,* 378.

church as a credit institution, notes briefly the role of the confraternities in lending money at interest, but does not apply to the confraternities the distinction between liens and loans he makes so clearly for censos.[72] In Quito the role of the confraternities in credit circulation appears to have been exactly analogous to the functioning of the censos, that is a system which in theory involved credit circulation had sometimes ossified into a system of permanent obligation.

Several of the features of festivals which have been found for parts of New Granada do not seem to be directly applicable to Quito. For several locations in New Granada, confraternities cut through class and ethnic boundaries, and festivals were events which mobilized the whole community, often in a symbolic inversion of the social order. Spaniards dressed up as Indians, men as women, and by releasing social tensions in this way, festivals reaffirmed the cohesion of the whole community.[73] Although there is obviously a sense in which all festivals and major collective rituals symbolically unite the community, the critical question here is the degree and character of the interaction of the different social strata.

All the evidence on Quito shows clearly that the elite did not mingle with plebeians in the kind of festival which characterized the New Granada coast. Two festivals organized on royal occasions—the birth of the son of Philip V in 1629, which was celebrated in 1631, and the celebration of the accession of Charles IV in 1789—provide a clear picture of the organization of these highly hierarchical and structured events. In 1631 the guilds of artisans, and the merchants paraded independently and indeed on separate days, prior to a symbolic reenactment of the conquest.[74] During the 1789 festival, doña Rosa Chiriboga went onto the balcony and threw money and sweets onto the crowd.[75] The fact that at least in the nineteenth century the aristocratic families allowed the Indians access to their balconies during the election of the Indian alcaldes, suggests a passive involvement in the ceremony, rather than a temporary inversion of the social order. Data from all periods therefore underline the strength of hierarchical traditions in Quito.

The closest we come to the form of inversion noted above may have been during the bull-fights, on the evidence of Stevenson's account, but this was certainly a highly sedate Quiteño version of what was happening on the Colombian coast. Although Stevenson's account came from the

---

[72] Bauer, "The Church in the Economy of Spanish America," 722.
[73] McFarlane, "Civil Disorders and Popular Protests in Late Colonial New Granada," 47–49; O. Fals Borda, *Mompox y Loba: Historia doble de la costa* 3 vols. (Bogotá, 1980).
[74] P. Herrera, *Apuntamientos* (Quito, 1851): repr. in E. Enríquez B. *Quito a través de los siglos,* Tomo II [Segunda parte] (Quito, 1942), 51 ff.
[75] *Ibid.*, 103.

early nineteenth century, we can corroborate the use of masks at the time of bull-fights from eighteenth century evidence.[76]

> At this time many of the nobility and grave ecclesiastics disguise themselves, and leave their galleries to mix in the motley group, and quiz their acquaintances in the galleries. This part of the diversion generally lasts for more than an hour, and after the whole is concluded, groups of masks parade the street with music and flambeaux .... Some of the natives are remarkably skillful in making masks, and a person may procure, at a few hours' notice, an exact representation of the face of any individual in the city; whence, it very frequently happens, that people are seen double, one very gravely seated in a gallery, and a facsimile dancing about the circus, to the annoyance of the original, and the diversion of the spectators.[77]

That religious festivals in eighteenth century Quito followed the first type of celebration rather than the extremely limited inversion described by Stevenson is suggested by the evidence of the weavers' festival cited above, which is confirmed by Jorge Juan and Antonio de Ulloa's account.[78] In this respect, it is possible that Quito with its substantial Indian population and conservative elite resembled Peru more than it did the rest of the Viceroyalty of New Granada to which it had been transferred. What festivals appear to have done is license excesses *within* the established order, with alcohol playing an essential role. The "drunkenness and disorder" which the Protector identified as an integral part of the festival was also noted by Juan and Ulloa,[79] while the open cabildo of 1765 which admittedly had its own reasons for deploring the effects of the *aguardiente* monopoly painted a bleak picture of the effects of drink.[80] Drink also forms one of the common threads which unites festivities and rebellions,[81] and its presence may be noted in the social disorders discussed in Chapter 8.

Another type of festivity may be mentioned which has the most direct interest for questions of rioting and the social hierarchy, namely the mock battles which were fought between the barrios of the city, and were stopped in the late 1760s as a threat to the social order.[82] It would obviously be fascinating to have more detail on these ritualized disorders for the city of

---

[76] AGI Quito 289, "Yndice de las representaciones que Don Serafín Veyan ..." (6 de Junio, 1768).

[77] W. B. Stevenson, *A historical and descriptive narrative* (London-Edinburgh, 1825), 308–309.

[78] Juan and Ulloa, *Relación Histórica*, 361–362.

[79] *Ibid.*, 373, 546.

[80] AGI Quito 398, "Testimonio ... echo por las Religiones y común de Quito" (1765), fols. 598–667, including numerous testimonies.

[81] Taylor, *Drinking, Homicide and Rebellion*.

[82] AGI Quito 289, "Yndice de las representaciones que Don Serafín Veyan" (June 6, 1768).

Quito. The socio-demographic evidence on the barrios of the city is, however, sufficiently clear to suggest that mock battles between districts is compatible with the interpretation adopted here. In Chapter 8 an attempt is made to correlate the class and barrio origin of disorders, underlining the role of the relatively homogeneous popular parish of San Roque as the "engine of unrest." The mixed independence, competitiveness, and rivalry of the barrios is certainly clarified by the existence of "el combate de barrios." Although it is difficult to assess the extent to which confraternity and parish structure interacted, it is certainly striking to compare the existence of mock battles with the competitive rivalries between artisanal groups which the weavers' petition revealed. Although fiestas in Quito may not have served as the "explosive suspension of everyday rules" and therapeutic release of tensions on a Mexican scale,[83] it is clear that the colonial order was reinforced by its absorption of conflicting tensions and rivalries.

The fact that we find late eighteenth-century weavers in a confraternity founded for acculturated Indians in the sixteenth century certainly suggests that this form of socio-religious organization had its role to play in preserving the "Indianness" of particular occupations. The church clearly played a major role in shaping social structure, and establishing or perpetuating caste-like distinctions in colonial society, a point which Hassaurek made for mid-nineteenth century Quito.[84]

---

[83] Taylor, *Drinking, Homicide and Rebellion*, 118, citing Octavio Paz.
[84] Hassaurek, *Four years*, 86.

PART II

✣ ✣ ✣

The Popular Dimension of Eighteenth-Century Fiscal Reform and Economic Change

✣ ✣ ✣

Chapter 5

THE INFORMAL ECONOMY: THE URBAN MARKETPLACE AND THE PETTY TRADERS

The Dual Economy: Preliminary Considerations

Studies of modern Third-World urban economies emphasize the contrast between the formal economy, based on rationalized production and capital reinvestment, and the bazaar economy, which draws on the logic of the household economy to make full use of family labor, and interrelates with the firm economy through goods and services based on exchange with peasant producers, ownership of "the tools of the trade" and the possession of urban plots of land. Rural forms of domestic economic organization are transferred to urban settings, and the suburbs of modern Latin American (or Asian) cities are the scene of small-scale agricultural work which supplements specifically urban forms of economic activity.[1] If this approach is particularly appropriate for the early stages of industrialization, and for smaller provincial cities, it is held here to be directly relevant to the (by modern standards) extremely small and non-industrialized urban society of colonial Quito. The characteristics of the barrios of the city as (although in varying degrees) semi-rural parishes have already been noted; houses had plots of land attached, while a certain amount of textile and quasi-industrial activity was located along the river Machángara outside the city, giving a centrifugal character to the city as a zone of economic activity and consumer of Indian and non-Indian labor.

The notion of the dual economy is used here as the point of departure for an examination of the systems of market distribution within the city of Quito. One of the most suggestive features of this model is that the urban

---

[1] I am here paraphrasing B. Roberts, *Cities of Peasants: the Political Economy of Urbanization in the Third World,* (London, 1968), 110 ff., summarizing the work of Clifford Geertz on Indonesia, McGee on South-East Asian cities, and his own research on Peru and Guatemala.

bazaar economy draws much of its strength from the vitality of the peasant economy around it.² The inter-relationship of peasant and bazaar economies in colonial Quito is, however, partly subsumed into the problem of the nature and effectiveness of official controls on commerce, as well as specific legal and fiscal distinctions. Indians were liable to the payment of tribute, a system which despite its often brutal realities retained at least traces of the ideal of reciprocity. In theory certain ecclesiastical and other benefits, such as the services of the Protector of Indians, were paid for out of tribute income, while in the symmetrically conceived division into parallel Spanish and Indian polities Indians were not liable to payment of the sales tax. This legal distinction between Indian and non-Indian presupposed the existence of parallel Spanish and Indian economies, the former involving more expensive foodstuffs or the import (in theory from the metropolis) of luxury items; the latter with subsistence items on which the sales tax was not paid.

Although the break-down of this legal distinction, as well as widespread tax evasion, will be documented here, it may be emphasized that the peculiarity of the highly regulated Spanish colonial economy contained certain inherent ambiguities which gave legal sanction to a form of bazaar economy. Exemption from alcabala payments was one device which enterprising Indians could use to play on some of the possibilities of the Spanish colonial system (and therefore has particular interest for the social history of the urban Indian). Within the urban economy, subsistence agriculture was an explicitly untaxed form of activity which constituted a safety net for much of the popular strata within an often difficult monetary economy. In 1765 the Crown did impose a tax on the urban plots, but this led to the outburst of rebellion in the very parishes in which the measure was first projected, and may therefore be taken as confirmation of their importance in the popular economy.³ The exclusion of Indians and Indian-type subsistence produce from alcabala payments means that there is an important level of economic activity which does not appear in the official indices of sales-tax payments. Quito's bazaar economy was based not only on local production in urban plots, but on an inter-relationship with both the Indian peasant economy—which supplied it with subsistence food products—and with the dominant urban economy.

The existence of different levels of supply and distribution within the urban economy, interacting and sometimes competing with each other, has to be set within the municipality's long-running attempts to regulate the city's market system. R. J. Bromley has summarized the evidence on colonial market regulation in the Audiencia which led to contraband to evade price and quality control and disputes over weights and measures.

---

2   Roberts, *Cities of Peasants*, 112
3   For the 1765 rebellion see Chapter 8.

With regard to the profusion of official controls on commerce:

> "From the Ordenanzas of the Viceroy Toledo in 1572 until the end of Spanish rule in 1821–1822, the legal apparatus of municipal controls on trading activity became more and more rigorous. Trade in colonial Andean America was not 'free' but rather a highly regulated and disciplined activity. ... a virtual municipal code ... An ordinance charged the ... inspector of the market with the changes in regulations regarding trade and business. He was obliged to fix prices for goods sold throughout the district ..., to visit each business establishment during the first week of each year, to examine all models of weights and measures against falsification, and to deal sternly with hucksters who had a propensity for overcharging .... Numerous decrees were drawn up to further the best interests of the (urban "white") community. They were intended to insure an adequate supply of pure drinking water, to prevent the adulteration of flour, and to provide sufficient meat through sanitary slaughtering of cattle and pigs."[4]

Toledo's decrees were supplemented by later Viceroys, by the decrees of the Audiencia, and by the many decisions of the local cabildos.[5]

The *Pulperías*, the Petty Traders and the Urban Market (Sixteenth and Seventeenth Centuries)

In Quito, as Salomon points out, there was never a municipal *acta* creating a market on its foundation in 1534. An exchange system centralized in the "tianguez," the term imported by the Spaniards from the Nahuatl for "market," existed in pre-Hispanic Quito, and the earliest references to market activity in the municipal records show that the Spaniards rapidly adapted it to the colonial market economy.[6] The Indian traders in the "tianguez," located in the square of San Francisco, were

---

[4] R. J. Bromley, "Precolonial trade and the transition to a colonial market system in the Audiencia of Quito," *Nova Americana*, (Turin) 1, (1978), 275–276.

[5] J. P. Moore, *The Cabildo in Peru under the Hapsburgs*, (Durham NC, 1966), 68–70; For a summary of measures in Lima see Iwasaki Cauti, Fernando, "Ambulantes y comercio colonial. Iniciativas mercantiles en el Virreinato Peruano," *Jahrbuch für Geschichte von Staat, Wirtschaft und Gesellschaft LateinAmerikas*, 24 (1987), 179–211.

[6] F. Salomon, *Ethnic Lords of Quito*, 145; AM/Q, LCQ, T 1, (1535), 79–81. Salomon's account includes archival findings which partly supersede R. J. Bromley's overview, 269–283.

subject to both European and Black slave interventions in the form of forced sales and ill-treatment, as well as to the economic pressures of the colonial market system which were still, however, not so overwhelming as to overcome the preference for barter over money transactions forty years after the conquest.[7] Although it was claimed in the late sixteenth century that the Audiencia had "fallen outside the mainstream of city life" because of its distance from the Indian market-place, commercial activity was progressively diffused to other parts of the city.[8] During the sixteenth century, new "tiangueces" were being established on such a scale that when the President of the Audiencia, Fernando de Santillán, received his *residencia* as early as 1568, witnesses affirmed that it was not always possible to establish those which had been established by the President and those which were "antigua cosa entre los yndios."[9]

For the late sixteenth century, the Anonymous description of 1573 underlines urban dependence on food-supply from Indian produce for the "tianguez," as well as on White farm production. This independent small-scale supply for the urban market was to be an enduring feature of urban supply, although not all Indian produce was channeled through the market system.

The Anonymous' clear description may serve as a summary of early colonial urban supply:

> "The city is supplied with wheat and maize by citizens and other land-holding residents; in addition, there are many Indians who usually bring their produce to the "tianguez," which is located in the square of the city, and where the fruits and vegetables which the land produces can be obtained. Beef is supplied from the municipal slaughterhouses, while sheep are killed by those who raise them ... Indians supply and sell rabbits, partridges and other fowl, and chicken and eggs in their "tianguez." On Mondays and Thursdays, the Indians of designated communities are required to bring rabbits, partridges, chicken and eggs ... People prepare salt pork in their houses, but salt pork and ham are also often sold. Those who want dried beef make it in their houses, and dried venison is often found in the market. Pulperos sell cheese, lard and fat. Fodder and firewood are brought by designated mitayos, who come from a distance of twenty leagues to be hired ...."[10]

---

[7] Salomon, *Ethnic Lords of Quito*, 146, 148–50; "La cibdad de Sant Francisco del Quito. 1573," *RGI*, 2:228. The interventions of slaves in the market-place which Salomon cites (*LCQ*, for 1535 and 1548) was to be the subject on ongoing municipal concern, as recorded in the *LCQ*. For a later example, see below.

[8] Salomon, *Ethnic Lords of Quito*, 149, citing AGI Quito 9.

[9] *Ibid.*, 150, citing the Vacas Galindo collection of AGI copies in the Dominican Archives in Quito 1 ser. vol. 27. (There are many errors in this collection.)

[10] "La cibdad de Sant Francisco del Quito. 1573," *RGI*, 2:220.

The overlapping of household food-preparation (*tocino*, salt pork) with a type of produce sold in the market may be an early indication of the interplay of domestic production with urban supply. Notes of attempts to control the movement of pigs in the streets of the city form a frequent entry in the municipal records, and complements the evidence for urban plots of agricultural land detailed in Chapter 2.[11] Taking domestic urban production with the rural (Spanish and Indian) supply, we have at least three sources of produce for urban consumption subject to differing official norms; to these we should perhaps add the independently marketed production from the estates of the religious orders.

Protracted litigation during the mid-colonial period shows, however, that the different forms of urban supply cannot be easily separated. In 1573 the Anonymous Observer, cited above, had already noted the role of the pulperos in marketing cheese and lard, and elsewhere mentioned retail commerce of cloth, cheese, sandals, ham and wine.[12] As retail merchants, the pulperos constituted a visible group operating through fixed outlets, and as such they were subject to the licensing and tax control of the municipality. In 1642, they brought an action against the Indian women of the city who were alleged to be selling products which only pulperos were licensed to sell (ham, salt, cheese, tobacco etc.) and thereby undercutting their commerce.[13] This case was mentioned in Chapter 3 because it suggested that the interaction of the slave population with the free urban lower strata was more complicated, notably through patronage and compaternity, than the periodic cabildo complaints of Black violence against Indians in the market might suggest. In this case the slaves were able to steal food from Spanish households, and sell it to the market-women. Specifically, the Indian women had been able to obtain *alfajor*, *bocadillos*, and *turrones*, (pastry, dried fruits, nougat etc.), all items which should have been subject to a specified tariff (*arancel*).

As a result of competition from the market-women, or *gateras,* it was claimed that many shops had gone out of business, and only twenty eight licensed shops remained in the city.[14] In the list of *composiciones* for the official confirmation of their pulperías on February 26 and May 20, 1642,

---

[11] e.g. AM/Q Cartas de Cabildo vol. 54, January 7, 1772, fol. 24, cited in Chapter 2, and many other examples for all periods.

[12] "La cibdad de Sant Francisco del Quito. 1573," 218, 220.

[13] ANH/Q Carn. y Pulp. 1 doc. 7–VII–1642, fol. 2. Other products which were also mentioned were soap, honey, sugar, ink and ribbons, (fols. 6-7); pita fibre, jewels, knives, string, fish, (fol. 10); rice, biscuits etc. (fol. 12).
These lists give us a clear picture of the produce theoretically marketed by the *pulperías.*

[14] ANH/Q Carn. y Pulp. 1 Doc, 7–VII–1642, fol. 3.

only the following names appeared:

TABLE 5.1 COMPOSICIONES OF PULPEROS OF QUITO, 1642

Pulpero	Shop-owner
Pedro de Vega, Mulato	Doña Francisca de Varas
Joan de Cassas	Gaspar Lazo
Joan de Salazar	Diego Ruíz de Padilla
Francisco de Toro	Pedro Bayllo
Francisco Gutiérrez	"En la calle de Carvajal"
Pablo Sánchez	Doña Clara de Peralta
Pedro de Avendaño	Cristóbal de Bastidas
Cristóbal Ruiz	Diego de Peralta
Joan de Yépez	Pedro de Molina
Diego de Betancur	Diego Gutiérrez Pinto
Pasqual Nabarrete	"En su cassa"
Gerónimo Correa	Diego Bautista
Lázaro Fernández	Cosme de Casamiranda

Source: ANH/Q Carn. y Pulp. Doc: 7–VII–1642, fol. 4; *Composiciones* of February 26 and May 20, 1642.

The list of pulperos paying fees for their title shows that only two of the thirteen owned their own shops, while the rest were owned by property-owners of the city such as Pedro de Dueñas Bayllo whose transactions as recorded before the notaries mark him out as one of the richer men in the city.[15] The presence of a free Black in the list of pulperos may be noted as one of the scattered pieces of evidence which tend to place this category in the lower intermediate, and often mercantile section of the population. Obviously, the evidence presented before the court was with the intention of proving that the pulpería category of small business was being squeezed by unfair competition, but whatever the real economic reasons—and the pulperos' own explanation seems a reasonable one—the low level of licensed pulpería activity in the 1640s suggests that it has been misleading to take licensed commercial activity as an index to the economic growth and decline of Quito. Although we have few reliable indices of the level of commercial activity in the mid-seventeenth century, Phelan, Tyrer and Ortiz all concur in making that period the heyday of Quito's textile economy, when we would expect to find intensive pulpería activity. What is clear is that the city's large Indian population, and part of White society, were conducting their commercial activity through other channels.

---

15 For example ANH/Q 3 Not. Tomo 1, Francisco Díaz de Asteiza, 1653, fol. 3, 32, 33.

Despite losing their case, Indian and Mestiza women continued to sell the same type of produce, and in 1667 the pulperos made a renewed appeal to have this activity stopped.[16] María Sinaylin and María Criolla, Indian market-women, prove that they have been enjoying a kind of *de facto* truce with the authorities, a neat example of the adaptation of colonial principles to local realities. Although not technically allowed to sell pulpería produce, they have been doing so; although as Indians they are not liable to the alcabala sales tax, they have been paying it—as a payment-slip of 6 pesos clearly shows.[17] The pulperos' petition virtually confirms the existence of a kind of local pact, by alleging that the Indians are protected by important landowners who are selling the Indians their produce, and effectively bypassing the controlled market.[18] Although the use by the land-owners of parallel informal channels of urban supply is certainly interesting, the aspect which most concerns the overall theme of this study is the light shed on the urban Indian and Mestizo population. A number of points may be sifted from this mid-colonial evidence, which, it is argued, sheds a general light on the plebe of the city.

The evidence reveals a network of complicated relationships which reach beyond the plebe and suggest that access to patronage was one of the key features of part of the urban lower strata, and one cutting across the obvious class boundaries. The market-women will have had ties with the Indian peasant economy (supplying chickens, eggs etc.) which had no reason to appear in the law-suits. Their other economic ties—with slaves, unspecified suppliers, and indirectly with the Creole elite—established them as a counter-weight to the pulperos. On this evidence, the pulperos do not emerge as a group which had enormous weight in mid-colonial Quito, neither owning their own shops, nor serving as intermediary in the most important transactions of the urban market. Access to patronage is obviously a difficult area to examine, but the evidence of compaternity (see Chapter 3) may help to clarify the role of important Spanish households with spheres of influence which reached beyond their actual members. These inter-locking ties certainly mean that class categories should be used with some flexibility.

The fact that the traders in question were women should be stressed. Abundant other documentation shows that women played a key role in the informal market economy.[19] The most obvious point, that market activity

---

[16]   *Ibid.*, fol. 16.

[17]   *Ibid.*, fol. 17–20.

[18]   *Ibid.*, fol. 27.

[19]   For a late-colonial case similar to that examined above, ANH/Q Gobierno doc. 28–VI–1784, the *franjeros,* (the people who make fringes for clothes) are complaining of market-women selling those made by three or four "oficiales vagos." For the demographic evidence, see, for example, the *padrón* de Santa Bárbara, cited below, and in Chapters 6 and 7. I have not attempted to examine meat supply in this chapter, but there was an interesting legal battle over the land-owners' forcing the

allowed (as it still does) the family to make full use of domestic labor may be briefly noted. Perhaps the most interesting question, however, turns on ethnicity. In Chapter 3 we found Mestiza women "dressed as Indians" in the city of Quito in the 1630s, and stressed the selective nature of colonial impositions in which tribute (and the mita) was a specifically male obligation. For urban market-women, on the other hand, the ethnic pressure was precisely the opposite, to be Indian, and avoid alcabala payments. Although the petitions of the pulperos allow for the possibility that some of the gateras and *regatonas* were Mestiza or Mulata, it is clear that these were usually Indian, but with a very loosely defined ethnicity. This ethnic ambiguity is clear from their surnames. María Criolla, a surname we also find in a later case,[20] is the classic evidence of an Indian undergoing the process of transculturation, belonging to the no-man's land between Indian and Spaniard.

The documentation of the 1640s and 1660s was incorporated into later lawsuits which turned on the obligation of Indians to pay alcabala, and there were limits to the possibilities of the popular strata to "play the system." Alcabala exemption was effectively accepted when applying to foodstuffs of prime necessity, but Indians who went beyond this risked the imposition of the sales tax.[21] Nevertheless, between day-to-day transactions and cases actually brought to the attention of officials, there was undoubtedly more room for maneuver as an Indian than as a Mestiza. Some of the flexibility of urban social stratification in its lower rungs can be measured by a law-suit from Riobamba in 1695. The case was brought by Felisiana de Mora for 400 pesos, but Antonio de Riofrío, defending, claimed that she was a Mestiza and not an Indian, and was pretending to be an Indian in order to take advantage of the services of the Protector of the Indians.[22] One inheritance of this ambiguity in socio-racial classification in urban popular society was to be some of the petitions to be declared Mestizo in the 1770s in the face of the effort of the reforming Bourbon administration to sort its way through this ethnic confusion.

---

indios carniceros to purchase offal from the meat they killed at exaggerated prices. The *carniceros* purchased low quality meat which was then re-sold to poor people by the market-women: "porque nuestras mugeres son las regatonas, que la menudean," ANH/Q Ind. 80, doc. 1764–17–V, fol. 2.

20 ANH/Q Carn. y Pulp. 1 doc. 7–VII–1642 fol. 32. Although preserved in the same documentation, this is a separate case from 1686; "Catalina Criolla." See also F. Salomon, "Indian women of early colonial Quito as seen through their testaments," *The Americas,* 40 2 (1988), 341, where he speaks of "a true strategy of innovation, a movement by which extant relationships of both native and colonial origin were reworked by women as entryways into a rapidly expanding market economy."

21 See the cases preserved in ANH/Q Carn. y Pulp. 1 doc. 7–VII–1642; ANH/Q Ind. 94 doc. 24–VII–1777.

22 ANH/Q Mz. 1 doc. 1695–VI–8.

The number of licensed pulperías as an index of the level of economic activity is certainly brought into question. If pulpería activity was only on the scale claimed by the pulperos in 1642, by far the greater part of the commercial activity of the city in its period of expansion, was passing through other channels. There are, however, more fundamental problems with regard to the official data in this area; they suggest possible strategies of the urban population in the face of economic difficulties, and therefore clarify the themes which will be examined in the remainder of this study.

Urban Commercial Activity and Economic Change in the Eighteenth Century

Quito's economic decline has been the subject of debate in Ecuadorian historiography, and turns in part on the still partly uncharted impact of the freeing of trade regulations after the 1770s.[23] For the period 1690–1765, Andrien's recent work underlines the decline of the textile industry after the late seventeenth century, and the limited success of attempts to shift from textile to agricultural production which was hampered by high transportation costs and ecological impediments to specialization.[24] His reconstruction of tithe remittances show that this index of agricultural production was mainly stable or rising in the three decades up to the mid-1750s, but went into decline in the years from 1756 to 1767; this trend specifically characterized sugar cane production for aguardiente which had risen in importance as textile manufacture had declined.[25] Comparing these tithe remittance figures with the demographic evidence (see Chapter 6), and with the auction values paid by tax farmers for sales tax collection, Andrien concludes: "the transition from textiles to agriculture resulted in some modest recovery from the reverses of the late seventeenth century, followed by a marked decline by the 1750s."[26]

In a broader sense, Andrien's work underlines the sense in which the Quito economy had failed to adapt to the decline of its textile industry. How does the evidence on the informal economy fit into the broader picture, and what light can it shed on the official indices? I wish to base my discussion, in part, on a padrón of the farms, obrajes, and commercial establishments of the city and its corregimiento in 1770 which formed the basis of the administrator of alcabalas Antonio Romero de Tejada's

---

[23] cf, for example, Carlos Marchán Romero, "Economía y Sociedad durante el siglo XVIII," *Cultura, Revista del Banco Central del Ecuador*, 24 (1986), 55–76.

[24] Andrien, "Economic crisis, Taxes and the Quito Insurrection of 1765," *Past and Present*, 129 (1990), 107–111.

[25] *Ibid.*, 112–115.

[26] *Ibid.*, 117.

summary of accounts for 1768–1775.[27] Javier Ortiz de la Tabla has published a summary and discussion of the padrón, and argued that it provided an index of the decline of the city. A different picture emerges, however, when it is integrated with other forms of official evidence, and with the evidence for the inter-play of the different levels of commercial activity in the urban economy.

Before turning to the evidence of the 1760s it may be noted briefly that the nature of urban supply for the late seventeenth and eighteenth centuries followed the pattern outlined above. The dependence on the Indian population for the marketing of food produce continued, and in 1716, we encounter accusations of ill-treatment of Indian market-women by slaves which take exactly the same form as those of the 1530s. It was claimed that this was on such a scale that the city was running short of food, which may indicate that these tensions tended to be aggravated by, and reflect more profound problems of dearth at periods of agricultural depression.[28] In 1714 there was a proposal, opposed by the cabildo, for a reduction in the number of pulperías from 30 to 16.[29]

One "new" development was the emergence of a distinctive small-scale grocery called *chagro*, although this was clearly based on the deep-rooted tradition of domestic production and marketing of produce. In the late 1680s the cabildo claimed that there were unlicensed pulperías in private houses. In defiance of official restrictions, wood and other products were being brought to the city and being marketed in private houses called chagras in the barrios of the city.[30] It may be that the attempts noted above to control the marketing of certain types of produce in the markets of the city, however partial they may have been, encouraged the formation of these household "markets." The revealing terminology (the word chagra means "field") underlines the point made at the beginning of this chapter about the close interaction of the "subterranean economy" with the peasant economy of the surrounding areas. By the eighteenth century, in any case, these chagras—normally described as chagros in the eighteenth-century documentation—had become an accepted part of the urban economy, dedicated to the supply of "different grain, bread and other foodstuffs ... for poor people."[31] That they had indeed become an

---

27 Javier Ortiz de la Tabla, "Panorama del corregimiento de Quito (1768–1775)," *Revista de Indias*, vol. 145–146 (1976), 83–98, based on the *padrón* preserved in AGI Quito 430.

28 AM/Q, LCQ September 19, 1716, fol. 53, and for the agricultural depression of this period, see Chapter 3.

29 Gustavo Chiriboga C. (ed.), *Libro de Cartas Escritas por los Reyes* (Quito, 1970), 158, for January 24, 1714.

30 AM/Q, LCQ (1686–90), fol. 9, entry for 1686.

31 "En su casa una tienda en que haze vender diferentes granos, pan, y otros comestibles en la misma forma ... que llaman chagro, para el abasto de la gente pobre, y veneficio del comun." ANH/Q Carn. y Pulp. 2, doc. 1760–V–23, fol. 1.

accepted part of the commercial activity of the capital is clear from the fact that their presence was noted in the official documentation of 1768, the padrón of alcabalas and in the padrón of the parish of Santa Bárbara in that year.[32] We will return to these "poor man's pulperías" when the post-1760s evidence on the commercial activity of the capital is examined.

In order to set the commercial activity of the capital around 1768 within a medium-term cycle we may note the sales-tax returns for the period 1751–1800, which are offered as a general guide to trade flows within the northern and central Highlands, as this was a tax on virtually all non-subsistence items, Table 5.2.[33] However, one should note that the major increase after 1778 may have been partly due to increased efficiency of collection once the reformed Bourbon administration had reassumed direct fiscal control. The low figures in the mid-1760s may be noted, because they suggest a short-term downturn in commercial activity which helps to clarify the economic background of the 1765 rebellion. During the seven years after 1768, the padrón of Antonio Romero de Tejada revealed the existence of four to six functioning workshops for the production and sale of hats (*sombrererías*), three to five tile factories (*tejares*), and only one pot-producer (*ollero*) in a sufficiently healthy state to pay alcabalas.[34] There were also 124 recorded "shops" (*tiendas*)—whether open or shut— and 48 pulperías which were open for all or part of this period, of which 31 for the full seven years. Only two urban obrajes were functioning out of eleven which were recorded as licensed factories. This certainly indicates a low level of commercial and licensed industrial activity in the capital. The decline of the hat-factories was particularly marked as 38 different hat-factories had been recorded in the near or distant past, suggesting that conspicuous consumption (of hats etc.) had undergone a major decline in the eighteenth century,[35] although this was probably also because this production was obraje-related. Although licensed obrajes were probably never a good index of the scale of textile manufacturing, the fact that only two were functioning in the 1760s certainly confirms the decline of the eighteenth century industry.

---

[32] See the *padrón* of AGI Quito 430, cited above. My comments, unless otherwise stated, are based on my own reading of this document. See also "Padrón de Santa Bárbara en 1768," *Museo Histórico* (Quito), 56 (1978), 93–122.

[33] AGI Quito 430, "Testimonio de expediente relativo a la presentación de las Cuentas de Alcabalas," fols. 18–19 lists the rates (normally 3%) on the products which entered Quito. I have included these as a "crude" indicator, but see however, Andrien, "Economic crisis, Taxes and the Quito Insurrection of 1765," 113 for some "deflated" figures.

[34] AGI Quito 430, "Padrón"; for the *olleros,* Antonio Romero de Tejada notes: "Asimismo consta en dicha certificación quanto se travaxo en solicitar la cobranza de las expresadas ollerías de que resultó el reconocimiento de los hornos arruynados, y miseria en que manifestaban en ellos."

[35] Quiteños had a preference for imported luxury goods over locally made items, but a decline on this scale seems unambiguous.

The problem with "decline," however, is deciding what the base for comparison is. What were the "muchos años atrás" to which the collector of the sales-tax made reference when he said a business had closed long ago? If we place the padrón within an infinitely longue durée, it is probably true that Quito had declined, but this should not blind us to the medium-term and short-term cycles which are after all the measure of the human life. What the padrón tells us is the number of years a particular business was functioning during the period 1768–1775, but it is wrong to assume, as Ortiz appears to do, that all those recorded for less than seven years were going out of business. This point applies with particular force to the tiendas and pulperías. According to Ortiz there were 70 pulperías in the city of which 54.8% closed, and of whom six changed to chagro. Ortiz notes that only 28.4% of the shops remained open for the full seven years, while 12% were totally closed.[36]

At least a few of those businesses functioning for only part of this period, however, were in fact new ones. Of the six people who were chagro for part of the period, and pulperos for the rest, at least one was a chagro who became a pulpero rather than the opposite,[37] while several of the others are unclear. If we return to the case of the 1640s it was claimed there were only 28 pulperos in the city in 1642, while in 1683 there were 46 pulperos, which may be an overcount for comparative purposes as the total appears to have included religious pulperías which were exempt from the sales tax.[38] In other words, unless the commercial activity of the city was expanding rapidly in the eighteenth century, and it would have to be the most implacable revisionist who suggested this, it is quite clear that the total of 70 pulperías does not mean that all these had ever been functioning simultaneously. On the contrary, there had been a considerable turn-over of pulpería activity, with some closing and others opening, and the expanded total of 70 was the accumulated total of the pulperías which had been kept on the fiscal record.

There is considerable evidence that business was conducted on a cyclical basis, and that people opened and shut their shops according to the state of the market, almost certainly retreating to other forms of activity, including urban plots when business was bad. This was later explicitly recognized by the cabildo when they said that "in some years there are more pulperías, in others less."[39] The proximity of chagro and pulpería emphasizes the interaction of the subsistence economy with urban

---

36 Ortiz de la Tabla, "Panorama económico y social," 97–98.
37 AGI Quito 430, "Padrón," entry number 66 under pulpería; "esquina de la ollería de Mora frente de Leyba en San Blas. Pagó dicha pulpería 6 pesos por un año y medio que empesó a vender en ella su dueño." Five and a half years as *chagro*.
38 Aquiles Pérez, *Las Mitas en la Real Audiencia de Quito*, (Quito, 1947), 358–359. Pérez suggests that some of these were owned by the Jesuits.
39 ANC/B Juicios Civiles del Ecuador, vol. III, fol. 833, "... el Escribano del Cabildo" (1803), for an annual number of 32 *pulperías*.

commerce. One of the entries in the padrón of alcabalas contains the revealing comment that at one stage a pulpero had simply had nothing to sell.[40] The Santa Bárbara census of 1768 does not include many dual occupations—perhaps simply because they were not required for its purposes—but those which are recorded are essentially for small-scale commercial activity: *barbero/pulpero; sombrero/pulpero; albañil/chichero; estanquero/ carpintero*.[41] Ortiz' work demonstrates the diversification of the economic interests of the elite, and the notarial records (see, for example, in Chapter 2, the tailor who purchased an orchard in Pomasque) suggest that this aim ran through lower levels of Quito society. Fortunately, the coincidence of dates between the padrón of Santa Bárbara and the padrón of the alcabalas allows to establish differences between the two series of census data which shows clearly that either—if taken alone—provides a highly misleading picture of the commercial activity of the city. Although the colonial form of designating streets and shops by varying criteria (the house of X, near the Convent of Y) make it difficult to compare the two censuses house by house, the essential point is quickly established. In the padrón of alcabalas of 1768–1775, there were only 124 shops (tiendas), most of them shut at any given moment whereas in the single parish of Santa Bárbara in 1768 there were 110. What was a "shop" in these circumstances? Not all the tiendas in Santa Bárbara were actually "shops" in which anything was sold, and tienda was almost certainly a highly elastic term. In a late eighteenth-century law-suit we find an inventory of what was actually sold in a shop, which was a little of everything—a great deal of old clothing of every kind, a "Christian Cato," two "saints' hands," and last but perhaps not least, vessels of alcohol ("botijas de chicha y guarapo").[42] In many cases, artisans worked in their own houses, and when they had products to sell, they did so. In the period of agricultural depression around 1723, (discussed in Chapter 3), witnesses claimed there were only eighty or ninety shops functioning, but perhaps more revealing is their commentary that many others had almost nothing to sell except a few products like salt or cotton.[43]

Similarly, the one ollería for making pots did not exhaust the number of pot-makers in the city. In the padrón of Santa Bárbara we find eight, half of them women, with the ambiguous ethnic classification we have already found in the market-women of the city. Interestingly, they were located in and around the area of the *carnicería* which straddled the parishes of Santa Bárbara and San Blas, and a major concentration of tiendas were located in this area. In Chapter 2, we spoke of possible sub-barrios, small districts which did not have parish status but which had a real socio-

---

[40] AGI Quito 430, "Padrón," entry 22, under *pulperías*.
[41] "Padrón de Santa Bárbara en 1768," op. cit. 94, 96, 116.
[42] ANH/Q Ind. 97 doc. 1779–IV–27, at original fol. 21.
[43] AGI Quito 181 "Autos sobre minoración de censos," testimony in 1723; fols. 107, 109.

economic meaning, and the slaughterhouse certainly seems to have generated its own zone of economic and market activity around the square of the slaughterhouse. The 1830 padrón would reveal the existence of a production of leather in San Blas,[44] while the notarial records reveal a residential specialization of the Indian butchers on the slopes of the hill of Ichimbía (San Blas), i.e. in the scattered popular district near the slaughterhouse.[45] It is likely that the ties we find between the barrios of San Blas and Santa Bárbara mask the common identity of a more restricted popular district which overlapped both.

We should certainly emphasize the low level of licensed commercial activity in the eighteenth-century city, when it is noted that in a city of comparable size such as Caracas, there were 134 pulperías in 1816, which Kinsbruner considers a low rather than a high total.[46] With regard to what might be termed industrial or quasi-industrial production in eighteenth century Quito, the padrón shows that this was extremely low and the city had clearly been reduced to essentially administrative, ecclesiastical and commercial functions. The padrón of the late 1760s shows evidence of long-term economic decline (the obrajes, sombrerías), and if the collector was only capable of finding one ollería able to pay alcabala, that is a clear measure of the short-term economic difficulties of the city. In this sense an emphasis on Quito's decline is not misplaced.

I would argue, however, that once the economic activity of a stagnant city falls below a certain level, the conventional indices begin to lose much of their value, and we should begin to look for other ways of evaluating the evidence. This is not so much a problem of fiscal fraud which exists with virtually all official data, as of the very nature of urban small-scale commercial activity in "tiendas," "chagros" or "pulperías." Quito seems to have had what we might call structurally low levels of pulpería activity. From the totals we have for the seventeenth and eighteenth centuries it appears that the vitality of the informal economy, as well as independent marketing by the major land-owners, were factors keeping this total low. Unlike Caracas, a city well-connected to its seaport La Guaira which had direct ties with international trade, and which had Catalans and Canarians who became its pulperos, the city of Quito's interaction was with the peasant economy of the countryside around it, and the chagros (the modern Quiteño word for peasant) are symptomatic of this relationship.

---

44 See Table 2.1.
45 ANH/Q 1 Not. vol. 246 (1728–31), fol. 77; vol. 276 (1754–55), fols. 582, 588–90. The "Padrón de Santa Bárbara en 1768," suggests the concentration of "tiendas" given in the text.
46 J. Kinsbruner, "The pulperos of Caracas and San Juan during the first half of the nineteenth century," *Latin American Research Review,* vol. III, 1978, 68; and his *Petty Capitalism.*

TABLE 5.2 ALCABALA INCOME IN THE ROYAL TREASURY OF QUITO, 1751–1800

Year	Income	Year	Income
1751	6,682	1776	16,911
1752	4,498	1777	12,169
1753	8,283	1778	15,956
1754	5,500	1779	22,701
1755	9,365	1780	25,457
1756	11,646	1781	16,823
1757	6,977	1782	26,169
1758	9,511	1783	30,388
1759	9,375	1784	25,435
1760	6,950	1785	24,860
1761	7,600	1786	28,520
1762	11,693	1787	29,565
1763	5,120	1788	10,439
1764	6,400	1789	24,365
1765	9,003	1790	29,467
1766	3,855	1791	28,348
1767	10,607	1792	32,261
1768	8,272	1793	20,946
1769	12,992	1794	21,712
1770	10,997	1795	20,791
1771	4,924	1796	19,757
1772	9,413	1797	17,038
1773	12,873	1798	20,854
1774	8,437	1799	23,668
1775	10,378	1800	22,834

Source: AGI Contaduría 1539; AGI Quito 416-424. Note: Income is in pesos. Totals have been rounded. The area covered is the northern and central highlands, excluding the treasuries of Cuenca and Guayaquil.

When commercial activity dropped there was the possibility of a retreat into a semi-subsistence economy, but by tracing records of sales-tax returns we have difficulty following those who took this route. This interaction of different levels of economic activity took place on a continual basis, rather than as a permanent retreat from one form to another.

Chapter 6

DEMOGRAPHIC CHANGE AND SOCIAL STRUCTURE

"The general numeration of Indians is the fundamental cornerstone of the treasury and all the governance of the Kingdom of Peru ... God commanded Moses to do the same when, instructing him on what he had to do with the Israelites, he ordered him to take a census of them all, house by house and family by family ...."

Juan Romualdo Navarro, "Idea del Reyno de Quito, 1761–64," AGI Quito 223; J. Rumazo González, *Documentos* ... Tomo VIII, 529.

The Sources

"Everything said ... about population in Spanish America is merely hypothetical,"[1] but this is peculiarly true of the late-colonial city of Quito. Many of the demographic sources for the city are defective or incomplete. The reconstruction of demographic structures is usually based on house-to-house census returns, but these are missing from the archives.[2] Nevertheless, for all their shortcomings, the demographic data form a reasonably coherent body of documentation, allowing us to chart population trends, and identify periods of recovery, stagnation or intensified demographic crisis after Quito's initial decline in the late seventeenth century.[3]

---

[1] Manuel María Lisbôa, *Relação de uma viagem a Venezuela, Nova Granada e Equador* [1853] (Bruxelles, 1866), 356.

[2] ANC/B, Censos Varios departamentos, Tomo 8; fol. 327, Quito, 3 de Marzo de 1783; "El Presidente remite el Padrón General de Habitantes de aquella Capital y Corregimiento del Distrito, correspondiente al año de 1782..." Folios 307–26 are missing, and there is the annotation that these had disappeared before Dec. 1971.

[3] For the demographic history of the eighteenth century Audiencia, see J. Estrada Ycaza, *Regionalismo y Migración* (Guayaquil, 1977), R. D. F. Bromley, *Urban*

The discussion which follows is based on parish, ecclesiastical and census data to the exclusion of published contemporary descriptions of the city. These have traditionally been used by historians to provide population totals for the city and have led to figures much higher than those given here.[4] As we cannot disentangle their genuine reliance on census data from pure guess-work, such contemporary descriptions are largely devoid of value. Where other types of data are lacking, what such accounts can do is provide a rule-of-thumb guide to comparative size. Caldas, for example,

---

Growth and Decline; M. Hamerly, "La demografía Histórica del Distrito de Cuenca," *Boletín de la Academia Nacional de Historia*, (Quito), vol. LIII (116), (Jul.–Dec. 1970), 203–229; *Historia social y económica de la antigua Provincia de Guayaquil, 1763–1842*, (Guayaquil, 1973); R. B. Tyrer, *The Demographic and Economic History of the Audiencia de Quito: Indian Population and the Textile Industry*, (Ph.D. Berkeley: University of California, 1976); M. Minchom, "Historia demográfica de Loja y su Provincia: Desde 1700 hasta fines de la Colonia," *Cultura, Revista del Banco Central del Ecuador*, (Edición monográfica dedicada a la Provincia de Loja), 15, (Quito) (1983), 149–169. Other studies are less reliable because they have mixed (reasonably) reliable census data with (highly) inaccurate observer's accounts to produce otherwise inexplicable fluctuations in population totals. For example, it was argued that the population of the Sierra rose from 405,000 to 515,100 between 1780 and 1810, only to plummet to 392,160 by 1825; N. D. Mills and G. Ortiz, "Economía y sociedad en el Ecuador poscolonial, 1759–1859," *Cultura, Revista del Banco Central del Ecuador*, 9 (Enero–Abril, 1980), 139. However, their figure for 1810 was taken from E. Ayala, Lucha Política, (Quito, 1978), 39, who gives no source. There was no census in 1810 and the only other source given for that year is Stevenson, for a clearly impossible figure of 75,000 for the city of Quito; Mills and Ortiz, "Economía y sociedad," 142.

New research is appearing on Ecuador's demographic history; see now S. A. Alchon, *Native Society and Disease in Colonial Ecuador*, (Cambridge, 1991); K. Powers "Indian migrations in the Audiencia of Quito: Crown manipulation and local co-option," in D. J. Robinson (ed.), *Migration in Colonial Spanish America*, (Cambridge, 1991), 313–323; L. Newson's forthcoming book and her articles "Old World epidemics in early colonial Ecuador" in N. D. Cook and W.G. Lovell (eds.), *Secret Judgements of God: Old World Disease in Colonial Spanish America*, (Norman, OK, 1992), 84–112; "Highland-Lowland contrasts in the impact of Old World Diseases in early colonial Ecuador," *Social Science Medicine*, 36 (1993), 1187–1195.

4 Juan de Velasco gives a post-1759 epidemic total of 70,000 in his *Historia del Reino de Quito*. vol. 3 (Quito, 1977–8), 119. Giandomenico Coleti, who lived in Quito, gives a total of 58,000 in his *Dizionario storico-geografico dell'America Meridionale*, vol. 2 (Venezia, 1771), 106, although this may have been for a wealthier past, when compared with other descriptions by the same author. See another description of the same author and those of Montúfar (Selva Alegre) and others cited by J. Ortiz de la Tabla, "Panorama económico y social del corregimiento de Quito," *Revista de Indias*, (145/146), (1976), 86–7, who gives a total of 44,000. C. Borchart de Moreno cites eighteenth-century descriptions and also gives population totals which are too high: *Pichincha*, (ed.) S. Moreno Yánez, (Quito, 1981).

who visited Quito in 1805 criticized Juan and Ulloa's estimates of around 60,000 by saying that the population was only 35–40,000.[5] In fact, although these estimates are too high, I believe they give a fair reflection of the city's decline between the 1740s and 1805, and halving both figures would bring Quito into line with the disparity between eye-witness descriptions and more apparently solid evidence found to exist for other areas.[6]

Another source of which only limited use has been made is tribute data. Changes in the fiscal returns often simply reflected distinct accounting or collecting procedures and this largely deprives them of demographic value, unless they were in effect Indian census data. Although this material can undoubtedly be used for to establish a tributary curve in rural areas, tribute evasion and ethnic change make it a less satisfactory instrument for the discussion of urban demographics.

For the period prior to the censuses of the late eighteenth century, reliance has essentially been placed on the parish registers. R. D. F. Bromley pioneered the use of these sources in Ecuador, calculating the changing total population of the central Sierra by relating annual baptismal rates to the known total in a census year. This method depends on a number of variables which may change the baptismal rate: epidemics, food shortages, age at baptism, geographical factors and ethnic differences may all be reflected in fewer births, or in a lower ratio of baptisms to births by allowing time for babies to die before baptism.[7]

Although I used this method in an article on Loja, there are certain difficulties in applying it to the much larger city of Quito. It depends, first, on the datum line of a reliable census, against which to examine the earlier evidence, and the censuses of the late 1770s by no means provide such a solid base. Second, there were significant changes in baptismal practice in Quito. The earliest parish records of El Sagrario (preserved from the mid-sixteenth century onwards) show that at that period, El Sagrario parish was registering the baptisms of infants from outside the city. Late baptism was common until at least the 1670s and 1680s: of the fourteen Spanish entries for Santa Bárbara in the first month and a half of 1666, those which specify age at baptism give two and nine months, and nine, thirteen, fourteen and twenty-six years! In contrast, by the early eighteenth century, early baptism seems to have become standard practice.[8]

The records were examined for four of the urban parishes—those of El Sagrario, Santa Bárbara, San Blas and San Marcos (the latter consulted in

---

[5] Francisco José de Caldas, "Viaje de Quito a Popayan," *Seminario de la Nueva Granada*, (Paris, 1849), 504.

[6] R. D. F. Bromley, *Urban Growth and Decline*, 56–8, and "Una acotación," by J. Estrada Ycaza, *Revista del Archivo Histórico del Guayas*, Año 3, (6), (Dec. 1974), 93–5.

[7] R. D. F. Bromley, *Urban Growth and Decline*, 52–4.

[8] Between one day and a week became usual.

the AHBC/Q)—while the material I collected on the three rural settlements of Tabacundo, Cayambe and El Quinche enable the Quito evidence to be placed in its regional perspective.[9] El Sagrario constituted such a major part of the city that even on its own, its evolution is of considerable significance. In the nineteenth century, it was to make up over half the population of the city,[10] although Figure 6.1 suggests that the proportion of the urban population being baptized in El Sagrario may have been rising during the eighteenth century. Santa Bárbara, as a socially mixed nuclear parish, provides a "typical" picture of Quito's evolution, and I established a relatively complete series of data (although the Indian registers were missing from 1740) from the seventeenth to the early nineteenth centuries. In view of the comparability of this parish's evolution to El Sagrario (see the very similar curves of recorded deaths in Figure 6.2), this series provides a good indication of predominant urban demographic trends. The evidence from San Blas allows us to make sure that the data from El Sagrario, Santa Bárbara and San Marcos were not being distorted by differential growth between the urban center and the outlying parishes. It is possible that San Roque, (whose records I was unable to consult along with those of San Sebastián) may have been declining more rapidly than other parishes. Generally described as the largest of the ancillary parishes in the mid-eighteenth century, it had fewer people than Santa Bárbara and San Sebastián by the end of the century.[11] A possible explanation could be that the observers who described it as the most populous parish were misled by its lower class character as reflected in a large number of small households. This does not appear to be so, since Jorge Moreno Egas informs me from his knowledge of the parish records that it had indeed been a large (and Indian) parish in the seventeenth century.

From the second half of the eighteenth century onwards, we begin to have detailed but not always reliable data from the censuses. Although Juan de Velasco cites a census of 1757, and there was certainly census-taking activity in the 1760s, much of this was almost certainly partial and incomplete; prior to 1776, most enumerations were more linked to the collection of tribute from the Indian population than to any attempt to assess

---

9   Documentation examined in each case in the AP except for AHBC/Q "Adquisiciones" 14.5.10 for "Libro de Españoles e Yndios de ... San Marcos" (1786–1835).

10 The proportion was 59.4% in the admittedly highly flawed census of 1825. ANC/B Miscelánea de la República, Tomo 123 (i): fol. 188.

11 See, for example, the letter of Dionisio de Alsedo y Herrera, President of the Royal Audiencia of Quito, June 18, 1732, AGI Quito, 132, which described it as the largest in 1732. According to AGI Quito, 206, Real Audiencia, Jan. 12, 1748, "este barrio de San Roque es el mas numeroso de esta ciudad." The same point was still being made in 1765, according to the officals reporting in AGI Quito 398.

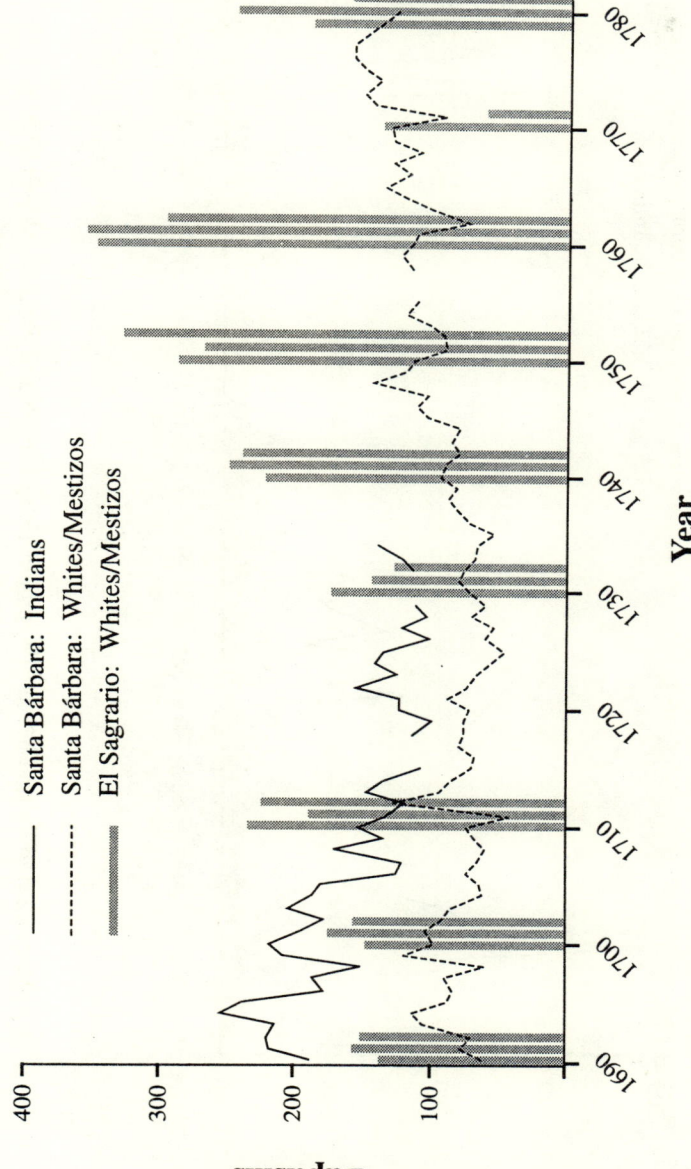

Figure 6.1 Annual Baptisms in El Sagrario and Santa Bárbara Parishes, Quito, 1690–1780

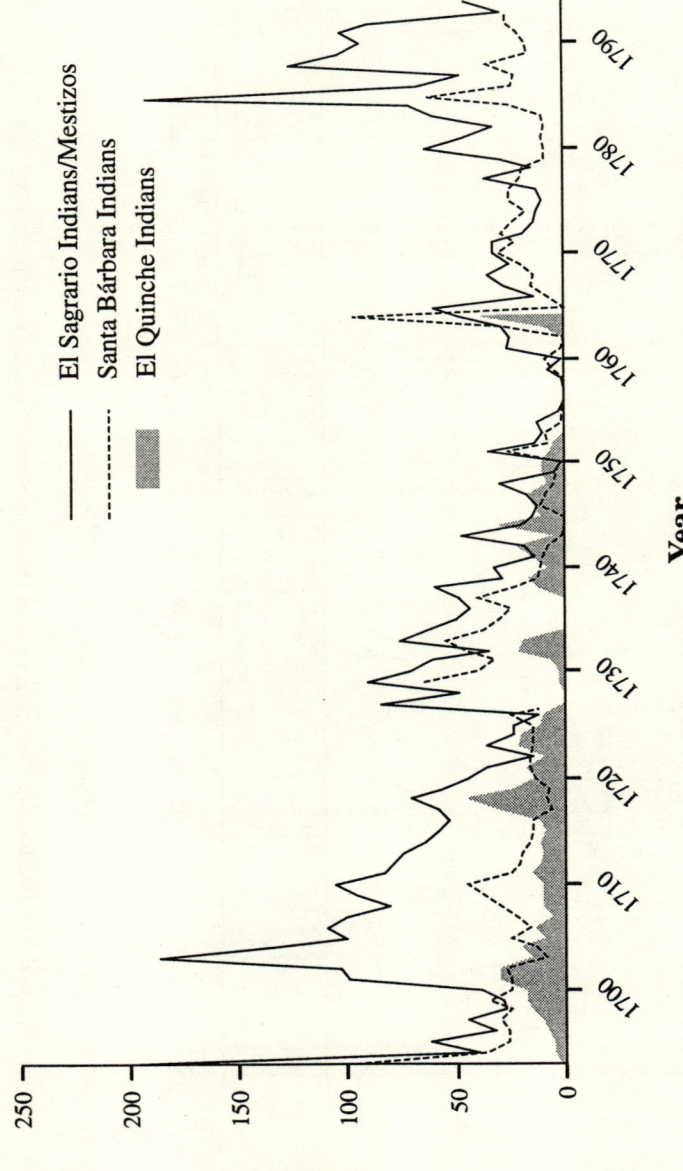

Figure 6.2 Indian and Mixed Burials in Urban and Rural Parishes, 1693-1793

the overall population.[12] It is probable that the census-taking which was carried out after the imperial decree of 1776 was reasonably accurate for the smaller urban centers.[13] A separate census which Villalengua carried out in the late 1770s was used by R.D.F. Bromley to corroborate the accuracy of the official *circa* 1780 series in the central Sierra. For Quito, however, it only sheds doubt; instead of a total of 24,939 for 1780, it gives one of 21,960 for only a very slightly earlier date.[14] In view of the climate of fear of fiscal exactions (see Chapter 7), it is in fact unsurprising that the census takers of 1780 had great difficulty in giving an accurate demographic picture of the capital. The greater size of the urban center made it easier to escape from the enumerators, and as a section of the city's population consisted of cholos who could be reduced to tributary status if they were identified as such, widespread evasion was inevitable.

Browning and Robinson have stressed the importance of working directly on census data rather than compilations,[15] and the census summaries which followed in the 1780s were not merely limited to adding and subtracting births and deaths, but saw major defects creep in.[16] These compilations have been excluded from consideration here, except for the census of 1781 which is an early one, and does not appear to have suffered the distortions which later compilations accumulated. The official who transcribed the 1814 census refused to believe the relatively plausible total

---

[12] Juan de Velasco mentions a census of 1757, *Historia del Reino*, vol. 3, 118, basing himself on the oidor Navarro. Navarro's "Idea del Reyno de Quito" (1761–4), in AGI Quito 223, (a document published by Rumazo González) is, however, quite inaccurate. The totals it gives are higher than those which census data located for the same period suggested; its totals may be compared with those in M. Minchom, "Historia demográfica de Loja," 149–169.

[13] R. D. F. Bromley, *Urban Growth and Decline*, 148.

[14] The Villalengua padrón is preserved in AGI Quito 381. Essentially a tribute document, it also includes figures for the overall population. There are multiple copies of the imperial censuses in Seville, Bogotá and Quito (see also B. L. Egerton ms 1809, fol. 45). The 1780 summary cited by M. Hamerly "La demografía," 210 is in the section of the ANH/Q now called Empadronamientos. The 1781 summary used here was taken from the ANC/B Hacienda Real, varios no. 2893, "Censos del Ecuador": "Ciudad de San Francisco del Quito y su corregimiento. Padrón hecho en el año de 1781 ..." The same volume includes later summaries. The apparent disappearance of census data on Quito from this archive was noted in the introduction. For a summary of 1782, AGI Quito 242; for 1783, AGI Quito 378A; for 1784, "Censos del Ecuador," ibid.; for 1785, AGI Quito 243.

[15] David G. Browning and David J. Robinson, *The Origins and Comparability of Peruvian Population Data: 1776–1815*, Discussion Paper, Syracuse University, 1976.

[16] The copies from 1783 onwards appear to have numerous insuperable defects. Between 1781 and 1783, there is an inexplicable drop in the number of Indian solteras from 2,007 to 308. In 1784, the total for the corregimiento is clearly erroneous, being over 87,000.

of 20,627 he encountered on account of the evasion which had occurred when people hid to avoid a military levy.[17] Consequently, he took the total of 65,133 from the entire corregimiento of the city in 1785, and gave this as his total, an inaccuracy which found its way into the secondary literature. The defects of the official censuses make a series of padrones carried out by the parish priests of Quito in 1797 all the more valuable at exactly mid-point between the major census-taking activity of around 1780, and the census of 1814.[18]

These padrones, however, pose their own problems. Although they list inhabitants, either they do not give occupational data, race and age, or this is highly incomplete, which means that they cannot form the basis for a full study of the demographic structure of Quiteño society. More particularly, the padrones were communion listings rather than genuine censuses; the purpose of the church padrón was pastoral, and all names were marked as to whether the person had attended annual communion the previous year. Adults and older children who were capable of attending communion were listed but not apparently younger children (normally under eight years of age) who did not receive communion. In the official censuses of around 1780, property-owners are unlikely to have objected to listing slaves, so the total of 588 slaves in the census total of 1781 was probably roughly accurate; yet in the church padrones of 1797 there were less than 200 Blacks including only 33 slaves. Were slaves, as "property," not worth declaring in a church census? As with all censuses there is evidence of evasion. The parish priest of San Sebastián complained that the heads of households were hiding people.[19] It was unfortunately possible to locate only part of the El Sagrario census and the total for that parish was provided by Moreno Egas, whose overall totals I have combined with my own reading of the padrones. The total of 5,890 for El Sagrario, however, is impossibly low in view of the annual baptismal rate in the parish. This is clearly an incomplete and defective series.

Nonetheless, what the church censuses *can* do, when carefully studied alongside other evidence, is to provide us with a rough estimate of the population of Quito in 1797. The importance of this is that in allowing us

---

17 ANC/B Misc. de la Rep. Tomo 123 (i), fol. 191.

18 These documents come from the unclassified ACM/Q lying in a box marked "Visita Pastoral- Ilmo Pérez de Calama (1790)," with the exception of El Sagrario parish, part of which was in one of the early boxes marked "Capellanías." The census for San Marcos is complete. I am greatly indebted to Sr Jorge Moreno Egas, of the Centro Nacional de Investigaciones Genealógicas y Antropológicas, for sharing with me the calculations in his "Estimaciones sobre la población de Quito de 1797" (manuscript deposited with the Ecuadorian National Academy of History). All the calculations relating to the Sagrario, (and therefore also the cumulative totals) are his, as I was unable to locate the whole of this census. I incorporated my own readings into his cumulative totals which explains minor discrepancies in the figures. I am equally indebted to Monsr. Cadena who directed me to this document.

19 Padrón of San Sebastián, ACM/Q, "Visita Pastoral-Ilmo. Pérez de Calama (1790)."

to examine demographic change in the last twenty years of the eighteenth century, they enable us to go beyond the general comparison of census data from a much earlier date with censuses carried out during or after the troubled Independence period which began in 1809. Consequently, it becomes possible to clarify the demographic consequences of the Independence wars, by having a clearer understanding of demographic trends in the late pre-Independence period.

In order to reach a population total for Quito in 1797, it is clear that we need to calculate the proportion of those too young to be considered capable of participating in religious practice. Two padrones of parishes have been used for comparative purposes, that of Santa Bárbara in 1768[20], and that of San Marcos in the 1790s. The complete padrón of Santa Bárbara was checked against the partial ecclesiastical one of 1797. The census of San Marcos appeared in the same group of documents as the 1797 census, but does not appear to belong to the same series of padrones.[21] It is certainly different in character, identifying Mestizos as such and specifying young children (*párbulos*), and appears to be a complete census, rather than a list of those eligible for communion. There is evidence that there was ecclesiastical census-taking activity in 1791 when the energetic Pérez de Calama was Bishop in Quito, and the padrón may have belonged to that series; on June 18, 1791, Calama wrote that he had completed this official visita.[22] It is possible that the census of 1797 was not carried out for San Marcos, and that the 1791 census was updated instead; unlike the other parishes there is a supplementary communion list for 1799. Obviously, if this padrón was indeed carried out six years earlier, the 1797 series is incomplete, but this is not a major distortion in view of the margin of accuracy within which we have to work.

Parish Demographics to 1780

The Ecuadorian highlands witnessed major demographic changes after the late seventeenth century. In the case of the central highlands, these have been carefully examined by Bromley, who identifies a process of urban recession, which constitutes a valuable model to test against the evidence for the region of Quito. In the late eighteenth century, the towns of Riobamba, Latacunga, and Ambato were declining in population, while the central highlands as a whole were already witnessing the beginnings of the

---

[20] "Padrón de Santa Bárbara en 1768," Museo Histórico (Quito), 56, (1978), 93–122. See Chapter 7 for the evidence of this census on socio-racial classification.

[21] Moreno Egas dated all the documents in the series 1797. On my reading, the date may have been March 30, 1791 (the other padrones were carried out in June/July), and I feel the points noted in the text make this date plausible. This difference does not significantly affect demographic calculations.

[22] AGI Quito 379, Letter of Joseph Pérez de Calama, Bishop of Quito, June 18, 1791.

Sierra-Coast emigration which was to be a major feature of nineteenth century Ecuadorian history.[23] Nevertheless, that area appears to have been much harder hit by catastrophes (such as earthquakes), as well as having a higher degree of dependence on the textile economy, than may have been true of parts of the North and the South of the Audiencia.[24] To what extent did the capital of the Audiencia participate in the demographic crisis which affected at least part of the Audiencia?

From the early data, we may pick out the impact of the epidemic of 1665 which led to 75 Indian and 27 Spanish burials in the parish of Santa Bárbara alone. In view of the changes in baptismal practice noted above, some caution is in order in comparing the mid-seventeenth century figures with those of the eighteenth century. There is no doubt, however, as to the major impact of the epidemic of the 1690s which is confirmed by other sources. Urban parish priests recorded 423 Indian tributaries dead in the city and there is evidence of major underreporting. Tyrer's estimate that the Indian population fell by 40 percent in the 1690s certainly suggests the scale of the disaster, which has been the subject of Alchon's research.[25] The evidence for high mortality in the 1690s is so strong that we do not need to rely exclusively on data from the parish registers to confirm it. The surviving register of deaths of "mestizos, montañeses, yndios, negros y mulatos, 1693–1729" of Sagrario parish begins during the epidemic, but shows the extent of its impact.[26] The relatively low number of baptisms in 1690 before the epidemic may have been the consequence of food shortages which preceded it, leading to fewer pregnancies or more miscarriages.[27]

Assessing the data in Figures 6.1, 6.2 and 6.3 together, it is clear that the city had undergone a major demographic decline between the late seventeenth century and the 1720s. During this period, the baptismal and burial registers reserved for Indians, Mestizos and Mulatos in El Sagrario were dominated by Indians and comparison of the different parish evidence suggests that it was above all the Indian population of the city which was declining. The relative impact of epidemics on the Indian population was commented on by many observers, and in a city like Loja where socio-racial segregation survived far better than in Quito, the existence of distinct Indian and White/mixed blood parishes made it possible to establish this

---

23   R. D. F. Bromley, *Urban Growth and Decline in the Central Sierra of Ecuador*, (Ph.D. University of Wales, 1977).

24   See M. Minchom, "Historia demográfica de Loja." M. Hamerly suggested that this might have been because of the role of the north and south as "regions of refuge" in the Wars of Independence, but Loja's growth antedates this period.

25   Tyrer, *The Demographic and Economic History*, 40–1; S. A. Alchon, "The Effects of Epidemic Disease in Colonial Ecuador: the Epidemics of 1692 to 1695," Paper presented at the Annual Meeting of the American Historical Association, 1982.

26   There were 90 recorded deaths during July, compared with 22 in August, 22 in September and only 10 in October.

27   R. D. F. Bromley, *Urban Growth and Decline*, 52–3.

differential impact very clearly.²⁸ The figures for burials in El Sagrario and Santa Bárbara show that after a brief recovery following the 1690s epidemic (probably because the most vulnerable groups such as infants had already been eliminated) there were high though steadily declining numbers of Indian deaths between 1700 and 1720 and then a new peak in the late 1720s. The evidence for an agricultural depression whose effects were reinforced by epidemic-induced labor shortages is therefore confirmed by the demographic evidence.

After the late 1720s Quito's population apears to have undergone some modest recovery, with the detailed figures for Santa Bárbara (Figure 6.3) confirming the broad pattern which had previously been established (Figure 6.1). In the case of Santa Bárbara, there were modest decreases in the mid-1730s, the early 1740s, and 1751–52, and there was stagnation in the 1760s. However, this did not affect the underlying trend upwards through to the late 1770s. The evidence assembled here is sufficient largely to discount as major demographic influences the earthquake of 1755 and the epidemic of 1759 described by Juan de Velasco.²⁹ The two major crises to be identified from the demographic data for the period from 1730 to the late 1770s are that of the mid 1740s, and above all, that of 1764–66. The evidence of food shortages and epidemics of the mid-1740s is not clear; to judge from Figure 6.2 this may have had more impact on the Indian population of the hinterland than on the urban population as there was a substantial rise in mortalities in the rural parish of El Quinche. On the other hand, Figure 6.2 shows that the epidemics of the mid-1760s had a major impact on both rural and urban parishes.

In examining the economic background of the Quito rebellion of the 1765 insurrection, Andrien emphasizes the unfavorable economic context. In particular, his figures for tithe remittances, which indicate agricultural production, show that these were mainly stable or rising during the 1730s and 1740s, but went into marked decline in the period 1756–67.³⁰ They also dipped slightly in 1741–2 prior to the earlier epidemics. The number of annual deaths in urban society (at least for the poorer Indian, Mestizo sectors recorded in Figure 6.2, although the White population in Figure 6.1 showed more stability) were therefore closely following the rhythms of agricultural production and scarcity. This correlation is not surprising in

---

28   M. Minchom, "Historia demográfica de Loja," for the figures of White (and mixed-blood) and Indian baptisms.

29   The 1759 epidemic caused few mortalities because of previous exposure to viruelas; S.A. Alchon: "Epidemics in the city of Quito: disease, population, and public health during the eighteenth century," Paper presented at the 46th International Congress of Americanists, Amsterdam, 1988.

30   K. J. Andrien, "Economic crisis, Taxes and the Quito Insurrection of 1765," *Past and Present*, 129, (Nov. 1990), 112–3.

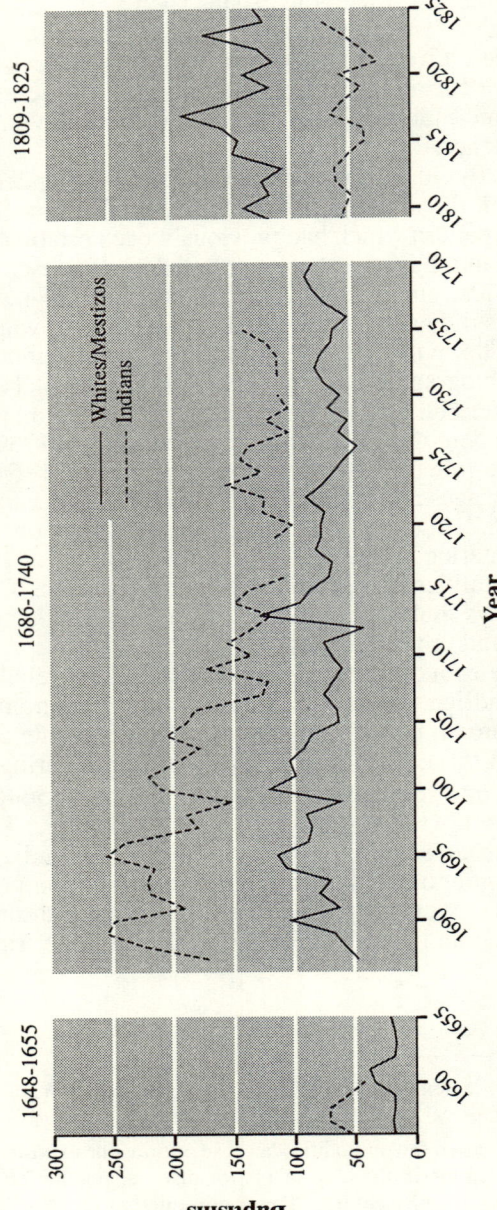

Figure 6.3 Annual White/Mestizo and Indian Baptisms in Santa Bárbara Parish, 1646–1825

view of the documentation on the early eighteenth-century agricultural depression cited in Chapter 3 which revealed the impact of the rural depression on urban society. Infants being abandoned at the doors of (generally) White households are a good indicator of economic hardship. In Figure 6.4 the proportion of these children being abandoned in the parish of Santa Bárbara shows a clear correlation with periods of high Indian mortality, and both the early 1740s and the late 1750s and the 1760s saw the rate rising substantially.

Nevertheless, allowing for short-term cycles and the impact of epidemics, Figures 6.1, 6.2 and 6.3 suggest that the period from the 1730s to the late 1770s was in general one of demographic recovery.

Demographic Change After 1780

Mortality in the 1780s and 1790s

The parish registers show clearly that the epidemic of 1785 was only the high point of a period of high fluctuating mortality, in which other epidemics had an impact on almost the same scale (see Figure 6.2 and Table 6.1). This may have been a consequence of another medium-term climatic and agricultural cycle similar to that of 1690–1720 since we know that epidemics were closely inter-related with agricultural shortages. For other regions, we have evidence of excessive rain in 1784–5, 1803–4, and 1817–21, and for droughts in 1771–2, 1790–1, 1792–3, 1794–5, 1804–5, 1808–9, and 1809–10.[31] In the case of Quito, the municipal records reveal that in the late eighteenth century, there was excessive rain in 1771, 1774–5 (with agricultural price rises), 1777, 1784–5, 1789, 1790 and drought in February 1774, 1780, 1783, 1787, 1792, 1793, 1797.[32] There were food shortages in 1783–5 [33] (preceding the 1785 epidemic), "many illnesses" in 1777, 1780, 1782, 1792 and 1800[34] and epidemics in 1785 and

---

[31] M. Hamerly, "La demografía," 210; most of these references are to the coast.

[32] AM/Q, LCQ, Aug 31, 1771, fol. 159; Feb. 5, 1774, fol. 91; August 22, 1774, fol. 104; Jan. 29, 1775, fol. 132; Feb. 7, 1775, fol. 134; March 10, 1775, fol. 138; Nov. 17, 1777, fol. 44; Oct. 20, 1780, fol. 186; Jan. 28, fol. 64v; Aug. 4, 1784, fol. 137; July 15, 1785, fol. 176 and other entries; Jan. 12, 1787 fol. 9; Feb. 2, 1787, fol. 13; July 3, 1789, fol. 123; July 6, 1790, fol. 173; Feb. 10, 1792, fol. 13; Oct. 18, 1793, fol. 62; Feb. 3, 1797, fol. 7.

[33] AM/Q, LCQ, Dec. 19, 1783, fols. 97–8, Feb. 1, 1785, fol. 165; and multiple entries.

[34] AM/Q, LCQ, Feb. 14, 1777, fol. 15r; Oct. 20, 1780 fol. 186r; March 2, 1782, fol. 15r; Jan. 28, fol. 64v; July 31, 1792, fol. 25; Jan. 28, 1800, fol. 118.

TABLE 6.1 MAJOR EPIDEMICS: THE CITY OF QUITO, 1690–1820

c1693	(Measles+). A major epidemic with multiple sources: see S. A. Alchon, "The Effects of Epidemic Disease."
1720s	R. D. F. Bromley, *Urban Growth and Decline*, 43–5, citing AGI Quito 129; Quito 204 for other areas. A major pan-Andean epidemic which had less impact on Quito than in Peru: see Figure 6.2.
1740s	*GS*, 2: 1049, preceded by food shortages in 1743 and 1744 according to Juan and Ulloa; see R. D. F. Bromley, *Urban Growth and Decline*, 45.
1759	B. L. Kings 219, fol. 40, and Juan de Velasco, *Historia del Reino de Quito*, 140. This probably had less impact than Velasco suggested.
1764–6	ANC/B Misc. de la Colonia, Tomo 60, fol. 441; Carta de Felix de Llano, Quito, Dec. 17, 1765. AGI Quito 398 fol. 495; Carta del Audiencia, Aug 25, 1765. A. Pérez, *Las Mitas en la Real Audiencia de Quito*, (Quito, 1947), 346, citing "Escritos de Espejo." See Figure 6.2.
1785	(Measles+). Parish reports, AHBC/Q, vol. 29, Libro Verde 1: 252ff.; ANC/B, Misc. de la Colonia, Tomo 2, fol. 814; Villalengua to the Viceroy, Sept. 18, 1785; ibidem. Oct. 18 and Nov. 18, 1785, AGI Quito 243. See Figure 6.2.
1788	APQ/ Sagrario, Register of deaths, (Inds.1767–1800) fol. 94.
1792	Tyrer, 90, citing ANH/Q Gobierno,1793.
1795–6	See Figure 6. 2 of recorded Indian/Mestizo deaths in the APQ/ Sagrario. AM/Q, LCQ August 14, 1795, fol.115.
1804	Tyrer, 90 citing ANH/Q varios, 1804.
1816	(Smallpox). M. Minchom, "Historia demográfica," for the south of the Audiencia. R.D.F. Bromley, *Urban Growth and Decline*, 197, for the central highlands. No specific corroboration for Quito.

Note: Although the nature of non-indicated epidemics is not known, the sign (+) acknowledges that the "peste" often included inter-related diseases; for example, Villalengua to the Viceroy, October 18, 1785, AGI Quito 243; "Sarampion complicada de otros graves males." For the background, see S. A. Alchon: "Epidemics in the City of Quito."

1795.[35] There were also problems with the water supply, according to the municipal records of 1787, with marsh water mixing with the water supply.[36]

Droughts in particular were liable to cause food shortages, and bring epidemics in their wake, and the municipal data correlate fairly well with the mortality fluctuations recorded in Figure 6.2. It is difficult to make

---

35 AM/Q, LCQ first entry is Sept. 6, 1785, fol. 180; August 14, 1795, fol. 115.
36 AM/Q, LCQ, Jan. 16, 1787, fol. 10 and subsequent entries.

comparative use of work on the central highlands, because other pressures—most notably the devastation of earthquakes—mean that the relative importance of these factors was diminished within a generalized demographic crisis. In the south of the Audiencia, however, I also found a similar change in mortality rates[37] so it is likely that much of the highlands entered a period of high mortality in the 1780s and 1790s. The link between demographic and economic change is a crude one, but it is worth noting that this was a period in which the liberalizing of trade regulations had hitherto unexamined consequences for the economy of the Audiencia, while trade patterns were also disrupted by the European wars of the 1790s. Agricultural and climatic changes are much more likely, however, to provide the essential explanation.[38]

The period of high fluctuating mortality of the 1780s and 1790s[39] was certainly felt most strongly in the youngest age groups who acquired less immunity to disease. The ratio of adult to child mortality was recorded during the 1785 epidemic in Quito.[40] During the months of September and October this ratio was 1:1.7 (1,166 recorded child mortalities out of a total of 1,859). Even this total slightly underestimates the impact on child mortality in the subsidiary parishes, as the adult to child death ratio was inverted in El Sagrario. In part this confirms the distinctive character of El Sagrario as the place of residence of the creole elite in which the low proportion of child burials reflected both better child health and superior food consumption.[41] It also reflected the demographic imbalance towards adults, created by the presence of a sizeable servant population, an imbalance documented by the reports of the parish priests of El Sagrario.[42] (See the high proportion of single Indian and colored women, probably domestic servants, in Table 6.2.)

---

[37] M. Minchom, "Historia demográfica de Loja," appendices.

[38] Andrien's work will clarify this problem. For the economic background prior to this period, K. J. Andrien, "Economic crisis." For the impact of comercio libre, *Relaciones de Mando*, (ed. F. Posada and P. M. Ibáñez, Bogotá, 1910), 108, cited by A. J. Kuethe, The Military Reform in the Viceroyalty of New Granada, 1773–1796, (Ph.D. University of Florida), 2. Numerous official reports commented on Quito's late-colonial predicament; see the "Informe" of Carondelet, Nov. 21, 1800, published in Documentos ..., (ed. J. Rumazo González), vol. 5, 290–307.

[39] Figures for the 1790s are in Minchom "Demographic change in eighteenth century Ecuador," *Equateur 1986*, (eds. D. Delaunay and M. Portais) (Paris, 1989), 191, Figure 2.

[40] Villalengua to the Viceroy, October 18 and November 18, 1785, AGI Quito 243.

[41] I have no evidence as to whether Quito families followed the widespread European practice of sending infants out to wet-nurses in rural areas which would also have influenced this ratio.

[42] Parish report, Aug. 23 to Sept. 4, 1785, AHBC/Q, vol. 29, Libro Verde 1, 255.

TABLE 6.2 DEATHS IN EL SAGRARIO IN THE EPIDEMIC OF 1785

	Españoles	Montañeses	Indios	Pardos y Negros
Men	11	7	7	0
Married Women	5	2	6	1
Single Women	6	7	26	5
Children	13	9	18	1

Source: Parish reports, AHBC/Q, vol. 29, Libro Verde 1: 252ff.

Note: The use of the category "montañés" reinforces the point that the Church had a major role in shaping socio-racial distinctions, given that this category did not exist in the official censuses (see Chapter 7). It also confirms that the root sense of "montañés" was "mestizo."

The change in the ratio was so extreme between the months of September and October (112 adults died out of 136 in September, the total dropping to 53 out of 84 in October), that it is appropriate to recall that El Sagrario was also the center of the city of Quito, receiving many of the bodies left in the streets or outside houses; comparing the parish report of El Sagrario with the official letters sent by the President to the Viceroy suggests that the President may have simplified his data by including as adults at least one mass burial of these abandoned corpses.[43] Whether children received the same attention as adults with regard to receiving a registered burial is a moot point, and may mean that an already high child mortality rate provides a minimum rather than a maximum estimate.

How severe were the epidemics of the 1780s and 1790s in Quito? The estimates of parish priests which were summarized by colonial officials give a clear picture of the epidemic of 1785 and can be correlated with the evidence of the parish records. The epidemic having begun in mid-August 1785, the President was already writing to the Viceroy on September 18, 1785, that a third of the inhabitants of the city (8,000 people) were sick with measles.[44] There were 1,859 burials in September and October, while the baptismal records of "Indians, Mulatos and some Mestizos" shows clearly that these were the peak months of the epidemic.[45] Allowing for

---

43 Ibid., fol. 256; "53 expuestos a las puertas de dicha Santa Yglesia." See also APQ/Sagrario, Libro de Muertos ("Indios ...") (1757–1800), fol. 94, for an example from the later epidemic of 1788; "tambien cinco cadaveres en el sementerio cuios apellidos se ignoran por ser botados, y se hase mencion de ellos aqui por curiosidad, y cuenta."

44 ANC/B, Misc. de la Colonia, Tomo 2, fol. 814; Villalengua to the Viceroy, Sept. 18, 1785.

45 Seven were buried in July, 19 in August, 48 in September, 61 in October and 11 in November. Villalengua to the Viceroy, October 18 and November 18, 1785, AGI Quito 243.

undercounting suggested by the picking up of bodies, and for some continuation of the epidemic outside the dates for which we have official totals, and it is reasonable to suggest that Quito lost around 10 percent of its population of about 25,000 in the 1785 epidemic.

CALCULATIONS OF THE POPULATION OF QUITO IN 1797

The defects of the 1797 censuses have been discussed above, and require little amplification. It is nevertheless believed that by relating them to other evidence, it is possible to establish a reasonable estimate of the population of the city at that date.

It is necessary to begin by discounting the figure of 5,890 for El Sagrario, because it is inconsistent with the baptismal rate of the parish. For the central highlands in about 1780, Bromley established baptismal rates of 41.9 baptisms per thousand for Ambato, 48.9 per thousand for Riobamba, and 69.7 per thousand for Latacunga.[46] For Santa Bárbara, the Indian baptismal records are missing in the late eighteenth century, but these had averaged 123.6 in 1732–34, falling to 51.5 in 1809–10 while there were 108 Spanish baptisms in 1768. A total of around 200 baptisms in 1768, for a total population of 2,757, would give a rate of roughly 70 baptisms per thousand; this may be too high, but provides us with an upper limit. At the other extreme, we have a minimum rate in the figure of around 39 per thousand for San Marcos.[47] The total of 665 baptisms in El Sagrario in 1797 suggests that the total of 5,890 in the Church *padrones* is implausible, even when young infants have been added to the total, and must have been based on incomplete census returns, or the special problems of census-taking in such a large parish. The range of 40–70 baptisms per thousand would theoretically give us a population range of 9,500–16,625 for El Sagrario, but 10,000–12,000 is a plausible "guesstimate," given the similarities with Santa Bárbara, the later evidence for the comparative size of the parishes, and the presence of only 5,890 names in the ecclesiastical censuses. For the other parishes, we can follow the evidence of either Santa Bárbara or San Marcos to calculate the fall-short caused by the exclusion of young children from the 1797 series.

We may take note of the age pyramids compiled from complete censuses for districts in the Province of Tunja, New Granada in 1777–8. These show the potential width of the age pyramid at its lower (i.e. younger) levels. In that area, 19.5 percent of the population was aged under 4, while 36.4 percent was aged under ten, and therefore probably already

---

[46] R. D. F. Bromley *Urban Growth and Decline*, 53–4.

[47] For 1,405 births, there were 55 births in 1797, or 54 in 1791, so for this point the dating of the document is not important.

including children of the age at which they would attend communion.[48] However, if in Quito children bore the brunt of the 1785 epidemic, this would be reflected in an age pyramid weighted towards the upper age groups. Cook has examined similar effects for early colonial Peru which was ravaged by the epidemics which followed (and preceded) the Spanish conquest. In the Peruvian community of Acarí in 1593, for example, only 14.21 percent of the population were aged under nine, and the age pyramid bears fully the marks of epidemics.[49]

The complete 1790s padrón of San Marcos lists only 206 párbulos, or young children, out of 1,405, some 14.7 percent. This figure is clearly a low one, which may have been influenced by epidemics and high child mortality. A comparable age pyramid for 1797 would add 15 percent to a total of 6,090, and including the 1,405 people of San Marcos itself this would raise the combined total from 7,495 to around 8,500 for parishes other than El Sagrario.

In the case of Santa Bárbara the census of 1768 means that we have two padrones of the parish at an interval of thirty years, and it is therefore possible to compare the two series. The record of White baptisms suggests that Santa Bárbara's White and Mestizo population underwent modest growth from the 1720s onwards. Although the baptismal records of the Indian population have not survived, it is probable from a comparison of the two padrones that the process of "whitening" which had characterized the early eighteenth century continued during the second half of the century. Some decline in the Indian population therefore probably partially offset the modest expansion of the White population. The comparable number of residential units in the two censuses (182 as against 188 in 1797) also suggests that the parish was relatively stable. It therefore seems likely that the total of 2,757 in 1768 was at least the same and perhaps slightly higher in 1797, while the church census gives a total of 1,984 at that date. Assuming that the totals of 1,541 for San Roque, 1,982 for San Sebastián and 579 for San Blas were similar under-estimates raises their combined total by a third from 4,102 to around 5,500, or just under 9,000 with San Marcos and Santa Bárbara included.

---

48 Hernando Gómez Buendía "Análisis demográfico y social de 7 poblaciones de la Provincia de Tunja en el Siglo XVIII," *Anuario Colombiano de Historia Social y de la Cultura*, (Bogotá), (1970), 26, Table 1.

49 N. D. Cook, *Demographic Collapse. Indian Peru, 1520–1620*, (Cambridge University Press, 1981), 166–170.

TABLE 6.3 THE POPULATION OF THE CITY OF QUITO, 1670–1814

Date	Census	Estimate
1670–80	—	40,000+
1740s	—	c30,000
1765	—	c30,000
c. 1780 (late 1770s)	21,960	25,000+
c. 1780 (1781)	25,325	25,000+
1797	—	20–22,500
1814	20,627	—

Sources: For population trends see Figures 6.1, 6.2 and 6.3. For around 1680, Munive's estimate of 30,000 Indians in the capital (or nearby areas?) may not be accurate, but suggests a much higher population than we find in the early eighteenth century (AGI Quito 69, Carta de Munive, July 30, 1681, fol. 332). For the 1740s, Juan and Ulloa's estimate of around 60,000 can probably be used as a guide to the relative size of the city (see above), and therefore halved in line with the evidence for other regions, and with the baptismal evidence of Figure 6.1. The lower estimate for c. 1780 is from the Villalengua enumeration carried out in the late 1770s, and preserved in AGI Quito 381, under a summary made in 1783. 1781: ANC/B Hacienda Real, varios no. 2893, "Censos del Ecuador": "Ciudad de San Francisco del Quito y su corregimiento. Padrón hecho en el año de 1781 …" 1797; ACM/Q "Visita Pastoral-Ilmo. Pérez de Calama (1790)," with the exception of El Sagrario, part of which was in one of the early boxes marked "Capellanías." 1814; ANC/B Miscelánea de la República, Tomo 123 (i): fol. 191.

To compare with the nineteenth century figures, see Y. Saint-Geours, "L'évolution démographique de l'Equateur au XIXe siècle," *Equateur 1986,* D. Delaunay and M. Portais (eds.) (Paris, 1989), 200.

In order to make the ecclesiastical census comparable to that of 1781, we should add 1,500 to include the slaves and many ecclesiastics who were excluded. Adding these to the combined totals of 10,000–12,000 for El Sagrario and 8,500–9,000 for the other parishes gives us a total for the city of 20,000–22,500 in 1797.

This is perhaps not the "real" population of the city at that date, but then no census in Ecuador has ever given the real population. The remarkably exact totals which colonial officials arrived at were often the product of quite arbitrary manipulation of the figures, and where data were inadequate, they did not resort to the practice of rounded approximations; in 1825, the compiler noted evasion, and suggested that the total for the Province of Pichincha should be raised by a third, i.e. by exactly 44,387.[50]

---

[50] ANC/B Miscelánea de la República, Tomo 123 (i): fol. 188.

136

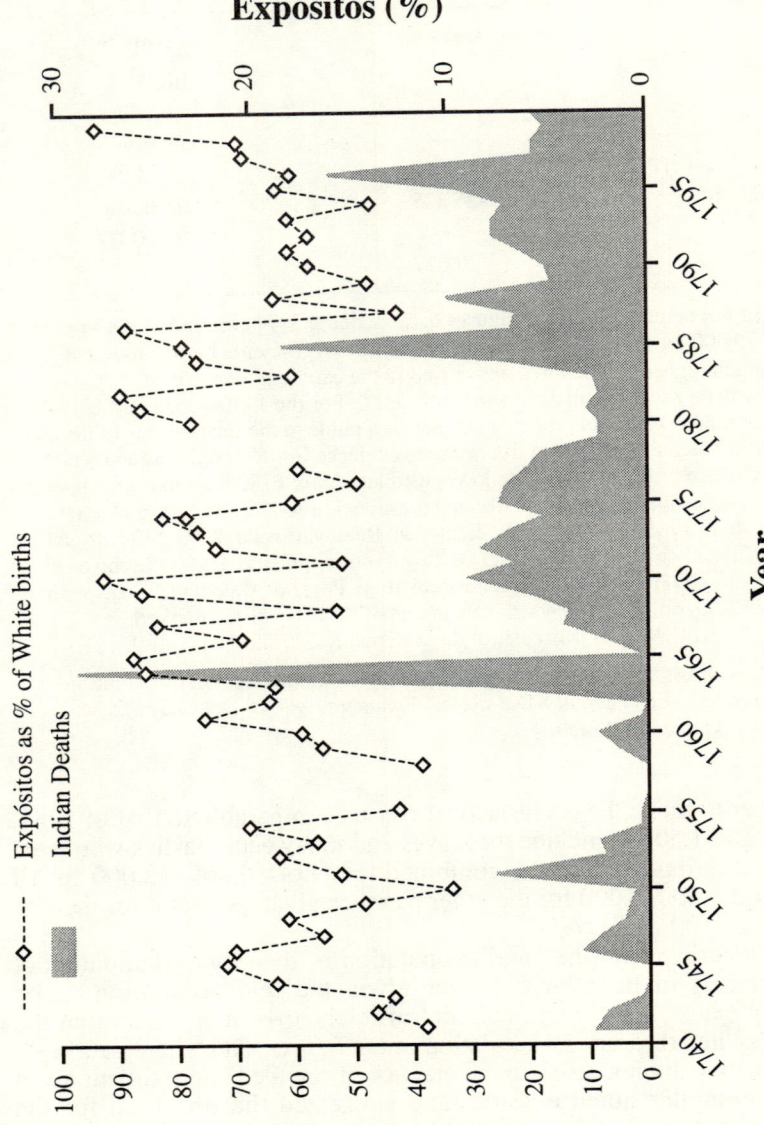

Figure 6.4 Indian Deaths and Foundlings (Expósitos) Among Spanish Baptisms in Santa Bárbara, 1741–1800

The value of the house-to-house data, when it survives, is that it demonstrates the existence of genuine census-taking activity and not a reliance on parish records and previous compilations.

Urban Decline and Urban-Rural Contrasts

Placing the calculations for 1797 alongside the official census data, and comparing the late eighteenth century data with the evidence from the parish registers allows us to compile Table 6.3.

A "rounded" figure for 1797 of just over 20,000 suggests a decline in Quito's population from the total of around 25,000 in the official series of *circa* 1780. There is evidence to confirm this fall which may in fact have been even more marked than these figures suggest in view of widespread evasion at the earlier date. The changing sex ratio supports the hypothesis of demographic decline between 1780 and 1797, as an increase in the surplus of women over men is consistent with the phenomenon of mainly male emigration from the city. The mid-1780s and 1790s were a period of high fluctuating mortality and epidemic impact (Figure 6.2). The figures for abandoned children in Santa Bárbara show that rates were very high in 1780–86 averaging 20–25 percent, and fell in the late 1780s and 1790s only to begin rising sharply 1794–1800, a rhythm of change which can be closely correlated to Indian mortalities in the parish (Figure 6.4).

The baptismal records of El Sagrario suggest slight decline at this period, although the sharp drop in White baptisms in the 1790s was due to ethnic reclassification. Those of Santa Bárbara show that a decline after the late 1770s was followed by a recovery in the late 1780s and early 1790s, but there was then a steady decline 1795–1813; this decline was paralleled by that of San Marcos (Figures 6.1, 6.3, 6.5). These parishes included a considerable elite presence; the evidence of San Blas suggests that the popular sectors were relatively more affected. In that parish, both Indian and White baptisms were in decline, but the decline in Indian baptisms was more pronounced.[51] The low totals for baptisms in 1797 suggest that the earthquake of that year may have been a marginal factor, but decline clearly precedes it. The tributary data confirms the parish records with regard to the decline of the Indian population. The rise in Indian tributaries 1779–81 is almost certainly the result of more efficient tribute collection rather than demographic change. Thereafter the number declines, notably after the 1780s, with the 1785 epidemic emerging as a watershed (Figure 6.6).

---

[51] Annual Indian baptisms were the following in San Blas: 1790–45;1791–42; 1792–40; 1793–38; 1794–54 ; 1795–42; 1796–31; 1797–20; 1798–27.

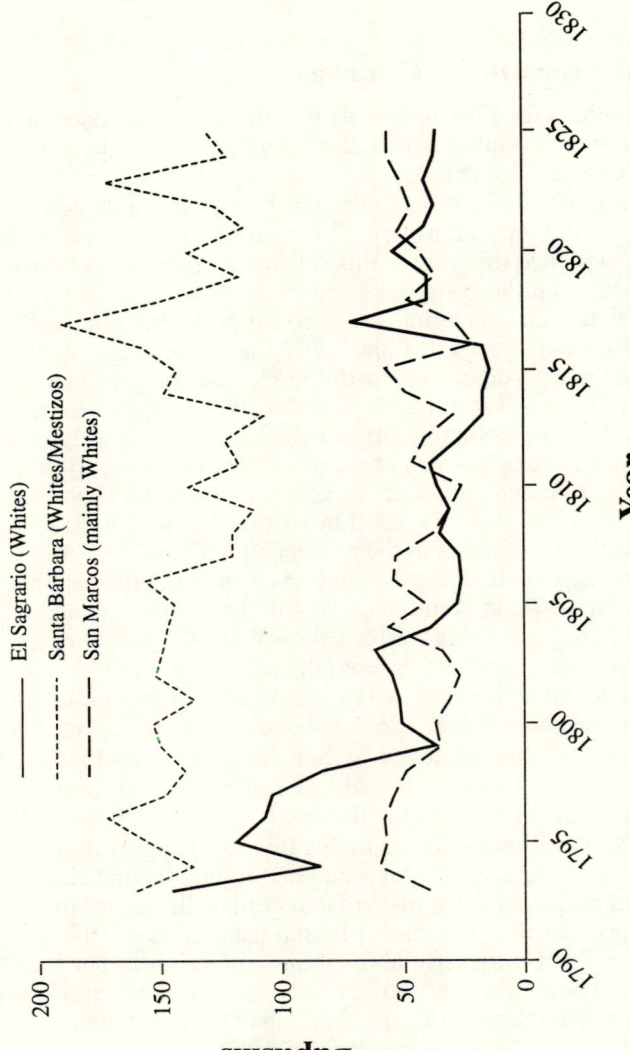

Figure 6.5 Annual Baptisms of the *"Gente Decente"* of Central Quito: El Sagrario, Santa Bárbara and San Marcos, 1793–1825

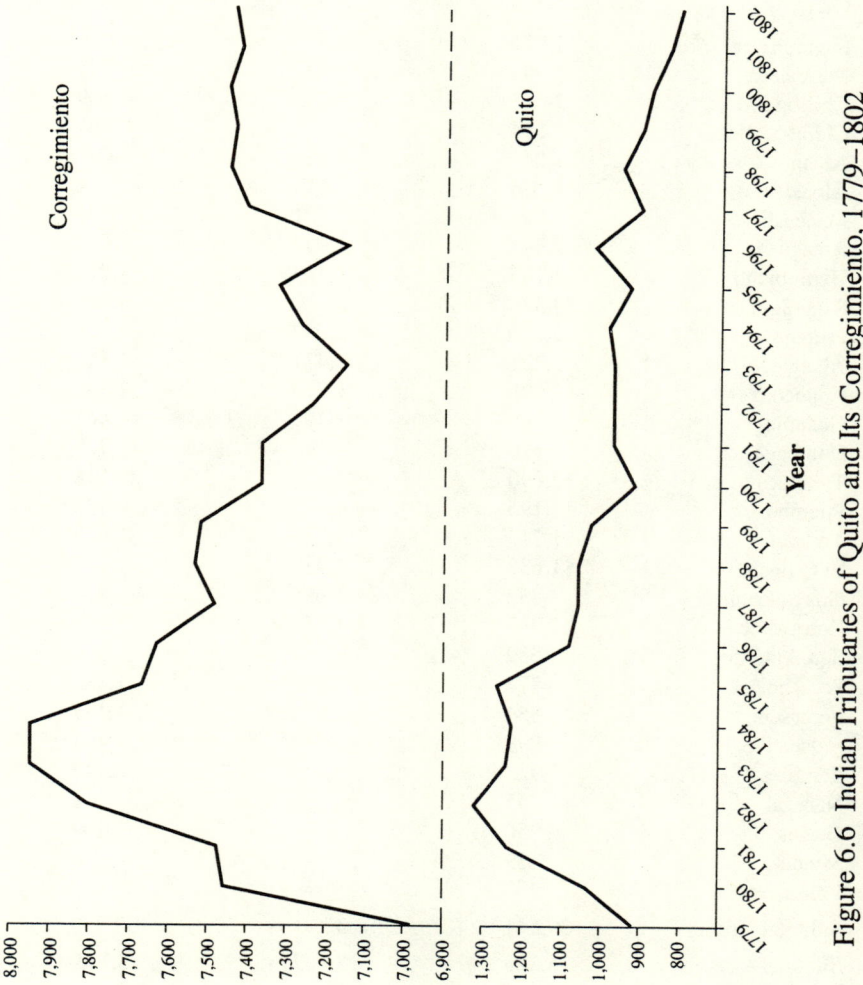

Figure 6.6 Indian Tributaries of Quito and Its Corregimiento, 1779–1802

TABLE 6.4 QUITO AND THE CORREGIMIENTO: POPULATION ESTIMATES PROVIDED BY OFFICIAL CENSUS DATA, 1781–1825

	1781	1814	1825
Quito	25,325	20,627+	13,374+
Santa Prisca	1,611	973	1,000
Magdalena	943	1,397	743
Chillogallo	2,023	2,583	2,559
Chimbacalle	614	815	935
Aloag	1,051	1,086	1,031
Aloasí	1,076	1,112	994
Machachi	2,041	2,721	2,535
Amaguaña	2,341	1,454	2,605
Uyumbicho	1,185	1,449	1,218
Sangolquí	4,536	3,178	4,076
Pintag	2,270	2,082	2,024
Alangasí	1,221	1,471	1,114
Conocoto	2,025	1,710	1,782
Guápulo	343	196	461
Cumbayá	616	—	728
Tumbaco	2,090	1,524	2,118
Puembo	1,195	1,295	934
Yaruquí	1,713	1,788	1,849
El Quinche	1,638	1,418	1,659
Guayllabamba	832	1,690	818
Cotocollao	1,907	1,750	1,625
San Antonio	559	739	796
Perucho	877	878	1,885
Pomasque	854	1,256	1,157
Calacalí	998	1,554	1,403
Zámbiza	2,923	2,353	2,547
Nanegal	255	—	111
Gualea	256	—	169
Mindo	229	—	—
Cansacoto	273	—	—
Subtotal—rural	39,641	37,216+	39,719
Subtotal—urban	25,325	20,627+	13,374+
Total	64,966	57,843	53,099

Source: ANC/B Hacienda Real, varios no. 2893, "Censos del Ecuador": "Ciudad de San Francisco del Quito y su corregimiento. Padrón hecho en el año de 1781 …"; ANC/B Miscelánea de la República, Tomo 123 (i): fol. 191; ANC/B Miscelánea de la República, Tomo 123 (i), fol. 188.

Possible explanations for Quito's population decline were suggested above. Quito can be said to have participated in the process of urban recession which characterized much of Spanish America at this period, and which has been documented for some parts of the Audiencia.[52] Comparing the evidence of the city of Quito and its corregimiento, it appears that the rural district weathered the period after the 1780s better than the capital itself. Figure 6.7 presents data reflecting the evolution of three rural parishes where it was possible to consult the parish records. To the north of the corregimiento, the Indian population of the village of Cayambe was in slow decline, while that of Tabacundo (where there were mixed entries) enjoyed stable growth, as it had since the 1740s. The apparent decline of El Quinche was in fact partly exaggerated by changes in the system of registration which mixed Indian and non-Indian entries in the twenty years after 1765. Confirmation of a slight decline between 1781 and 1814 comes from the official censuses (Table 6.4).

Table 6.4 shows clearly the demographic stability of the rural district of the capital after 1780. Given that the total of 1814 for Cumbayá is missing, the differences between the censuses are very small indeed, in a period when the totals for the capital underline a process of urban recession. In one sense, this is surprising at a time when the rural textile industry was probably unable to absorb urban migrants, and officials claimed that rural farms were actually cutting down on labor requirements.[53] In the region of Quito neither the positive pull of the countryside, nor the impact of catastrophes are entirely sufficient to explain the ruralization of the district, and it is probably better to stress the parasitic nature of the urban center, whose expansion, monetary circulation, and commercial role for the neighboring region were all dependent on the vitality of the regional economy. Mobility, as a response to economic and other pressures, emerges clearly from the documentation.[54] This was both permanent and seasonal, with the beginnings of migration to the coast, and with continual movement between the capital and its rural district.

This demographic inter-dependence is suggested by the data in Table 6.5. The fact that different censuses for almost the same date produced such distinct urban/rural ratios suggests that place of residence was being defined in different ways as a result of residential and occupational mobility between the city of Quito and the rest of the corregimiento. This point may help to explain some of the contradictions between the different totals recorded in the censuses.

---

[52] See R. D. F Bromley, *Urban Growth and Decline*.

[53] "Informe" of Carondelet, Nov. 21, 1800, published in Rumazo González, *Documentos*, vol. 5, 290–307.

[54] For the wider implications of such mobility see Robinson, *Migration in Colonial Spanish America*, passim.

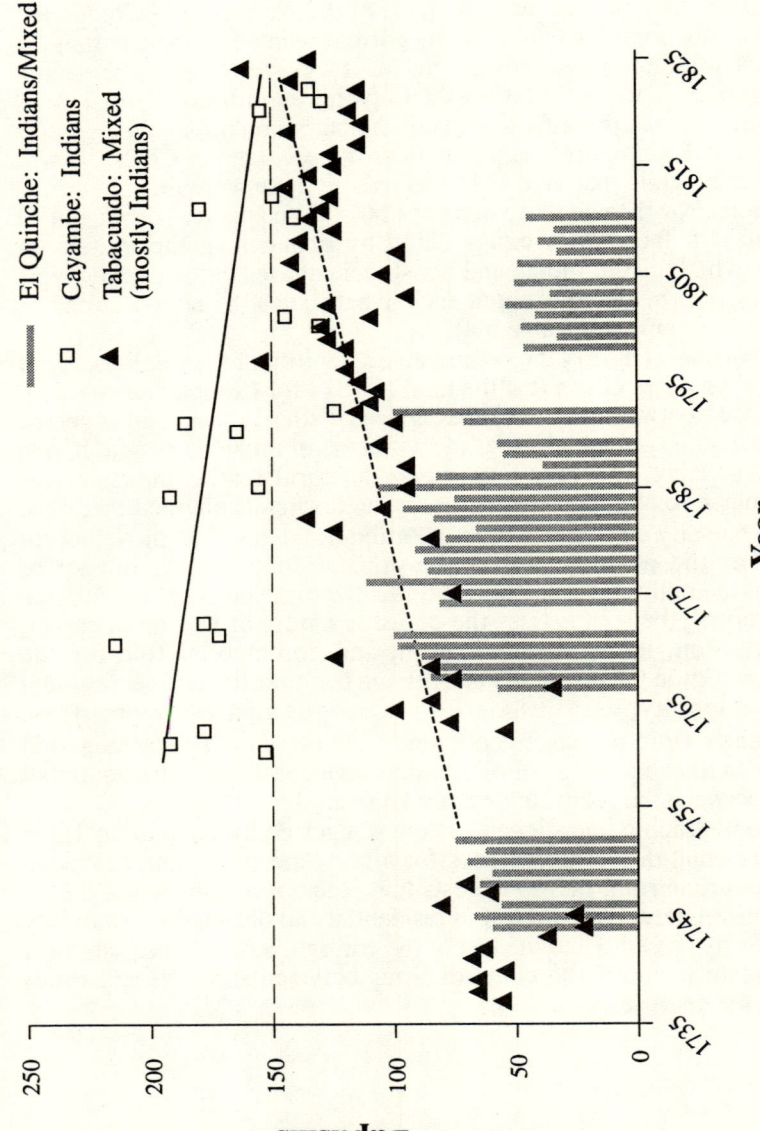

Figure 6.7 Annual Indian Baptisms in Three Rural Parishes, 1737–1825

TABLE 6.5 ETHNIC CLASSIFICATION OF THE POPULATION OF QUITO
AND ITS CORREGIMIENTO, C. 1780*

	Source A		Source B	
	% INDIAN	% NON-INDIAN	% INDIAN	% NON-INDIAN
City (Six parishes)	30	70	24	76
Corregimiento	79	21	92	8

* Percentages Rounded.

Source: Source A is the "Villalengua enumeration" carried out in the late 1770s, and preserved in AGI Quito 381, under a summary made in 1783; Source B: ANC/B Hacienda Real, varios no. 2893, "Censos del Ecuador"; "Ciudad de San Francisco del Quito y su corregimiento. Padrón hecho en el año de 1781 ...."

One of the most striking urban-rural contrasts was ethnic, the rural district being overwhelmingly Indian (Tables 6.5 and 6.6). In contrast, the low proportion of the city's inhabitants who were Indian around 1780 confirms the long term decline of the urban Indian population (Tables 6.5 and 6.6). This is also apparent from Figure 6.1. The breadth of the category of "Indians, Mestizos and Mulatos" in the baptismal records of El Sagrario imposes caution in handling the El Sagrario data. In this respect, the figures for the parishes of San Blas and Santa Bárbara are initially more revealing, showing the extent of the decline during the eighteenth century. Figure 6.6 shows that in the 1790s the urban Indian population was falling at a faster rate than that of the rural areas.

The reasons for this change in the ethnic composition of the city are suggested by the evidence cited above: selective epidemic impact, the decline of the urban economy, and ethnic transformation. With regard to the more contradictory evidence of El Sagrario, I believe it monitors two independent processes: first, the absolute decline of the urban Indian population, and second, the growing selectiveness of the category "White" which meant that the Mestizos and poor Whites were progressively excluded from the baptismal register which became increasingly reserved for the White elite. Until the 1730s, there was a clear and significant decline in the Indian population (Figure 6.1); thereafter, this process was being hidden by this registration factor. Some confirmation of this is clear from the social exclusiveness apparent in White early nineteenth century baptisms.[55]

---

[55] J. Moreno Egas, *Vecinos de la Catedral de Quito bautizados entre 1801 y 1831*, (Quito, 1984).

TABLE 6.6 ETHNIC CLASSIFICATION OF THE POPULATION OF QUITO AND ITS CORREGIMIENTO, 1781

	A	B	C	D	E	F	G
Quito	1,112	7,129	9,526	2,615	3,495	1,448	25,325
Santa Prisca	1	24	27	743	812	4	1,611
Magdalena	1	16	14	449	454	9	943
Chillogallo	2	55	66	1142	752	6	2,023
Chimbacalle	2	10	7	394	196	5	614
Aloag	2	57	45	409	530	8	1,051
Aloasí	1	41	35	562	435	2	1,076
Machachi	2	84	73	974	894	14	2,041
Amaguaña	1	44	54	1,115	1,121	6	2,341
Uyumbicho	2	49	48	531	550	5	1,185
Sangolquí	2	68	78	2,684	1,698	6	4,536
Pintag	2	62	59	1,054	1,091	2	2,270
Alangasí	2	18	21	577	595	8	1,221
Conocoto	2	40	47	1,160	771	5	2,025
Gúapulo	3	9	14	151	166	—	343
Cumbayá	2	25	24	335	230	—	616
Tumbaco	1	77	109	799	1,104	—	2,090
Puembo	1	84	62	508	535	5	1,195
Yaruquí	1	61	81	785	781	4	1,713
El Quinche	3	84	128	540	873	10	1,638
Guayllabamba	3	60	162	287	310	10	832
Cotocollao	2	56	65	890	889	5	1,907
San Antonio	2	10	34	286	225	2	559
Perucho	1	65	75	392	341	3	877
Pomasque	21	50	85	364	329	5	854
Calacalí	2	76	60	460	400	—	998
Zámbiza	1	53	36	1,391	1,436	6	2,923
Nanegal	2	12	10	113	116	2	255
Gualea	2	13	14	109	118	—	256
Mindo	2	7	8	102	107	3	229
Cansacoto	2	7	5	115	144	—	273
Total	1,185	8,446	11,072	22,036	21,486	1,583	1,583

A: Ecclesiastics, B: White men, C: White women, D: Indian men,
E: Indian women, F: "Castas" and slaves, G: Total

Source: ANC/B Hacienda Real, varios no. 2893, "Censos del Ecuador": "Ciudad de San Francisco del Quito y su corregimiento. Padrón hecho en el año de 1781 ...."

Note: Total slightly corrected for the district: census total 65,933; 296 *libres casados* and 221 *libres solteros* were calculated to be a total of 617 instead of 517. (There were also 10 too many female slaves). In Chillogallo, there were only 82 Indian single women compared with 670 married women, so this may be a mistake unless Chillogallo had a particular role in supplying female servants to the capital.

Gender and the Male : Female Ratio in Relation to Family Structure

The male–female ratio is only one aspect of many in family history but it is given importance here for the information it provides on the position of women in Quito society, and on demographic change in the late-colonial period, as well as for the clues it provides for family structure. Two factors, male emigration and higher male mortality in wars and civil disorders, were offered by Bromley as possible explanations for the changes in the urban sex ratio in the central sierra, 1780–1825.[56] Although the focus here is on the period 1780–1810, some data will be give for 1825 to establish comparability with her work.

It is worth mentioning some of the factors which may have distorted the figures. The phenomenon of tribute evasion probably exaggerated the male:female imbalance in the late 1770s and 1780s, and the avoidance of conscription certainly did so in 1814 and 1825. The church was a mainly, although not of course exclusively, masculine vocation, so this also influenced the figures. The official censuses show a number of defects with regard to the urban sex ratio in the capital, but their evidence may be examined even if we subsequently choose to ignore it. Table 6.7 presents the evidence of the official censuses, and the church census of 1797:

TABLE 6.7 SEX RATIO IN QUITO, 1781–1825 (MEN PER 100 WOMEN)

Year	Urban	Barrios	Rural (corregimiento)
1781	75.8	—	106.6
1797	53.3	55.8	—
1825	(97.5)	63.4	102.7

Source: ANC/B, Hacienda Real, varios no. 2893, "Censos del Ecuador"; "Ciudad de San Francisco del Quito y su corregimiento. Padrón hecho en el año de 1781 ..."; Church padrones of 1797, ACM/Q, "Visita Pastoral, Ilmo. Pérez de Calama (1790)"; ANC/B Miscelánea de la República, Tomo 123 (i), fol. 191.

Note: This total excludes the clergy. "Urban" means the six parishes of the city, i.e. excluding Santa Prisca. The "barrios" means all parishes excluding the central one of El Sagrario. The 1797 total includes the census for San Marcos.

How far does Table 6.7 reflect the real sex composition of the city? It is probably best to take the most reliable data as a fixed point before attempting to interpret more questionable data. Comparison of the 1781 census with the Villalengua enumeration suggests that it provides an essentially accurate picture of the rural corregimiento of the city. Although

---

[56] R. D. F. Bromley, "Urban-rural demographic contrasts," 288.

its data for the city are somewhat less reliable, the broad pattern of a masculine dominated countryside, and a female dominated city is extremely clear. Latacunga, Ambato and Riobamba also had a higher proportion of women in the urban centers than in the countryside around 1780, but the pattern there was by no means as marked as in Quito.[57] Unlike those urban centers, Quito's immediate rural hinterland had a surplus of men, which suggests that at that date the rural district of Quito was not losing as many men through out-migration as the central Sierra, and that as a larger urban center, Quito was absorbing a higher proportion of the female population of its rural hinterland for domestic service. The broad pattern of male countryside and female city is nicely illustrated at an individual level by the example, cited by Cushner, of the laborer Pascual who worked on the Jesuit estate of the Chillos in the early eighteenth century, while his wife lived in the city.[58] The scale of the imbalance around 1780 also documents the process of male Indian tribute evasion in the capital, the cultural dimension of which will be examined in the next chapter.

The padrones of the 1790s, however, suggest that domestic service and male tribute evasion were factors which cover more profound explanations for imbalance in the urban sex ratio. Table 6.7 records an increasing surplus of women over men in the 1797 series, compared with 1781. Can this be accounted for in terms of the incomplete character of the series? The fact that women attended communion more frequently than men may suggest that there was an inbuilt bias towards women in ecclesiastical head-counts, in the same sense that tribute lists sometimes maximized male figures by omitting elderly widows etc.[59] On the other hand, men had less to fear from a church census than a civil one. The census of 1797 did not include young children, but at its lower levels a population pyramid tends to be relatively balanced between the sexes, and major imbalance only comes later, with differential mortality rates, migration patterns etc.[60] The contrast between 1781 and 1797 appears considerable, but taken together the two censuses show conclusively that there was a major surplus of women over men in late-eighteenth century Quito. San Marcos presents few features in its social composition which suggest it was likely to be much out of line with the city as a whole; the ratio of 67 men to 100 women in 1791 may therefore be cautiously taken as a link between the higher ratio in 1781 and the lower one of six years later, suggesting also that much of the change was in the 1790s.

There was high fluctuating mortality in the 1780s and the 1790s and calculations for 1780–1797 suggest some demographic decline between

---

[57] Ibid., 288–9.

[58] N. P. Cushner, Farm and Factory: *The Jesuits and the Development of Agrarian Capitalism in Colonial Quito*, (New York, 1982), 128.

[59] M. Minchom, "Historia demográfica de Loja."

[60] See I. Langenberg, *Urbanisation und Bevölkerungsstructur der Stadt Guatemala in der Ausgehenden Kolonialzeit*, (Köln- Wien,1981), 117, 124.

those two dates. A falling male:female ratio is consistent with the hypothesis of absolute demographic decline. What is extremely striking in the 1797 censuses is that the sex ratio was uniform across the parishes, despite their range of social composition. Only San Sebastián came close to the ratio of San Marcos of six years earlier (at 66.9), but that may reflect its semi-rural characteristics. In the other parishes the rate was virtually uniform: 50.5 in El Sagrario, 46.1 in Santa Bárbara, 48.1 in San Roque, 53.2 in San Blas. The ratio in Sagrario and Santa Bárbara is easily explicable in terms of the domestic servant population, but these figures show clearly that domestic service is only a very partial explanation. The lower class parish of San Roque was characterized by small households in the 1797 series, and must have had a low servant population, and yet it had a comparable male:female ratio to the other parishes.

In the latter part of the eighteenth century, Guayaquil began to receive both long-term and seasonal migration from the Highlands[61], and the Quito evidence suggests that the city's female surplus was beginning to be emphasized by male migration to the coast during the 1780s and 1790s. If, as the demographic evidence suggests, the effects of economic depression may have been felt in the corregimiento of Quito at the end of the eighteenth century, migration could have been the parallel process of males to the coast, and some females from the rural district to the capital. The changing sex ratio in Table 6.7 is compatible with this hypothesis; some female immigration would also have softened the impact of male migration on the total of the urban population, although that impact remained considerable.

For the period after the 1780s, and sifting the solid evidence from the unreliable, it is clear that the proportion of men in the city of Quito was falling, while its rural district retained a higher ratio of men to women. What is equally clear is that this process antedates the effects of the wars of Independence and is primarily due to other factors. The relative demographic stability of the rural district certainly suggests that the effects of war were felt more in the cities than in the countryside, but the war was more the agent of disruption and temporary evasion than the cause of high numbers of male deaths; it may have reinforced but it did not initiate more deep-rooted patterns of migration. The proportion of married women to married men dropped between 1781 and 1825, which suggests the presence of some war widows, but this change was slight; in 1825, there was still a ratio of 95.5 married men to 100 married women in the city and natural longevity may explain part of the difference.

Although changes in the sex ratio can be documented, the demographic preponderance of women seems to have formed a permanent feature of eighteenth and early nineteenth-century Quito. It was, at any rate, sufficiently marked to be noted by observers prior and subsequent to the periods for which census data was examined. The Spanish observers Jorge

---

[61] M. Hamerly, *Historia social y económica*, chapter 2.

Juan and Antonio de Ulloa had already noted this imbalance in the 1740s:

> "It may be noted that in that country (describing the city of Quito) the feminine sex is more abundant than the masculine; and this stands out all the more because there is not the movement or absence of men which is common in those of Europe. It is customary to see families full of women and rarely men; in the same way, it is in the nature of men raised at ease that they are normally unhealthy from 30 onwards, while the women maintain more health and vigor. Perhaps the climate contributes, and food may also be a factor, but I attribute the principal reason to the excess of abandoning themselves from a very early age to sensuality; so that their stomachs declining in vigor, they do not have strength for their digestion, and many of them bring up their food half an hour or an hour after eating it ...."[62]

Nineteenth century observers of Quito made similar observations.[63] Although influenced by a number of different factors—domestic service, differential mortality, church influence, some migration—Quito's demographic structure struck contemporary observers as essentially homogeneous; the sex ratio was naturally tilted towards women by a law of nature.

At the lower levels of society, it would be unwise to follow Juan and Ulloa too rapidly in denying the role of migration even as early as the 1740s. The symbiotic relationship of city and country mean that short-term and seasonal movement certainly took place on a scale which the static nature of the censuses, as a series of still-photos, cannot catch. The inverse correlation of changes in urban and rural sex ratios in the censuses of Quito and its corregimiento underlines the demographic interdependence of city and countryside, the city continually absorbing and "rejecting" its rural population. On the Quito evidence we should add gender to the familiar demographic contrast between the White Spanish colonial city and the Indian countryside.

---

62 "Se nota en aquel País, que abunda mas en él el Sexo Feminino, que el Masculino; y es esto mas reparable por no haver alli el extravío, ó ausencia de Hombres, que es regular en los de Europa. Suelen verse las Familias cargadas de Mugeres, y ser raros los Varones: assimismo la Naturaleza de los Hombres por lo regular entre la Gente criada con regalo es endeble desde los 30 años en adelante: al contrario las Mugeres mantienen mas salud, y robustéz; puede contribuìr el Clima, y pueden coadyubar los Alimentos: pero yo atribuyo la causa principal al excesso de entregarse desde una edad muy corta à la Sensualidad; de que proviene, que descaeciendo el vigor de los Estomagos, no tengan fortaleza para hacer la digestion, y muchos vuelvan la comida à media hora, ò una, despues de haverla tomada diariamente ..." Juan and Ulloa, *Relación Historica*, 372.

63 See, for example, H. E. Bates, *Central America, The West Indies and South America*, (London, 1882): 336, an observation possibly taken from the traveller Orton. Many nineteenth century observers continued to plagiarise Juan and Ulloa, but surely in this respect they followed the evidence of their eyes.

Female-headed households appear to have been far more important in eighteenth and nineteenth century Latin America—where they varied between 25 and 45 percent of the total—than they were in Europe or North America.[64] In the case of Quito, 41.3 percent of households appear to have been headed by women in the parish of Santa Bárbara in 1768. Indeed this proportion was to rise to 58.2 percent in the parish by the time of the 1831 census.[65] This suggests that households headed by women were relatively more important in Quito than in many parts of Spanish America, while their increasing predominance is consistent with the changing male:female ratio. The social composition of Santa Bárbara suggests that some at least of the female heads of households corresponded to the pattern of Mexico city at the beginning of the nineteenth century where widowed White women over forty predominated.[66]

In societies where migration meant that men were often absent, whether permanently or seasonally, the demographic preponderance of women and their role in domestic industry must have been translated into a distinctive socio-economic position of which the documentation can only provide hints. The documentation assembled by S. Moreno Yánez includes frequent references to the role of women in riots and it is certainly worth reconsidering that participation in the light of the economic and demographic evidence cited here.[67] Female resistance to fiscal reform must have owed much to the centrality of women in the household economy, and also to their small-scale market activity.

Tyrer summarized the partial Indian censuses of 1733, noting that many Indian men delayed marriage until they were in the 25–29 age group, and had children in their thirties; "Thus, in the most active years of an Indian male's life, he was very often childless."[68] In strict logic, Tyrer's own objection to this argument—that we do not know the age at which Indian women married—is not merely a minor reservation, but sufficient to invalidate the argument. In the turn-of-the-century rural Ireland depicted by the playwright Synge men stayed unmarried until their late thirties or early forties, and then married women half their own age; the only impediments to demographic growth in these circumstances would be economic rather than biological. Unfortunately, the marriage registers consulted (El

---

[64] E. Kuznesof, "Household, Family and Community Studies 1976–1986: a Bibliographic Essay," *Latin American Population History Newsletter*, (Fall 1988), 9–10.

[65] "Padrón de Santa Bárbara en 1768," *Museo Histórico* (Quito), 56, (1978), 93–122; AM/Q "Padrón de población ... de Quito y Latacunga y Ambato" (1830–1), vol. 64.

[66] S. Arrom, *The Women of Mexico City*, Stanford, 1985.

[67] Segundo Moreno Yánez, *Sublevaciones indígenas en la Audiencia de Quito, desde comienzos del siglo XVIII hasta finales de la Colonia*, (Bonn, 1976; 2nd. edn. Quito, 1978).

[68] Tyrer, *The Demographic and Economic History*, 59.

Sagrario) did not give age at marriage. Few censuses specify age and sex before the mid-nineteenth century, but one of the exceptions, that for the town of Riobamba in 1836, suggested that urban white women married at 22.8 on average and their rural white women at 26.8, while urban Indian women married at 19 and their rural counterparts at 23.3. Nevertheless, it was also found that fewer women married in the city than in the countryside.[69]

Since the urban parishes had a high proportion of unmarried women it is reasonable to hypothesize a low rate of marriage for the city. According to the 1781 census—later compilations show wild fluctuations—fractionally 2,007 out of 3,495 Indian women were single and over 6,000 out of 9,523 White women. The high proportion of unmarried domestic servants in El Sagrario was suggested by the high number of deaths in the 1785 epidemic (see Table 6.1). High illegitimacy rates may have been influenced by this imbalance. In Santa Bárbara in 1760, the baptismal register of "Españoles" revealed that only 51 percent were legitimate, although only 28.5 percent were illegitimate, the difference comprising abandoned children, *hijos expósitos*, a category discussed in Chapter 7.

The factors noted above may have played a role in restricting family size to judge from the census of the same parish in 1768. 78.9 percent of both Indian and non-elite households had four members or less, while as many as 32.9 percent of Indian households appear to have had only two members. These were relatively small by the standards of colonial Spanish America, although still within the accepted range, where households commonly had between four and six free members.[70] As elsewhere, elite households (those with members titled "Don") had larger numbers (Table 6.8).[71] In the corregimiento as a whole, the census aggregation of 1781 suggests that White matrimonial units had 4.7 members, compared with figures of 3.6 for Indians, 3.4 for libres and 4.7 for slaves.[72]

---

[69] R.D.F. Bromley, "Urban-rural demographic contrasts," 289.

[70] E. Kuznesof, "Household, Family," 9.

[71] See for example R. D. Anderson "Race and Social Stratification: A Comparison of Working-Class Spaniards, Indians, and Castas in Guadalajara, Mexico in 1821," *HAHR*, 68 (1988), 223–4.

[72] Calculated by dividing the total of the non-ecclesiastical population by the total of "matrimonios."

TABLE 6.8 NUMBER OF PERSONS PER HOUSEHOLD,
SANTA BÁRBARA, 1768

	1–2	2–4	5–8	>8	Total	Percent
Elite	18	13	16	17	64	20.9
White/Mestizo	60	67	26	8	161	52.6
Indians	25	35	13	3	76	24.8
Mulatos	—	3	1	1	5	1.6
Total	103	118	56	29	306	
Percent	33.7	38.6	18.3	9.5		

Note: "Elite" is here defined by titles such as "Don" etc. Many households were grouped together in the same residential unit.

* For large Indian households, c.f. a *pregonero,* (6, p. 101, house 32), a *tejedor,* (14, p. 103, house 42), a *cantor* (7, p. 104, house 51), a *frutero,* (7, p. 104, house 52), a *barbero* (9, p. 112, house 109), a *maestro barbero,* (9, p. 117, house 141)

Source: "Padrón de Santa Bárbara en 1768," *Museo Histórico* (Quito), 56, (1978): 93–122.

THE URBAN CENTER AND THE BARRIOS

Periods of urban decline appear to have been above all those of the lower class barrios. San Blas was undergoing a major decline at the end of the eighteenth century, and one which San Roque had already undergone at an earlier date. In periods of crisis, El Sagrario, or Santa Bárbara as it became a more élite parish, followed the same trends as the other parishes only in a less extreme form. Their growth was not absolute but relative.

The data in Table 6.9 help in the definition of the social composition of four parishes for which the 1797 church padrones provides useful information. It is not directly comparable with Table 6.8 because the padrón of Santa Bárbara of 1768 allows us to identify households within residential units, which is not always possible for 1797; in 1797 residential units are described as "Casa de X," and may include several households. For the purposes of Table 6.9, an "elite" household was one with the presence—usually as owner but sometimes as resident—of someone with the title "Don," "Captain" etc. Some of these households also included Indians (as servants etc.) but have not been classified as Indian. In the case of San Roque, the lower-class character of the parish makes it difficult to assign ethnic status to households: almost certainly some of those not specifically indicated as such were in fact Indian (for example, those with Indian surnames).

TABLE 6.9 THE SOCIAL COMPOSITION OF FOUR QUITO PARISHES, 1797

| | \multicolumn{6}{c}{Occupancy of Residential Units} | |
| | ELITE | | WHITE/MESTIZO | | INDIAN | | AVG. PER UNIT (NON-INFANTS) |
	NO.	%	NO.	%	NO.	%	
San Marcos	70	77.8	18	20.0	2	2.2	15.6
Santa Bárbara	133	70.4	42	22.2	14	7.4	10.5
San Sebastián	17	9.3	154	84.6	11	6.0	(11.5)
San Roque	23	11.4	151	74.8	28	13.9	8.6

Note: In San Sebastián eight *haciendas* have been included as elite households, and this has slightly icreased household size. The proportion per household for San Marcos has been raised by the fact that it is a complete padrón (i.e. includes párbulos, or young children) unlike the other parishes.

Source: Church census of 1797, ACM/Q "Visita Pastoral- Ilmo Pérez de Calama (1790)."

El Sagrario was not included in Table 6.9 because of the incomplete character of the data, but the presence of much of Quito's elite there is clear from its parish records. For San Blas, there is an independent census of a later date[73] which confirms its lower class character. What emerges clearly from Table 6.9 is the lower-class character of the parishes of San Roque and San Sebastián in comparison with San Marcos and Santa Bárbara. The data of the 1797 censuses are defective and not helpful for the absolute size of residential units. In particular, I have not attempted to correct the data with regard to a small number of elite residential units which artificially increased the unit size in San Sebastián. The median size of residential units in San Roque was certainly smaller than the urban average. Nevertheless, for comparative purposes I believe Table 6.9 provides a representative picture of the social composition of these parishes.

Table 6.9 shows that the houses in the popular parishes (but especially San Roque) did not include the great houses which Caldas likened to villages, with a multiplicity of families in them (see Chapter 2). There, residence was in small lower class households, and socially mixed residential units with an élite presence were virtually absent. Whereas in Santa Bárbara and San Marcos, these were virtually the norm at 70.4 and 77.8 percent respectively, in San Roque and San Sebastián, they were virtually absent at 11.4 and 9.3 percent. This has important implications for the social geography of the city. It suggests a much lesser degree of elite-plebeian interaction in these parishes, and in Chapter 8, I will argue that this was translated into a reduced degree of social control at times of popular unrest.

---

[73] ANH/Q "Empadronamientos" 26, Doc :1826, San Blas.

Chapter 7

SOCIO-RACIAL STATUS AND MOBILITY: THE DECLARATIONS OF MESTIZO

Sources and Possibilities of the Declarations of Mestizo

It is widely recognized today that the boundary between Indians and Whites in Andean society is, after extensive race mixture and cultural cross-influences, largely socio-cultural rather than racial.[1] The colonial law-suits whereby those considered to be Indian by the tribute-collecting authorities attempted to establish themselves as mixed-blood, show the extent to which socio-racial boundaries had already become fluid and confused before, and probably well before the 1770s. These law-suits, entitled "Declarations of Mestizo," (*Autos sobre declaratoria de mestizo*) illuminate the social attitudes of the popular sectors going before justice to define themselves socially and racially, as well as providing a multiple perspective (witnesses, Crown officials) which allows us to see how other groups respond to those pretensions. In comprehensiveness and detail they provide virtually a prosopographical picture of a section of the lower strata, clarifying some of the mechanisms of social mobility within what tends to appear in macro-analyses an immobile, hierarchical system. The series of documents also adds an unusual perspective on the social and economic consequences of the Bourbon program of administrative reorganization, offering a micro-level view of the consequences of fiscal reform on the individual lives of some of Charles III's most humble and remote subjects.

Examples of this type of document were located for Ecuador, Colombia, and Peru, and almost certainly the problem of sorting their way

---

[1] For what defines ethnicity in the present-day Andes, there is a voluminous literature. Language and dress form essential elements, although language was by no means a solid guide in colonial Quito. There is general agreement that "la raza de un hombre no coincide con su raza," J. Ossio, "Relaciones interétnicas y verticalidad en los Andes," *Debates en Antropología,* 2 (Quito, 1978), 7, here citing Fuenzalida.

through an ethnic maze was posed to administrators, caciques and tax-farmers in other parts of colonial Spanish America. No systematic attention, however, appears to have been given to this type of document.[2] The quantity and quality of the material on the northern and central highlands in the late-colonial period stands out in comparison with the data located for other areas, and as they form a single body of documentation, they will be examined as such. Nevertheless, both the content and geographical spread of the cases gives them a particular interest for the study of the urban popular society of the city of Quito, demonstrating the "hidden" migration of Indians to the capital, and the role of the city as an agent of acculturation. Many socio-racial attitudes were common to urban and rural society, and cannot be arbitrarily separated; where they differ, those differences require attention. The cases selected for detailed attention are from urban Quito itself.

The superior quality of these documents reflects, in part, the legalistic scrupulousness of the Spanish colonial authorities who were prepared to go over individual cases with considerable care, first calling three witnesses and then often another set on appeal. Although cumbersome and liable to delays, the Spanish colonial system was enormously thorough, and a comparison with a similar series of documents on nineteenth-century Peru reveals the extent to which more summary administrative procedures would deprive the historical record of much of its richness; in the colonial Declarations much more evidence emerges about the social and cultural background of those involved.[3] With regard to the quantity of cases preserved in the Ecuadorian archives, the flurry of law-suits corresponded to a particular conjuncture of the late 1770s and 1780s in the Audiencia of Quito. Since the response to the same fiscal pressures in most of Peru, as well as parts of the Audiencia of Quito, was full-scale rebellion rather than litigation, the greater number of cases found for the Audiencia of Quito is probably not accidental.

Although a number of other examples were located in other sections and different archives, the bulk of the Declarations are in the section "Mestizos" of the Archivo Nacional de Historia, Quito, which consists of seven boxes containing 266 cases in 252 folders.[4] In the Audiencia of Quito, the earliest cases date from the 1680s and the latest from 1815; the earliest cases come from the whole of the Audiencia including Popayán, the

---

[2] J. Estrada Ycaza has called attention to this type of document; see "Petición de Juan Tomás Alvarez para que no se le cobre tributo por no ser indio" (Guayaquil, 19–III–1789), *Revista del Archivo Histórico del Guayas,* no 13, (1978), 113, a document of the same archive (EP/J) 158. The ongoing published indices to this archive in the same review list a handful of cases.

[3] See, for example, AGN/L Legajo 3, Cuaderno 63, Año 1842, Tributos, Informes, Cajamarca, "Expedientes de algunos indígenas que han seguido para pasar a Castas del Distrito de Cajabamba," (1841–42), fol. 105.

[4] ANH/Q Mestizos (Mz). Throughout this chapter, references to documents from this section will be given as a case number in parenthesis.

coast and the extreme south, while after the 1770s the cases are nearly all from the northern and central highlands. Only 34 petitions are preserved from the period prior to 1776; there are 210 cases between 1776 and 1787, and the cases become more irregular after that date.[5] Thus the spread of the cases gradually narrows, both temporally and spatially, towards Quito and its region. The explanation for the decline of cases from outlying regions may only partly lie in the creation of the *gobernaciones* of Cuenca and Guayaquil.[6] A decree of 1776 specified that decisions on tribute exemption because of Indians being injured would be heard by corregidores *in situ* when they were in isolated areas; it can be assumed that the different forms of tribute exemption were considered equivalent for official purposes, as a number of exemptions on other grounds were included in the main series of Declarations of Mestizos.[7]

The concentration of the cases into a little over a decade after 1776, corresponded to a period when the reinvigorated Spanish Crown assumed a more direct control over tribute collection, and began in colonial Quito, as in the rest of Spanish America, the census-taking which reinforced its drive to establish—or, from an official view-point, reestablish—its fiscal rights. During the 1770s the definition of the tribute-paying Indian became a matter of official concern, throwing into high relief the long period of official neglect which had preceded it.

The position prior to 1776 was one of official laxity, widespread tribute evasion, confusion between the socio-racial categories of Indian and Mestizo and variations in local customary practice. Within the capital, acculturated Indian residents had acquired the clothing and sometimes the skills which enabled them to "lose" themselves in the city, although no legal exemption from tribute existed for urban Indians.[8] Official reports

---

[5] In the case extracted below, the dates (1–IX–1686, etc) are references to the folder in the section of Mestizos of the ANH/Q in which the document is held. There is a complete listing of this section is in M. Minchom, *Urban Popular Society in colonial Quito, c. 1700–1800*, doctoral dissertation, University of Liverpool, 1984, 253–276, and I have followed its classification; the numbers of the cases represent the order in which they appear in the series. Cases 1–35 were in Box 1; 36–84 in Box 2; 85–121 in Box 3; 122–158 in Box 4; 159–185 in Box 5; 196–235 in Box 6; 236–266 in Box 7.

[6] A. Pareja Diezcanseco, *Las Instituciones y la Administración de la Real Audiencia de Quito* (Quito: Ministerio del Tesoro, 1975) for the different jurisdictions, especially 224-227.

[7] AGI Quito 248 "Relación que forma el Sr. don Juan Josef Villalengua y Marfil, Presidente," "Yndice de los Autos Acordados" (1783), decree of April 26, 1776 referring to Indians of Loxa, Cuenca, Riobamba, Quijos and Macas.

[8] There were various reports of these *cholos*. See AGI Quito 138, Carta de Don Nicolas Ponce de Leon, n.d. but received 1736, fol. 63. Indians of Lima, for example, were in quasi-possession of the right not to pay tribute in the late eighteenth century, see BNP/L Año 1797, c931, "Juan de Dios Chubirayco, yndio originario del pueblo del cercado, sobre que se ampare en la posesion de no pagar los

emphasized that this form of evasion was on a wide scale, and over six hundred of these Indians were picked up in the early 1760s.[9] This numeration of the cholos, as they were pejoratively called, generated the tensions which are examined in Chapter 8. The same groups, and in at least one documented case the same person, were one of the most obvious targets of the renewed census-taking of the late 1770s. It is difficult to quantify these cholos, because they are precisely the Indians who escaped the enumerators, but there are various indices which suggest their presence, notably an exaggerated female/male ratio, which may have been due, amongst other factors, to male census evasion.

In rural areas, the problems of tribute evasion were of a different order, involving Indians hidden by landowners on their haciendas or in remote villages.[10] Customary practice on the eve of reform varied considerably from one area to another. The Audiencia reported that "in some *pueblos* it is the custom that sons of an Indian woman and White man pay the Royal tribute, while others of the same condition do not pay."[11] This confused situation on the eve of reform can only have been encouraged by irregular practice in tribute collection, which varied in the intensity of its application from one region to another. Crown revenues from tribute were diverted into the hands of tax-farmers and local officials, and the inadequate, or sometimes deliberately misleading, summaries of tributary data provided an inadequate base for the Crown's systematic exploitation of its tribute revenues.[12]

The official inspection in the late 1770s involved the overhaul of the fiscal administration, and the establishment of the imperial census in the territory of Quito in order to establish tribute collection on a firmer footing. In the Audiencia of Quito, the reorganized administration did not attempt to impose the separate census category of Mestizo, as it did in Peru and Colombia, nor did it, in principle, attempt to bring new groups into the tribute-paying population. The attempt to "follow custom" can be seen in the series of Mestizo law-suits, where a certain number of illegitimate sons of Indian women were given interim judgments in their favor, if they were

---

reales tributos," Lima, Feb. 16, 1797, fol. 9. This exemption was, however, a quid pro quo for labor services rendered by the urban Indians, (fol. 7).

[9] AGI Estado (1792–1817), No. 137, fols. 12–15, and case 61, below.

[10] For a discussion of the functioning of the tribute system, see Tyrer's introductory essay on demography in his "*The Demographic and Economic History*," 2–78, which is based on tributary data. See also the discussion in Chapter 8 of tensions between local interests and the Crown in the early eighteenth century.

[11] ANC/B Colonia Tributos XVI, "La Real Audiencia de Quito sobre que se declare si los Mestisos de aquella Provincia deben pagar tributo," fol. 567, (1777).

[12] For a different region see Minchom "Historia demográfica de Loja," 149–169. In this case, comparing the official estimates with the original *padrón* suggested that the *corregidor* may have been deliberately under-estimating tributary population to maximize profit.

commonly considered Mestizos. This category normally had to pay tribute, and after 1787, the more restrictive classification was generally adopted.[13] The aims of the Bourbon reform policy in colonial Quito were therefore relatively modest, and can therefore best be categorized as an attempt to impose order on a confused social reality for strictly fiscal purposes, rather than a full-scale recreation of caste society.

Despite this measure of flexibility, defining custom was not necessarily an easy matter, and the mere act of counting heads and extracting nominally owed tribute threatened certain groups. The urban cholos were simply Indians from the point of view of official policy, while the *forasteros,* or Indian migrants, enjoyed a privileged tax status, and therefore felt vulnerable to strict census control which could lead to their relegation to the category of *llactayos.*[14] In certain rural areas, customary practice had gradually blurred the cultural distinction between Indians and poor Mestizos, and these Mestizos ("dressed as Indians") were clearly vulnerable to a reinvigorated tribute system. Other groups can be identified which were incorporated by efficiency rather than design into the tributary population such as the foundlings, or hijos expósitos, the determination of whose ethnic status had not come up before the tribunals prior to the late 1770s.

The most important instrument of effective tribute collection was adequate demographic evidence, and the censuses were rightly seen by the popular sectors as a highly dangerous device to impose additional fiscal burdens. The connection between the Mestizo law-suits and census activity is explicit in the documentation: the petitioners sometimes state that they have been picked up and identified as Indian during the census, while the series includes a number of somewhat summary hearings which the Visitor and Enumerator Juan Josef Villalengua y Márfil heard while he was actually carrying out the census in the area of Ambato in mid-1777.[15] The two major phases of census activity in the early/mid-1760s and late 1770s, both met with violent if localized resistance. Guano, where the attempt to carry out the census in 1778 met with armed rebellion, produced no litigation: the Mestizos and Indians there argued their case with stones.[16] The Mestizo petitioners, on the other hand, came from areas where the census had been successfully carried out. Those who went to the time and expense of bringing their complaint before justice constitute a self-selected group; they were not normally vagrants or the lumpen poor, and thought they could

---

[13] See cases 208 and 214.

[14] For a discussion of these categories see M. Minchom, "The making of a white province: demographic movement and ethnic transformation in the south of the Audiencia de Quito, 1670–1830," *Bulletin de l'Institut Français d'Etudes Andines,* (Paris-Lima), XII (3–4), 1983, 23–39.

[15] Cases 36–52.

[16] For an account of this uprising see S. Moreno Yánez, *Sublevaciones Indígenas,* 196 and *passim* for other uprisings.

probably win their cases, as indeed they often did. The Declarations of Mestizo and rebellions therefore provide mutually complementary evidence, allowing us to see how the Bourbon system rode out the difficulties in its administration of the reform program, and showing the impact on different groups and areas. For the city of Quito, the rebellion of 1765 was followed by relative tranquillity during the second wave of rebellion in the late 1770s; along with the stifling of unrest in 1780 examined in Chapter 8, the Declarations of Mestizo complete the evidence for the city around that date.

Declarations of Mestizo Sought in Quito and the Audiencia of Quito, 1686–1800.

1) Blas de Horta (1–IX–1686), of Licto (Riobamba), legitimate (or illegitimate?) son of Captain Antonio de Orta and Doña Joana Buesten of Lito (cacica). Declared free of tribute.

According to a witness, Joan de Torres, (fol. 1), his father "had him in his power and company in Spanish dress, and they called each other father and son. And because he fled from his power, he was raised in Indian dress." According to another witness, (fol. 3), "he fled so as not to learn to read, and went away to another province and was raised in Indian dress."

2) Juan de Horta (1–IX–1686), a case from 1772. The Ortas have again married into the family Buesten, once again marrying cacicas (see the previous case.) He is variously the son of Españoles, or of a Spaniard with a cacica.

According to Nicolas de la Torre, scribe, resident in Quito, "they inferred that he was Indian by the clothing in which they saw him and his office of carrier (*cargador*)." Juan de Horta says (fol. 15): "I declare that because of my utmost poverty, orphanism and misery, although I have always been known as montañés ... going a stranger in far-off lands, I have always carried my baptismal certificate."

3) Diego de Velasco (1706–1–19), son of an (important?) father and cacica in Popayán was educated and socially accepted as white. Declared free of tribute.

A witness said he had "seen him many times in the city of Popayán wearing shoes and stockings and carrying a sword and dagger in the public streets and square of the said city where he has been seen and held for Mestizo and white man by all the creoles of the said city." (*The law did not permit Indians to carry arms.*)

6), 7), 27) The long-running case of the Aguilar family in Guaranda (1707–72) Children of Indians with Mestizas, and later of poor Mestizos.

In 1707 (fol. 3, of 25–11–1736) the ancestor "is a 'Mule' mixed-blood ('Mestizo Romo') because his father was Indian." In 1772, the whole family have fled to the mountains (1772–11–28): the cacique has been persecuting them. Pedro and Manuel say (fols. 7–8): "... so much so that even our wives with whom we are married are Mestizos, and the marriage was in the good faith that we are Mestizos and not Indian tributaries."

10) Manuel Alvares, (1747–XII–20), natural child of a silversmith and both parents "Españoles." Declared free of tribute.

He declares that he holds "the office of carrying letters from one place to another on the road from this city (Pasto) to Cartagena, using that clothing which belongs to the Monastery, on account of which they judged me Indian."

13) Ysidro Barionuevo, (21–VI–1751), resident of Quito, harpist and "maestro de capilla" ("the master of music, who beats time ... in church"), appealed for his four sons, through his "Spanish" wife. Declared free of tribute.

His wife's father (fol. 4) had been "Pedro Espinosa de los Monteros, Spanish man, in the sense in which they say Spaniards in contrast to Indians and Mestizos, because he was a very White man, and fair. He was married with Ysidora Solano, also a White woman."

14) Mariano Ortiz' wife (21–VI–1751, but actually 1789), from Guayllabamba within the Corregimiento of Quito.

Her husband presented himself with his documents of Declaration of Mestizo, and these were given to the Financial Administration of Tributes. "They've had the dossier two months, with the secretary keeping it back, claiming the papers have been transferred, so that my husband would pay four reales for one of his officials to look for it. Meanwhile, my husband returned to the town of Guayllabamba to sow, and look after a growing number of children perishing in his absence. Nobody has stayed here in his place except myself and I find myself consumed by misery, begging for alms, without the officials of the secretary Don Luis Cifuentes, wanting to hear me."

36) Mariano Alvarez, (14–III–1777), of Latacunga, a poor Mestizo.

According to a witness (fol. 3), his father "with his White and well-covered beard and his clear eyes and his office of artisan of leather trunks (*petaquero*) and saddler, was known by all as a White man, although dressed as an Indian.. He doesn't know if his parents paid tribute or not, but what the witness can affirm is that everybody knew them for Whites." A clergyman says (fol. 4) that he baptized the son of a White man, and next day, he offered to dress him as a Spaniard, but Alvarez refused, saying he was dexterous in the said clothing."

54) Pedro de la Peña, (15–XI–1777), Quito. Declared free of tribute.

Captain Don Ventura Guerrero Ponce de Leon says (fol. 3) that the mother is the "sister of a mestiza servant in his house, and although in reality, he can't say if the said Manuela Asencia Zambrano is Indian or Mestiza (but her said sister is held and known for mestiza, as her color shows) referring only to a certificate which the said Pedro has shown him, which says that the entry is found in the Spanish register."

Pedro de la Peña claims he is clearly Mestizo, and then adds a quite distinct supplementary argument (fol. 6): "I say that I am a descendant of the caciques of the Governance of this Province ... and I should have the protection of being a subject of recommendation by virtue of being a descendant of the Titisuntos ... in the descent of Pillas Ynca Ango de Salazar ... I am a descendant of the Caciques of Angamarca and Chicayza, nobles by nature, and since I am descended from all the cacicazgos of this territory I should enjoy the Royal Accord ... which those of my nation hold, and not be held as an Indian tributary."

59) Juan Francisco Xavier Guebara, (9–XI–1779), Quito, son of Mestizos. More proof needed on the legitimacy of parents.

He says (fol. 2) that "the deputy Collector of Royal Tribute, of this city and its Corregimiento, without more justification than the dark color of my skin, which by accident, cannot be construed either Indian or Spanish, reduced me to this Royal Prison."

61) Juan de Dios Guzman, (1779–XI–15), Master Organist, Quito, foundling. Exempt on appearance.

Juan de Dios was abandoned at the doors of a Spanish house and raised by an Indian. According to Don Manuel Coronel, Cacique of El Sagrario (fol. 5), "about eighteen years ago Don Josef Llanes and ... Don Francisco María de Larrea Zurbano were collectors of tribute in this city and its Five Leagues ... and with the order ... to enumerate the Indians for payment of tribute, as the said Governor, he went out to this purpose in company of Don Leandro Sepla y Oro, Cacique of various "parcialidades," and Don Gregorio Silvestre, who was the then Governor of the parish of Santa Bárbara of this city; and they enumerated 510 persons who were dressed as Spaniards, and among them the present party, who having shown himself to be Hijodalgo, and foundling ... stayed free." It was claimed that Indian mothers were using the device of abandoning their children to evade tributary status for them.

62) Antonio de Ortuño, (22–XI–1779), Quito, barber. Declared free of tribute.

Antonio de Ortuño, barber of the city of Quito petitioned to be recognized as mestizo on November 26, 1779, claiming to be the illegitimate son of Manuela Sumbe, a mestiza, by a Spaniard Antonio de Ortuño. What he termed "mistake or accident" meant that his baptismal entry was in the book reserved for the Indians, but three witnesses backed up his story. Next, there were delays until on February 29, 1780 when the General Administrator of Tribute demanded that he present the baptismal certificate of his mother. Many of the petitions end at this point, and it proved difficult; his mother was brought to Quito at the age of two, and it is not known where she was baptized; in any case, claimed the defense, the parish priests simply said what those who assisted at the baptism told them to.

Three more witnesses were summoned, this time to establish whether his mother had been brought up as a young mestiza in the house of Doña Manuela de Ontañan. The first of these, apparently White, did not seem to know whether she was mestiza or Indian; the second witness was a black slave who had worked in the same house, and said she was mestiza; the third a montañés confirmed this version. According to the treasury representatives, the Indian had been denounced as one of those who had hidden during the census; the mother had been brought as a servant "that she came given ("regalada"), and it is known that for this purpose they always seek Indians and not mestizas"; and her surname was Indian. On December 19, 1780, the decision went against Ortuño, until more proof was offered.

On August 31, 1781, three more witnesses were heard and this time the defense had done their work, bringing in more prestigious witnesses; Don Josef Paliz, vecino and master silver-smith had often gone into the house of Doña Manuela, and "saw that by her color and condition the mother didn't have a trace of Indian but was mestiza, and was treated as such in the said house, with esteem and love, and not with rigor and violence like the Indians" (!) Two more witnesses, one a saddler, confirmed this version, and Antonio de Ortuño refuted the argument that only Indians were taken for service; the young Indians rarely left their villages because of debt, being sold into textile factories. Finally Ortuño was asked to make a personal appearance so that the Court could judge his "quality" and on September 17, it decided in his favor.

Antonio de Ortuño's mother had been integrated as a servant into a wealthy Spanish household. Its wealth is suggested by the presence of a black slave. In eighteenth-century Quito, there was only a very small-scale, almost exclusively feminine slave market for domestic labor and slaves were expensive. The practice of using very young Indian children as domestic labor raised almost within the family and subject to strong acculturating influences was noted in the sixteenth century,[17] and continues in present-day Ecuador. While this would not make the son less Indian from a legal point of view, it would effect a single-generation transformation from rural Indian to acculturated urban resident. The

---

17 See *RGI*, II, 319, for Indians given as servants when young so that they acquire "good customs" ("buenas costumbres").

barbers constituted an Indian occupation, although an acculturated elite one with clothing at the limit of Spanish dress; apart from this ambiguous case, there was little evidence for the existence of Mestizos in this occupation. For the social position of the barbers, and the evidence that this was an Indian occupation, see Chapter 4.

In view of the shortage of documentary proof, and the fact that the barbers were an overwhelmingly Indian occupation, it is clear that this case turned almost exclusively on social acceptance. An unusually large number of witnesses were produced, and the case only decided when the court saw the "quality" of the petitioner. The evidence of the third set of witnesses appears to have been decisive, because of their social prestige as established artisans. That a member of an elite Indian occupation should be opting to be Mestizo rather than Indian should not pass unnoticed, this being a parallel rather than superior status from the point of view of the upper Indian elite, evidence of the extent to which tribute was a burden in the cold fiscal climate of the late 1770s. Ortuño had been denounced as an Indian who had hidden during the census, confirming the atmosphere of fear and evasion surrounding it. Other features of the case which may be noted are the differential treatment meted out to Indian and Mestiza servants, and the evidence of debt-peonage.

64) Francisco Xavier Hidalgo, 22–XII–1779, resident in Quito but originally from Latacunga, violinist.

According to a certificate of the parish priest of El Sagrario, Quito, an abandoned child called Francisco Xavier was baptized in the cathedral parish on January 18, 1743. Thirty years later Francisco Xavier Hidalgo, a good Spanish name, appeared before the court to petition for exemption as one who has enjoyed the "privilege of gentleman (*hidalgo*) by virtue of being a foundling," an abandoned child who was brought up and given the necessary education by a Spanish woman. In spite of claiming to have enjoyed exemption from tribute all his life, he had been pressured by the tribute collectors. The three witnesses located by the treasury officials gave quite a different story. Juan de Navarrete, citizen of Quito, testified on December 16, 1779; "that he knew Xavier, whose surname he does not know, but that it is the same who produced the preceding text, and that he is the same who was held and commonly reputed in Latacunga to be an Indian, and was called cholo, which name is given to those who are legitimately Indian; that he is native of Latacunga where the witness knew the mother of the said Xavier who was clearly Indian, known and held as such; for this motive, apart from the aforementioned reputation, they called him *yapango.*"[18]

---

[18] *Yapango, llapango,* (quichua), barefooted. Stevenson says this word was used of the Mestizos in the early nineteenth century, but it is clearly close in sense to *cholo*. See Stevenson, *A Historical and Descriptive*, 303.

The second witness, Josefa Leon, also of Quito, confirmed this version; "She knew Francisco Xavier, the violinist, whose surname she does not remember, knows he is Indian, because he was the son of an Indian she knew, called Maria, *papacato*[19] by office which is how they call the market women (recatonas y gateras), that the said Indian, held and commonly reputed as such, lived in the house of the deceased Don Diego Donoso; that he was not native of this city but from Latacunga."

The third witness, Juan de la Cruz, added that Xavier was falsely calling himself Cárdenas, that his father was an Indian tailor who sewed shirts; and his maternal aunt still a petty trader. With this evidence, the Court had little doubt in arguing that the person he calls "Francisco Xavier Hidalgo, alias the violinist Hidalgo" has managed to procure the baptismal entry of some other inhabitant of the city, and on February 5, 1780, the President ordered that he pay tribute.

The same month, Hidalgo appealed with a new version of his past: he is the son of Fernando Cardenas and Maria Santos Narbaez, known to be pure-blooded Spaniards, who had never held mechanical offices, and if they had left him at the doors of Doña Juliana Gordillo, this had been because she was an appropriate choice for bringing him up. Three witnesses, two from Latacunga, and one from Quito back up this version. In Hidalgo's petition of March 1, 1780, he signs with an expanded name, Francisco Xabier Hidalgo y Cárdenas. The case was not immediately decided, but Hidalgo badgered the court officials and finally repetitioned the President late the same year. In November the court finally came to a decision. Yngacio Montes de Oca, representative of the tribute branch of the treasury, delivered a blistering attack on Hidalgo's evidence, picking out contradictions in the evidence of the second set of witnesses, and showing the extent to which plebeian pretensions to *hidalguía* were contemptuously viewed :

> "[The first witness] wants us to understand that legitimacy and a consummate nobility were the offspring of the collusion of these fellows (*estas gentes*) ... He certainly believed in the beginning that someone else's birth certificate would save him, and tried to acquire his liberty, making use of his quality of foundling; further, when it was revealed that his mother was called María la Gatera, María the market-woman, devoid of means, he added Doña, and the surname Santos, with which, and by his friendship with the witnesses, he ennobled her; and in this way, he who a little earlier did not know his parents, and was hijodalgo found them shortly afterwards, and adorned with a brilliant nobility, no less."

On December 11, 1780, the court asked Hidalgo to supply his parents' birth certificates, and this time we lose trace of him definitively. If, as

---

[19] *Papacato,* (quichua), one who sells potatoes in the marketplace. "En *quíchua*, mercado es *ccatu,* vocablo que también se vulgarizó, así en *Quito* como en el *Perú* propio, en la forma ridícula de *gato,"* note of Jiménez de la Espada, *RGI*, II, 220, note 1.

seems most logical, we follow the Court in considering Hidalgo to belong to the category of cholo from the sierra, he can be considered the prototype of the emigrant to the urban centers who was able to escape the restrictions of race and tribute in the relative anonymity, as this case clearly demonstrates, of the urban centers. Two of Hidalgo's close female relatives (mother and maternal aunt) had been market-women, confirming in an individual case the evidence of Chapter 5. Only the officials called him a violinist, not the defense, so he was clearly a street musician rather than the more protected category of church musician. (See cases 61, 25, and 244 for example, for musicians who won their cases.)

Hidalgo was a resourceful fellow, who knew how to sign his own name (although rather badly), organize a lively defense and persuade witnesses to testify on his behalf; the cholo living off his wits had taken on many of the traits of a Spanish urban resident, even if his pretensions did not go down well in court. The documentation reveals enormous fluidity in eighteenth-century surnames; a change of surname was one of the essential features of a successful transition into White society, and "Hidalgo," of course, signified the minor Spanish nobleman class. In a modern ethnological study, *chalashca* was one of the names for urban Mestizos recorded for the central sierra, meaning "collector of other people's surnames."[20] The ambiguity of the expósito, (foundling) category may also be noted.

74) Pedro Rodrigues, (18–VIII–1780), Quito, legitimate child of Spaniard and cacica. Declared free of tribute.

In his petition, Rodrigues (fol. 9) argues that "the proof based on color is mistaken and inconclusive because there is nothing more ordinary than very dark Spaniards, and extremely White mulatos, who in places far from their homelands can comfortably deny their plebeian origin."

89) Francisco and Manuel Sanches, (20–III–1781), Ibarra.

Was the mother Indian or Mestiza? In any case (fol. 5), she wore a pleated Spanish-style skirt (*faldellín*) and not the garment which Indian women wrapped around themselves (*urco*). They had a cousin, a merchant, who was married to a "señora." Relatives of the father in Quito were of "good color."

98) Damacio Caceres, 14–V–1781, Quito, son of a Spanish mother. Declared free of tribute.

His defender (fol. 11) speaks of the tribute collection of 1779 in which many were taken unprepared, and were now trying to prove they were White, handicapped, or deaf and dumb; "In all philosophy, color is an accident, which none can doubt .... One should not decide by the color of

---

[20] P. Peñaherrera de Costales and A. Costales Samaniego, *Katekil, o Historia Cultural del Campesinado de Chimborazo*, (Quito, 1957), 235.

the subject, to place him in this or that sphere. My party, if it were permitted and caused no shame to the noble families of the city could name subjects individually, but nonetheless, Your Excellency himself will reflect briefly on one or another distinguished subject, who if he were brought low by poverty, or more exactly dressed in a rough cloth vest (*capisayo de gerga*), who would know that it was Don So-and-so, and perhaps he would be the first to pay tribute in the mind of the collectors ...."

99) Thomas Robles, (4–V–1781), barber of Quito, originally from Latacunga. A foundling, declared free of tribute after the court had examined his physical appearance.

Denounced as an Indian by his mother-in-law!

107) Faustino Camelo, (9–VI–1781), Alaquez (Latacunga). They need to present more documents.

No one in the family paid tribute, and (fol. 4), "they were only known to pay the alcabala, sales tax, as Mestizos, without having exercised the ministries which the Indians occupy."

109) 9–VI–1781, Augustin Calderon, of Ibarra, originally from Guápulo near Quito. Declared free of tribute.

His parents were both White, he says; "... and I have withdrawn to these lands because I took the surname Sarabias because I felt like it (*por gana*). For the relativity of anonymity in a medium-sized urban centers see the testimony of Vicente Sisneros (fol. 2); "... as a Quiteño he knows almost all the people of the city ... and knew Esteban Calderón, White man, married to Pasquala Seballos, a White woman, who lived in the barrio of la Merced of the said city." It was worth stressing (fol. 4) that not only his parents, but also his godfather were all White, a detail which underlines the importance of compaternity.

116) Manuel Justo and Martin Bonifacio Mosquera, 1781–IX–13, Quito, legitimate children of the cacique of Cotocollao and a Spanish woman. Declared free of tribute.

This case illustrates the cautious approach of Villalengua and the higher levels of fiscal administration, attentive to possible repercussions in the form of social disorder. (Other cases attest to the lack of restraint of lower-level officials.)

The court was prepared to follow custom in this case; but what was the custom? According to the auditor, (fol. 8), "the custom observed in this province with regard to the collection of tribute of the legitimate children of Indian in White woman, or mestiza ... It happens that they have collected in some towns from this class of Mestizos, but not in others," sometimes following the fathers and sometimes the mothers (Quito, 1781).

The "fiscal" said that:

> "Having taken note in the visit and enumeration of his charge the variety with which in the same communities, the legitimate children of an Indian with a mestiza or White woman, or of Mestizos with an Indian woman paid tribute without causing any problems, while others resisted, he felt he should inform Your Excellency ... to delay a possibly dangerous innovation (*una novedad poco segura*), while the correct practice was established. But as the court consulted the Superior Government, the present Minister continued enumerating the Mestizos of the said class for greater security, so that this would facilitate the collection when the decision was made; and since the Government decided to follow custom ... which was not solidly established ... a decision must be made on how to proceed given the diversity encountered. Can Your Excellency provisionally relieve Manuel Justo and Martin Bonifacio Mosquera of the obligation to pay tribute."

The administrators should proceed "without violence" to standardize practice, using moderation, or "... above all as Your Excellency considers conform to Justice without introducing great innovations (*novedad considerable*) for those in possession of the right not to pay tribute." (Villalengua, Quito, November 27, 1781)

118) Marcos Hidalgo, (25–IX–1781), of Lulumbamba in the Corregimiento of Quito.

He was a foundling. Ten pesos had been collected in tribute, even though "all the town knows I am not Indian" (fol. 8). He was found in a doorway in Quito by the cacica of the village when he was a day or two old, and brought to the village to be baptized. 21 pesos and 7 reales were demanded in back tribute and his (Indian) guarantor was imprisoned in the obraje of San Roque.

120) Martin Alvarado, (1781–X–5), resident of Gualaseo, illegitimate. Declared free of tribute (1781). Case reheard (1785).

This case shows the extent to which the climate had changed since the more relaxed climate of cases 1) and 3) in the late seventeenth and early eighteenth centuries. "New" Indians were being created, but in 1779–81 the fiscal administration was still "feeling its way." By the mid-1780s, however, the courts had tightened up their procedures, and had perhaps by then got accustomed to some of the anomalies created by the revived tribute system.

Martin Alvarado was the son of a noble father and Indian mother, the "first generation" type of Mestizo who would have had few difficulties a century earlier. "My father," he says (fol. 1), "was Spanish and noble, the legitimate son of well-known parents, so I enjoy the genealogy of 'fine' Mestizo (*Mestizo fino*), and accordingly I have the honor to be entitled to rise to any estate; for which the proof is the resemblance to my said father, for I am his very portrait; and as such when he had procreated me, he brought me up, recognizing me as his natural child." Now the collectors wanted to collect tribute, and had registered him on their listings. This is a difficult case, he recognizes; "I am a natural child," he says, "I can't deny it" (fol. 1). His own father testifies that he recognized him as a son and had "fed" him (fol. 2); the father's conversation with a friend that his son should be defended from being bothered or imposed on as an Indian. In 1781 this was enough.

Four years later, however, there was a further petition by Martin Alvarado; despite his Declaration of Mestizo he had been asked for tribute. It was pointed out that the Viceregal Administration in Santafé de Bogotá had now decided that exemption should only go to legitimate children (fol. 6, Quito, September 22, 1785.) More details were needed on whether the mother was mestiza or Indian. Case abandoned?

125) Francisco Xavier Villamarin, (1782–1–18), Quito, although his parents were from Ibarra. A musician. Declared free of tribute.

The evidence here underlines the distinction between "new" mestizos, with Indian parents or grandparents, and those who were further removed from Indian society. According to Felipe Briones, a montañés tailor, his parents were "not even treated as Mestizos, as their colors and persons attested, and it was never noted that they were descended from Indians."

126) Mariano Damacio Chaves (1782–1–18), Quito, Legitimate child of Mestizos. Declared free of tribute, after initial reservations on account of his appearance.

For the barrios as villages, compare the testimony of Pedro Gonsales, aged 60, (fols. 1–2), who said that "because he was from the same barrio, and the immediate neighborhood, he knew Felipe Chaves" and his grandfather and other relatives.

145) 1782–VIII–1, Fabian Mora, Cuenca, natural child of a Spaniard and a cacica. Case denied.

The sons of an unmarried woman follow the mother, while the exemption of the cacique only applies to the eldest son; and in any case, an illegitimate son being a Mestizo should not inherit a Cacicazgo (fol. 9). In other words, this category falls between two stools, and the petitioner gets caught despite obvious claims to exemption.

153) Atanacio Bonifacio and Francisco Muela, (26–III–1783), brothers of Pintag, in the Corregimiento of Quito. Interim Declaration of Mestizo granted in 1776: case denied in 1783.

What should petitioners make of claims to distinction which were those of Indian and not White society? This question arose for those who were of cacical descent, and similarly in this case where the brothers had served in a (presumably Indian) confraternity.

The brothers declared in 1776 (fol. 1): "Although we have had and continue to enjoy the status of montañeses, we have served in the said village as stewards (*priostes*) in the brotherhoods which the Church holds, spending, and offering our personal work." The theme of matrimonial alliances was stressed (fol. 2): "We have married with White women known in the said village, as our ancestors have also been married to White women."

In 1776, these children of an Indian woman with a Spanish father received an interim Declaration of Mestizo. In 1783, they were picked up again, and the fiscal administration wanted to know more about the mother, apparently unmarried; this time they lost.

196) Juan de Dios de la Cruz, (1–VII–1786), resident of Quito, militiaman. Declared free of tribute.

He was picked up in Latacunga where he had been selling. He had left fine pearls with the *cura*, who had then paid his tribute for him. In a number of cases, witnesses seem to have been a kind of guarantor, sharing economic interests, and otherwise having dealings with the petitioner; the witnesses here, for example, are two plateros and a person who drills holes in pearls for necklaces (*taladreador de perlas*). His baptismal entry cannot be found; "He said he had been baptized in the year 1758 in the chapel, which as a hut they made in the Plaza mayor on account of the earthquakes."(fol. 4).

198) Ramon Hati Villalba, (16–VII–1786), Quito.

"Hati" was a clearly a non-Spanish surname, which was used against him (fol. 8). The ambiguity of cacical descent, which was a form of nobility but also associated a person with Indian, and therefore tributary status, is clear from this case. Hati Villalba denied that he had claimed to be the son of a Cacique of 7 pueblos (fol. 8).

200) Antonio Hidalgo, (23–IX–1786), Quito, a tailor, prisoner in the obraje of Añaquito. Asked to appear so that they could examine his appearance, and declared free of tribute.

Hidalgo was a tailor, button-maker, or maker of adornments for clothing. The witnesses say he was Mestizo, but he may have been brought up by Indians. It was at an Indian's house that a witness, a tailor, saw him (fol. 2) learning one of his offices when he was seven or eight years old, dressed as a Mestizo in his blue cloth waist-coat (*chupa azul de paño*).

201) Thomas Bermeo, (5–X–1786), Loja, claimed on the basis of services rendered. Case abandoned?

This case was heard in Loja, and sent to Quito, which makes it the most geographically remote case of the series. Thomas Bermeo adduced, in support of his Mestizo status, his services as an interpreter and canoeist/ ferryman (*balsero*) on the expedition "to reduce the Indian infidels" down the rivers of the Amazonian region of Samora (fol. 1). With regard to his services, one of the witnesses asked him how much he earned, "... to which the said Bermeo said nothing, that he had done it to gain "merit" (*por hazer merito*). According to another witness (fol. 2), the canoe overturned "so that he lost all his goods and everything which was in it."

Thomas Bermeo's petition states "... Although I am not Indian, because my parents weren't, it is rather difficult for me to prove so, as they died years ago, and were migrants (*forasteros*), and each from different areas" (fol. 4). The Court in Quito was not impressed by the testimony and affidavits made in Loja, and asked (fol. 6) for further inquiries from the Corregidor, notably on the possible Mestizo parentage of Bermeo. It refused in effect to allow the category of Mestizo to serve as a cover for other types of claim to tribute exemption.

208) Manuel Garrido, (7–I–1787), Quito, Legitimate child of an Indian tiler (texero) and a White woman. Case denied.

According to the decision of the Junta of the treasury (1787), the legitimate children of Indians with non-Indian women will now pay tribute (fol. 6). In this case, the mother was the sister of a noble (fol. 4), "known, reputed and held to be a señora," who on account of her "total indigence and bad judgement married Luis Maita, Indian" (fol. 2). Garrido therefore came within the terms of this decision, and the case failed.

241) Francisco Binuesa (23–VI–1789), Mira, Ibarra.

Socio-racial downgrading accompanied downward social mobility. A witness said (fol. 4): "he doesn't know why the said Francisco Binuesa was subject to the Royal Tribute, and it has only come to his notice that the said Francisco Binuesa was poor, and for this reason went to work in the Hacienda of San Nicolas and as they put him in the book of "consierto" workers, they classified him as an Indian without him being one."

242) Carlos Herrera, (15–VIII–1789), born in Quito. Declared free of tribute.

This case provides a note of caution with regard to baptismal practice; he was born in the Barrio de la Loma, Quito, but baptized in the pueblo of Zambisa. He was adopted by Padre Fray Juan de Herrera, and understood that his father was "a subject of distinction and honor." The petition dated October 13, 1790 (fol. 5), claimed he was being persecuted in Pelileo, alone as a forastero.

244) Rafael Garses, (13–X–1789), from near Ambato. Natural child of Spanish parents. Declared free of tribute.

According to Mathias Ortiz (fol. 4) "he made music in the Church ... and in virtue of this ... has always been held, treated and reputed to be a Mestizo."

251) Thomas Gutierrez and relatives, (7–IX–1793), Jipijapa, legitimate child of Mestizos. Declared free of tribute.

According to Don Ygnacio Barveran, "they are Mestizos of very good presence and color (fol. 4)." "They have never occupied the offices or charges (*cargos*) of Indians. (See Chapters 7 and 8 for what constituted "offices" and "charges" of Indians.)

257) Domingo Maria Alvarado, (23–X–1797), Quito, foundling, given an interim Declaration of Mestizo.

According to the administrator of tribute, the Indians, too, had natural children, and this must be one of them, according to his physiognomy. Juan Romualdo Ortiz gave the following testimony (fols. 6–7): "He remembers ... that he heard a commotion (*novedad o bulla de gente*), and passed a shop of the said Don Ramon, and they told him they'd just left an infant in the doors of one of those shops, but he can't remember the name of the woman they left the child with. He asked her to raise him, and if he lived, to give him to the witness to teach him the same office of saddler. He remembers, too, that in the baby's clothing they found a paper which said that he was already baptized. And indeed with this boy growing up almost within his sight, he asked his adoptive mother to fulfill her word, and let him learn his office, little by little, which she did. And he took the said boy for himself, and up to today he has maintained him in the said office, and that he's a really good saddler, for his customs and application ... He is known as a Mestizo and gentleman (*mestizo e hijodalgo*)."

The Language of Race: A Discussion of Socio-racial Terminology

The petitions which are discussed here form the plebeian counterpart to the genealogical preoccupations which ran through much of the intermediate and higher strata of colonial society, the transposition of the traditional Spanish concern with *limpieza de sangre* as an expression of honor, to the racially diverse society of Spanish America. Jaramillo Uribe has assembled for New Granada rich material on the litigation which the usurpation of the title "Don" caused, as well as that caused by "offenses to honor."[21] When we find the same values at a lower social level, this is testimony to the osmosis by which Spanish ideals and values penetrated into much of the popular strata of colonial society, not least of course because these paralleled so closely the hierarchical values of traditional Andean society. Blood, honor, office: the concern with what constituted "vile and mechanical offices" was an entirely Spanish one which in both Spain and

---

21 J. Jaramillo Uribe, "Mestizaje y diferenciación en el Nuevo Reino de Granada en la segunda mitad del siglo xviii," *Anuario Colombiano de Historia y de la Cultura*, 1:2 (1964), 21 ff. Similar preoccupations can be found in the cases of opposition to childrens' marriages cited by S. Socolow, "Acceptable partners. Marriage choice in colonial Argentina: 1778-1810," Working Paper, Augsberg, 1987.

Spanish America was reinforced by a quasi-racial dimension (New and Old Christians in Spain/ Indians and Castas in Spanish America).

It was in the nature of the legal process that the petitioners should attempt to make their self-assessments intelligible to Court officials, but the language of the petitions nevertheless illuminates unconscious values, and provides a means of access into one dimension of popular ideology. The linguistic confusion is striking; the documentation of the Declarations reveals a world of subtle gradations, shades of meaning and, to our logic, plain contradictions:

- "Mestizo y hombre blanco" (3)
- "Hombre muy blanco" (13)
- "De buena color" (89)
- "Christianos viejos" (95)[22]
- "Hera blanca, tenida por mestiza" (96)

In one sense, although rich, the language of these petitions is far less developed than the extraordinary compilations of caste distinctions which have been recorded for Spanish America as a whole. The paintings in the Museo de América in Madrid, for example, represent a series of Mexican caste distinctions which bear little resemblance to what we find in the Quito documentation.[23] In part, this is because they are highly schematized, and probably did not accurately describe the reality in any one region in Spanish America. Nevertheless, the absence of Blacks or part-Blacks from the Declarations certainly simplified things. Of the 266 cases, only 8 turned on petitioners of Black or part-Black origin, some three percent, roughly the proportion of Blacks in Quito society as a whole.

The relative absence of Blacks only throws into sharper relief the polarization of the popular sectors into Indians and non-Indians. For the region of Quito there was no legal category of Mestizo in the official censuses, and I would argue that this lack of legal definition is an accurate reflection of the socio-racial nature of Quito society. The absence of the category of Mestizo may of course have been both cause and effect; it is probable that official efforts to push people into census or tax categories was itself a major factor in shaping social differentiation. Although the categories of "poor White" and Mestizo are often set in contra-distinction to each other, no clear borderline emerged from the Declarations. A person was of more or less "good color" as he distanced himself socially and racially from the category of Indian. The attempt to define this distance formed the terrain of the lawsuits: few were sure how they defined themselves, but all were sure that they were not Indian.

---

[22] For Mexican examples of this claim see D. López Sarrelangue, "Mestizaje y catolicismo en la Nueva España," *Historia Mexicana,* 1 vol. XXIII, (1973), 21.

[23] See, for example, the painting "Castas," Inv. 26, Esc. Mex S. XVIII in the Museo de América, Madrid. These paintings have been widely reproduced, for example, by Mörner in his book, *Race Mixture in the History of Latin America,* (Boston, 1967).

Thus we find few of the elaborate subdivisions which existed—whether theoretically or in reality—elsewhere in Spanish America, and it may be no coincidence that almost the only exception came from one of the few cases (29) which was heard from the more ethnically diverse coastal region, where we find a "cuarterón" (one quarter Negro). Quite certainly, the "rules of the game" changed considerably in those few parts of the Audiencia with a substantial Black presence, and the need to define ethnicity twice over, in relation to both the Indian and Black population, produced a more complicated language of race. We should not forget the peculiarity of a Peruvian-type society (White minority and large Indian peasantry) belonging to the Viceroyalty of New Granada with its more substantial Black population. Greater stigma was attached to a degree of Black ancestry than to part-Indian descent. In the case of Loja, where the city had a relatively significant Black presence, we find both the cases of insults to honor examined by Jaramillo Uribe for the rest of New Granada, and an attempt to interpose a mixed Mestizo/Free Colored category between the White elite and the Indian and Slave populations.[24]

Although we encounter a relatively narrow range of socio-racial terminology, the language of race is highly revealing, and requires some attention if we are not to misread the data. Four key terms will be noted here: Cholo, Don, Mestizo, and Montañés. Although the first three terms are common to a larger area, the term "montañés" seems to have been used more in the Audiencia of Quito than in most areas of Spanish America, although it was certainly used more widely in the early colonial period.[25]

CHOLO/LLAPANGO For the early colonial period, one definition of cholo was given in Chapter 3. However, in the late-colonial documentation, cholos were acculturated Indians, perhaps on their way into Mestizo society. For a classic example of the urban cholo see the petition of Francisco Xavier Hidalgo, (case 64). Although the ambiguous status of this category meant that cholo tended to be assimilated into "mestizo," the term still referred essentially to the Indian population; "cholo which is how they call the Indians" (see the petition of Hidalgo, above). In the early nineteenth century, Stevenson found that the term *llapango*, (barefooted) was used of the Mestizos, whereas its prime sense was clearly cholo. Whether this was an evolution from the eighteenth-century meaning, a reflection of the fluidity of socio-racial terms, or perhaps an oversimplification (or misunderstanding) of the terms used in Quito, it is difficult to say. Stevenson's description is interesting and may be cited in full:

---

24 See Minchom, "The making of a white province," 36–38.
25 For the term's use in the early colonial period, see the quotation from Garcilaso de la Vega, below. The term does not appear much in Mörner's discussion of socio-racial terminology for Spanish America as a whole, (Mörner, Chapter 5), although a Paraguayan example is cited for the early colonial period.

> The dress of the mestizos is composed of a jacket and small-clothes; a long Spanish cloak of blue cloth, manufactured in the country, and a Black hat; these are called *llapangos,* a Quichua word signifying barefooted. The females often wear a large hoop, and a gaudy petticoat made of English flannel, red, pink, yellow, or pale blue, ornamented with a profusion of ribbon, lace, fringe, and spangles, wrought into a kind of arabesque about half a yard deep, near the bottom of the coat, below which a broad White lace hangs, attached to an under garment. The bodice is generally of brocade or tissue, or of embroidered satin, laced very tight round the waist; the bosom and sleeves of this are ornamented with White lace, ribbons and spangles; a narrow shawl of English flannel to correspond with the petticoat is thrown over the shoulders; the head is uncovered but ornamented with a fillet, ribbons, and flowers, and the hair hangs in small tresses down the back. Like the men, the women seldom wear shoes or stockings, and it is considered a trait in their beauty to have small White feet, and red heels, to procure which cosmetics and rouge are often called in to lend their assistance: the practice is very common among a certain description of females.[26]

Although Stevenson describes these llapangos as Mestizos, it is probable from the dress of the masculine llapangos that they were essentially cholos in the process of transculturation. "Upper" Mestizos often wore more European-style trousers and sometimes had shoes.[27] With regard to the feminine category of llapanga it is, as always, rather harder to fix them in a clear ethnic category, and their dress is totally acculturated. Stevenson's final hint of an association of at least part of the category of llapanga with prostitution may also be noted. In 1861 Holinski remarked only on the llapangas and not the llapangos, and made similar comments, so it may be that the former were closer to becoming an urban "type," while the latter were indeed a transitional category on its way into assimilation into White society.[28]

DON/DOÑA Jaramillo Uribe has documented the lawsuits created by the usurpation of the title "Don," which was technically a mark of nobility, although it had been somewhat democratized in its actual usage.[29] For the region of Quito, we may emphasize the continuation of its use by important Indians to the extent that a tribute collector (see case 117) identified someone as Indian almost entirely because his mother had this title. In the baptismal register of for Whites in El Sagrario, Quito (1762–70), we find at

---

[26] W. B. Stevenson, *A Historical and Descriptive Narrative,* vol. 2, 303–304.

[27] To judge by later paintings, in any case: see *Imágenes del Ecuador del Siglo XIX. Juan Agustín Guerrero,* (Quito, 1981), 106, for an artisan explicitly "vestido a la Antigua," (although in this case with bare feet), as well as the paintings of Mestizos in the collection Castro y Velázquez, Guayaquil.

[28] A. Holinski, *L'Equateur. Scènes de la vie sud-américaine.* (Paris, 1861), 161–163.

[29] For a discussion of the title "Don," see Jaramillo Uribe, "Mestizaje y diferenciación," 43–48.

folio 179 the baptism of a child of Don Miguel García and Doña Josefa Jara y Almeida, written in different handwriting from that of the priest. The entry which follows states that the baptismal entry for the son of Miguel Chuquimarca had been torn out of the book of Indians, and a new entry written in for him in the book of Whites, "aumentado con muchos dones." The importance of the Church as the *de facto* arbiter in determining social distinctions is thus reemphasized.

MESTIZO An official writing in the late 1770s at the time when the administration was concerned about real and potential threats of disorder distinguished between three types of Mestizos. The first were "cholos," Indians seeking to avoid tribute obligations, the second were children of "plebeian" fathers and Indian mothers, and the third were the illegitimate offspring of noble fathers; the former two categories were afraid of censuses for fear of being reduced to tributary status, while the third were considered a naturally lively and scandalous group.[30] The first two categories of Mestizos emerge clearly from the documentation, although it may be appropriate to call attention to Martín Alvarado (120) who belonged to the third category, and whose fortunes were markedly different in the 1770s and 1780s than they would have been in an earlier period (compare with cases 1, 3, 12, 32, 106). This "first generation" type of Mestizo forms a link with the material of Chapter 3, but he is clearly a very small part of the total Mestizo population by the late eighteenth century.

The term "mestizo" had pejorative associations. In the padrón of Santa Bárbara in 1768, if Xavier Casas, street seller, has been classified as Mestizo, while everybody else is Indian, Mulato or unspecified, this is clearly not because the Mestizos are a tiny minority, but because the categorization as Mestizo is a comment on his unstable way of life (Table 7.1). In this sense, the early colonial definition of the Mestizos as idle and potentially seditious (see Chapter 3) had a long life and requires little additional comment. There was relatively little self-identification as Mestizo in the petitions, and "Mestizo" was clearly a category which pulled towards White society when it could.[31]

One important distinction should be stressed as regards internal differentiation within the popular Mestizo sectors, namely the distinction between new Mestizos, and those who were further removed from Indian society. The designation of a person as a "Mestizo Romo,"[32] comes up in one of the earlier cases (6), but it is clear that the distinction remained an important one. Case 125 was merely one example of many who stressed the remoteness of Indian ancestry, and the phrase "mestizo limpio" signified those who were not the illegitimate offspring of White and Indian but the

---

30 Manuel Ponton to the Audiencia, December 1, 1778, ANH/Q Pres. 1778, vol. 12, doc. 150, letter cited by S. Moreno Yánez, *Sublevaciones Indígenas*, 218.

31 See *inter alia*, cases 13, 97.

32 "Mule," because of the divided ancestry, and with an Indian father.

children of Mestizos on both sides. The putative plotted uprising of these Mestizos against the cholos of the city in 1762, shows that this distinction was a real one. How many generations separated a cholo from a "Mestizo limpio" is another difficult question, and what is striking in the ethnic tensions in San Roque is that a parish which may have been quite strongly Indian in the second half of the seventeenth century acquired such a strong "Mestizo" identity during the first half of the eighteenth century.

Some degree of racial mixture affected different social strata, and left its mark in a consciousness of socio-racial gradations within White society. The defender of Damacio Cáceres observed: "one or another distinguished subject, if he were found downcast by poverty, or to be more exact, dressed in a rough cloth poncho, who would believe that he was Don So-and-so, and perhaps in the mind of the collector, he would be the first to pay tribute" (case 98). Although there may not have been "insults tò honor" cases on the scale of much of New Granada, this racial consciousness is nevertheless revealed by quarrels brought before the law-courts, in this case, an ecclesiastical one, when unspoken racial attitudes were brought to the surface. In 1805, in Sidcay (near Cuenca) a coadjutor and his priest were engaged in a furious dispute: "... saying he was senile, a scoundrel, a thief, cholo, Mestizo, and other equally outrageous insults."[33]

MONTAÑÉS Tyrer defines "montañés" in terms of the "gente decente," arguing that it was a "term which in Quito literally meant a mountain man, usually applying to a mestizo but including poor Whites as well."[34] In a study of the present-day Province of Cañar, Muñoz-Bernand refers to "montañeses" as coming from the wooded zones of Dudas and Zhoray, or being laborers on the haciendas, but does not specifically identify them as Mestizos.[35] Although we often find terms such as "White," and "Mestizo" used interchangeably, this should not blind us to their root meaning, and there is no doubt that from the sixteenth to at least the nineteenth century (and I suspect beyond) the prime sense of montañés was Mestizo. Garcilaso de la Vega gives an extremely clear definition of this term for the sixteenth century, and his sensitivity to racial differences—as the son of a Spaniard and Inca princess—give his testimony particular interest:

> "... if a person is told: "You're a mestizo" or "He's a mestizo" it is taken as an insult. This is the reason why they have adopted with such enthusiasm the name montañés which some potentate applied to them, among other slights and insults, instead of the word mestizo. They do not stop to consider that, although in Spain the word montañés is an honorable

---

[33] AA/C, unclassified, "Dr. Don José Raymundo Perez v. Prev° Don Agustin Checa" 1805. "Palabras de que el Dr. Pérez era un Viejo, Pícaro, Ladrón, Cholo, Mestizo, y otras injurias igualmente enormes."

[34] Tyrer, *The Demographic and Economic History*, 97.

[35] C. Muñoz-Bernand, *Les Renaissants de Pindilig*, doctoral thesis, University of Paris, 1981, 39, 109.

> appellation, on account of the privileges that have been bestowed on the natives of the Asturian and Basque mountains, if it is applied to anyone who is not from these parts, it assumes a pejorative sense derived from its original meaning "something from the mountains." This is brought out by our great master Antonio de Lebrija, to whom all good Latinists in Spain are indebted in his vocabulary. In the general language of Peru the word for a mountaineer is sacharuna, properly "savage," and whoever applied the word montañés was privately calling them savages: those of my own generation, not understanding this malicious implication, took pride in the insulting insult, when they should have rather avoided and abominated it, using the name our fathers bestowed on us rather than accepting new-fangled indignities."[36]

In Spain "la Montaña de Burgos" was the region where even the lower social strata were considered not to have Jewish or Moorish blood, because the Arab conquest had not reached the extreme north-east of the country.[37] The new lease of life of this Spanish term in the Indies was therefore a direct expression of the traditional Spanish concern with purity of blood as an expression of honor. Distant echoes of this preoccupation can be found in the Mestizo law-suits of the late-eighteenth century, when petitioners pleaded as *mestizos limpios,* of "pure mixed-blood." Montañeses were Mestizos of an "honorable," middling status in society, and in the late-colonial period, people of this status could be labeled either "White," "montañés," or "mestizo." Although it may certainly be argued that there was no clear borderline between montañés and "poor White," and we can find abundant contradictory usage, the term still carried the root sense of mixed-blood, (and had nothing to do with the Ecuadorian *montaña);* "Montañés, which is how they call the Mestizos" (71). At least in the registers of El Sagrario, this was quite an explicit category, and in the nineteenth century, the term continued to be used in the same sense.[38] The self-identification of mestizos as Whites or near-Whites, was already in evidence in the eighteenth century petitions. The term may have survived better outside the capital. In view of the colonial and nineteenth century meaning of the term, it is likely that the people of Dudas and Zhoray, cited above, are in fact present-day montañeses, (or descendants of montañeses) in the sense discussed here.

---

36 Garcilaso de la Vega, *Royal Commentaries of the Incas,* Part 1, Book 9, 607.
37 See, for example, the definition in the *Diccionario de Autoridades.*
38 See Hassaurek, *Four years,* 85. The present-day Ecuadorians I asked were unable to explain the term (not apparently through any reluctance to discuss the subject). This is perhaps unsurprising since racial terms are sustained mainly by abuse (*cholo,* etc.).

SOCIO-RACIAL CATEGORIES

The cases presented above may be disaggregated into the following categories:

1) The children of Spaniard and Indian mother, the latter often belonging to the class of the cacicas.

2) The children of Indian fathers and White mothers, (6, 34, 116, 208). For the legal position, see case 116. Case 208 appears to be an unusual example of this form of matrimonial alliance, and shows that inter-ethnic marriages could be a reflection of downward as well as upward social mobility.

3) "Indians dressed as Spaniards." Indians who have assimilated urban skills and adopted Spanish culture. Statistically, the "real" cholo was less likely to bring his case before the tribunals than a person who was Mestizo.

4) "Spaniards dressed as Indians." These were usually Mestizos in rural areas who are partly assimilated into Indian culture, or who for reasons of poverty go "dressed as Indians," but who have enjoyed recognition of their Mestizo status until over-zealous caciques or tax-collectors try to reincorporate them into the category of tribute payer. The long-running battle of the Aguilar family exemplifies this group (cases 6, 23, 28, 36).

5) Hijos expósitos, foundlings, for whom there was no easy criterion for establishing ethnicity.

6) "Poor Whites" were normally people who found themselves before the law-courts because their low economic status made it difficult for census takers to separate them from Indians; they had also been sometimes subject to denunciation of evil-wishers.

7) The Declarations also merge into other kinds of document relating to tribute exemption, such as those who have served the Church in varying capacities, serving on a dangerous expeditions into the jungle or hacing fought the English in Guayaquil.[39]

The case studies cited earlier serve as a warning against attempting any clear separation of these categories. In the course of an inventive defense a petitioner might—and often did—advance many different explanations of why he was not Indian, some of them quite contradictory. The advantage of setting out the cases is that it allows us to establish discussion on a solid documentary base, without being dependent on the presentation of a series of tables which a more restricted format requires. A degree of flexibility in handling this data is certainly in order. If we calculate the illegitimacy rate, for example, we find that only 31 percent of the petitioners were legitimate.

---

[39] Cases 16, 201: see also for the importance of church service cases 153, 244.

It is appropriate, however, to emphasize the legal background. The viceregal decree of September 1774 specified that illegitimate children followed the mother, and despite some elasticity in the application of this decree (in the light of variations in local custom (fol. 49), this was the guideline in the majority of the cases in the series. The decisions of the Junta of the Treasury on December 22, 1787, and of the viceroyalty on June 23, 1789, specified that the legitimate sons of Indian men and White women would follow their father, while the illegitimate sons of White men with Indian women followed the mother. In a sense, it was true that a son raised by an Indian woman, but who was biologically Mestizo, might be closer to Indian than to White society. On the other hand, as noted above in case 120, the illegitimate son who was recognized and raised by his Spanish father, would certainly have had no problems with tribute collectors prior to the 1770s. In effect, it was precisely illegitimacy which formed the legal basis of decision-making on ethnic status in the 1770s and 1780s. The evidence on legitimacy is therefore necessarily the most oversimplified aspect of all the data: some of the cases described here as "legitimate" turned precisely on the question of whether they really were.

The quantification of the data poses problems in other respects, and the absence of firm occupational data for all cases is certainly a handicap. Although a Lockhart-style "Men of Quito" study may be somewhat beyond the possibilities of the documentation, the existence of a major series serves to prevent the evidence from being merely anecdotal. I would argue that this is one of the defects of an interesting collection of life stories on "Struggle and Survival in Colonial America," which shows the survival strategies of "ordinary people" in colonial Spanish (and North) America.[40] It is clear that the petitioners were a self-selected group, and the loose sheet which found its way into one of the lawsuits (14), is eloquent on the sufferings which a legal action could entail: delays, loss of money, and absence from home for those who attempted to bring an action from outlying areas (14, and also 96). Those who did bring an action were those who thought they could succeed, and there were certainly many others who did not bring actions, (or whose cases were not located) who were equally affected.

In view of these points, it is difficult to provide statistical answers to a number of relevant questions: Was it becoming more difficult to obtain a favorable decision from the law-courts after 1776? Can we consider the 200 and more petitioners brought before the law-courts after the late 1770s (or the 68 from Quito) to be a significant or a small total? It is certainly clear that in the fiscal climate of the late 1770s, more people were being turned down than prior to that date. Although it is not always clear how a case ended, the pre-1776 cases were successful, whereas a small but steady

---

40 D. G. Sweet and G. B. Nash, *Struggle and Survival in Colonial America*, (California, 1981).

minority of petitioners were turned down from the late 1770s onwards. The great flurry of law-suits in the late-1770s itself attests to increased official pressure, but we should not ignore one caveat, namely that some of the cases from the period before 1776 which we find in the series are there precisely because they succeeded, and are brought in evidence by their children, or grandchildren. Although those actually going before the tribunals were probably less than one percent of the total adult male population, the atmosphere of denunciations (99, 100 etc.), fear and evasion complements the evidence of a climate of repression around 1780.

It is argued that whatever the flexibility of official practice, it is clear that new groups were in reality being incorporated into the tributary population. Chapter 6 describes a major increase in the tributary population of the city at exactly the time the Mestizo petitions were being brought, and for a period for which there is no evidence of a sudden increase of the population. The rise in the number of tributaries suggests that the enormous income in tribute income at the same date [41]was not therefore simply a consequence of increased efficiency, but of a real widening of the tribute net. Case 116 includes the explicit testimony of Villalengua that in the face of variations in local custom he had "enumerated" the indeterminate

---

[41] Tribute income entering the Royal Treasury in Quito rose to an extraordinary degree:

1773	46,115	1776	52,032	1779	113,570	1782	112,880
1774	49,020	1777	41,678	1780	97,017	1783	106,410
1775	64,892	1778	51,050	1781	91,386		

Source: AGI Quito, 417, 418, 419, 420, 421. These figures are for the whole of the northern and central highlands, and changes in accounting procedure around 1779 do not appear to have been a major factor. Although tribute income stayed at between 100,000 and 150,000 *pesos* in the 1790s from this area, Royal officials regarded this as inadequate. The Audiencia, as a whole, produced 210,347 *pesos* in 1790, but this was argued to be a low total for a region with 60,000 Indians which allegedly ought to produce 260,000 *pesos*. The lack of specie made money payment difficult, and it is rather a mark of the efficiency of the reformed fiscal administration that the shortfall was so small. See ANC/B, Cartas de Contrabandos, Tomo XI, Carta del Contador General de Tributos de Quito, Quito, July 3, 1792, fols. 104–6; also for the difficulty of paying tribute in specie after the late 1770s, see the "Cedula Real del 5 de Octubre de 1776 sobre petición de los Indios que se les cobre el tributo como antes," doc. from ANH/Q Cédulas Reales, repr. in *Eugenio Espejo, Conciencia Crítica de su Epoca,* (various authors), (Universidad Católica, Quito, 1978), 48.

For evidence of the pressures to which Mestizos were subject, see Espejo's "Defensa de los curas de Riobamba" (1786), *Escritos,* Tomo III (Quito,1923), 8, where it is claimed that Mestizos have been forced into tribute payment in the region of Riobamba by the collector Barreto, while the better-off ones have had to pay 50 *pesos* clandestinely to avoid being classified as tribute-payers. In other words, the documentary proof (Espejo, the petitions) confirms the statistical data that there were new tribute paying groups despite relative official flexibility.

Mestizos, and the possibility that he counted them as Indian may help to explain the fact noted by Bromley for the Central Sierra that his enumeration uncovered more tributaries than the parallel imperial census.[42] In the case of Quito, the Villalengua enumeration gave a total of 2,944 Indian males and 3,674 females, compared with 2,615 Indian males and 3,495 Indian females in the 1781 census summary.[43] We can interpret the difference either in terms of the greater efficiency of Villalengua's efforts to identify Indian tributaries or, more particularly, the inclusion of these marginal Mestizos. The fact that the difference in number of males was slightly greater than that of females emphasizes the fiscal character of the Villalengua enumeration. In either case, it is difficult to believe that we can advance much closer quantitatively to the problem of either evasion or the number of "new" Indians, except to say that both undoubtedly existed.

Who were the "new" Indians? Obviously, from the point of view of Crown officials, the cholos were simply tax evaders, and greater efficiency was by definition a widening of the tribute net. The "poor Whites" are interesting because they underline the relativity of socio-racial categories. Francisco Binuesa is obliged by poverty to work as a laborer on an hacienda and finds that downward social mobility is accompanied by a weakening of his ethnic status (241; see also, 177). In the atmosphere of denunciations, some who were probably Mestizo were reclassified. Although smaller categories than the cholos, two other groups need to be discussed, as they shed a revealing light on the process of ethnic classification (and reclassification) in the 1770s and 1780s:

FOUNDLINGS (HIJOS EXPÓSITOS) The foundlings represent a group, a section of which can be shown to have been directly threatened by incorporation into the Indian tributary population in the period of Bourbon fiscal reform. None of these cases arise before the late 1770s whereas after 1776, they form around ten percent of the total.[44] Clearly in pre-reform days, categories like this passed relatively easily into the non-tribute paying sector of the population, whereas after the 1770s, they were subject to official scrutiny. One tribute official had no doubt that this category was quite simply one of tribute fraud: "the Indians defraud ... the Treasury placing their children at the doors of their neighbors, or abandoning them entirely."(61).

The descriptions of how babies were found (118, 257) are particularly interesting in one respect, because they specify that the infants had been found with a paper indicating that it had already been baptized. Although in one sense this is confirmation that baptism was indeed a virtually universal practice, in another sense it suggests that some caution is in order before

---

42 Bromley, *Urban Growth and Decline*, 151.
43 AGI Quito 381; ANC/B Hacienda Real, Varios No. 2893, "Censos del Ecuador."
44 23 cases: 61, 64, 78, 97, 103, 114, 115, 118, 128, 129, 137, 170, 174, 190, 221, 229, 237, 238, 239, 241, 243, 248, 257.

using the hijos expósitos as a clear index to periods of economic difficulty.⁴⁵ In Quito, many babies were being baptized and only then abandoned, and these baptisms would not then presumably reappear in the registers. The fiscal in case 221 specifies the inexactitude of the classification of the different types of non-legitimate children. The essential correlation of the proportion of hijos expósitos with periods of economic crisis may well be correct, but this evidence suggests that our figures for foundlings are often minimum rather than maximum estimates, and that foundlings may well have been a far more considerable presence in Spanish American society than has generally been argued.

A high proportion of both illegitimate children and foundlings was noted for Santa Bárbara in the previous chapter, and there are other indices to indicate a high rate of abandoned children in Quito. In 1765, a period of dearth, epidemic and rebellion, 24.5 percent of baptisms in the book reserved for Whites were foundlings, 59 percent being legitimate. Comparing this with the figures in the same register for the early nineteenth century, admittedly at a time when the category of White had become more socially exclusive, suggests that this was indeed a large total, and a small point to be taken into account in relation to the socio-economic background of the Quito rebellion.⁴⁶ At the same period, the proportion of abandoned children in the book reserved for Indians, Mestizos and Mulatos was much lower, only 7.8 percent of the total although in view of the official's comments noted above about the difficulty of separating hijos expósitos from illegitimate children, we should perhaps pay attention to the rate of "natural children" *(hijos naturales)*, which was high at 30.8 percent. Were Indian and Mestizo children being left at White doors as the official cited above obviously believed? In other words, did the placing of foundlings at the door of Spanish households, keep the total of Indian and Mestizo hijos expósitos remarkably low?

During the law-suits differing views were expressed on this point (compare 239 to 257); there was sometimes the assumption that children belonged to the same race as the doors they were left at (170). In any case, the courts were not greatly influenced by this point, and the foundlings were the one category decided essentially on the grounds of physiognomy;

---

[45] The possibility of using *expósitos* as an index to times of dearth etc. has been noted by a number of historical demographers. See E. Malvido, "El abandono de los hijos—una forma de control del tamaño de la familia y del trabajo indígena—Tula (1683–1730)," *Historia Mexicana*, 4, vol. XXIX, (1980), 521-561. For a general model of parish demographics, see N. D. Cook, "La población de la parroquia de Yanahuara, 1738–47: un modelo para el estudio de las parroquias coloniales peruanas," in *Collaguas 1*, (ed. F. Pease, Lima, 1977), 13–34. For the documentation on Mexican *expósitos*, see "Expósitos e Hidalgos, la polarización social de la Nueva España," *Boletín del Archivo General de la Nación, Mexico*: Tercera Serie, Tomo V, Num. 2 (16), (1981), 3–34.

[46] See J. Moreno Egas, *Vecinos de la Catedral de Quito Bautizados entre 1801 y 1831*, (Quito, 1984). The proportion rarely rose above 10 percent during that period.

the foundling was asked to make a personal appearance so that the court could judge his appearance. Whatever the actual racial origin of the foundling, there can be little question that the role of the Spanish household served as a transitional stage in his assimilation into White society. The case of Antonio de Ortuño above can be cited as a similar example of the acculturating role of the Spanish household. It is clear from surviving civil lawsuits, that hijos expósitos had a status which was often distinct from that of servant, and could reach that of adopted child. Actions with blood relatives over inheritances underline the ambiguity of this category.[47] In this respect, it is interesting to note the claims to hidalguía of the hijos expósitos; (cases 64, 78, 115, 118, 170, and 238) all had the name Hidalgo or were alleged to have taken it.

THE OFFSPRING OF SPANIARDS AND CACICAS The series of petitions uncovers another special group which may be briefly noted. During the mid-colonial period, matrimonial alliances between Spaniards and cacicas permitted the White or Mestizo to integrate himself as an "intruder" into positions of authority within the Indian communities, and was also a factor which was ultimately to play an important role in the transfer of land from Indian to Spanish hands.[48] This was not a process which stopped in the eighteenth century, but the series does allow us to take stock of some of its unforeseen consequences in the late-colonial period.

The offspring of Spaniards and cacicas appear relatively frequently in the series, and it is probable that many of those classified here as the children of Spaniards and Indians belong to this category. Those petitioners with clear cacique links were included in some 21 cases.[49] This was by no means a new category, and indeed the earliest examples tend to be examples of this process (1, 3 etc.). There was, nevertheless, certainly a

---

47 These law-suits are relatively numerous in the section Hijos Expósitos y Naturales of the ANH/Q. The same point can be made through the evidence of testaments in the notaries; see, for example, ANH/Q 1 Not. vol. 246, fols. 67–69, for the testament of Doña María Romero: "Declaro que desde que nació Pedro Ponse, lo he criado a mis espensas, por havermelo botado, a las Puertas de mi cassa, y como a hijo, que hubiera nacido de mis entrañas, lo he querido manteniendolo con mi pobreza ..." (May 14, 1728).

48 For a brief mention of this point see the Introduction above. For land transfer see C. Borchart de Moreno, "Composiciones de tierras en el valle de los Chillos a finales del siglo XVII: una contribución a la historia agraria de la Audiencia de Quito," *Cultura, Revista del Banco Central del Ecuador*, (Quito), 5 (1980), 139–178; and "La transferencia de la propiedad agraria indígena en el corregimiento de Quito, hasta finales del siglo XVII," *Caravelle: Cahiers du Monde Hispanique et Luso-Brésilien*, 34 (1980), 5–19.

49 Around 8 percent of the total, although probably in reality somewhat greater; they were cases: 1, 2, 3, 9, 19, 32, 54, 56, 74, 90, 93, 96, 105, 106, 124, 145, 171, 184, 188, 191, 195. One may also take note of 116 for the rarer example of a *cacique* married to a white.

sense in which the fiscal reforms of the late 1770s may have had the long-term effect of leveling out the distinctions within Indian society, both by assuming a more direct control of tribute collection, and partly bypassing the caciques, and by gradually imposing uniform criteria of tribute eligibility. Although this meant that the caciques and their eldest sons continued to be exempt, association with the cacique class (which was also association with nobility) was not a decisive advantage, although it might be adduced as an additional argument (54, 145). In other words, noble Indian ancestry as such provided no special protection by the late 1770s, unless the petitioner could validate his claim on other grounds.

"Vile and Mechanical Offices"

One of the repeated refrains in the documentation is that the petitioner and his family have never "exercised the offices which belong to Indians" (107). The association of occupation with ethnicity is so strong that some people seem to have been apprehended largely because of their occupation, these exceptions to caste-like distinctions therefore in certain measure proving the rule (2, 241). What were the "offices" of Indians? To answer that question, the evidence of the petitions can be somewhat misleading, because all the cases are by definition the marginal ones, and it is therefore appropriate to turn to the demographic evidence which is not affected in the same way. The only known full house-to-house census for eighteenth-century Quito, providing relatively complete ethnic and occupational data is the padrón of Santa Bárbara parish in 1768.

With regard to the data in Table 7.1, it is appropriate to stress that, although socially mixed, Santa Bárbara was an elite parish, and the economic activities of the popular sectors were more oriented around elite consumption and requirements than they would have been in San Roque, San Sebastián or San Blas. The occupational data are certainly different from the other parishes to judge from the padrones of the Indian population in 1733. The fact that tailors were White in Santa Bárbara is derived essentially from the parish's elite character. In San Roque, for example, we find Indian tailors serving the more popular sectors in 1733.[50] In a parish like San Roque, tailoring was probably more clearly linked to weaving which the padrón of Santa Bárbara confirms to be an exclusively Indian activity. The data on the small-scale production for popular consumption in Table 7.1 are more mixed, but since this was a more female activity, ethnic classification is less reliable for the reasons given in previous chapters.

---

[50] These *padrones* were cited by Tyrer, "The Demographic and Economic History," 410, and have been reclassified in the boxes of Indígenas 46, 47, 48, 49 of the ANH/Q. Tyrer calculated six tailors for the whole of the city, and I counted six and one "sastre y tratante" for the parish of San Roque alone, so it is clear that the Indian tailors were concentrated in this parish.

TABLE 7.1 OCCUPATIONAL AND SOCIO-RACIAL CLASSIFICATION: THE PARISH OF SANTA BÁRBARA, QUITO, 1768

	ETHNIC CLASSIFICATION		
Occupations	**Indian**	**White***	**Don****
PRODUCTION FOR INDIAN/POPULAR CONSUMPTION			
Weaver *(tejedor)* [a]	11	—	—
Producer, maize beer *(chichero)*	7	2	—
Fireworks-maker *(cohetero)* [b]	—	(1)[b]	—
Pot-maker/dealer *(ollero)* [c]	—	(8)[c]	—
FOOD/MARKET			
Baker *(panadera)* [d]	—	1	—
Market-woman *(gatera)* [e]	1	—	—
Market-woman, red pepper *(vendedora ají)* [f]	1	—	—
Street-seller *(vendedor, calle)* [g]	—	1 Mestizo	—
Butcher *(carnicera)* [h]	1	—	—
Fruit-seller *(frutero)* [i]	2	—	—
Sugar dealer *(tratante azucarero)*	1	—	—
Chagro [j]	1	2, & 2 mulatas	—
SERVICES TO WHITE SOCIETY			
Mason *(albañil)*	2	—	—
House-servant *(huasicama)*	1	—	—
Servants *(sirvientes/criados)*	—	45+	—
Town crier *(pregonero)*	1	—	—
Coachman *(reatero)*	1	2	—
Clothes-presser *(prensadora)*	—	1	—
Barber/minor surgeon *(barbero)* [k]	6	—	—
SERVICES TO THE CHURCH			
Chorister *(cantor)*	1	—	—
Sacristan *(sacristán)*	1	2	—

*"White" means unspecified non-Indians and non-Blacks who did not have the title "Don," it thus includes Mestizos.

** The use of the title "Don" is here taken to denote upper-class status, although this is by no means an exact category. Indians are those specified as such, although a number of others (especially women) with Indian names may also have been so. It may be stressed that the above are data on a partly elite parish, and occupational categories were therefore largely oriented around White consumption and requirements. Occupational data in this padrón are incomplete.

	ETHNIC CLASSIFICATION		
Occupations	Indian	White	Don
ARTISANS			
Leather			
Cobbler *(zapatero)*	9	1	—
Artisan, damask *(damasquero)*	1	—	—
Saddle-maker *(sillero)*	—	2	—
Furniture/Construction			
Carpenter, cabinet-maker *(carpintero)*	3	3	—
Varnisher *(barnizador)*	1	—	—
Clothing			
Embroiderer *(bordador)*	2	1	—
Tailor *(sastre)* [m]	2	15	—
Hat-maker *(sombrerero)*	—	3	—
Button-maker *(botonero)*	1	—	—
Specialized production			
Guitar-maker *(guitarrero)*	—	1	—
Lantern-maker *(farolero)*	—	1	—
Cigar-maker *(cigarrero)*	—	1	—
Jewelry/ Metal			
Crucifix-maker *(crucero)*	—	1	—
Rosary-maker *(rosariero)*	—	1	—
Blacksmith *(herrero)*	—	7	—
Silver-smith *(platero)*	—	3	—
Artists			
Musician *(músico)*	—	2	—
Painter *(pintor)*	—	1	1
COMMERCE[n]			
Chagro: *see Food/Market*			
Pulpero [o]	1	6	—
Monopolist *(estanquero)* [p]	1	7	—
Merchant *(mercader)*	—	1	4
CHURCH			
Priest *(curas, presbíteros)*	—	8	—
Obrero? [q]	—	1	—

Continues

| | ETHNIC CLASSIFICATION | | |
Occupations	Indian	White	Don
OFFICIALS, LIBERAL PROFESSIONS			
Scribe *(plumario)*	—	1	2
Notary *(notario)*	—	—	1
Lawyer *(abogado)*	—	—	1
Military Officer *(militares)*	—	—	5
Royal Officials *(funcionarios Reales)*	—	5	—
LAND-OWNERS/USERS[f]			
Farmer *(labrador, chacarero)*	—	5	1
" *(granjero)*	—	—	1
Sugar-producer *(azucarero)*	—	—	1

Source: based on the "Padrón de Santa Bárbara en 1768," AM/Q published in: *Museo Histórico* (Quito), 56 (1978), 93–122.

SOURCE NOTES:

a   These weavers are placed in this category, because the absence of textile specialization (tintorero, hilador, etc.) suggests they were involved in small-scale domestic production, rather than employed in workshops. There were probably more independent weavers in the more lower-class parishes than in Santa Bárbara, weaving cotton cloth for trousers and woolen *ponchos* for Indian clothing.

b   This cohetero has an Indian name although he is not identified as such. See the portrait in: *Ecuador Pintoresco. Acuarelas de J. Pinto*, (Barcelona–Quito, 1977), Illustration 1 (1901). Such later pictorial sources often provide the only non-census data on some of the more popular occupations, which generally escape the notarial records. Fireworks were an essential part of Indian festivals, (as well as eighteenth-century riots).

c   Five had no specified surnames, and may have been Indian (or perhaps, more strictly cholo?); four of the eight were women. Indian women involved in small-scale commercial activity were classified less rigidly than men, as non-tribute-payers. The *olleros* were all near the slaughterhouse where there was water from the *quebrada*.

d   *Panadero de Quito* in *Ecuador Pintoresco*. Ill. 9.

e   "En quichua, mercado es ccatu, vocablo que también se vulgarizó, así en Quito como en el Perú propio, en la forma ridícula de gato," *RGI*, II, 220, note 1.

f   Portrait in the collection Castro y Velázquez, *Guayaquil*, number 22. (Nineteenth century *costumbrista* (customs) paintings). *Ají* was often consumed with *chicha*, and formed a key part of the Indian diet see W. Stevenson, *A historical and descriptive narrative*, vol. 2, 315.

g   Explicitly Mestizo, whereas nearly all poor non-Indians were not classified in ethnic terms, i. e. the street-seller did not have a fixed place in a hierarchical society, and this classification was a value-judgment on him.

h   Collection Castro y Velázquez, Guayaquil, number 85.

i   *Acuarelas,* Ilustr. 32 (1900). *Imágenes del Ecuador del Siglo XIX, Juan Agustín Guerrero,* (Quito, 1981), 58.

j   Women. Chagro, deriv. quichua, *chagra,* field; "a shop in which is sold different grains, bread and other foodstuffs, which they call chagro, for the provision of poor people" ("una tienda en que haze vender diferentes granos, Pan y otros comestibles ... que llaman chagro, para el abasto de la gente pobre" (ANH/Q Carn. y Pulp. 2: Doc. 1760–V–23, fol. 1).

k   See Chapter 4. These barbers have Spanish surnames, which reinforces the point that this was a highly acculturated Indian occupation.

l   67 artisans, a significant artisanal production for White consumption, and urban tastes, but in a parish with a population of 2,757. Whether this is considered a large or a small total depends of course on the degree of parish specialization in artisanal production, whether Santa Bárbara's artisans were also supplying the Cathedral parish, or whether popular parishes such as San Roque were supplying the city as a whole, including a relatively White parish like Santa Bárbara. Only the localization of similar padrones for the other parishes could answer this question.

m   In Santa Bárbara in 1768, the tailors were overwhelmingly White, and the two Indians had Spanish names. On the other hand, the padrones of 1733, cited in the text, revealed 7 Indian *sastres* in San Roque, but apparently none in the surviving padrones for the other parishes. This occupation was obviously "whiter" in an elite parish than in San Roque, where the tailors were supplying poor quality products to the popular sectors, and where it may have been more closely linked to weaving activity.

n   Four people involved in commerce had dual occupations (p. 94, barber/pulpero, sombrerero/pulpero; (p. 96) albañil/chichero; (p. 116) estanquero/carpintero). Furthermore, commercial activity was certainly not restricted to those in this category (or food-market above), as many of the above artisans also commercialized their products through the tiendas which they owned or rented.

o   Pulperos owned or rented licensed retail outlets for knives, cheese, alcohol, etc. Some pulperos converted to chagro in economic difficulties (see Chapter 5).

p   The estanco was notably the brandy monopoly, but tobacco, playing cards and official paper *(papel sellado)* were also state monopolies.

q   Probably a *demandero* (or alms collector) for the church rather than a manual laborer, in view of the ethnic classification. In *Acuarelas,* and in *Imágenes,* 98, he is represented as a poor White.

r   Many of the most important landowners were resident in the El Sagrario parish, not Santa Bárbara.

The padrón of Santa Bárbara confirms the descriptions of Jorge Juan and Antonio de Ulloa in the 1740s and Stevenson in the early nineteenth century with regard to ethnic classification. According to Juan and Ulloa, the shoemakers, masons, weavers, and barbers were all Indian, the barbers constituting the most elite acculturated group. Mestizos were picked out for their talent as silversmiths, painters, and sculptors, the Quiteño school of painters being one of the most celebrated in Spanish America.[51] Stevenson's account follows Juan and Ulloa, and may have been partly inspired by them, but he incorporates material from his own experiences:

> Indians, both men and women, are of a low stature, well proportioned, very muscular and strong; they bear a general resemblance to the Indians in Peru, but they are more subject to their masters. Those that are employed in the city are household servants, in which capacity they are very useful, partly on account of the equanimity of their temper and their blind submission to their masters ... They are capable of supporting very heavy burdens; a man will carry on his back during the greater part of the day a large earthen jar holding from twelve to sixteen gallons of water ... The Indian women who employ themselves in bringing from the surrounding villages any produce to the market at Quito, carry their burdens in the same manner as the men. I have often seen them so covered with a cargo of brushwood, lucern, green barley, or other light bulky articles, that the load seemed to move along of itself, the carrier being completely enveloped. Many Indians in the city become butchers, weavers, shoemakers, &c. ... Some of the Indians are barbers and manage the razor with the greatest dexterity.[52]

The Santa Bárbara padrón confirms that the shoemakers, masons, weavers, and barbers were Indian occupations, with just one shoemaker out of ten apparently being Mestizo. Stevenson's account stresses the association of Indians with domestic service and with carrying, an "office" which was so closely associated with Indian ethnic status, that a Mestizo was picked up by the tribute collectors for exercising it (see case 2 above). His account also reminds us that a padrón of one urban parish does not provide an adequate delineation of the social characteristics of the city as it neglects the interaction of the city with its rural district, an interaction which was stressed in Chapter 5. In general, the Quito evidence shows an extremely high correlation of ethnicity and class/occupational criteria. Along with manual labor which was exclusively Indian, the "vile and mechanical offices" were largely the artisan occupations which occupied the same place in sixteenth century Spanish society. In this sense, urban Quito continued to be a colonial society, and one which maintained the distinctions and notions of honor which were characteristic of Medieval Castile. The popular strata was as highly imbued with the Castilian ideal of office as an expression of honor as any other strata in colonial society, and perhaps

---

[51] Juan and Ulloa, *Relación Histórica*, 365–66.
[52] Stevenson, *A Historical and Descriptive Narrative*, 298–300.

even more so because it was this which marked them off from the allegedly inferior Indian society:

- "He was a musician for the Church ... and has therefore always been esteemed to be a Mestizo" (244).
- "Mestizos of good color ... They have never occupied offices of Indians" (251).

"Indians Dressed as Spaniards": The Urban Center as an Agent of Acculturation

Although the demographic evidence might suggest a fairly rigid system of social stratification, the evidence of the Declarations suggests that this is too static a view. Mörner's argument for colonial elites that "social mobility or circulation within the established structures is far more striking than structural change"[53] seems to me entirely applicable to the lower strata in colonial quiteño society. Despite the city's structural immobility, there is ample evidence of considerable fluidity in the functioning of what is often oversimplified as a caste system.

As one petitioner put it, "there is nothing more ordinary than dark Spaniards and extremely White mulatos, who in places far from their patrias can easily deny their plebeian origin"(case 74). The five hundred or more cholos apprehended in the city in the early 1760s (61) attests to a hidden migration to the city of Indians who passed into the Spanish world and therefore testifies to one of the mechanisms of social mobility in colonial society.[54] These cholos do not appear in the censuses, so it is difficult to quantify them: the demographic evidence suggests that the Indian population of the city was undergoing a decline relative to the total population and ethnic transformation may have played some role in this. It is equally clear that the city was not expanding, and that its capacity to absorb new immigrants was limited in the late-colonial period. The real agent of social mobility and ethnic change was to be the great migration to the coast in the nineteenth century.

The violinist Hidalgo, (64) certainly provides us with the prototype of one kind of social climber. A change of surname formed one indispensable element, but often enough there would be several changes of surname, and confusion as to what the real one was, a reminder that this was inherently less fixed in colonial society than it is today. One petitioner changed his name "because I felt like it" (109), while another explicitly builds his defense on the fact that he does not have a name like those of the Indian "nation" (166). One of the very few Indian surnames in this series did not

---

[53] M. Mörner, "Economic Factors and Stratification," *HAHR*, 63 (1983), 368.
[54] Such hidden migrants are mentioned in David J. Robinson (ed.), *Migration in Colonial Spanish America* (Cambridge, 1991), Introduction.

fail to give its holder problems (198). Clothing formed another essential element: a loose vest of fine blue cloth and a pair of shoes would make an Indian unrecognizable as such, as many cases testify. The petition of Hidalgo is also interesting because it also allows us into the world of the street-wise lower strata, those living off their wits who do not often appear in the documentation. Lisbôa, visiting Quito in the nineteenth century was struck by the number of beggars, and there were certainly many in the eighteenth century.[55] This substratum of Quito society lay beyond the usual criteria of ethnicity, as the periodic attempts to "enumerate" and fix these groups in the more organized structure of (Indian) society clearly shows.[56]

The transforming role of the urban center is one of the most striking features of the documentation. Although this initially suggested an analysis along the lines of the medieval German city in which "city air" was creating "freemen," (i. e. providing the anonymity which allowed Indians to escape tribute), this is by no means the only perspective, not least because the demographic evidence cited above does not fully support it. Reading the documentation closely, what is striking is the extent to which a city of 25,000 and divided into several smaller barrio-villages was not in fact an anonymous entity. Witnesses stress that they know X "because he lives in the same barrio" (108, 126). Vicente Sisneros testifies that "as a Quiteño he knows almost all the people in the city" (109). Prior to the 1770s a forastero could and (probably did) escape tribute obligations as easily by moving to another rural area as he did by moving to an urban center.[57] If the urban cholo succeeded in evading the tribute collectors, he was nevertheless familiar enough to his neighbors and did not blur automatically into a homogeneous mass with the rest of the urban population. For evidence of this, there are the ethnic tensions between "pure" Mestizos and the new arrivals, who were perceived as a danger which might pull the entire Mestizo population into the tribute paying class (see Chapter 8). Nor in a wider sense, is it necessarily best to approach ethnicity in terms of a linear advance from Indian to White society; the "Spaniards dressed as Indians," the Mestizos who are culturally very close to Indian society, shed an interesting counter-light on colonial society. Even urban society had its own equivalents to the "Spaniards dressed as Indians" like Lyman Johnson's Mestizo shoemaker in Buenos Aires who pretended to be an Indian and became an officer in the militia reserved for the Indians.[58] In Chapter 5, Felisiana de Mora was mentioned, the Mestiza who was alleged to have pretended to be Indian to avail herself of the services of the

---

55 M. R. Lisbôa, *Relação de uma viagem a Venezuela, Nova Granada, e Ecuador,* (Bruxelles, 1866), 357. *GS,* 2, 953, for an early eighteenth-century testimony.

56 For example AGI Quito 248 "Yndice de los autos," decree November 13, 1789, that the *Alcaldes de barrios* should enumerate the "vagos, borrachos y malentendidos."

57 See Minchom, "The making of a white province," *passim.*

58 L. L. Johnson, "Francisco Baquero" in *Struggle and Survival,* 86–101, but especially 91, 95.

Protector of the Indians. There were many ways of "playing the system" in colonial society.

The tightening up of custom and the pressure on part of the lower Mestizo class in the 1770s and 1780s only throws into relief the fluidity of colonial society prior to that date. Caste was not functioning as a legally sanctioned system, essentially because the mechanisms which kept it in place, notably tribute collection, were not of a type or efficiency to operate with any rigidity. Migration was probably the simplest and the most important device for changing ethnic or tax status, both between Indian and White society, and within the Indian population itself by means of the separate tax-category of the *Corona Real*.[59] Although Quito society was in this sense quite flexible, the actual degree of movement across ethnic frontiers is quite a different question. The Declarations of Mestizo show that this movement existed, but its scale is harder to assess. The demographic evidence suggests that although real, it was never of an order to substantially modify Quito's social structure which remained conservative, inward-looking. In Chapter 4, we already noted the existence of an urban confraternity for acculturated Indians which seems to have fulfilled the same role throughout the colonial period.

A Parallel Life: The Ethnic Background of Eugenio de Santa Cruz y Espejo

The career of Eugenio Espejo, the Enlightenment propagandist whose polemical career had him in jail only a few days before his death in 1795, links the socio-racial questions of this chapter with the discussion of disorder and rebellion which follows. On the one hand, his career has been taken as symptomatic of the tensions generated by the caste system in the late-colonial period in which a talented Mestizo ran up against the barriers of colonial society.[60] His life and writings have also been viewed as a manifestation of Creole consciousness which anticipated the Independence movements of the early nineteenth century. Indeed in his dual role as a prominent Mestizo figure and precursor of Independence (and therefore, with later attempts to forge a distinctive national identity, doubly Ecuadorian "before the letter") he has attracted an attention only matched or surpassed in Ecuadorian history by the highly controversial and more immediately imposing figures of García Moreno, the President who dominated Ecuador

---

[59] Minchom, "The making of a white province," 28–35.
[60] M. Mörner, *Race mixture in the History of Latin America* (Boston, 1967). *La mezcla de razas en la historia de América Latina*, (Buenos Aires, 1969), 83. Mörner calls him a "zambo" because of his possible African ancestry.

in the 1860s and early 1870s, and Eloy Alfaro who presided over the Liberal revolution at the end of the nineteenth century.[61]

What are particularly interesting aspects of the career of Espejo are the parallels and contrasts it offers with the humbler Mestizo petitioners caught up in litigation in the late eighteenth century. According to his biographers, who have stressed his humble Mestizo extraction, Eugenio Espejo was born in Quito in 1747 to a father, originally called "Chusic," who was an Indian from Cajamarca and to a mother who may have been a Mestiza or free Mulata.[62] We may now add, on the evidence of this chapter, that in some regions of the Audiencia this could theoretically have made Espejo a tribute-paying Indian. Yet during his lifetime Dr. Don Eugenio de Santa Cruz y Espejo, as he was later to style himself, became a doctor and later Quito's first public librarian, publishing a pioneering "journal" and moving in important aristocratic circles prior to his final imprisonment and death (recorded in the register for "Mestizos") in 1795. Here, on the face of it, was an example of vertiginous social mobility worthy of a Balzac hero forcing his way into salon society on nothing but charm and talent: his biographers have given prominence to this dimension and one study, for example, was entitled "The Mestizo who overcame prejudice."[63] Looking more closely at Espejo's background, however, with the optic provided by other socio-racial documentation, allows us to see that the conventional picture is misleading.

It is worth recalling, as a preliminary caveat, that a known admixture of non-European blood did not preclude membership of established White society. By the eighteenth century this was perhaps merely a recognition that the evolution of colonial society had outstripped racial sensitivities. At higher levels of society, recent non-European blood could nevertheless be brought into play to block a marriage, while racial insult was a weapon to be used against a segment of White society from the popular strata upwards, particularly those with alleged part-African ancestry like Espejo.[64] The series of polemics in which Espejo was involved throughout his career earned him more than enough enemies for rumors to be floated and his background exposed to critical scrutiny. When Espejo accused Doña Maria Chiriboga of adultery in Riobamba in 1787 it is hardly

---

[61] See the entries in R. E. Norris, *Guía bibliográfica para el estudio de la Historia Ecuatoriana* (Austin, 1978). For Espejo as a precursor in Latin America's movement for liberation see A. V. Efimov, *Ecuador* (Moscow, 1963), 153.

[62] P. Astuto, "Eugenio Espejo: A man of the Enlightenment in Ecuador," *Revista de Historia de América*, 44 (1957), 370–371. Isaac J. Barrera, *Quito Colonial. Siglo XVIII, comienzos del siglo XIX.* (Quito, 1922), 109.

[63] M. Albornoz, "El mestizo que venció los prejuicios," *Revista Nacional de Cultura* (Caracas), 7, 48 (1945), 63-75.

[64] See the interesting article by J. Jaramillo Uribe, "Mestizaje y diferenciación en el Nuevo Reino de Granada en la Segunda mitad del siglo xviii," *Anuario Colombiano de Historia y de la Cultura*, 2 (1965), 21-48.

surprising that he himself should be tarred as a Mestizo.⁶⁵ Polemics such as this, however, expose the cracks in Creole society: what they reveal may indeed be accurate, but the information provided is of a selective and highly charged type which has wrongly been assimilated raw into social categorization. Unlike the "Declaration of Mestizo" lawsuits they provide only half the picture, the accusation without the defense, because the gap between Espejo's birth and his aristocratic pretensions has been too extreme for the latter to be taken as a corrective.

The testimony which appears to have carried most weight in establishing Espejo as the "poor Mestizo" is that of the family's former patron, the Spanish-born Bethlemite Fray Josef del Rosario during the lawsuit of 1787. According to Fray Josef, a well-placed, if now hostile, witness:

> "He knew the grandfather of Eugenio Espejo, an Indian who worked in his convent in the material construction of the Church as a stone-mason; that he can't remember his name, only his surname which was the "national" [i. e. Indian] one of Chusic, but he was generally known as Cruz, a surname which the Indians are fond of. That he wore a cape, and not cotton or an Indian shirt; that this was the father of Luis, that he doesn't know how he came to be called Espejo, but he was known as Benites ... [possibly because of his godfather] ... That the said Luis came to this city [Quito] as the servant of the informant [Fray Josef] at the age of fourteen or fifteen and he wore shoes and was dressed in the normal way; That he was married in this city to Cathalina So-and-so, mother of Eugenio, who was reputed to be a mestiza or a mulata, from whom came Eugenio in the quality of cholo or zambaygo with respect to his father and grandfather having been Indians." [After signing his declaration Fray Josef added for good measure that Chusic meant Lechusa (owl).]⁶⁶

With this biographical data we are on familiar ground, that of the socio-racial litigation of this chapter, with similar criteria being used to assign ethnicity: name, clothing, occupation, public opinion. As with the cases of "Declaration of Mestizo," the transition across ethnic boundaries was here too reflected in the abundance and confusion of surnames (Chusic, Cruz, Benites, Espejo), the characteristic so marked that it had led to the epithet for the Mestizo of chalashca, or name-collector. Other elements, the church and geographical displacement as agents of mobility, were also present. Fray Josef's testimony clearly provides a classic account of socio-cultural mobility over three generations.

---

65   ANC/B Miscelánea de la Colonia 77, fol. 510ff. "Petición de Doña Maria Chiriboga en que le acusa al Dr Eugenio Espejo por haverle injuriado gravamente su honor" Quito, November 27, 1787 (copy March 8, 1789).

66   ANC/B Miscelánea de la Colonia 77, fol. 510ff. "Petición de Doña Maria Chiriboga"; "Ynforme del Reverendo Padre F. Josef del Rosario, Religioso Betlemitico" (Quito, December 2, 1787), fol. 512.

In the secondary literature, however, these changes have been telescoped into Eugenio's lifetime. Fray Josef's account specifies that both father and grandfather were Indian, but all the other evidence suggests that with regard to Eugenio's father, Luis, this was a hostile interpretation based on the narrowly racial meaning of "Indian," (or more exactly, the narrow definition as one of Indian parentage). In fact, it is clear from Fray Josef's account that Espejo's grandfather was already an acculturated Indian wearing Spanish-influenced dress and with some contact with the church through his occupation as stone-mason, while the essential change from a Quechua name (Chusic) to an acculturated one (Cruz) took place during his lifetime. Eugenio's paternal grandmother had a traditional Spanish name, Doña Antonia Ruiz, according to Luis' testament, though this could well have been a later attempt by Luis to improve his parentage. It is not clear that Luis, Eugenio's father, "changed his name to Benítez."[67] It seems more likely that he was "given" to the church, and could have been baptized with some variation of Luis Benítez: Fray Josef seems to consider that his name was connected with that of his godfather the priest and vicar of Cajamarca, Doctor Don Luis Benites de la Torre. This hypothesis, made plausible by his father's professional contacts with the church, and his own early accompaniment of Fray Josef to Quito at the age of fourteen or fifteen, would imply that the essential leap into church and therefore non-Indian society had been made at birth or in infancy. The cases above, of foundlings in a White household, legally accepted as non-Indian, provides an analogous secular example of the way full absorption into Spanish culture eased the ethnic transition out of the Indian population.

Other evidence concerning Espejo's father confirms that in all but strictly racial terms he maintained himself at a considerable distance from the tributary Indian population. When he was taken to Quito it was as Fray Josef's "servant," which led to hospital work and the position of administrator/surgeon and it was here, according to Astuto[68], that Eugenio could observe the inadequacies of the medical practice of his day. The council minutes record proceedings against Luis de Santa Cruz y Espejo himself for the death of one of his patients.[69] Perhaps more revealing, however, was the simultaneous action against the barber Vicente for his medical and surgical work, which suggests that tighter controls were leading to the rise of the status of the medical profession as a whole. Data are available on Luis' wealth from his testament in 1778 and related documentation. While the problem with this material is that it reflects what is accumulated over a lifetime—and does not necessarily establish Luis' status during Eugenio's formative years—there are nevertheless indications of his earlier situation. We learn that no dowry was given at his wedding

---

[67] Astuto, "Eugenio Espejo," 371.

[68] *Ibid.*

[69] AM/Q, LCQ, May 29, 1767, fol. 23r; July 24, 1767, fol. 23.

If the names given here alongside those used in the testaments of Espejo and his father are tabulated we have a good picture of change over three generations:

Paternal Grandfather	Paternal Grandmother	Maternal Grandfather	Maternal Grandmother
ACCULTURATED INDIAN • Chusic / Cruz • Don Juan de la Cruz y Espejo	• Doña Antonia Ruiz	unknown	• Larraincar
Father		**Mother**	
• Espejo/Benites • Luis de la Cruz y Espejo *(own testimony)* • Don Luis Santa Cruz y Espejo • Luis de Santa Cruz y Espejo		• Cathalina de tal (so and so) • Doña Cathalina Aldaz y Larrayncar • Doña María Catalina Larraincar	
Espejo			
• Eugenio Espejo • Dr. Don Eugenio de la Cruz y Espejo • Dr. Don Francisco Xavier Eugenio Santa Cruz y Espejo			

(*Pseudonyms: Javier de Cía, Apéstegui y Perochena in "Nuevo Luciano"*)

Sources: ANC/B Miscelánea de la Colonia 77, "Petición de Da Maria Chiriboga" fol. 512; "Ynforme del Reverendo Padre Fray Josef del Rosario (Quito, December 2, 1787); ANH/Q 4 Not. (1776–78), fols. 147–149 Testamento de Luis de la Cruz y Espejo, November 9, 1778; ANH/Q 4 Not. (1794–7) fols. 456–57, 467. Testamento de Dr. Don Francisco Xavier Eugenio Santa Cruz y Espejo. December 23, 1795; LCQ/ AMQ, 24 Julio 1767; AHBC/Q Jijón y Caamaño vol. 2, fols. 88. "Nueva demanda puesta por el Dr. Dn Eugenio de Santa Cruz y Espejo."

because he "married poor" (Doña Cathalina in fact already had a natural child).[70] A more concrete piece of evidence is offered from 1766 when Espejo was not yet twenty. According to his testament, Luis placed the considerable sum of 1,000 pesos with the Procurator of the Jesuits, Marcos Bonilla, as a life censo on April 25, 1766 on which he then received the annual five percent interest. The Jesuits were already subject to the anti-Jesuit campaign which was to culminate in their order of expulsion and it is difficult to say whether local arrangements were being made in advance, and whether Luis really had this money; it clearly didn't come out of his

---

[70] ANH/Q 4 Not. (1776–78), Testamento de Luis de la Cruz y Espejo, fol. 148.

official salary of 50 pesos per year. There is other evidence of accumulated family wealth.[71]

According to Astuto, Espejo was to attempt to "shake off" his Mestizo background.[72] He requested recognition of *limpieza de sangre* claiming through his maternal grandmother a connection with Navarre (considered one of the noblest of Spanish regions) and would later show his certificate in 1791 when he wanted the position of librarian. Similarly, when he published the *Nuevo Luciano*, considered by Astuto to be an attack on Jesuit teaching, he did so under the rather grandiose and sarcastic pseudonym of Javier de Cía, Apéstegui y Perochena. It seems to me illogical to dismiss Espejo's claims, and follow only his enemies' accounts; there is no inherent reason why despite his other family origins, he should not also have had Navarre Spanish ancestry through his grandmother, which is the kind of contrast we find in the series of "Declarations of Mestizo." However, he may have overplayed his hand and opened up himself to counter-attack by the scale of his pretensions.

While the contrast between Espejo's origins and later career is less remarkable than traditionally presented, it remains nonetheless of great interest. A full account of Espejo's career and writing lies beyond the scope of this study, but the dependence on patrons is a recurring theme: he sought a dangerous upward mobility, based on the risks he took as polemicist for those who themselves chose to stay in the shadows. (See Chapter 8 for some episodes). If Espejo had kept his head low and enjoyed a traditional career as doctor, we would have had no knowledge of the "flaws" in his ancestry, which could have been papered over by genealogies and his low profile. Without denying his ultimately humble origins, or attempting to claim that his was a "typical" background, I would argue that it is exaggerated to label him "the son of an Indian from Cajamarca" in any analysis which is attentive to colonial socio-racial realities. The cases of "insults to honor," in which members of creole society had "flaws" in their ancestry thrown at them as insults by their enemies are analogous to the treatment received by Espejo, and show that his case was not unique.[73] All the usual documentary evidence of his later life and that of his relatives (the names given in testaments, property held etc.) are fairly typical of those of members of the middle ranks of Creole society. In other words, there was a sense in which Espejo was a "Mestizo" because he made enemies.

Espejo's recorded burial in the register for "mestizos, indios, negros y mulatos"[74] has figured largely in the biographies, but there has been little appreciation of the context, which makes this categorization less surprising.

---

71   *Ibid*. and AHBC/Q: Jijón y Caamaño vol. 2, 88ff. "Nueva demanda puesta por el Dr Don Eugenio de Santa Cruz y Espejo..."

72   Astuto, "Eugenio Espejo," 374.

73   J. Jaramillo Uribe, "Mestizaje y diferenciación" cited above; M. Minchom, "The making of a White province," includes a couple of examples.

74   Astuto, "Eugenio Espejo," 374.

In fact, my examination of the registers of El Sagrario, Quito, shows that from precisely 1795 onwards, there is a dramatic fall in "Spanish" baptisms. From a figure of around 120 White baptisms in 1795 the figure declines to only thirty or so a year from 1805 onwards. Thus there were only a quarter as many White babies being baptized in El Sagrario in 1805 as a decade earlier, which demonstrates an extraordinary trend towards social exclusiveness. In other words, Espejo was very far from being the only member of "respectable" Quito society to be excluded from White society at this period, even if his "trouble-making" did make him vulnerable. This point provides a chronological link with the tensions and alleged conspiracies of 1795 and allows us to interpret those tensions as a watershed after which the Quito aristocracy withdrew in on itself: in the intense period of social reaction in the Sagrario after 1795, "White" was practically made to be synonymous with "aristocratic."

How far does this evidence on Espejo's background support Mörner's description of a talented Mestizo running up against the barriers of caste society with all the ensuing tensions which were generated: "the humiliations individuals suffered in caste society"[75]? In the next Chapter I examine the tensions of the 1790s in which Espejo played a role, but here I would stress one sense in which I would argue exactly the opposite of Mörner's view. If we study Espejo's family over three generations what is remarkable is the fluidity of the pre-reform "caste" system which permitted their successful integration into early and mid-eighteenth century society. Even in the 1780s and early 1790s Espejo enjoyed access to wealthy Quito society, under a succession of patrons. Ironically, it was precisely on Espejo's death that a climate of reaction turned him into the "humble Mestizo" which he has remained.

In the light of the "Declarations of Mestizo" and other evidence (such as the absence of the category "Mestizo" in the official 1780s documentation), I would argue that the historiographical treatment of Espejo's life shows some of the problems the historiography of Spanish America has faced in coming to terms with its "Mestizos." In the treatment of Espejo's career, polemical evidence has not been treated cautiously enough and biological race and socio-racial classification have been assimilated and confused on the incorrect assumption that White and Mestizo were substantive and autonomous categories.

---

75 Mörner, *La mezcla de razas,* 83, retranslated from the Spanish.

Conclusion: The Indian/White Dichotomy in Ethnic Classification

The corpus of Declarations of Mestizo underlines the White/Indian borderline as the essential polarization in colonial society, one which can be traced back to the colonization as an inheritance of the Spanish preoccupation with "purity of blood" and the necessary separation of the races which precluded the "integration" of the concept of race mixture.[76] In rural society this polarization persists in the late twentieth century Northern Ecuadorian Andes where the line of demarcation is Indian/White ("runa/mishu" for the Indians and "indio/blanco" for the rural "Whites").[77] I found this dichotomy in colonial rural parish records, where the category "Mestizo" might be a negative value judgment on an individual, but where the essential categories in the registers were "Españoles" (including, for example, Blacks), and "Indios." I did come across the energetic rural parish priest of Tabacundo carefully classifying his flock into "Españoles, Montañeses, Mestizos" and (one) "Pardo,"[78] but this was in 1783 which may make it part of the wider late eighteenth-century attempt to discover "order" in chaos. In any case, few rural parish priests made this effort which meant one pressure less towards a complete and identifiable system of socio-racial classification.

We also find the Indian/White dichotomy in eighteenth-century urban society with its more complex social stratification. At the very highest levels of Quito society, I found a trend towards social exclusivity, indicated by the increasingly restrictive category of "White" in El Sagrario parish. However, the creation of a narrow social category of "White noble" only underlines the absence of a frontier between Whites and Mestizos by placing the rest of the White and Mestizo population in the single, undifferentiated category of non-Indian.

The Audiencia of Quito did not have the highly diversified racial classification depicted in the paintings of Mexican society,[79] and it is striking to observe how narrow was the vocabulary of the Audiencia of Quito for indicating socio-racial variations. The "rules of the game" may have been different for areas where the racial mix was more varied and there was a more substantial Black presence. Nevertheless, the Ecuadorian evidence should clearly be kept in mind by historians of Peru, where the "accident" or tactic of the inclusion of a separate Mestizo category in the censuses may have disguised similar realities. In theory, we must allow for the possibility that where, as in Peru, the category of "Mestizo" was

---

[76] C. Caillavet and M. Minchom," Le Métis Imaginaire: idéaux classificatoires et stratégies socio-raciales en Amérique Latine (XVIe–XXe siècle)," *L'Homme*, 122-124 (1992), 115-132.

[77] *Ibid.*

[78] AP/Tabacundo, Baptismal register for 1783.

[79] Mörner, *La mezcla de razas,* 78,109; however this provide an idealized picture.

recognized by the State, it could also have generated a corresponding identity, but the strength of the Mestizo petitioners' "Spanish" identity in the Audiencia of Quito makes this interpretation improbable. One way of testing the wider applicability of the colonial Ecuadorian evidence is to contrast it with the nineteenth-century evidence when tribute was reclassified as the "contribution" and the category of "Mestizo" was included in the censuses.

Caillavet and Minchom examined the data for a group of villages south of Quito in 1862 and found contradictions in the new classification of "Mestizo" which shows that the fundamental Indian-White dichotomy survived under the Republic.[80]

Thus the official category of Mestizo was very little used in either colonial or Republican Ecuador, and when it was this was in such varied forms that it can be considered a kind of fictitious category to be invented or reinvented by officials, ecclesiastics or outside observers, according to different criteria. I believe the Ecuadorian evidence has wider implications for the Spanish American social and demographic studies: when we find striking fluctuations in the population of the *castas*, we are likely to be rarely observing "real" change if we accept that, unlike the "pure" Indians, the Mestizos corresponded to no clearly established classificatory definition.[81]

---

[80] C. Caillavet and M. Minchom, "Le Métis Imaginaire," 115-132.

[81] For shifting categories in Loja, see Minchom, "The Making of a White Province," 23–39; and for the fluctuating Mestizo population of Durango in Mexico: Michael M. Swann, *Tierra Adentro: Settlement and Society in Colonial Durango*, (Boulder, 1982), 334.

Chapter 8

RELIGIOUS RIOTS AND CIVIL DISTURBANCES[1]

"Fuenteovejuna !
¡ Viva el rey Fernando!
¡ Mueran malos cristianos y traidores!"

Lope de Vega, *Fuenteovejuna*, Act III, Scene VII

The plebe, the amorphous lower social strata, took on a very real meaning for colonial administrators at moments of extreme social tension; they became the "vulgar and licentious plebe," prone to outbursts of drunken and irrational violence, easily led astray by troublemakers. Relatively structured patterns of behavior have been traced in what contemporaries and many historians thought of as the random violence of the mob. Since the 1970s, studies of popular movements in early modern Europe have emphasized that "popular violence is often the organized—and ritualized—expression of particular aims, and also that it has its own calendar, tending to occur at major festivals" dividing as to class oriented interpretations, and those based on community cohesion.[2] Once the

---

[1] The importance of the 1765 uprising in comparison to earlier disturbances is clear, but to avoid continuous repetition I have not tried to define the different disorders by using distinct terminology ("rebellion" as against "riot" etc.).

[2] P. Burke "The Virgin of the Carmine and the Revolt of the Masaniello," *Past and Present*, 99 (1983), 3. I found this article highly suggestive for the interpretation of Quito riots. For an overview of Andean rebellions, see L. G. Campbell, "Recent research on Andean Peasant Revolt, 1750–1820," *Latin American Research Review*, 14 (1979), 3–49. A. McFarlane shows that many of the insights of European historiography can be extended to Latin America: "Civil Disorders and Popular Protests in Late Colonial New Granada," *HAHR*, 64 (1984), 17–54. See also, W. B. Taylor, *Drinking, Homicide and Rebellion in Colonial Mexican Villages*, (Stanford Univ. Press, 1979). The connection between riots and festivals

"spasmodic view of history" is laid to rest, in which popular riots appear as aberrant deviations from normality, the patterns of collective behavior which are uncovered make it possible to integrate much more closely the study of riots with the examination of the society which produces them.[3] The social organization of the popular sectors, their religious beliefs and forms of association become directly comparable with their usually coherent behavior in disturbances. From this perspective, the evidence from the riots supplements and draws together a number of threads from earlier chapters; it also provides a way of measuring communal cohesion and testing it against the evidence for class antagonism.

The 1765 Quito rebellion, provides the most obvious vantage point from which to view the urban popular society of the city, for it was then that the barrios were fully mobilized in a major eruption of popular disorder. Historians of the 1765 rebellion have pointed to the possible connivance of the Creole elite and sought explanations based, in greater or lesser measure, on community cohesion.[4] I am unconvinced by this approach, in part because of the light a number of lesser riots and disorders shed on the major outbreak of 1765, and in this chapter I review all the disturbances I have been able to identify in the period 1700–1810. I examine the following questions:

- Rebellions in late-colonial Andean society have been seen as a response to fiscal pressures from the reorganized Bourbon monarchy, a description which clearly applies to the rebellion of 1765. Identifying riots from the period which predates the Bourbon reforms may not necessarily weaken this connection, but may suggest transformations in the forms of popular protest, as well as clarifying the extent to which the economic decline of the city was linked to social unrest.

- Can the influence of the demographic and social characteristics of the popular districts of the city be detected in differential participation in riot and social disorder? What light does barrio identity shed on social disorder, and conversely, how far do Quito's riots clarify the nature and social function of the barrios, and the inter-relationships between them?

- It is argued here that the riots of the 1740s constituted a major outburst of class antagonism, albeit provoked by, and closely linked to, religious factors. The 1765 rebellion has been seen as the expression of local class alliances, with probable Creole complicity. How far, if at all, can

---

which these authors emphasize is also implicit in much of the documentation on rural rebellions in: S. Moreno Yánez, *Sublevaciones Indígenas* .

[3] The phrase is from E. P. Thompson, "The Moral Economy of the English Crowd in the Eighteenth Century," *Past and Present*, 50 (1971), 76–136.

[4] For an interpretation along these lines see A. McFarlane, "The 'Rebellion of the Barrios': Urban Insurrection in Bourbon Quito," *HAHR*, 69, (1989), 283–330.

we synthesize these two approaches into a coherent record of class relations in late-colonial Quito?

- Festivals have been linked to riots. This connection has been used to support of a community cohesion interpretation of social disorder, that is both riots and festivals forming part of a collective act of communal affirmation, and spilling over into each other. The detailed data on Quito suggest that festivals there did not break or invert the social order, and are not incompatible with the class, more exactly barrio, interpretation of riots adopted here.

Traditions of Popular Protest

Almost three years to the day before the great Quito rebellion of 1765, two fly-posters appeared in the parish of San Roque: "Mestizos of San Roque, by Father and Mother, let us all be one ... Rise up! Let those who pay tribute perish under fire!"[5] Fly-posters were the common prelude to rebellion, and the Spanish authorities expressed concern despite the extravagant protests of loyalty of 48 leaders of the parish. According to the *fiscal,* "the insolence of some bad arrivals, with such laudable virtues that instead of exercising them, they disseminate offensive broadsides and stir up the vulgar and licentious plebe, without more cause than the laxity, and lack of punishment experienced *in other past occurrences.*"[6] The scare of 1762 is of interest in its own right, but of particular interest is the fact that officials were already identifying a clear tradition of urban street disturbances even before the great Quito rebellion of 1765. What were the "past occurences" mentioned by the fiscal ?

Although his comments suggest there had been several previous disturbances, it is likely that the Franciscan riots of the late 1740s were uppermost in his mind. These mobilized the same parish of San Roque, and were indeed dealt with by the relative "laxity and lack of punishment" to which he referred, when a general pardon was issued to the whole parish. It is difficult to identify all minor rioting, and for colonial officials, any collective gathering involving drink and festivities could involve a threat to the established order. In order to classify the different forms of unrest, I found it helpful to identify all known eighteenth century riots, religious

---

[5] ANH/Q Reb. doc. 1762–V–24, fol. 1.
[6] *Ibid.*, fol. 5; (emphasis added).

TABLE 8.1 SOCIAL TENSIONS, 1700–1780

Date	Nature	Participation	Creole	Barrio	Background
1717[a]–1726	suppression Audiencia social unrest	E/P	—	San Roque	economic crisis agricultural dearth epidemic
1718[b]	ecclesiastical schism	R	localism	—	—
1725[c]	San Luis seminary	R/S	Creole?	—	festival
1734[d]	election rector	R (Jesuits)/S	Creole vs. Peninsular	—	—
1747[e]	Franciscan visitor	R/S/P	localism	San Roque	food shortages epidemics New Year
1762[f]	census/fiscal	P (attempted)	Mestizo vs. Indian	San Roque	preparation for Corpus Christi festival
5/22/1765[g]	fiscal	P/E/R?	anti-Peninsular	San Roque/ San Sebastián	food shortages epidemics preparation for Corpus Christi festival
6/18/1765[h]	election of cura release of prisoner	P/R	—	Santa Bárbara/ San Blas	breakdown of authority
6/24/1765[i]	as 5/22/1765	P	anti-Peninsular	barrios	San Juan festival
1779[j]	fiscal	P(R ?) (attempted)	—	San Sebastián	fiscal reform census tensions throughout Andes

Abbreviations: E= tensions between the local elite and royal authority P= popular tension or riot
S= secular support of one side in an ecclesiastical dispute R= religious involvement

Sources: [a] AM/Q, LCQ, 5-2-1726; P. Herrera "Apuntamientos," (1851), 91; AGI 206, RI. Audiencia, January 12, 1748, fol. 14; [b] GS, 2, 930 ff; [c] Ibid. 946 ff; [d] Ibid 993 ff. [e] Ibid. 1089 ff; ANH/Q Reb.1 Doc. 1748–1–1; AGI Quito 206, 207; [f] ANH/Q Reb. 1 Doc. 24-V-1762; [g] Multiple sources, especially AGI 398, 399; [h] AHBC/Q vol. 10, fol. 1, "Diario de lo acaecido desde el día 22 de Mayo," fol. 1; [i] AGI 398, 399; [j] ANH/Q Indígenas 97: 1779-IV-27. For the sources on epidemics, see Table 6.1.

disturbances and near-riots. These data are presented in Table 8.1, terminating in 1780, the year in which the second wave of Bourbon fiscal reform generated riots and rebellions throughout the Andean region. Discussion then continues with the events of 1809, when an autonomous junta was established, while the alleged conspiracy of the philosopher, doctor and propagandist Espejo forms a link between the eighteenth-century disturbances and the Independence period.[7]

How comprehensive are the data in Table 8.1? It is likely that only the Franciscan riots of 1747, and the Quito rebellion of 1765 brought the urban crowd fully into play. The list of religious disputes closely follows those identified by González Suárez, and the ecclesiastical orientation of his writing mean that he was unlikely to neglect any major outbreaks. The examples of "attempted" disturbances obviously reflect the possibilities of the material localized. Their inclusion, and that of some of the religious disputes, requires the clarification that Table 8.1 is not so much a "list" as a kind of barometer of social tension. Frequent attempts have been made to compile such lists of Andean rebellions to see how far they were provoked by particular economic and political conjunctures. Although it is certain that no two historians would establish even loosely comparable lists, there is a broad consensus that the latter part of the eighteenth century was a period of widespread rebellion throughout the Andean region, partly in response to fiscal pressures.[8] An over-rigid quantification of riots and rebellions can prevent us recognizing social tensions in unfamiliar dress. I suspect that if we had more studies of the seventeenth and early eighteenth centuries, and recognized that disorder does not have to take a single form, the disparity with the well-studied late-colonial period might seem less extreme. My list partly antedates the main period of fiscal reform. Differing criteria of selection, notably the inclusion of religious disturbances, exaggerate the contrast while urban riots do not of course have to obey the rhythms which have been established for rural rebellions. Nevertheless, while accepting the broad hypothesis for the Andean region, that a wave of riots and rebellions were caused by fiscal pressures in the late eighteenth century, it is clear that in the case of Quito these were preceded by social tensions generated, in part, by the process of economic decline.

In order to map out the social history of eighteenth-century Quito, apparently different types of occurrence have been grouped together, but

---

[7] The post-1780 events, and particularly 1809–10, belong to the history of Quito's elite, but it is the interaction with popular society which will be stressed in this account.

[8] Campbell, "Recent research on Andean Peasant Revolt," 4, cites the list of Carlos Rama. See also A. Flores Galindo, "La revolución tupamarista y los pueblos andinos (una crítica y un proyecto)," *Allpanchis* (Cusco) XV (1981), 254. Particularly important for Peru (and including earlier disturbances) is S. O'Phelan Godoy, *Rebellions and Revolts in Eighteenth-Century Peru and Upper Peru* (Cologne, 1985). Pérez and McFarlane both stress the impact of the Bourbon reforms in their analysis of the 1765 Rebellion.

these are far less dissimilar than they tend to appear in an historiography polarized between the ecclesiastical disputes described by González Suárez, and more recent ethno-historical interests. The term "religious dispute" is itself misleading. These were by no means sedate affairs, and were frequently very violent; in the controversy in the Jesuit seminary of San Luis in 1725, for example, swords, blunderbusses, pistols and shotguns were used.[9] More important for the purposes of this study was the mobilization of social groups outside the religious orders (or the secular clergy). Close familial ties between the church and Creole society may partly explain this capacity of religious disputes to mobilize a wider society. The demographic importance of the church and notably the religious orders in Quito has already been noted, as has the economic symbiosis of the Creole elite and the church.[10] The Franciscans were a more strictly evangelizing order than the others, and the evidence of 1747 suggests they had more direct ties with the popular social group. In a city where church and society were closely interdependent, religious institutions mirrored the social preoccupations of the society around it, and nearly all the elements which we find in secular disorders can also be found in religious disturbances.

This point can be illustrated by virtually all the religious disputes listed here. In the ecclesiastical schism of 1718, the localism of a society which rejected the alien intrusion of outside authorities or groups (whether religious inspector, state official in 1765 or peninsular Spaniards) also seems to have come into play, to judge from the account of González Suárez.[11] The disorders at San Luis in 1725 were provoked by seminarians who participated in festivals against the permission of the Rector, but ethnic and class prejudices appear to have influenced the dispute.[12] Above all, religious disputes provided a forum for the tensions of Creoles and peninsular Spaniards, and one which extended well beyond the bounds of the religious orders. There was nothing new in Creole-peninsular confrontations in the religious orders which had often turned on the system of rotation of the leading posts known as the *alternativa*.[13] But even if behind the eighteenth-century disputes lay a long process of maturing of Creole consciousness, it is equally clear that the early eighteenth-century religious disputes reveal a degree of animosity towards peninsular

---

[9] See the references in Table 8.1. For an earlier (1679) example of an ecclesiastical riot, see L. Martín, *Daughters of the Conquistadores. Women of the Viceroyalty of Peru*, (Dallas, 1989), 247–257.

[10] See above, Chapters 4 and 6.

[11] See the references in Table 8.1.

[12] AGI Quito 203, (on San Luis, 1725), Testigos: Juan Agustín de La Rosa, and Maestro don Fernando Ladrón de Guevara.

[13] B. Lavallé, *Recherches sur l'apparition de la conscience créole dans la vice-royauté du Pérou: l'antagonisme hispano-créole dans les ordres religieux (XVI-XVIIs.)*, (Lille, 1978).

Spaniards, which directly anticipates the anti-Spanish rioting of 1765. The 1730s religious confrontations, in particular, led directly into violent tensions between Creoles and peninsulars in which the secular cabildo became closely involved.[14]

The scope of this study does not require detailed examination of the above disturbances. The Franciscan riots of the 1740s, on the other hand, will be discussed in detail, because they mobilized an entire barrio, revealed profound class tensions, and had the highest degree of popular participation. It may be reiterated that demonstrating the existence of early eighteenth-century disorders, notably religious ones, by no means "disproves" the correlation of late eighteenth century rebellions with Bourbon fiscal reform, but it can certainly sharpen our analysis of that late-colonial conjuncture. What were the differences and the similarities with earlier disorders? How far were both phases of disturbances linked to Quito's economic difficulties? The immediate cause or "trigger" is known for all eighteenth century disturbances, and in no case do these correspond, although perhaps only at first sight, to "hunger riots."

Certain correlations with economic change can be suggested, even if it is emphasized that these always interacted with political, fiscal or religious factors. Economic difficulties in the 1690s and 1720s have already been suggested.[15] Although the result was not open rebellion, the latter part of this period witnessed certain tensions which in many ways foreshadow the major outbreak of 1765. In 1717, the Audiencia was suppressed and formed part of the Viceroyalty of New Granada from 1718 until 1722, when it was reestablished and again formed part of the Viceroyalty of Peru. Like the later phase of intensified bureaucratic vigor in the second half of the eighteenth century, early reformism took place at a time when the Creole elite considered itself in a disastrous economic state. A cycle of bad harvests is attested during the later appeal for the lowering of censos,[16] and the cabildo complained about rising sugar prices in August 1717, referring to the "notorious" lack of specie of the Audiencia, which was to become a constant refrain in the late-colonial documentation.[17] From 1716 to late 1719, there were continual confrontations between local and official interests, including on February 1, 1718, cabildo complaints of the "calamitous state" of city and Province, and the convening of an open cabildo against the wishes of the corregidor.[18] The *casus belli* turned, unsurprisingly, on the economic interests of the elite, notably the projected inspection of haciendas, obrajes, and mills, and official attempts to control

---

[14] GS, 993 ff.
[15] See above, Chapters 3 and 6.
[16] See Chapter 3.
[17] AM/Q, LCQ, August 3, 1717, fol. 76.
[18] AM/Q, LCQ, February 1, 1718, fol. 98.

the tribute system, regulate Indian labor against the wishes of the landholding elite, and collect from the hacendados on "dead souls."[19]

The tensions of this period never constituted a direct threat to royal interests but they are suggestive in showing the way that economic crisis could provoke or reinforce a clash of local and official interests. The convening of an open council meeting was one of the devices by which local groups expressed grievances and was to be reused in the 1765 rebellion, and the 1809 uprising. Most interestingly, the political tensions of 1716–19 seem to have interacted with popular unrest on a major scale. Thirty years later the Audiencia recalled disturbances from San Roque during the transit of the Viceroy Villalonga on his way to Bogotá in 1719.[20] The people of San Roque had "insulted" the Viceroy on that occasion ("le perdieron el respeto"). Unfortunately the way in which this "disrespect" was expressed is not specified, but we may suspect it was tumultuous as similar disrespect was shown to the recently appointed peninsular Bishop, Dr. Don Luis Francisco Romero,[21] allegedly to the extent of trying to burn down his house and kill him. If this was the local popular response to major political changes and ecclesiastical schism, it shows clearly that elite division and resistance helped to stimulate popular disorder at moments of economic crisis and, given the background of the suppression of the Audiencia, that notions of local autonomy ran deep in Quito society. The rioters of San Roque, however, certainly do not seem to have been respecters of persons, to judge from the brief summary of a generation later: when the President of the Audiencia put an end to their action, they also "... le perdieron el respeto."

The continued economic difficulties of the 1720s involving a sharp frost and a drought in 1723–1724, and high rising mortality in the late 1720s, also seem to have stimulated popular unrest.[22] The cabildo, usually more concerned with elite than with popular matters was sufficiently concerned to discuss the state in which the "Vulgo y Barrios" of the city found themselves, as a result of the "lamentable poverty" of the province.[23] Perhaps they had little choice: popular agitation was expressed in a mass demonstration in support of a petition presented by the leaders of the barrio of San Roque. The petition was against independent collectors of payment for burials, arguing that the parish priests should collect payment otherwise poor people would go unburied.[24] Once again the refrain is the poverty of the city and province. The parish of San Roque again played the dominant role, and the presence of an organized barrio leadership drawing up an

---

19 "Indios ausentes y muertos." AM/Q, LCQ, March 4, 1716, fol. 39.
20 AGI Quito 206, Rl. Audiencia, January 12, 1748, fol. 14.
21 *GS* 2, 935.
22 For the background, see Chapters 3 and 6.
23 AM/Q, LCQ, February 5, 1726, fols. 54–55.
24 *Ibid.*, fol. 56.

extremely well conceived petition, appealing for an open cabildo, and urging the council to support the familiar formula of "obeying but not carrying out" the decree, shows that this was a highly organized, settled leadership "knowing the ropes" in the Spanish colonial system.

In the 1710s and 1720s potential disorders of a political dimension were largely defused, by the diversity of Spanish colonial institutions, in which legal devices (the open cabildo, petitions), and often competing authorities (cabildo, corregidor, Audiencia) formed a mesh of overlapping interests into which tensions could be absorbed. Official pressures were certainly negligible in comparison with the major reforms of the 1760s and 1770s. The official *visita* does not appear to have been carried out, and the tribute reform of 1718, which initially permitted high profits for the corregidores, ultimately led to the partial transfer of tribute-collection to tax-farmers up to the reforms of the late 1770s.[25] Nevertheless, the pattern of future disturbances was set: the background of declarations of impending economic catastrophe, the clash of local and outside—or official—interests, the use of the open cabildo, and, not least important, popular unrest and the particular role of San Roque. Similar checks did not operate on religious disputes, which may help to explain why they were so relatively unrestrained at this period. Perhaps the religious disputes of 1718 or 1725 can be related to the economic and political climate of that period, but there is no known exacerbation of economic difficulties or political background to explain those of the 1730s. On the other hand, the religious and social tensions of the 1730s do not seem to have had a major popular dimension, and the plebe seems to have been notably quiescent in the 1730s and 1750s when the demographic evidence suggests the city was stable or growing.

For both the main popular riots, there is clear evidence of a short-term deterioration of conditions immediately prior to their outbreak. Historians working on Latin-American materials for the colonial period have tended to argue that rebellions were largely independent of crises in agricultural production.[26] It may be that far less importance has been attached to this factor than in Europe because the agrarian history of Latin America is so much less well-known. The chronology of urban rioting certainly suggests that urban society was closely responding to the economic rhythms of the countryside. The major outbursts of the 1740s and 1760s both followed food shortages, and epidemics.[27] Quito's long-term decline and short-term

---

[25] The tribute reform of 1718 led to *corregidores* making underestimates on their tributary lists, and large profits; see Tyrer, 47; AM/Q, LCQ, March 4, 1716, fol. 39, for Indians hiding on haciendas.

[26] In addition to the literature summarized by Campbell, see W. B. Taylor, *Drinking, Homicide and Rebellion*, 129. Florescano's work may be correct for Mexico without being transferable elsewhere.

[27] See the references in the list of epidemics in Chapter 6.

economic difficulties have now been linked by Andrien to the outbreak of the rebellion of 1765.[28]

The rest of this chapter seeks to shed more detailed light on the main "popular" disorders in the eighteenth century, those of 1747 and 1765. It continues by examining Quito's "missing" revolution, the relative calm around 1780 when the riots and full-scale rebellions swept the rest of the Andean region, and concludes with an account of the tensions of the 1790s and the early Independence movement which discusses the degree of popular participation.

Much of the analysis which follows will focus on the barrio of San Roque. Characterized by virtually endemic disorder which periodically erupted into major disturbances, that parish emerges as the key to an understanding of social disorder in the late-colonial city. The agitation of the plebe in 1719 and 1726 involved this parish. In 1747, the parish rioted on a major scale, and San Roque's seditious character was already sufficiently notorious to attract the critical comment of the Audiencia that San Roque was the "most populated" parish, where "the lads have always been the most audacious" ("y siempre los mosos de el los más atrevidos"). In 1762, the authorities feared another uprising from the same source, and the *fiscal* referred to the "past occurences."[29] From this perspective, it is clear that the outbreak of the 1765 rebellion in the same parish was by no means fortuitous, and that uncovering the origins of San Roque's seditiousness will clarify the nature and purposes of popular participation in the 1765 rebellion. What, one may well ask, made San Roque so distinctive?

The Barrios and Social Order: The Franciscan Disturbances and the Parish of San Roque, 1719–1765

The Plebe of San Roque: Socio-Demographic and Religious Background

An attempt will be made here to draw together and synthesize the data on San Roque included in earlier discussions of the spatial characteristics of colonial Quito, religious compliance and demographic decline, in order to see what peculiarities of its social structure, if any, underlie such a distinctive tradition. If we wish to uncover patterns which have validity for the plebe of the city as a whole, it is not only the character of San Roque which requires examination, but its articulation with the other barrios of the city. The broad division of the city into two halves—San Roque/San Sebastián, on the one hand, Santa Bárbara/San Blas, on the other—has

---

[28] See the study of Andrien: "Economic crisis, Taxes and the Quito Insurrection of 1765," *Past and Present*, 129 (1990), 104–131.

[29] ANH/Q Reb. doc. 1762–V–24, fol. 5.

already been noted. This upper/lower division was not only a ritual one, a colonial perpetuation of pre-Hispanic divisions, but also a geographical one. El Sagrario, and parts of the other parishes (notably San Marcos, and parts of Santa Bárbara) formed a nucleus of "white" settlement to which each popular parish was connected in a radial fashion. But the interaction of the popular parishes with each other provided an intermediate stage in the building-blocks (parish, aggregation of parishes, city) upon which Quito was built. Alliances, or attempted alliances, between barrios formed a clear feature of social disorder. The fact that the central parish divided the two main concentrations of popular residence—San Sebastián/ San Roque, and San Blas/the slaughterhouse district of Santa Bárbara—tended to restrict the geographical scope of potential disorder and reinforce these lateral connections. San Roque's links with San Sebastián were notably illustrated in the May rebellion of 1765, when San Roque's action was supported by San Sebastián. In 1748, however, there were also suggestions of an alliance with San Sebastián (and also with San Blas).

If we place the San Sebastián scare of 1779 alongside the predominant role of San Roque, it becomes clear that virtually all disturbances originated in the south of the city, with the exception of the period of generalized breakdown of order which followed the May uprising in 1765. It is therefore appropriate to consider whether San Roque's apparent particularity does not simply mask a broad difference between the north and south of the city. On the evidence of the 1733 padrones, which unfortunately date from a period well after the main period of textile activity, it is probably unwise to seek a direct explanation in changes in the weaving industry. At that date 51 percent of surviving recorded male adult Indians were in obrajes or weaving activities in San Roque; but these figures were greatly swelled by a single obraje, that of don Antonio Pastrana, and the proportion in the city as a whole was a comparable 49.5 percent. San Sebastián was more textile related.[30] It is possible that the decline of the obrajes affected parts of the city more than others, but changes in the structure of the urban economy may also have owed much to the wider reorientation of trade routes in the eighteenth century. In the seventeenth century, the great export market for Quito's textiles had been Lima, while the decline in their competitiveness was (inadequately) compensated for by the markets of southern Colombia. If it may reasonably be hypothesized that most commerce entered by the south of the city in the seventeenth century, the alcabala records show clearly that at the end of the eighteenth century most commerce passed by San Blas.[31] The demographic data suggest that this commerce did not generate much urban occupational specialization—no "urban" *arrieros,* or muleteers, were found

---

[30] Tyrer, 414–415; my own calculations for San Roque and San Sebastián.

[31] For example see AGI Quito 432, año 1793, Pliego 1. San Blas seems to have received around 70 percent at that period. The other entrances were Magdalena and Recoleta.

in any of the admittedly incomplete eighteenth-century padrones—but must have been a stimulus to the local economy. To judge from the padrón of Santa Bárbara in 1768, the meat market generated activity in an area overlapping the parishes of Santa Bárbara and San Blas, and this commercial activity was probably reinforced by trade with the north. This did not prevent San Blas from declining in the eighteenth century, but almost certainly San Roque's decline preceded it. It may be that after around 1700, Quito was beginning to look north rather than south in more ways than one.[32]

But the north-south dichotomy is adduced here only as a background factor, and it is argued that the essential distinctiveness of San Roque can be found in the parish itself. In the absence of the equivalent of the Santa Bárbara padrón, a number of points can nevertheless be deduced from admittedly incomplete demographic evidence relating to size, social composition, and demographic change. San Roque was the largest parish in the sixteenth and seventeenth centuries,[33] but all the eighteenth century evidence suggests major demographic decline. Although the demographic assessments of contemporary observers have to be used with caution, they are probably reasonably accurate with regard to the *relative* importance of districts; from 1730 to 1765 they were unanimous in commentating that the parish was still the largest of the popular barrios, although they were probably not taking into account the Cathedral-parish of El Sagrario.[34] On the other hand, the flawed series of padrones of 1797, and 1825, demonstrate clearly that San Roque no longer enjoyed its predominant role by that period, trailing El Sagrario, and also Santa Bárbara and San Sebastián. San Roque was declining, and it appears that, as with the rest of the city, a concomitant of decline was ethnic transformation. San Roque was a highly Indian parish in the sixteenth and seventeenth centuries,[35] while the parish of the eighteenth century riots was ethnically mixed, with Mestizos predominant. In 1733, an incomplete Indian padrón included 150 adult male tributaries in the parish. By the 1797 census only 28 households out of 202 in the parish appear to have been Indian, although some Indians lived in other houses. As the 1762 scare will show, ethnic change has to be considered with economic and demographic change as a potential cause of social disorder.

Despite the absence of full occupational data for the relevant period, clear distinguishing features emerge from the demographic evidence. San Roque was characterized by small, usually nucleated households instead of

---

32 That is resulting from the transfer to New Granada.

33 Personal communication of J. Moreno Egas based on data from the parish registers.

34 AGI Quito 132, Carta de Dionisio de Alsedo y Herrera, June 8, 1732, fol. 5, "El Barrio de la más numerosa Parroquia de San Roque." AGI 206, Real Audiencia, January 12, 1748, fol. 14, "el más numeroso de esta ciudad," at the time of the Quito rebellion in 1765, according to the reports in AGI Quito 398.

35 For example ANH/Q 3 Not. 1 February 21, 1656, fol. 96.

the two-tier socially mixed households of the elite parishes. Caldas' characterization of houses in the latter as "small villages" is completely borne out by the Santa Bárbara padrón, where occupational and ethnic diversity accompanied shared residence. The social interaction which this presupposed in the elite districts, the annual permission of Indians to mount to the second floor on the election of the alcalde, for example,[36] can be equated with a degree of social control. One of the clearest testimonies of this came in 1779 when it was argued that a certain defendant had not been involved in disorders, by virtue of the district he lived in. In San Roque there were few persons with the title of "don."

Once the popular character of the parish is emphasized, the hypotheses already advanced for the absolute and relative decline of the parish (weaving, regional commerce) can be put in their correct perspective. Although in European cities groups like the silk-workers played an important role in urban riots, their real equivalents in social terms in Quito were not obraje or chorrillo weavers, whose Indian quasi-rural characteristics were emphasized in Chapter 3, but the independent artisans linked to the urban monetary economy. Far from being the parish of weavers, San Roque's real importance was precisely the opposite, as the parish of the popular artisan groups, who were probably more affected by economic decline than the weavers—more exactly the non-independent weavers, because they could be less easily, or willingly, reabsorbed into the rural economy. This point emerges with particular clarity in the 1762 petition cited below. The 1733 Indian padrones are unfortunately incomplete, but the relatively high concentration of Indian tailors, carpenters, and barbers in San Roque may be noted.[37]

The location of San Roque reinforces this point. Major parts of San Sebastián and San Blas lay at some distance from the main nucleus of the city, and were marked off by quebradas. San Roque, on the other hand, gave directly on to the center, and except for a small extension over the quebrada Jerusalén, it was not a disguised semi-rural parish. In terms of the social geography of rebellion, this is not a minor point, as riots turned on the control of the central district, the locus of authority. Defining our question in negative terms, the semi-rural or elite character of the rest of the city may help to explain why the other parishes did not rebel, and this in turn, by a process of elimination, leads us back to San Roque. It may be that we should paradoxically stress the typicality of San Roque, rather than its exceptional character. A large, urban parish, popular and declining, connected directly to the city center and with a restricted elite presence—

---

[36] See Chapter 2.

[37] Tyrer, 414-415, counted 483 recorded Indian occupations in the whole of the city; in the original documents I counted 150 recorded occupations in the surviving *padrones* for San Roque. I counted 7 sastres, (one with dual occupation) whereas Tyrer found 6 (?) for the whole series; 5 carpinteros, out of 10 found by Tyrer for the whole city; 3 barberos, compared to 8; and 5 zapateros, compared to 12.

here we have a partial explanation for why San Roque should play such a leading role.

The demographic and socio-economic evidence culled from the main body of this study and discussed above, nevertheless provides only the most general background unless we resort to a purely mechanistic interpretation of social disorder. There are two areas where we can stress the interplay of San Roque's socio-economic characteristics with considerations of an ideological dimension, namely religion and "community." The idea of the *común,* the commonwealth, had a legitimating function in rebellion. The common good of the community, a kind of "unwritten constitution," in Phelan's phrase, formed the basis for the conservative appeal against irregular Bourbon innovations in taxation, or perceived abuses in the body politic. Just as local interests "obeyed without complying," rioters divorced royal authority from their attacks on royal policy (or its local representatives). "Long live the King and down with bad Government" formed the refrain in popular riots in the King of Spain's more distant dominions, just as it did in Spain and Europe itself. The ideal of the commonwealth which was notably invoked at elite level during the open cabildo which preceded the 1765 rebellion can also be found in the popular defense of customary arrangements which characterized that major outbreak.[38]

The ideal of the común has normally been used to reinforce interpretations of rebellion as the expression of class alliances,[39] but some caution is in order in relating an ideology as general as the "public good" to the specific motivations of the popular sectors. There is certainly a sense in which the whole community rejected "alien" intrusions, notably "inspectors," whether religious or fiscal, but the ideal of the común operated at many different levels, and took on different shades of meaning in different hands. At least for the plebe of Quito, this ideal becomes a more flexible instrument for analysis of social disorder when it is transferred to barrio level. Who, for the men and women of San Roque, were the "community"? Although the concept certainly evoked a larger ideal, all the evidence from the unrest in San Roque reinforces the sense in which "community cohesion" is better described as barrio cohesion. The appeal for an open cabildo in 1726 was certainly to the wider community of the city, for the bypassing of official justice within the ideological framework noted above; even more striking is the fact that it was a barrio petition submitted by a clearly defined popular leadership. The same organized communal leadership emerges from the 1762 documentation, and evidence from the 1747 riots attests to the remarkable identity of the barrio. If we note San Roque's identity as a fairly homogeneous popular parish with clear collective leadership and a strong sense of community, we perhaps approach the distinctiveness of the barrio. San Roque, unlike any

---

38 See McFarlane, "The 'Rebellion of the Barrios.'"
39 See also J. L. Phelan, *El Pueblo y El Rey*, (Bogotá, 1980).

other parish in the city, was both a community and a social class, and to locate the origins of social disorder in that district is also to underline the popular roots of social disorder.

San Roque's particularity, however, was clearly reinforced by religious factors. In Chapter 4, it was noted that the parish of San Roque bordered on the monastery of San Francisco, and that the most evangelizing of all the religious orders was linked to the Indian population of that district in the early and mid-colonial period, possibly partially supplanting the secular clergy in ministering to the local population. This localized influence of the Franciscans may be taken as the counterpart to the absence of elite control in the parish if we wish to seek a "hidden hand" interpretation of social disorder. It is argued, however, that the Franciscan riots of the 1740s suggest a more complicated symbiosis of barrio and religious order. The problem of interpreting the riots of the 1740s is that San Roque allied itself with one faction of the Franciscan movement so it would be inappropriate to oversimplify the interaction of religious order and barrio. Taken together, the disorders of San Roque constitute such a coherent yet varied tradition, with religious, fiscal, and ethnic motivations involved, that it is logical to make the men and women of San Roque the principal agents of their collective actions.

The place of religion and "community" in San Roque can notably be elucidated from the pre-1765 disorders before the role of San Roque was subsumed in the more general rebellion of that year. While there is no evidence of unrest in the parish during the 1730s, during 1747 the parish became directly involved in a Franciscan schism, and a close examination of the disturbances of that year sheds an extremely interesting light on the parish.[40] González Suárez' late nineteenth century account emphasized the sense in which this was a religious dispute, and his account was largely followed by the few Ecuadorian historians who commented on the disturbances, while its popular dimension appears to have been entirely overlooked.[41] González Suárez' account will be mainly followed for the Franciscan background, before we examine the documentary evidence for bringing this dispute directly into line with San Roque's traditions of sedition and "disrespect."

"VIVA MARIA, AND THE BARRIO OF SAN ROQUE": THE RIOTS OF 1747–1748.

This dispute began, like so many disturbances in Quito, with the arrival of an "alien" although in this case he was neither tax inspector nor enumerator. In 1747, the Franciscan authorities in Lima sent a *visitador* to

---

[40] The account in *GS* is essentially based on AGI Quito 206–207.
[41] *GS* neglects the popular dimension and has been largely followed by later Ecuadorian historians.

carry out an official inspection despite an initial local reluctance to accept this; the visitador was eventually received but immediately became embroiled in a direct confrontation with the local Franciscans. After duly excommunicating them all, he sought refuge with the Jesuits. Why the Franciscans were so averse to an official inspection can only be conjectured; the general denunciations of the religious orders, or the denunciations of illicit bootlegging of brandy in monasteries in 1765,[42] suggest possible explanations, although probably the intrusion of official controls from outside was in itself unwelcome to the religious orders. From St. Francis' own lifetime onwards, the Franciscan movement had been characterized by opposing currents of more or less strict adherence to the rule of poverty, and on the evidence of the riots, the more severe tendency was emanating from Lima. The potentially damaging nature of an official inspection was in any case revealed when the Commissary of Lima, Ibáñez Cuevas arrived from Lima to take direct control of the situation, and after a period of calm, proceeded to take the residencia of the ex-Provincial, Fray Bartolomé de Alácano, who had instigated early resistance to the visita prior to 1747, as well as Fray José Morrón who had occupied the post at the beginning of the inspection.

Both were imprisoned and brought to Quito from the Franciscan seminary in Pomasque, amidst a major schism of the Franciscan Order. The schism hardened with the liberation of Padre Alácano as he was being escorted south to exile, and Padre Morrón's release by a mainly secular group which included some friars on December 2, 1747.[43] Padre Morrón's release was the catalyst for major disturbances. The Commissary engineered a purge of the Franciscan order, and led his followers, loyalists and plebeians, in a procession through the city, ropes round the neck in penitent fashion. Plebeians carrying the statue of Saint Francis led the way, followed by the Commissary carrying the Blessed Sacraments. As they went, they sang *In exitu Israel de Ægipto,* from the psalm used for the last offices and included in prayers for the dead from early medieval times onwards, and women followed the procession with rags and junk crying out that religion was finishing, that the world was coming to an end. In the Square of Santo Domingo, the Commissary, brandishing the Sacraments, issued ritual curses against Padre Morrón, the Audiencia, the President and the city itself, before leading the procession back to San Diego.[44]

As we will see, the "plebeians" accompanying Ibáñez Cuevas were the people of San Roque, and the Commissary's procession already provides interesting evidence of the dimensions the schism was beginning to take.

---

42 McFarlane, "The 'Rebellion of the Barrios,'" following AGI Quito 398.

43 *GS* 1089 ff.

44 *GS* 1093, AGI 206, Rl. Audiencia, January 12, 1748, fol. 14. I do not know if this changed during the Counter-Reformation, but for the mediæval use of the psalm cxiv see Dante, *Purgatorio*, canto ii. (OUP, London, 1971 edn.), notes at 41–42.

How far we can take the chiliastic overtones is difficult to say, and there is little evidence that unrest took the form of a full-scale messianic movement. Dearth and epidemic in the city of Quito in the mid-1740s[45] may have sharpened religious sensibilities in this respect just as they did in medieval Europe. It is clear, however, that religious ritual was playing a role in legitimizing the popular violence which was to ensue. The Commissary's move to the Franciscan retreat of San Diego just outside the city involved the symbolic act of closing San Francisco, and the patronage of a statue of St. Francis in the procession underlined the Commissary's claim to set true Christianity against the wicked city which was being abandoned (Quito=Egypt). Already, the action was going beyond a Franciscan dispute to take on a clear social dimension, and in this process, the plebe of San Roque were being mobilized not only behind one faction of the Franciscan movement, but also with the outsider and against the status quo. Behind the religious motivation lay class-antagonism, which the Commissary seems to have been only too happy to play on.[46]

This was heady stuff, and during December, the parish became an almost autonomous district. Using what colonial officials saw mainly as an excuse for "scandal" and "tumult," large crowds from San Roque guarded San Francisco and the Commissary in his retreat in San Diego, and royal officials had great difficulty doing their rounds.[47] On December 31, 1747 Manuel de la Parra, variously described as a *zambo* or mulato tailor of San Roque was arrested for attacking an official, the Lieutenant of the *Alguacil Mayor de Corte*. In view of the correspondence of both major outbreaks in 1765 with festivals, the timing of the outbreak was no coincidence; New Year was a religious festival, and coincided also with municipal elections.[48] It is possible, however, that in this case the link between festivities and rioting was an indirect one. Rioting did not directly spill over from festivities, but was certainly lubricated by the drinking which formed an integral part of both types of collective occurrence. It may be that the arrest of Parra was symptomatic of the rising tensions prior to New Year, and expectations of trouble on both sides. The actions of rioters from San Roque, who on the December 31, 1747 liberated Parra, and two days later attacked the President's house formed the subject of an inquiry by the Audiencia; at this point we must therefore part company from González Suárez, who made only a brief (and inaccurate) reference to the crowd's

---

[45] See the list of epidemics in Chapter 6.
[46] According to *GS*, 1093.
[47] ANH/Q Reb. 1: doc. 1748–1–1, Don Joseph de Quintana y Asevedo, fol. 52 ff.
[48] C. de Gangotena y Jijón, "Fiestas que se celebraban en Quito a fines del siglo XVIII," *Boletín de la Academia Nacional de Historia*, (Quito), VII, 1923, 263, the festival of the Circumcision, January 1.

"drunken fury"[49] and turn to the evidence collected by the Audiencia which gives a clear picture of popular action.[50]

The first disturbance, the attack on the prison to liberate Parra, was the subject of a graphic account by one of Parra's fellow-prisoners, Miguel Falcon, a brocade maker, who found himself imprisoned for debt.[51] Falcon's inside account shows clearly that this was a carefully planned attack rather than "blind fury." Prior to the attack, Parra was visited at the grills of the prison by Feliciano Chuquilargo, a gilder, and the timing of the attack was carefully coordinated to coincide with the departure of the guard. The main doors of the prison were assaulted, but since they had been shored up with stones, firewood was brought to burn them. The rioters (or rescuers) entered the prison carrying bared swords and cutlasses, faces partially masked by handkerchiefs. The first to arrive at the inside bars were the gilder Chuquilargo and Francisco Marques, a carpenter who used his professional skills with chisel and mallet to set to work on the interior grill. When this did not go quickly enough, they both smashed a hole in it with a rock and told Parra to come out, "... for this is how one behaved with friends, and how should he sleep in prison, being of the parish of San Roque."[52]

The attack was extremely well organized with a commando group of around twenty-five men carrying out the assault on the prison while a larger crowd which may have been several hundred strong lent moral support in the street outside.[53] The total defiance of the rioters was reflected in violence to symbols of property and authority, although not to persons, when the locks of the prison were smashed on the way out, that is after the aims of the rescuers had already been accomplished. Other prisoners were invited to leave but refused. The crowd left *"vitoreando,"* celebrating the victory of the barrio of San Roque.

Although we cannot know in detail the socio-ethnic composition of the crowd, a major clue is provided by the role played in releasing a mulato tailor by a gilder (with an Indian name), and with the participation of a carpenter (who was probably Mestizo to judge from his surname). The riots certainly seem therefore to have been multi-ethnic (a fact to be kept in mind when we turn to the 1762 tensions) as well as strongly rooted in the artisan class, at least at its leadership levels. The little additional occupational data which is available confirms that it was by no means the lowest social strata who were involved. Later the same night, for example, Manuel Zapata, nicknamed Capulí, claimed that he closed down the shop

---

[49] *GS*, 1094.

[50] ANH/Q Reb 1 doc. 748–1–1; witnesses heard mainly January 9, 1748 onwards. The citations that follow are from this document unless otherwise specified.

[51] *Ibid.*, fol. 12–13.

[52] *Ibid.*, fol. 13.

[53] According to the Audiencia there were more than a thousand (fol. 3). Don Joaquín de Alava (fol. 32) estimated some 400 people were involved.

where he sold aguardiente while the rioters passed, and two of them, one a painter, came in to request drink.[54] An alternative version by the witness María Josepha made Manuel Zapata himself one of the rioters, visiting a shop where brandy was sold and explaining that he had rescued Parra because he was his "friend."[55] The same witness later identified Vasilio and Eusebio, hat-makers as rioters in the second disturbance. The quest for ringleaders of a higher social class uncovered relatively little,[56] while the pulperos who animated the "lads" of San Roque by giving them drink in the second disturbance do not carry the social composition of the rioters into the higher reaches of Quito society. As well as confirming the connection with drink, the witnesses' accounts emphasize the popular community character of the riot. Although the data cited above provide only a fractional sample of those involved, a list of the occupational data shows an extremely coherent pattern: tailor, gilder, carpenter, painter, shop-keeper, hat-makers, pulperos.[57]

In the first riot, the slogans were against specific targets notably officials, and the traditional slogan of "Long with the King and Down with Bad Government!" was shouted, along with a more interesting variation: "Viva el Varrio de San Roque, muera el mal Govierno y el Theniente Matta, *y aquí ya no hay justicia*" (my italics).[58] The same sense of popular action as a legitimate form of informal justice, directed not against the King, but his evil counselors was vividly expressed by one rioter when he returned excited from the riot and exclaimed that "breaking an old animal-pen like the prison wasn't a crime."[59]

As in 1765, there was not one but two popular actions, the second being more violent than the first, and the difference between the two riots shows the pace with which popular motivation could change. The second attack began with fireworks (as had the first) and with the ringing of church bells. One witness recorded that a child from his house had gone to San Sebastián and heard that they were being convoked for a riot by the people of San Roque. The sign to join was to be three fireworks, first one flash, then two with the second, and three with the third.[60] The fact that the fireworks were being used more for their coded meaning than for their festival dimension sounds a note of caution against overemphasizing the symbolic function of the fireworks, although the two ideas are not

---

[54] Testigo Manuel Zapata, fol. 33.

[55] Testigo María Josepha, fol. 39.

[56] Manuel Guerrero y Ponse, testigo, Jan. 9, 1749, fol. 13–14 saw only one person of "distinto fuero."

[57] Testigo María Josepha, fol. 40.

[58] "There is no justice here now."

[59] Testigo Francisca Goribar, fol. 45–47; testimony confirmed by the Indian and his wife, fol. 49.

[60] Testigo Doctor Don Rafael de Ortega, fols. 43–44.

contradictory. The testimony is interesting because it confirms the San Roque-San Sebastián axis which was emphasized in Chapter 2 and was to come into play in the 1765 rebellion. Although there was concern that San Sebastián and also San Blas might be implicated,[61] all witnesses stressed the role of San Roque in the 1747–8 disorders. The fact that the three barrios considered to be potential sources of disorder were San Roque, San Sebastián and San Blas may be considered a confirmation of their popular nature.

What is striking in the disorders of 1747–48 is the combination of unity of spirit with diversity of motivation. To judge from the slogans shouted, as recorded by nearly all the witnesses, the popular ideology of San Roque was a syncretic mix of Franciscan religious influence, leveling ideas of justice and dreams of acquisition of wealth at the expense of the rich, combined with anti-peninsular Spanish sentiment and a generalized hatred of the authorities of the city. The one common thread was loyalty to the parish of San Roque, and perhaps to the King. Although González Suárez' account emphasized both the dominance of the Franciscan Commissary and the role of Parra as a popular leader, both these elements seem to have been less important than he suggested in explaining popular action. Parra was explicitly a "friend," a person of San Roque who should not have to sleep in prison. Although the quest for "hidden hands" may have led towards the Franciscans, the first riot at least was clearly a collective action of the "lads" of San Roque. It is difficult to say how far we should take the Marian dimension or the Biblical language, but this seems to have been effortlessly integrated into the traditional expressions of popular protest: "... against the *chapetones* [peninsular Spaniards] saying here come the Jews, Long Live the Law of God, Long Live the Church and Down with Bad Government."[62]

The people of San Roque blockaded themselves in the square of San Francisco, but were dislodged by thirty or forty men with firearms and swords. The end was to be flight via the quebradas, and the virtual abandonment of the parish in a climate of fear.[63]

CONSPIRACY AND ETHNIC TENSION, 1762

Document 61 of the Declarations of Mestizo[64] was the case of Juan de Dios Guzmán, who was picked up once as an Indian in the enumeration of the early 1760s and again in the next wave of census-taking around 1779. This enumeration was the cause of the fly-posters (cited above) which appeared on May 19, 1762, that the Mestizos on both sides of the family

---

[61] Doctor Don Gabriel de Piedrahita, fols. 34–35.

[62] *Ibid.*, fol. 44.

[63] *Ibid.*, fol. 56.

[64] Detailed in Chapter 7.

should rise up and kill the cholos of the city. There is little evidence that such an uprising was close to realization, but the existence of an alleged conspiracy suggests a number of interesting points.

The date is significant. The first rebellion of 1765 was to break out almost exactly three years to a day later, which suggests that the run-up to the festival of Corpus Christi which formed the background to the 1765 rebellion was indeed no coincidence. The next interest of the document comes from the rare light it sheds on inter-ethnic identity in the lower strata. The Quito rebellion was to reveal possible tension between the urban Mestizos and the Indian population of the corregimiento but the conspiracy of 1762 shows that these tensions existed within a differentiated Mestizo/Cholo urban population. Forty-eight leaders of the guild from San Roque sign their names well, as they make extravagant claims of their loyalty to royal authority. It is explained that the fly-posters have appeared because of the numeration of "the cholos who are the kind of people who being by their nature Indian, dress as Mestizos," and are promptly exempt from tribute; Mestizos do not "work the fields" and do other mechanical offices which are only for Indians.[65]

The case is a small one, and there were to be no known repercussions, but it is nevertheless highly revealing when placed alongside the riots of the 1740s and the great eruption of 1765. Once again San Roque was the source of tension, and the case demonstrates that it had a highly organized leadership and well-defined character. The fact that Mestizos were appealing for action as such is of particular interest because the Declarations of Mestizos—due account taken of their judicial character—suggest that there was little self-identification by the Mestizo class who saw themselves as White or near-White. Here the popular parish of San Roque appeared to have a specifically Mestizo identity, although the circumstances of a census may have helped to create this. It was noted by officials that there was a popular belief that the Mestizos were going to be enumerated along with the Indians, an example of the role of rumor which we find in all the eighteenth-century disturbances. Obviously, it is possible that the fly-posters had their own coded meaning, and that the possibility of disturbances of a different order were what really concerned the officials. Nevertheless, the simplest reading of the document is that in their fear of being reduced to the status of the cholos, the Mestizos directed their aggression against the groups who were on the rung beneath them, rather than against the colonial system as such. In this sense, one dimension of eighteenth-century civil disorder, its conservative, literally "reactionary" side, is confirmed.

---

[65] ANH/Q, Reb. doc: 1762-V-24.

The Impact of the Bourbon Reforms and the 1765 Rebellion

THE "REBELLION OF THE BARRIOS"

The last and greatest uprising of the "lads of San Roque" was to be the Quito rebellion of May 22, 1765, that broke out in that parish, initiated once again with fireworks and the ringing of bells. The "rebellion of the barrios," however, was to have a much wider-scale and significance: there were two great riots in 1765 as well as a virtually generalized breakdown of order. An initial attack against the customs house in May was followed by a major battle for control of the main square in June, and by the temporary expulsion of peninsular Spaniards from the city. Only the year afterwards was order fully restored after a period of great tension. Unrest on this scale has not escaped the historical record, and the Quito rebellion has been given a prominent place in the historiography of colonial Ecuador.[66] It has been described as "the first of the major insurrections provoked by the Caroline reforms of the later eighteenth century" with a notable place in that "second wave" of disturbances which culminated in the rebellions of the Comuneros in New Granada and Tupac Amaru in Peru in the 1780s.[67]

Andrien's study of the socio-economic background to the 1765 rebellion shows that "the transition from textiles to agriculture resulted in some modest recovery from the reverses of the late seventeenth century, followed by a marked decline by the 1750s."[68] These difficulties worsened after 1763 with the end of the Anglo-Spanish war, and the renewal of international trade competition for Quito's textiles.[69] A sharp deterioration of the situation in 1764–66 emerges from the figures for hijos expósitos which shows that children were being abandoned in Quito at this "conjuncture" (Figure 6.4). 1765 was also the year of a major epidemic. Pérez, drawing on Juan de Velasco, argued that the earthquake of 1755 and the epidemic of 1759 may have been background factors to the Quito insurrection.[70] In any event, the 1765 epidemic shows up far better in the demographic indices and clearly has a more direct relevance for the rebellion (Figure 6.2). Recio, a Jesuit who lived in Quito at the time of the Quito rebellion, specifically remembers this as running prior to, during, and after

---

[66] K. J. Andrien, "Economic crisis," 104–131; A. McFarlane, "Civil Disorders and Popular Protests, 17–54; "The 'Rebellion of the Barrios'," 283–330; J. Pérez, *Los movimientos precursores de la emancipación en Hispanoamérica*, (Madrid, 1977).

[67] McFarlane, "Rebellion," 283.

[68] Andrien, "Economic crisis," 117.

[69] *Ibid.*

[70] Pérez, *Los movimientos precursores*, 48. The 1759 epidemic caused few mortalities because of previous exposure to *viruelas*. S. A. Alchon, "Epidemics in the city of Quito: Disease, Population, and Public Health during the Eighteenth Century." Paper presented at the 46th International Congress of Americanists, Amsterdam, 1988.

the Quito rebellion, but there is other documentary proof as to its impact.[71] The importance of the epidemic was probably two-way; in the aftermath of the rebellion, the Audiencia was to claim on August 25, 1765, that the epidemics were having a tranquilizing effect on the population by immobilizing many households through sickness; at that date the epidemic was affecting much of the highlands.[72]

At this difficult conjuncture came the application to Quito of the much wider Bourbon attempt to tighten its imperial control over the colonial economy. In 1764 don Pedro Messía de la Cerda, the viceroy of New Granada decided to introduce direct administration of the aguardiente monopoly and sales tax. In Quito, these were administered privately by tax-farmers with all the indifference to royal interests which this supposed, and as part of a web of local interests which the royal administration would have to cut through. Thus the administrator of the aguardiente monopoly was Mariano Solano de Salas, an official of the Audiencia and associate of don Félix de Llano and don José de Cistue, judge and attorney of the Audiencia respectively; while it would be claimed later that sales tax collection had been rented out to the friends of the audiencia judges.[73] In late 1764 the viceroy's nominee, don Juan Díaz de Herrera arrived in Quito fresh from the successful application of similar measures in Popayán.

The opposition he was to meet was broadly based, but in the first instance, as would again occur in 1809, the initiative came from the highest levels of Quito society. McFarlane examines in detail the build-up to the rebellion and identifies distinct sources of opposition. Firstly, there was the Creole patriciate, with the cabildo as its instrument, where Francisco de Borja, connected to several of Quito's noble families, campaigned against the fiscal measures. Next, there was the ecclesiastical community which on November 14, 1764, pushed for a cabildo abierto, which would allow "creole opposition to move into a new arena ... a general congress which claimed to represent the interests of the entire community." Finally, there may have been opposition from within the ranks of royal government with four of the six serving ministers being Creoles, and the other two long-established in the city. Díaz de Herrera seems to have been suspicious of all the audiencia officials, and at the very least counted on little local cooperation.[74]

---

[71] B. Recio, *Compendiosa relación* ... (Madrid, 1947), 402. ANC/B Misc. de la Colonia, Tomo 60, fol. 441; Carta de Felix de Llano, Quito, December 17, 1765. AGI Quito 398, fol. 495; Carta del Audiencia, August 25, 1765, "Escritos de Espejo"; A. Pérez, *Las Mitas en la Real Audiencia de Quito*, (Quito, 1947), 346.

[72] AGI Quito 398, fol. 495; Carta del Audiencia, August 25, 1765, mentions Latacunga, Ambato and also Zambisa in the Corregimiento.

[73] D. A. Washburn, *The Bourbon Reforms: A Social and Economic History of the Audiencia of Quito, 1760–1810*, doctoral dissertation, University of Texas at Austin, 1984, 171.

[74] McFarlane, "Rebellion," 287–292.

An open cabildo, held on the December 7, 1764 was the forum in which elite grievances were aired. Earthquakes, lack of specie, redirected trade routes, poverty and misfortune, the pleading is eloquent:

> "... so the community (*vecindario*) cannot get over the travails caused by the earthquakes in many years nor recover from its poverty and misfortune. Next, the devaluing of the paños and state of ruin is not only in (la)Tacunga but in all the Province, since they do not buy them in Perú, nor pay their usual value as before because the paños of England which they call seconds ('de segunda') which are cheap, are caused by the ease with which the licensed ships come by Cape Horn, and this should be resolved ... because it is against the interests of the defense of Cartagena and Santa Martha and their defenses, and the lack of money is such that within three or four years there won't be specie left ...."[75]

Ecclesiastics argued for the suppression of the aguardiente monopoly on moral grounds, and whether or not they were also affected as producers, their arguments provide a detailed testimony of one of the negative pressures of colonial institutions on Indian society. According to Fray Marcos León, for example,[76] the monopoly was rented out in the villages to people with "little fear of God," who incited the Indians to drink on credit with clothing as security. Little by little, the Indians were indebted, losing their pawned goods and even livestock. The Creole elite advanced a series of arguments against the aguardiente monopoly based mainly on the alleged economic difficulties of the region.

The pressures of Quito's elite do not seem to have had any influence on the royal administration. On February 1, 1765, the viceroy took note of the difficulties Díaz de Herrera was experiencing, and his reaction to the opposition was to order an increase in available troops to 200.[77] On March 1, 1765 the aguardiente monopoly was inaugurated. In mid-May Díaz de Herrera set about the establishment of the reformed sales tax administration and on May 21 plots were registered in San Roque for tax purposes. Tax began to be collected from those hitherto exempt from the alcabala: the ecclesiastics and the Indians who supplied the urban market with subsistence agricultural produce. Meanwhile, rumors, the invariable harbingers of rebellion, began to spread through the city: the administration was going to tax the stones in the river or babies in the womb.[78]

The rebellion broke out on May 22, 1765. I have linked this timing with the preparations for Corpus Christi, having noted that the preparations took place weeks before the event, while the festival of Corpus Christi fell

---

[75] AGI Quito 398, two copies; here doc. 148, "Testimonio del discurso echo por las Religiones y Communidad de la Vezindad de la ciudad de Quito," Quito, Dec. 14, 1764, fols. 149/1598 ff., double numeration.

[76] AGI Quito 398, fol. 610–611.

[77] Washburn, *The Bourbon Reforms,* 172.

[78] Andrien, "Economic crisis," 125.

on June 6 in 1765.[79] The riot of May 22 was therefore well within the build-up period for that festival, one of competitive rivalries which mobilized a large part of the population of the city; one witness commented on the atmosphere of that night, which made him think the crowds were in fact going to celebrate festivities. [80] On the evening of May 22, crowds summoned by church bells and fireworks set out from the parishes of San Roque, San Sebastián and San Blas to converge on the customs house and distillery on the square of Santa Bárbara.[81] At least one account, however, specifies that the rebellion began in San Roque, and describes the crowds descending from San Roque to the plaza of Santo Domingo, where a contingent set off to fetch the people of San Sebastián, with rebellion subsequently spreading to the rest of the city.[82] The token force assembled by the Audiencia was unable to prevent the rioters demolishing the customs house and distillery, and only ecclesiastical intervention calmed spirits sufficiently for the crowd, several thousand strong, to disperse during the night. The Audiencia now had to "submit to a humiliating process of negotiation with a turbulent populace, in an atmosphere charged with excitement, fear, and suspicion," agreeing, firstly, to an ambiguous pardon which failed to convince the populace, and subsequently, after the bishop had been to San Roque to negotiate, to a full general pardon, and the suspension of the aguardiente monopoly and alcabala administration, proposals which were offered to a public meeting on the main plaza.[83]

In the weeks which followed there were further signs of instability. There was a "commotion" in the barrio of San Blas on May 26, and on the 29th "all the barrios assembled," and there were reports that they were stoning the house of an official, the *alguacil mayor de corte,* until the Mercedarians stepped in to intervene; a day later it was the turn of the Dominicans and the Colegio de San Fernando (Franciscan) to help Don Antonio Arango.[84] On June 18, 1765 the barrio of San Blas rose to impose their choice of parish priest, and the next day to rescue a prisoner from jail.[85] One official claimed that the state of anarchy was such that the people of the barrios themselves solicited the "rounds" of the royal officials:

---

[79] See Chapter 4 for Corpus Christi and Minchom, *Urban Popular Society in Colonial Quito*, 350–351, which suggested a link between the preparations for Corpus and the rebellion. (I calculated the date for 1765 from John J. Bond, *Handy-book of Rules* (London, 1875), 140.) McFarlane agrees, "Rebellion," 308.

[80] ANC/B Historia Civil Tomo 4, fol. 951.

[81] McFarlane, "Rebellion," 302.

[82] AGI Quito 398, "Relasion individual ... de lo acaecido en esta ciudad de Quito ... por el Dr Don Gabriel Alvarez del Corro," doc. 150, copy of 149, (received January 18, 1766): fol. 1.

[83] McFarlane, "Rebellion," 303–304.

[84] BN/Bogotá (Libros Raros), Ms. 179: 5, fol. 3.

[85] AHBC/Q Fondo Jijón y Caamaño, vol. 10, "Diario de lo acaecido en San Francisco de Quito desde el día 22 de Mayo ...," (n. d. but 1765), fols. 1–2.

"the evils we saw that night" led to the arrest of 44 people.[86] For all the intermittent eruptions of tension and small-scale criminality, this willingness to call on royal authority to maintain order demonstrates the underlying strength of conservative moderation in the barrios. The Marquis of Villarocha, describing this period between two rebellions, emphasized that the treasury was defenseless "and if the barrios had wanted to commit any excess, they would not have encountered the slightest resistance."[87] Popular moderation, however, was not reciprocated by the corregidor of the city who punished his new prisoners with floggings, duckings in water, telling them as they were beaten: "Take [this for the] Customs, take [this for] the monopoly, take [this for] the uprising: and in this way the rest fall."[88]

This official vindictiveness sparked off the second major rebellion which broke out on June 24, 1765, amid the rowdiness of the festival of Saint John; the Bishop of Quito was to comment on the drunkenness of the plebeians which may have spilled over from the festivities.[89] Once again a festival played a key role. The fact that Saint John's festival was the time at which ritual battles ocurred reinforces this link and defines the role of the barrios.[90] Rumors had run through the city on the 24th, with fly-posters appearing in San Roque calling for a union of the barrios against the corregidor of Quito.[91] Events were sparked off, however, in late evening when the corregidor and a group of peninsular Spaniards sought to make a demonstration of official authority by shooting into the crowd in San Sebastián, killing two or three people.[92] What followed took on the characteristics of an anti-Spanish riot. The houses of peninsular merchants were sacked, and attacks were launched against the Audiencia palace. With the Audiencia isolated and suspicious of the attitudes of the Creole elite, it had little choice but to agree to a virtual capitulation, which consisted of the surrender of official weapons, the expulsion of unmarried peninsular Spaniards and a general pardon.

Effective authority in Quito—insofar as it existed at all—was now in local hands, with royal officials biding their time. The Creoles appointed as

---

[86] *Ibid.*, fol. 2.

[87] BL Egerton 1808: "Información y probanza de la fidelidad de los oficiales reales ...," Quito, December 14, 1765; witness heard, October 29, 1765, fol. 459.

[88] BN/Bogotá (Libros Raros), Ms. 223, doc. 2, "Diario de la segunda sublevación," fol. 1. "Toma Aduana, toma Estanco, toma alsamiento, y asi van cayendo todos los demas."

[89] AGI Quito 398, Bishop of Quito, July 9, 1765, fol. 390.

[90] C. Caillavet, "Ex-voto coloniaux et pensée andine: une iconographie du syncrétisme religieux," in *Religions des Andes et Langues indigènes. Equateur. Pérou. Bolivie. Actes du IIIe Colloque d'Etudes Andines,* Université de Provence, 1993, 263-279.

[91] McFarlane, "Rebellion," 310.

[92] BN/Bogotá (Libros Raros), Ms. 223, doc. 2: "Diario de la segunda sublevación," fol.1; AHBC/Q Fondo Jijón y Caamaño, vol. 10, "Diario ...,"

the new captains of the barrios at the beginning of July 1765 attempted to channel the aggression of the populace which periodically manifested itself in renewed attacks on property, and attempts to control the movement of Europeans; there were even calls for independence from Spain with the Count of Selva Florida proposed as monarch.[93] This kind of radicalism, however, helped to reunite Creole leaders with royal authority, and a joint Creole and official policy of avoiding confrontation led to a gradual calming of spirits in the months which followed. Fears of generating violence which might bring the Indians of the hinterland into action (there were rumors to this effect several times in 1765)[94] undoubtedly contributed to this change of atmosphere. A turning-point may have been the ratification in mid-September of the general pardon previously offered by the Audiencia in July, and by October the President was reporting stability in the city.[95] A visitor to Quito in July 1766 reported on the security which the people of the barrios seemed to feel at the approach of Royal troops[96], and there was popular enthusiasm when the Royal troops entered the city on September 1, 1766.

The Rebellion as Seen by the Quiteños: The Official Investigation and Local Testimonies

Who, then, were those who participated in the rebellions of 1765? In the official documentation, there were repeated suggestions by officials that important Creole leaders may have been directly involved, and, at the very least, failed to rally effectively to the royal cause.[97] During 1764–65, church leaders were also heavily involved in local opposition to official reform, which affected them as landowners and producers.[98] If we should look for any "hidden hands," a comparison with the disturbances of the 1740s suggests that the Franciscans are among the more plausible candidates. During incidents in the Franciscan schism which do not directly concern this study, the Franciscans carried out a rescue wearing masks,[99] while the presence of masked men among the rioters was considered one of

---

[93] Andrien, "Economic crisis," 128; with a different emphasis to McFarlane, "Rebellion," 324.

[94] McFarlane, "Rebellion," 305–6; 312; 314.

[95] *Ibid.*, 322.

[96] The Royal Library of Copenhagen, "Cuaderno de Guachucal en la Provincia de los Pastos hasta la ciudad de Cuenca y Quito," (1766), Ny kgl. Samling 568 (4). Consulted in the transcription of Juan Castro y Velázquez, fol. 12.

[97] AGI Quito 398, Letter of the Viceroy, July 5, 1765, fol. 358. McFarlane, "Rebellion," for earlier suspicions, 305; Andrien, "Economic crisis," 125–6.

[98] AGI Quito 398, "Testimonio del discurso echo por las Religiones ...."

[99] This is a detail from AGI Quito 206, which *GS* omitted from his account.

the suspicious features of the 1765 rebellion.[100] The chronological link of the May uprising to the forthcoming festivities of Corpus Christi, with much of the populace collectively organized in their preparation, is also consistent with possible clerical involvement. All this evidence on elite and clerical involvement is, however, highly indirect.

While there is no doubt as to the involvement of the "people of Quito" in the rebellions of 1765, there are no trial records or other direct evidence on the socio-economic status of the rioters, although we know from the scattered evidence on the 1740s rioting that settled artisans or petty traders, rather than dispossessed marginals, tended to be in the forefront of the action. McFarlane cites Juan de Velasco for the participation of 60 butchers who attacked the excise house during the first rebellion and were then joined by people from other barrios; he argues that while "it is not entirely clear how [the] different groups were brought together," the mixed social composition of Santa Bárbara where the riot started, may suggest creole political influence.[101] Although Juan de Velasco is the least sound of eighteenth-century chroniclers, it is inherently plausible that the butchers did play a role.[102] I would argue, however, that it would be misleading to see Creole influence refracted through Santa Bárbara. The slaughterhouse area seems to have been a kind of sub-barrio straddling Santa Bárbara and the more popular parish of San Blas.[103] Furthermore, the fact that "the riot started in the slaughterhouse district"[104] simply reflects the location of the customs house on the plaza of Santa Bárbara; the official correspondence or narrative accounts compiled soon after the event nearly all stress the predominant role of San Roque and to a lesser extent San Sebastián, while, significantly, they also mention the popular parish of San Blas but not neighboring Santa Bárbara.[105] The Jesuit eyewitness Recio specifically picks out San Sebastián and San Roque, the latter described as the most "combative" (*aguerrido*) barrio.[106]

---

[100] On the other hand, masks were of symbolic importance in the Andean tradition as well as of obvious practical value, so this detail is scarcely conclusive. See R. T. Zuidema, "Masks in the Incaic Solstice and Equinoctial Rituals," in N. Ross Cumrine and Marjorie Halpin (eds.), *The Power of Symbols: Masks and Masquerades in the Americas*, (Vancouver, 1983).

[101] McFarlane, "Rebellion," 305–7, citing Juan de Velasco.

[102] C. Borchart de Moreno has noticed that Juan de Velasco copied extensively from Jorge Juan and Antonio de Ulloa (personal communication). He also "invented" an Ecuadorian pre-history which has had little echo among serious modern scholars. However, the butchers may have played a similar role in 1809.

[103] See Chapter 5.

[104] McFarlane, "Rebellion," 305.

[105] See precisely McFarlane's own work, "Rebellion," 302, while AGI Quito 398, "Relacion individual ... por el Dr Don Gabriel Alvarez del Corro," fol. 1, specifically states that the rebellion broke out in San Roque.

[106] Recio, *Compendiosa relación*, 517 ff. and 526.

To clarify the nature of popular and elite participation in the Quito rebellion, I am now able to contribute the major documentary evidence of an official investigation into its causes and nature. McFarlane mentioned a secret investigation sent by the oidor Hurtado de Mendoza to the viceroy in August 1765 with the testimony of witnesses, which has not been located.[107] However, the oidor Doctor Don Josef Ferrer sent a report from Quito, dated November 14, 1768, which contains the testimony of witnesses on the Quito rebellion, and must therefore have formed part of the ongoing official investigation.[108] Twenty-five witnesses were questioned in secret, amongst whom there were six merchants and two notaries. Only one was an artisan, a silversmith and therefore from the upper reaches of non-elite society, who was heard last, and took pains to distinguish his own like from the "more rustic people of the barrios." [109] Twenty-one of the witnesses were apparently Quiteños, while one was from Panamá and another from Popayán. Although there were also two peninsular Spaniards, and one witness had apparently had to seek refuge from the rioters[110], we clearly have to allow for an in-built bias towards Quito's creole elite.

Witnesses were asked "if they knew the origin of the revolt[111] which took place on May 22." Don Juan Matheo Navarette, a notary, testified that he had heard both in the city and in Sangolquí (in the corregimiento), fears "that they were going to tax the vegetables which the poor produced for their food, and likewise having gone out to enumerate the lots of land (*solares y corrales*) they were fixing the taxes they should pay. What was more, (they were going to tax) the women giving birth." All this exasperated the plebe of the barrios and the Mestizos of the countryside "who communicated with each other by letter."[112] Other accounts stress the critical importance of "the grains which they bring to the square for the common consumption."[113] "Some cried, others said they would vote with their feet (*mudarían de patria*), and another that the day was arriving when they would die of hunger."[114] It was specifically the fear that they were about to begin collecting taxes, presumably in the form of produce, which sparked off the rebellion; the evidence for this was not only the registering

---

[107] McFarlane, "Rebellion," 305.
[108] ANC/B Historia Civil Tomo 4, 917 ff. To judge from my notes, the "lost" testimonies are not in the same section.
[109] *Ibid.*, fol. 979, "la gente más rústica de los barrios."
[110] *Ibid.*, fol. 973 ff. Testimony of Don Bernardo Legarda.
[111] "*Alboroto*," "*inquietud*," o "*sublevazión*."
[112] *Ibid.*, fol. 955.
[113] *Ibid.*, fol. 925.
[114] *Ibid.*, fol. 928.

of plots, but the stocking in the Customs House of the bags and trunks which would be used for collection.[115]

What is striking in the testimony on the origins of the first riot is the frequency with which two points were mentioned; specifically, the threat to the urban lots, and the rumors that women would pay tax on births.[116] The first point, on which witnesses were practically unanimous, underlines the crucial importance of the threat to the underground economy. The prevalence of the second rumor, typical of those which circulated before Andean rebellions, suggests that it was perceived as a genuine threat, unlike the rhetoric about taxes on stones in the water, or on the air people breathed. The most plausible explanation is that what the populace meant by a "tax on babies" was a back-door attempt by the royal authorities to introduce some form of tribute or head-tax for urban plebeians. These were highly sensitive to any attempt to assimilate them to the Indian population; indeed, the Mestizos of San Roque had threatened to rebel on this very point three years earlier.[117] The testimony, by emphasizing the importance of the urban lots to the urban populace, underlines the role of San Roque and San Sebastián where officials had just begun recording them.

The role of San Roque as the "engine of unrest" is further corroborated by three replies to the second question which asked if witnesses knew who were the "tumultuados" and whether "disguised" ringleaders circulated among them. Doctor Don Matheo Joseph de Aizpuru, originally from Panamá, saw a large crowd of both sexes, youngsters included, going down the street from San Roque, shouting and carrying lighted candles. The atmosphere is nicely conveyed by his reaction that these were festivities; he spoke of the "alegría" of the plebe, going to another barrio.[118] Another witness, Don Bernardo Legarda, who lived in the Plazuela de San Francisco peeked through his window and saw a great number of people passing through the crossroads, shouting "Viva el barrio," and stoning the streetlights. They came "off the volcanoes and out of stores" and he didn't see any ringleaders: his vantage-point in the Plazuela of San Francisco means that he, too, was presumably seeing rioters from San Roque.[119] Finally, Fernando Solís, master silversmith, said that the rebellion was sparked off when it was rumored that they were threatening people with the gallows in the barrio of San Roque and "without waiting for prudent confirmation or Christian reflection" they invaded the royal customs house.

Some evidence emerges on the interaction of the barrios with each other and with the Indian population. The barrios may have communicated

---

115   *Ibid.*, fols. 964; 968.
116   *Ibid.*, fols. 920; 923; 925, multiple testimonies.
117   See above in this chapter.
118   ANC/B Historia Civil Tomo 4, fol. 951.
119   *Ibid.*, fol. 974.

with each other through church bells and fireworks,[120] while fly-posters may in fact also have been a method for inter-barrio communication.[121] Posters were fixed on church doors and at cross-roads.[122] As in the 1740s, the distinctive social geography of the city played its role with the quebradas serving as hiding-places and indeed improvised cemeteries.[123] The notary don Juan Matheo Navarette, claimed he saw an unsigned paper in which the barrio of San Roque threatened the Indians that if they did not come in their defense, they would burn their houses, and kill them.[124] Another witness also claimed that the Mestizos called in Indians from the Corregimiento,[125] and another "from his balcony saw a multitude of Indians who came shouting and throwing stones," but didn't know who summoned them[126]; they came in traditional Indian rebellion style playing conches and drums.[127] There was one suggestive comment on the divisions of the urban plebe, with some uniting with the Indians, while others did not wish to get involved.[128] These tensions may help to explain the break-up of the rebellion's impetus after June 1765.

The St. John's uprising was generally attributed to fears of a massacre by the Europeans[129] amid concern that the pardon over the first rebellion would not be respected.[130] Don Gerónimo Pérez de Grado, a peninsular witness, gave the impression that it was relatively organized; crowds assembling in San Sebastián were advised that the corregidor was doing his rounds. The first to resist was a fireworks maker, and the others followed with stones.[131] Another claimed the crowds knew in advance of the approach of the royal officials because they had "outlying spies" to warn them.[132]

---

[120] *Ibid.*, fol. 962.
[121] *Ibid.*, fol. 922.
[122] *Ibid.*, fol. 979.
[123] *Ibid.*, fols. 956, 981.
[124] *Ibid.*, fol. 957.
[125] *Ibid.*, fols. 944, 946.
[126] *Ibid.*, fol. 919.
[127] *Ibid.*, fol. 940, "churos y tambores."
[128] *Ibid.*, fol. 921, 924.
[129] *Ibid.*, fols. 918, 921, 923.
[130] *Ibid.*, fol. 929.
[131] *Ibid.*, fol. 948.
[132] *Ibid.*, fol. 969; my translation of "espias perdidas."

With regard to violence, the rebels used stones[133] and sticks[134] and thick wet cloths to defend themselves against bullets and fire.[135] Women and children picked up the stones to give them to the rioters,[136] "stones which rained better than bullets."[137] The silversmith reported a crowd coming to his house, because he made bullets for royal justice against the people of the barrios, and was saved by the troops.[138] As in the attack on the customs house and the property of peninsular merchants, this example of popular violence was controlled and directed against a specific target. All the witnesses knew the story of the gallows which was taken away from the main square and installed in Santo Domingo where a loyalist mulato, already dead, was hung by his feet.[139] This had therefore presumably become part of Quito folklore; it is revealing of a restraining sense of order and hierarchy that the most extreme symbolic violence should be directed only against the very lowest (and racially distinct) echelons of royalist authority.

Who were those responsible? The witnesses had no doubts: the rebellion was the work of "la ínfima plebe"—of Indians, Mestizos, women and children—and no-one went among them disguised.[140] They were driven by their desperation, shouting that it was better to "die killing than die of hunger."[141] Nobody influenced them, there were no disguises. It is not surprising to find the Creole elite closing ranks and blaming the "rabble" (*la gentalla*).[142] On the other hand, here were twenty-five witnesses, all of them testifying in secret, and yet we cannot find just one or two of them—even among the peninsular Spaniards—to point fingers, for the sake, for example, of a private grudge. Equally relevant is the fact that, despite their rather general accusations in the official correspondence, the royal officials had themselves been unable to do any better three years earlier; were they attempting to exculpate their own lamentable handling of fiscal reforms by magnifying the social scope of the Quito insurrection?

The clear identification of the popular homogeneous "Mestizo" barrio of San Roque as the "engine of unrest," building up contacts with other barrios such as San Sebastián, provides a new perspective on the social composition of the Quito insurrection. In the place of the Creole

---

[133] *Ibid.*, fols. 919, 921.
[134] *Ibid.*, fol. 930, 932.
[135] *Ibid.*, fol. 972.
[136] *Ibid.*, fols. 924, 927.
[137] *Ibid.*, fol. 927.
[138] *Ibid.*, fol. 981.
[139] *Ibid.*, fols. 919, 921, 924.
[140] *Ibid.*, fol. 920.
[141] *Ibid.*, fol. 928–929, "mejor es morir matando que de hambre."
[142] *Ibid.*, fols. 923, 925.

involvement to which McFarlane points when he attributes a possible leading role to the socially mixed parish of Santa Bárbara, it emerges that the insurrection was firmly rooted in precisely those popular sectors of the city which were outside aristocratic influence. And this provides one explanation for the total inability of the Royal administrative machinery to come up with plausible creole suspects, let alone institute trial proceedings. The rebellion may have thrown up an informal leadership, as implied by the rudimentary organizational structure of the rebellion; the barrio roots of unrest, however, show that this must have been at the lower levels of Quito society, beneath and beyond the "known" Quito society which its officials could investigate.[143]

The Political Landscape After 1765: Reaction and Conspiracies

QUITO IN 1779

The Quito insurrection shaped the political landscape for more than a generation. "A legacy of mistrust and fear remained after 1765, dividing the city's social groups and inhibiting concerted resistance to crown policies."[144] While the rest of the Andean region was swept by major rebellions around 1780, both to the north (with the Comunero rebellion), and to the south (with the Tupac Amaru and Tupac Catari rebellions), both the city of Quito, and to a lesser extent the Audiencia, were in a state of uneasy peace. This tranquillity was specifically commented upon by the Audiencia when they received news of the revolt in Pasto in 1781 and were worried about the risk of contagion to the capital. The creole elite had now seen what its populace was capable of and for "decades ... continued to fear the plebeians more than the fiscal exactions of the state."[145]

The Royal authorities, too, had learnt their lessons from 1765. Fiscal reform had been pushed through with deliberate insensitivity to local conditions, using Juan Díaz de Herrera, the Viceroy's own representative, to bypass a divided Audiencia.[146] In contrast, Villalengua's implementation of a new system of tribute collection in the late 1770s was far more attentive to local custom, precisely no doubt because of the unhappy precedent. It is difficult to imagine a conversation in the late 1770s along the lines reported

---

[143] Royal authority clearly had not learnt to make use of spies in the eighteenth century to judge from its performance in the 1740s or around 1779, when it appears to have relied on intimidation rather than stealth. Núñez del Arco's report (1813) belongs to a different period.

[144] Andrien, "Economic crisis," 129.

[145] *Ibid.*, 128–129. For the revolt in Pasto see R. E. Mond, "Indian Rebellion and Bourbon Reform in New Granada: Riots in Pasto, 1780-1800," *HAHR,* 73: (1993), 99-124.

[146] *Ibid.*, 120–121, and McFarlane, "Rebellion," 286–7.

in 1768 by the Quiteño Don Bernardo Legarda who had told Juan Díaz de Herrera of fly-posters threatening rebellion on the very eve of May 22, 1765. Díaz de Herrera's reaction was to "make light of this news, he told him they'd just throw four stones."[147] By then the authorities had assimilated the lesson that stone-throwing could shake the edifice of colonial order.

Indeed, the measures of security taken in Quito around 1780 underline the gradual emergence of a system of public order, which conforms to the broader imperial pattern of militia reform in the late eighteenth century.[148] The heavy measures of security which emerge from a case in 1779 provide a contrast to earlier disturbances such as the riots of the 1740s when officials were forced to do their rounds with a single black slave.[149] In 1779, Francisco Xavier de la Cruz and his companions were tried for having beaten a drum in the barrio of San Sebastián, allegedly in order to call for a rebellion. A patrol of eight soldiers and a lieutenant had picked Xavier up when he shouted "Brothers, bring the Virgin of Quinche."[150] The Virgin of Quinche was brought to help Quito in times of difficulty, and the defendant said people were dying of hunger.

The background to this case was the new wave of fiscal reform in the later 1770s and there were alleged fears that the authorities were going to introduce monopolies on bread, water and tallow fat.[151] We may note the occupations of the suspects, who were Indian and Mestizo hat-makers and an Indian tailor, of comparable artisan status to the rioters of the 1740s. From both the measures of security, the pains taken to investigate a relatively small-scale incident and indeed from the interrogation of witnesses, it is clear that the rebellion of 1765 was on everybody's mind. The question of whether one of the suspects had been involved was directly put to witnesses, and the reply—that "since he lives inside the city he was not a companion of the "mosos" of the barrios"[152]—is an eloquent comment in favor of the view that the roots of social disorder did indeed lie in the more popular barrios.

---

[147] ANC/B, Historia Civil Tomo 4, fol. 974. "Depreciando las noticias."
[148] A. Kuethe, *Military Reform and Society in New Granada, 1773–1808*, (Gainesville, 1978).
[149] See above in this chapter.
[150] ANH/Q Ind. 97 doc. 1779–IV–27, fol. 3.
[151] *Ibid.*, fol. 1.
[152] *Ibid.*, fol. 43.

Eugenio Espejo, The Economic Society of the Friends of the "Country" of Quito, and the Tensions of the Mid-1790s

Although the reform program associated with the Bishop Pérez de Calama in the 1790s was very much an aristocratic affair, we can find ideas crystallizing at this period which appeared to find a broader echo in Quito society. The elite dimension of Enlightenment ideology and its reception in Quito lies beyond the scope of this study, and here I wish to place the emphasis on the surfacing of Creole frustrations with roots deep in Quito society. These provide a link between the insurrections of 1765 and 1809-10, allowing us to see how barriers were emerging between the elite and the "people of Quito." The chronology of reform and repression in Quito in the 1790s provides a modest confirmation from the periphery of Palmer's hypothesis that the North American, French and other "Atlantic" revolutions were a series of inter-connected events sending out shock-waves and developing on parallel lines.[153]

Eugenio Espejo was to play a prominent role in the events of the 1790s, but his career as a hired pen, lent to the services of enlightened patrons, ecclesiastics or local factions, had already given his work an ambiguous character, notably present in his relations with the church.[154] From the early 1780s onwards he was involved in a series of controversies, taking the form most typically of a published polemic followed by trouble with the authorities, none of which, however, appears to have closed the doors of Quito society to him prior to his final disgrace and imprisonment. After "El retrato de Golilla" had attacked Charles III and Gálvez, Espejo began to have a questionable reputation and was arrested for the first time in 1783, the year he was named, against his wishes, medical director of an expedition to the Marañon. "Reflexiones ... viruelas," commissioned in 1785, showed the poor state of medicine. Espejo, *persona non grata* in Quito, had to leave for Riobamba where he drafted the reply of the priests to the report of the tribute official Ignacio de Barreto alleging abuses of the indigenous population. In 1787 Espejo wrote *Cartas Riobambenses,* taking on María Chiriboga, from one of Riobamba's most important families, whom he accused of adultery. Once again, Espejo had to move, receiving instructions to continue to Lima, or return to Quito from Riobamba. From 1788 to 1790 Espejo was in Santafé de Bogotá. By then he had acquired enough of a reputation as a troublemaker for Villalengua to write from Quito

---

[153] Palmer, *The Age of Democratic Revolution*. See also David J. Robinson, "Liberty, Fragile Fraternity, and Inequality in Early Republican Spanish America: analyzing the impact of French revolutionary ideas," *Journal of Historical Geography*, vol. 16 (1990), 51-75.

[154] Espejo defended the clerics of Riobamba; but the "Representation" written on their behalf has been seen as an attack on officials which only "ostensibly" defended clerics, while attacks on the clergy made him enemies. R. J. Shafer, *The Economic Societies in the Spanish World (1763–1821)* (Syracuse, 1958), 169; and the concluding discussion of P. Astuto, "Eugenio Espejo," 369-391.

warning the viceroy of Espejo's "objectionable life-style and practices."[155] He had what appears to have been a seminal stay in Bogotá where he was in contact with enlightened circles, meeting Nariño and the Marquis of Montúfar: in Astuto's opinion he came back a revolutionary.[156] When he returned to Quito in 1790, it was to make his contribution to a heady atmosphere of reform.

This was given its impetus by Bishop Pérez de Calama who assumed his post in February 1791 and attempted to shake the Quito diocese out of its lethargy with a major pastoral "visit," or inspection, in 1791, attacks on clerical absenteeism, and a sketch for the development of university education, the "Plan de Estudios de la Real Universidad" (1791).[157] On a broader front, it was Pérez de Calama who presided over the inauguration in 1791 of the Economic Society of the Friends of the "Country" of Quito[158] in which the philosopher and propagandist Eugenio Espejo played an important role. The Economic Societies, a reflection of Physiocrat influence and in principle among the more practical offshoots of Enlightenment thought, were centers for the exchange of social and political ideas ranging from the improvement of commerce and agriculture to politics and industry.[159] The emergence of an energetic new Bishop patronizing advanced European ideas seems to have had the effect of a breath of fresh air on the Quito equivalent of salon society, with Pérez de Calama himself paying tribute to the distinguished ladies present at the inaugural meeting on November 30, 1791.[160] The Peruvian journal *Mercurio Peruano* [161]noted the influence of the Count of Casa Jijón, another indication of aristocratic interest. The declared goals of the Society, announced in its proposed statutes were the advancement of Agriculture, Science, Arts, Industry and Commerce, Politics and Fine Arts.

As might be expected, Espejo had an important role to play in the Quito association, and indeed in the new journal *Primicias*. In 1792, he claimed credit for its creation, recalling his 1786 call for patriotic societies in all the American dominions to remedy the ills of the colonies.[162] When Quito's first Public Library was opened in May of 1791 to an address by Pérez de

---

[155] ANC/B Miscelánea de la Colonia 139, Villalengua to the Viceroy, November 3, 1789, fol. 868.

[156] Astuto, "Eugenio Espejo," 383.

[157] J. T. Lanning, "La oposición a la Ilustración en Quito," *Revista Bimestre Cubano*, 53 (1944), 225.

[158] "Sociedad Económica de los Amigos del País de Quito."

[159] E. Beerman, "Eugenio Espejo y la sociedad económica de los amigos del país de Quito," in: A. G. Novales (ed.), *Homenaje a Noël Salomon: Ilustración española e Independencia de América*, (Barcelona, 1979), 380.

[160] *Ibid.*, 383.

[161] Shafer, *The Economic Societies*, 171.

[162] *Ibid.*, 169.

Calama, it was Espejo who was its director. Espejo's writings had already, and would now continue to, set out the ills of the Audiencia in line with the goal of reanimating "the dying realm" which the *Mercurio Peruano* had defined as the goal of Quito's Economic Society. "Escuela de Concordia," a discourse written at the behest of the marquis of Selva Alegre depicted Quito on the verge of ruin and in spiritual decay. "Voto de un ministro togado de la Audiencia de Quito" reviewed the economic conditions of the Audiencia.

Within months of its creation, the Economic Society had already run out of steam. The Bishop, who had anticipated and condemned the "envy [and] discord" which might impede progress,[163] soon met with opposition from within the church. Lanning has traced some of the antagonisms in the local church, amongst which, the clash between the University of Santo Tomás and the Dominicans (who opposed to the secularization of education) was one of the most important. The strength of factionalism, which Lanning stresses was more important than liberalism or intellectual reaction (describing the "acrimonious debates" over the Ptolemaic system or Aristotle), must have played against Pérez de Calama's attempts to introduce a fresh approach (in this case through his plan for university education). In 1792 the ecclesiastical cabildo declared the bishop's chair empty, in what could be considered a miniature, ecclesiastical counterpart to the secular process whereby Spanish American provinces—preferring inefficiency and neglect—came to resent the new, enlightened Bourbon broom which was sweeping away what they saw as their customary rights. With Pérez de Calama relieved of his post, the Economic Society had lost its most dynamic patron.

The Economic Society held its last meeting on March 10, 1792. A royal order closed it on November 11, 1793. Its short life corresponded to the intellectual impulse generated by the early stages of the French Revolution, and its demise reflected the European, and therefore imperial, wide reaction to the course that the Revolution had taken by 1793. The Economic Society collapsed under its own weight as much as by virtue of official repression. Nevertheless, the reactionary policy of blocking all channels for creole resentment, and splintering circles which could express constructive ideas, hardened and drove underground critical opinions. The extent to which the international climate of the 1790s was directly conditioned by reaction to the French Revolution can be simply established by taking bearings from two radically different viewpoints. Thus both Quito and England followed exactly the same cycle: enlightened debate, followed by reaction (including in England, too, the dissolution of voluntary associations), which finally culminated in a climate of repression denunciation, and real or imagined conspiracies.[164]

---

163   *Ibid.*, 175.

164   Compare, for example, E. P. Thompson, *The Making of the English Working Class* (London, 1963).

In Quito, this last phase was in 1795 a year which also saw "pre-revolutionary" events in New Granada (with the arrest of Nariño) and Peru.[165] Already on October 14, 1794 the cabildo had complained that the plebe was becoming insolent and that disorders had increased. This was attributed to the suppression of the patrol of the dragoons, and the despatch of one of the three fixed companies which also assisted in patrols to Guayaquil.[166] During 1795 fly-posters and broadsheets (some penned by Espejo) appeared in Quito, Guayaquil and Cuenca. Belonging to the same climate of opinion were the extreme declarations of Eugenio's brother, Juan Pablo Espejo, which led to his arrest in the same year. The wider dimension of international unrest and reaction, in which rumors from abroad fed local resentments, can be seen in these events. In the first of Juan Pablo's two conversations ("roughly a month" before the second on January 28, 1795[167]) he mentioned that he was waiting for correspondence from a rich gentleman in Santafé de Bogotá offering them possibilities of benefiting from the "much progress" made there. The fly-posters in Quito[168] appeared with the "rumor funesto de motín, y cedición" in New Granada while those fixed in public places in Cuenca explicitly invoked the example of Peru in their call for rebellion against Spain:

> From Lima has arrived this faithful recipe: Die or conquer in accordance with our law and not the taxes of the King; Indians, Blacks, Whites and Mulatos now, now, now. He who betrays, wants to die; one cannot suffer; like valiant citizens joined to conquer or die, we have to be unanimous.[169]

Similarly, the French Revolution inspired presbyter Juan Pablo Espejo's declaration that the "French Nation acted justly in aspiring to Liberty which was in conformity to the Law of God and natural reason."[170] Clearly, the Creole anti-Spanish sentiments which had been such a driving force in 1765 had been redirected into a new and heady consciousness of hitherto unimaginable possibilities. According to McFarlane, the 1765 rebellion had a conservative, Royalist character while Andrien argues that a much more radical strain may already have emerged.[171] Now, in either case, a taboo had been broken with the execution of Louis XVI, the

---

[165] E. Keeding "La polémica del nuevo mundo en la literatura de Quito del siglo XVIII: Americanos y pardocracia," *Memorias del primer simposio Europeo sobre Antropología del Ecuador*, S. Moreno Yánez, (ed.) (Quito, 1985), 250.

[166] AM/Q, LCQ, October 14, 1794, fol. 88.

[167] AGI Quito, 363, "Compendio de los puntos vertidos ... por Don Juan Pablo Espejo," Quito, April 21, 1795," fol. 2.

[168] AGI Quito 363, "Copia de la vista fiscal," (1795), fol. 1v.

[169] E. Keeding, "La polémica del nuevo mundo," 250.

[170] "Vista fiscal," fol. 1r. We find him denying that the French were heretics in the "Compendio," fol. 2v.

[171] Andrien, "Economic crisis," 128.

symbolism of which was translatable at any level of social and political understanding. Regicide was on the popular political agenda. A lad ("chiquillo") in the street could say that if he were in Spain he would ask permission from the sentinels and stick a dagger in the King. Juan Pablo Espejo could find that this attitude was not merely not an aberration but widespread and defensible; "most people in this city were determined to demand liberty."

The arguments of Juan Pablo Espejo in conversation with Doña Francisca Navarette, here transferred into direct speech, allow us to gauge the extent to which anti-peninsular sentiments were crystallizing into a nascent Creole ideology.

> — I have heard a lad in the street say at night that if he were in Spain he would ask permission and kill the King with a dagger.
>
> — That's not the invention of the boy, I have heard this in various houses because most people in this city are determined to ask for liberty.
>
> — This liberty, they say it's heresy.
>
> — Ignorant people think it's heresy: Liberty of Conscience is one thing, and liberty of Person is another, because here they're bribed by the King's Government—for who doubts that the King is our father?—but this King is no father but a tyrant, and for a son to demand liberty is no sin. We are sons of the earth, we work, we are bribed and everything is for the peninsulars Spaniards. All the rent leaves, with just the other day Don Agustin Martin de Blas, without being assigned revenue ("situado"), taking many thousands. There are subjects of merit who cannot get to be anything because everything is for the chapetones; you'll soon see the government removed.
>
> — And how is that?
>
> — Because we're guarded in Quito like in a box, that closing the roads, they don't have any way of entering. With the few peninsulars there are, by nightfall we arrange that in the morning there are six soldiers at the door of each one, entering all their houses at the same time. And they're asked to show their capital ("caudal"), and for each they're given a thousand pesos to go back to their land. If they're married their wives are asked if they want to follow. If they say yes, give them a thousand more.
>
> — And the children?
>
> — These, no. They would stay in Quito because they have the right to the "patria" because they are born here.
>
> — What would be done with the President and his wife?
>
> — The same ....
>
> — What about me and my mother? And the deaths and the massacre there'd have to be?
>
> — What massacre?
>
> — And will the peninsular Spaniards defend themselves or go quietly?
>
> — He who wishes to die will die, we're not making war. There shouldn't be officially stamped paper ("papel sellado"), Audiencia or scriveners. The Government's very bad, it keeps people prisoner for years at a time, killing

them with hunger. These things have got to stop. There's got to be a judge and not just for a fixed period, so that if he governs badly he can be rapidly relieved and another put in. (Let me put it this way) so that you understand better. Imagine a man brings a girl low. They go before a judge, he wants evidence, witnesses, and let's everyone know it, and so the case drags on. That's not right. Straightaway, if its a person of standing ("decente") who did this crime, and he's got the means, he's ordered, according to her quality, to pay her, and if she's poor and of low birth the solution is getting her out of the Republic and punishment for him. That's how all the suits will be resolved, and there'll be fewer crimes because there won't be poor people or lazy ones, because everybody would be occupied and the Christian Religion would govern better. The monks will be made to follow the common life, giving them an Administrator. If they reply that their income isn't enough for the common life, they'll be given a certain amount, enough to keep them, and when one dies, another will replace him. The soldiers are of the "patria"; they all have relatives, wives and children. Its precisely them we have to make our own to throw out the peninsular Spaniards, close the roads and then we'll govern well. There wouldn't be people living together out of wedlock, they'd have to marry ....

— And should there be a Bishop?

— Everything has to be the same. Only there musn't be commerce, no clothing from Spain, we will dress with what the earth gives: we won't have reason to be jealous for we'll all be equal ....[172]

Juan Pablo Espejo was an ecclesiastic a generation away from the lower reaches of Quito society, but some of his arguments, notably on the functioning of justice, have the feel of street language. The tone of the conversation ("I heard a lad in the street ..."), suggest that it was in certain measure, a commentary on, and a reflection of what "ordinary" Quiteños were saying. A Creole utopia, with a strong strain of French Enlightenment radicalism, had been given a form intelligible to them. Natural rights, liberty against tyranny, commercial links as the reflection of a colonial imbalance: Quiteños had come to understand these in a way which sustained their animosity against peninsular Spaniards and prepared them for the break with Spain.

Suspicions, probably justified, of Eugenio's own role in stirring up unrest in the Audiencia led to the imprisonment from which he was released only a few days before his death on December 26 or 27, 1795. According to traditional accounts, his burial was recorded in the register of "Mestizos, Indians, Blacks and Mulatos." He was not, however, the only person to be excluded from "established" Quito society in the 1790s, at a time when the registers of El Sagrario show a trend towards social exclusiveness. When Juan Pablo Espejo was imprisoned in 1809 for his participation in the Quito revolution he reported that since the death of his brother, he had no contact

---

[172] AGI 363, Quito November 21, 1795, "Compendio."

with Montúfar, the Marquis of Selva Alegre, because, along with other aristocrats, they looked on him with "aversion." [173]

After 1795, then, the Quito aristocracy shut its doors to interlopers like the Espejos, and closed in even more on itself; almost a decade and a half later it was to take its own political route away from imperial authority. Other groups were excluded from this closed circle, and the Quito movement of 1809–10 was characterized by the polarization between narrow aristocratic maneuvers and popular tensions which were never fully mobilized in their favor. Nevertheless, in 1813 when Don Ramón Núñez del Arco compiled his report on the revolutionaries of the period 1809–1812, he was to argue that Selva Alegre had been planning his insurrection since 1794, which suggests that the tensions of 1794–95 had indeed left their mark in the political memory of Quito.[174]

The Quito Revolts of 1809–1810

Aristocratic Maneuvers: The "Shout" of August 10, 1809, and the First Quito Junta

There was little in the social panorama of the early nineteenth-century Audiencia to make independence from Spain seem imminent, even if an evolving Creole identity, a crystallizing consciousness of the "separateness" of the region as a homeland, and real or imagined economic grievances against the domination of the metropolis were all preparing the terrain. It was precisely the tranquillity of Ecuador, the absence of other than local, speedily repressed, Indian uprisings, the most recent that of Guamote and Columbe in the central highlands 1803, which meant that the Quito aristocracy now felt free to take on a new political role.[175] Unlike the Peruvian Creoles, still haunted by the nightmare of the great Tupac Amaru rebellion of 1780, they had little to fear from "their" Indians; they had still less to fear (or respect) in the divided local authorities with an incomplete control over the local garrison and led by an aged and incompetent new President, not least as Creole aristocratic influence reached into the command of the Quito garrison. President Ruiz de Castilla, who according to the Bishop of Quito, spent his mornings pottering around in the garden

---

[173] ANC/B Anexo (Historia) Tomo 6. Quito, December 17, 1809, "Confesión del Dr Don Juan Pablo Espejo, de edad de 50 años," 689–691.

[174] AHBC/Q, Jijón y Caamaño, 1a col. vol. 0010, doc. 38, 243–271. "Estado general ...," Entry 188, fol. 254.

[175] Segundo Moreno Yánez, *Sublevaciones indígenas*, 257ff. For administrative aspects of the Independence period, see Demetrio Ramos Pérez, *Entre el Plata y Bogotá. Cuatro claves de la emancipación Ecuatoriana*, (Madrid, 1978). The attitudes and activities of Quiteño deputies in Spain are mentioned in M-L. Rieu-Millán, *Los diputados americanos en las Cortes de Cádiz*, (Madrid, 1990).

and cooking lunch and the rest of the day gambling[176] saw his hopes of an enjoyable semi-retirement in these peaceful imperial backwaters cruelly frustrated by the chain of events set in motion by Napoleon's invasion of Spain in 1807–8. The abdication of Charles IV in favor of his son Ferdinand VII, and the subsequent replacement of both by Joseph Bonaparte led to the creation of a central junta acting in the name of Bourbon continuity: here was a series of events which posed in an acute and tangible form the question of where legitimate authority was invested at a moment of grave imperial crisis. The reaction in Quito was swift, and was to give Quito a pioneering role in the chain of events which was to culminate in the Independence of nearly all Spanish America.

On August 10, 1809, Quito's Creole elite deposed President Ruiz de Castilla and created an autonomous junta, an act of resistance for which the events in Spain had provided a quasi-legal cover, and which could rally Quiteños, even those not yet prepared for full Independence, to the cause of self-government. The "shout" (*grito*) of August 10, as it is now known, proved to be the prelude to two interruptions in the continuity of Spanish colonial authority, the first from August to October 1809, and the second for a period of over two years after September 1810. As in the rest of Spanish America, the form in which Independence arrived mirrored wider social forces at work, from Mexico, where the Independence movement took on the hues of a social revolution, to Peru, where Creole fears of the Indians were stronger than their resentment of the Spaniards, and Independence required an external stimulus.[177] Quito's revolt was, like the society which produced it, and above all in its inception, the closed, aristocratic affair characteristic of a hierarchical, inward-looking region with a white elite and substantial Indian population. When Don Ramón Núñez del Arco looked back on the events of 1809–12, and reviewed the conduct of all the "noteworthy" survivors in Quito, the most prestigious titled aristocrats, a group of seven with "Titles of Castile and Crusade"— admittedly highly visible and therefore likely to attract strong adjectives— emerged as the most strongly implicated secular group. Don Juan Pío Montúfar, the Marquis of Selva Alegre was described in the following terms:

> "Don Juan Pío Montufar, Marquis of Selvalegre, Knight of the Royal and Distinguished Order of Charles III, Knight of the Royal and distinguished order of Charles III, author of the insurrections, who planned it ('meditó') from the year 1794. President of the first with the title of Most Serene Highness ('Altesa serenísima'). In the second [he was] Vice-President, and had himself similarly elected to executive power in the Independence

---

176 José Gabriel Navarro, *La Revolución de Quito del 10 de Agosto de 1809* (Quito, 1962): 43, printing Carta del Obispo Cuero y Caicedo, May 21, 1809.

177 For a synthesis, see John Lynch, *Las revoluciones hispanoamericanos, 1808–1826* (Barcelona, 3rd edn., 1983).

movement. In short, a contentious intriguer ("caviloso, intrigante") and the cause of the ruin of Quito and the disturbance of all America. All his family insurgent and very bad ...."[178]

The Marquises of Villaorellana, Miraflores, Villarocha y Solanda, the Marquess of Maenca, and the Count of Casa Jijón were also berated[179]. Twelve relatives of these were also named separately as being deeply implicated.[180] The initial impulse came from the very highest reaches of Quito society, although popular participation was to follow.

Ramón Núñez del Arco, in his description of Montúfar, could claim, with the benefit of hindsight, that the revolt of 1809 was the fruit of a long conceived conspiracy going back as far as the period of tension of 1794–95. Although the rebels' speed of action was to prove their psychological readiness, more concrete evidence of preparations goes back, more modestly, no further than 1808, with a chronology which inter-relates suggestively with the information arriving from Spain. News of the abdication of Charles IV to Ferdinand VII reached Quito on September 19, 1808, while knowledge of the imprisonment of both followed in February 1809: early in 1809 there were fly-posters and alleged plots against recognizing Ferdinand VII.[181] On Christmas day, 1808, a group met at the estate of the Marquis of Selva Alegre in the valley of the Chillos near Quito and agreed on future action to depose the authorities. This chronology suggests that if the Quito aristocracy founded the first autonomous junta in Spanish America this is because they were, as it were, jumping the gun at the starting line. The December conspiracy took place after the Bourbon abdications had breached the established order, and with the Creole leaders hypothesizing the potential consequences of a complete Spanish collapse in the peninsula. With the delay in the arrival of news from Europe, Quiteños would not at that stage have known of the creation of the central junta in Spain which had, to a certain degree, institutionalized alternative vehicles for political authority in late 1808, although this was subsequently to provide them with one of their justifications in their manifesto. The Quito elite had seen their opportunity, and clearly required no prodding, and only the most summary legal cover.

The Christmas plot was uncovered in March 1809, but the handling of the trial of six of the plotters, which aristocratic influence guided towards an

---

[178] AHBC/Q, Jijón y Caamaño, 1a col. vol. 0010, doc. 38, 243–271. "Estado general que manifiesta a los sugetos empleados en esta ciudad y su provincia ... con las notas exactas y verdaderos de la conducta que ha observado cada uno de ellos," (compiled by Ramón Núñez del Arco, Quito, May 20,1813). Entry 188, fol. 254.

[179] *Ibid.*, entries 188–194, fol. 254. A seventh noble, Don Luis Cifuentes, of the Order of Charles III, was a loyalist.

[180] *Ibid.*, entries 39, 111 (Sanches de Orellana); 7, 27, 245 (Carcelen); 167b, 215, 216 (Montúfar); 239, 240 (Quiñones); 217 (Jijón); and 219 (Herrera). Entry 310 (Herrera) presumed to be unrelated.

[181] Washburn, *The Bourbon Reforms*, 221.

acquittal, can only have fortified their determination; the loyalist Don Pedro Calisto y Muñoz was later to claim as much.[182] They were back to their ruminations in the house of one Doña Manuela Cañizares near the Presidential palace when in early August, an alleged peninsular plot against Creole leaders preceded, or perhaps retrospectively justified, action by the rebels.[183]

During the night of the 9th–10th of August members of the local garrison secured government buildings and arrested royal officials and overnight Quito had its bloodless coup. This was strictly a conservative transfer of local authority, assured by aristocratic influence in the military. Structurally, the new government was the old Audiencia under a new name with only minor modifications such as the designation of the new President, the Marquis of Selva Alegre, as Most Serene Highness, the creation of the position of Vice-President, Bishop José Cuero y Caicedo, and the appointment of Ministers, all from the Creole elite. The narrow range of measures taken also reflected the concerns of White Quito society: the reduction of taxation and censo debt, the abolition of the monopolies on tobacco and spirits.[184]

The Creole elite do not seem to have considered that their actions, directed against the Spanish authorities but not against the social order, were of a type which posed the question of popular support. "Manifestos,"[185] or public declarations, were issued. These declarations attacked officials for incompetence (all the more dangerous in view of the state of the homeland) and enumerated offenses including the misdeeds of certain peninsulars, the contempt towards Creoles, and "the trampling of the sacred rights which Nature has conceded us,"[186] while still affirming loyalty to the King. But the affirmation that the vecinos of Quito were "for the most part descended from the same Spaniards (who conquered the region)" [187] suggests that it is misleading to take these manifestos as a bid for popular support. They could equally well be taken as an affirmation of the basis of the rebels' action to white society, not all of which assembled in Doña Manuela Cañizares' house or was party to what was being prepared. Most revealing is that those who were to represent the barrios of the city in the newly created government in 1809 were either marquises (in four cases)

---

[182] Alfredo Ponce Ribadaneira, *Quito 1809–1812, según los documentos del Archivo Nacional de Historia*, (Madrid, 1960), 22.

[183] R. L. Gilmore, "The imperial crisis, rebellion, and the viceroy: Nueva Granada in 1809," *HAHR*, 40, 1960, 1–24.

[184] "Informe," in Ponce Ribadaneira, *Quito 1809–1812*, 188. Washburn, *The Bourbon Reforms*, 229, citing Julián Fuentes-Figueroa Rodríguez, *La emancipación del Ecuador*, (Caracas, 1974), 39.

[185] Ponce Ribadaneira, *Quito 1809–1812*, 136–139, 142–144.

[186] *Ibid.*, 137.

[187] *Ibid.*, 142.

or related to them (in two)[188]. This was an ostentatious display of aristocratic domination rather than of a co-option of local leadership, an indication that the Quito rebels were not merely intent on preserving the social order but represented that current of conservative reaction and social exclusion, one trace of which was encountered in the parish records of El Sagrario from the late eighteenth century.

The first autonomous junta lasted two and a half months until October 1809. There was little sense of direction, and growing dissension within rebel ranks as to the next step to be taken. The loyalist dimension was still strong, and the first junta did not turn into an Independence movement. In their manifesto the rebels referred to Quito as "withdrawn (*retirado*) in a corner of the earth,"[189] and it may be that there was an unrealistic sense of the significance which would be attached to their actions and how far the perceived separateness of Quito could insulate it from external reaction, however well placed the Creole elite might be in relation to local peninsular authorities. Montúfar himself does not seem to have thought that his actions presupposed an irrevocable breakdown of relations with the imperial authorities, and wrote to the viceroy of Lima on September 9, 1809, affirming his loyalty and claiming that he had only accepted office to avoid tumults and restore order.[190] Little attempt was made to recruit outside support, and the one military action of the junta, an expedition to the north to secure Pasto, proved ineffective. In the face of the imminent arrival of troops from Guayaquil and Cuenca and reinforcements from the viceroyalties of New Granada and Peru, contact was made with Ruiz de Castilla, and capitulations were offered on October 24th and signed three days later.[191] Ruiz de Castilla was to become President of the undissolved junta which would be subordinate to the Central Junta in Spain, while there were to be no reprisals against the rebels in advance of the King's judgment. Thus some of the forms were kept, although the taxation measures were rescinded.[192]

The reconciliation between the President and the leaders of the former junta lasted only until the arrival of reinforcements strengthened the hand of the loyalists. Colonel Manuel Antonio de Arredondo y Pelegrín, heading a regiment of 400 soldiers from Lima, entered the city on November 25, 1809.[193] Just under two weeks later, Ruiz de Castillo, in breach of his agreement, wrote to the Governor of Popayán that he had ordered the arrest

---

[188] *Ibid.*, 144.

[189] *Ibid.*, 143.

[190] *Ibid.*, 162–163.

[191] Navarro, *La Revolución de Quito*, 105–106. However, capitulations were signed on the 24th, according to Washburn (following Fuentes-Figueroa Rodríguez, 46–51), and on the 28th according to Ponce Ribadaneira, *Quito 1809–1812*, 41.

[192] AHBC/Q Col. Jijón y Caamaño, 1a col. vol. 0003, fol. 31ff.

[193] Navarro, *La Revolución de Quito*, 126–127.

of the "principal authors of the scandalous revolution of the August 10, 1809."[194] Although the Marquis of Selva Alegre managed to stay free, (and later arranged for the escape of his brother) the eighty or so who were imprisoned constituted an important component of Quito's elite. The death sentence which Arredondo initially demanded for forty-six of them[195] was ultimately placed on all their heads.

THE MASSACRE OF AUGUST 2, 1810 AND THE EMERGENCE OF POPULAR PARTICIPATION

With the full reassertion of imperial authority in December 1809 and with an important section of Quito's Creole elite now threatened with liquidation, events had clearly gone beyond the gentlemanly maneuvering of the first junta (August–October 1809). According to Washburn, it was the "sentences against the elite [which] stirred the first popular outrage against the local peninsular officials."[196] However, it was some months before there was an attempt to rescue the prisoners which ended in a bloody massacre by loyalist troops on August 2, 1810. Moreover, there is evidence to suggest that the attack was an operation planned and financed by the Quito aristocracy, while popular motivation had distinct origins.

A new perspective emerges when the events of August 2 are not examined in isolation, but viewed instead against a broader atmosphere of mounting tension. It is not easy to penetrate to the level of popular ideology, but the deposition of royal authority must have been heady stuff, and it was in San Roque that these radical sentiments, based on an invocation of natural law, appeared in 1810: "There is no King, no legitimate owner, no father ... Everything is lies, fraud ... imposture. There is nothing more than intruding usurping tyrants. We have naturally stayed free."[197] More specifically, there was a feeling of alien occupation in the period immediately preceding August 1810. The hearings into the conduct of Doctor Mariano Batallas during a disturbance in Quito in July 1810 emphasize the role played by military repression in stoking up popular hostility towards the Lima troops stationed in Quito. The references in this case to the "mulatos of Lima" or to the "mulato soldiers" suggest that friction was sharpened by racial antipathies against a colored regiment which was doubly "foreign" by virtue of both race and place of origin. As

---

[194] Ponce Ribadaneira, *Quito 1809–1812*, 199.

[195] *Ibid.*, 55.

[196] Washburn, *The Bourbon Reforms*, 232.

[197] M-D. Demélas and Y. Saint-Geours, *Jerusalén y Babilonia. Religión y política en el Ecuador, 1780–1880*, (Quito, 1988), 102, citing AHBC/Q "Convite del barrio de San Roque a los demás barrios de Quito," (1810) vol. 27, fol. 281. See also Keeding, *Das Zeitalter der Aufklärung in der Provinz Quito*, (Köln-Wien, 1983), 508 ff. on "natural rights."

with some of the earlier moments of tension (1762, or 1779–80), the events of July 7, 1810 are more noteworthy for what they reveal than for their consequences. They consisted of the posting of fly-posters preceding the gathering of a "movement of the city" which advanced on the main square.[198] It was later to be claimed that those involved numbered 30,000, a near-impossible assessment which nevertheless shows the scale of the movement.[199] Although the crowds soon dispersed, according to one account, under the persuasion of the President, the military Commander Arredondo and others,[200] they displayed enough hostility for the sergeant who testified at the Batallas hearings to say that he would have asked his men to open fire if any of the populace had been armed.[201] The subsequent reaction is suggestive of the degree of suspicion with which the authorities now viewed Creole society. One José Yánez was whipped for spreading false rumors.[202] An action was brought against Batallas, identified in other sources as a loyalist,[203] for allegedly standing on a corner, denouncing the burglary of his house by four Limeños and arguing that the "sons of Lima were responsible for the tumults in Quito."[204] In his defense, Batallas claimed that the disturbances of that morning were caused by the "mulato Lima soldiers" with their insults, even though "some ... [of these soldiers were] ... honorable." He had been in his house when his maid had told him that there was a "movement of the city" and he had gone out to hear that the mulatos of Lima were plundering the city. By his own account, Batallas had attempted to pacify spirits saying that there could not be a sack of the city, and those who had put up fly-posters were "enemies of tranquillity." To which came the reply: "No, señor, the spoliation (*saqueo*) is now coming by San Roque." In the square itself, Batallas claimed he reassured a minister of the Audiencia that this was only a protest against robbery.

Depositions concerning Batallas' role in this unrest were taken on August 1, 1810 from a series of witnesses, many of them important white Quiteños. They constitute a catalogue of troop robberies and aggressions against the full range of Quito society, property-owners and aguardiente drinkers alike: these included forcibly expropriating livestock from the Indians on Iñaquito, and raiding the shops where spirits were sold (and

---

[198] AHN/M Consejos 21677 "Real Carcel de Corte. El Sargento de Guardia ... (sobre declaraciones del) Señor Batallas," Quito, July 7, 1810 (copy), fol. 3.

[199] Carlos de la Torre Reyes, *La revolución de Quito del 10 de agosto de 1809*, (Quito, 1961), 513; Letter of José Gonzales Bustillo to D. Carlos Montúfar, Guayaquil, October 30, 1810, published in *Museo Histórico*, 1957, (Nos. 27–8), 40–45.

[200] Letter of Gonzales Bustillo, *loc cit.*,.

[201] "[Sobre declaraciones del] Señor Batallas," fol. 1.

[202] Torre Reyes, *La revolución*, 520.

[203] "Estado general," fol. 262, entry 351.

[204] "[Sobre declaraciones del] Señor Batallas," fol. 1.

consumed) and detaining clients against payment.[205] With regard to the chronology of the disturbances, it is significant that the provocations of the Lima troops not only preceded the unrest of the July 7, but continued unabated thereafter, with don José Baquero, testifying on the August 1, 1810, reporting incidents from only the previous day.[206] In the absence of any serious attempt to curb excesses, the hearings themselves can only have reinforced Quiteño frustrations and sharpened a sense that the Lima troops were the cutting edge of a foreign occupation.

From this perspective, the events of the July 7, and August 2, appear less as separate events than as part of a chain of disturbances with troop aggressions preceding and succeeding the Creole ripostes which they helped to provoke. The events of August 2, can be seen as both an elite-backed rescue operation and a wider, popular anti-troop "tumult," with the force of popular resentment partly channeled towards a political goal. The attack on the prison itself had all the hallmarks of a carefully planned operation, not least in its timing at 1:30 in the afternoon on August 2, when as the Bishop of Quito remarked, most people were eating. According to the Bishop, who provides the most plausible eyewitness account[207] twenty-five men arrived at the prison, disarmed the colored guards, wounded the sentinel and an officer and released the prisoners. This much was clinically carried out and with a minimum of violence. Simultaneously, however, a second group made its way to the barracks, and of these, just six forced their way in and began killing soldiers with their knives. According to lieutenant Juan de Celis, writing to his commander, those who attacked "sacrificed themselves with the blindest impetus" and seemed to be drunk.[208] Rebel numbers were reinforced with the release of former members of the garrison from the presidium. The loyalist reaction came with soldiers near the barracks shooting to disperse people, and with the carnage carried out by guards in the prison leading to the death of most of the prisoners. Some soldiers were killed in the streets. According to the Bishop, this was by the lads (*mozos*) fleeing the prison, although their numbers may have been swollen by the "many Mestizos" mentioned by the President [209] and by now church bells had, as in 1765, "moved the barrios" to action.[210] The Lima troops moved onto the streets of the city killing whoever they encountered, "like wild animals (*fieras*) in search of the

---

205 *Ibid.*, fol. 5.

206 *Ibid.*

207 AHN/M Consejos 21677, Letter of José, Obispo de Quito, Virrey de Santa Fe, Quito, August 6, 1810 (copy).

208 AHN/M Consejos 21677, Letter of Juan de Celis to Comandante, Quito, Agosto 16, 1810 (copy).

209 AHN/M Consejos 21677, Letter of the President El Conde Ruiz de Castilla, Quito, August 6, 1810, fol. 1.

210 AHN/M Consejos 21677, "Conmovió a los varrios ...": Letter of José, Obispo, fol. 1.

tumult of people in the street."[211] The President's assertion that only a "little over" a hundred died, most of them prisoners and troops, hardly squares with the eye-witness accounts, even if, as he claimed, casualty figures were minimized by people hiding in their houses.[212]

The "2 de Agosto" has been described as the work of "authors unknown" and it was a secretive and ultimately tumultuous operation. Nevertheless, the thorough 1813 report of Ramón Núñez del Arco, himself a Creole and "inside" observer,[213] on the political conduct of 565 people during both phases of the Revolution identifies ten of 341 secular names as having participated in the events of August 2, 1810, (excluding those who were rescued). Of these, two—don Joaquín Sánchez de Orellana and don José Burbano—figured among the 214 mainly elite office-holders, while the eight others belonged with the more socially mixed 127 non-officeholders. The presence of don Joaquín Sánchez de Orellana, who was a member of an important aristocratic family is in itself sufficient to establish elite participation. Indeed the fact that an officer should be one of the rare members of the Creole elite to whom an active role in the "2 de Agosto" was ascribed (Sánchez de Orellana served as colonel in the second junta and was later commander-in-chief of the expedition to Pasto) is in itself a strong indication that the attack of August 1810 was planned as a military operation with explicit, if necessarily veiled, Creole aristocratic support. This interpretation is supported by the remaining entries, which are detailed enough to touch on the financial preparations and include, in the case of the second officeholder, don José Burbano, a similar example of "professional" specialization. Don José was an official at the treasury, and it was he who provided money and arms to "the lads of the plebe" to commit the assault. Don José Alvares was also credited with contributing financing to the assault on the barracks.

The other entries also underline the military back-up; one man had "armed men in his house," while another led a band of armed men from Machachi, demonstrating the scale of the enterprise. Most revealingly, José Xeres led a *cuadrilla* to rescue the former garrison and killed a sentry during the events of August 2, but was still close enough to the Montúfars to be "oficial de las confiansas" of the family. This, too, points to a large-scale operation and makes the connivance of the Montúfars highly plausible.

With regard to popular participation, the evidence, as always, has to be sifted more indirectly from a variety of sources. In Ramón Núñez' report

---

211 AHN/M Consejos 21677, Letter of Ruiz, fol. 2.
212 *Ibid.*, fol. 2. M-D. Demélas and Y. Saint-Geours, *La vie quotidienne en Amérique du Sud au temps de Bolivar, 1809–30* (Paris, 1987), 81, mentions 300 dead. The same authors have now published *Jerusalén y Babilonia* which examines religious and ideological aspects of the Independence movement.
213 AHBC/Q, Jijón y Caamaño, 1a col. vol. 0010, doc. 38, 243–271. "Estado general que manifiesta a los sugetos empleados en esta ciudad y su provincia ... con las notas exactas y verdaderas de la conducta que ha observado cada uno de ellos," (compiled by Ramón Núñez del Arco, Quito, May 20, 1813).

we do find an organist, a silversmith and a tailor Ramón Núñez, known as "Blackbeard."[214] It was specifically stated in the 1813 report that the lads of the barrio were paid and armed, although this must have been those most directly involved in the assault on the prison and barracks. Nevertheless, the disturbances grew wider than this and the Bishop reports that when troop violence reigned in the center, the barrios were seething and required ecclesiastical intervention (including his own) to calm their spirits. There are suggestions in the documentation that butchers from the slaughterhouse area which straddled Santa Bárbara and San Blas were involved in antitroop fighting. Although not specifically referring to the unrest of August 2, and couched in general terms, there are four mentions of barrios in Nuñez del Arco's report and it is unlikely to be a coincidence that these were to San Roque (twice) and to Santa Bárbara (twice). With San Roque we are back on familiar ground: the fact that the earlier disturbance of July 7 seems to have broken out with the rumors of the sack of this barrio links the events of 1809–10 with earlier disturbances. José Paz de Albornoz was described as a Creole insurgent, who was "captain of the troop of 'cuchilleros' of the barrio of San Roque" although it is not clear how literally we should take this.[215] And it was specifically in San Roque that the radical polemic against "intruding usurping tyrants," cited above, was recorded. It is worth stressing that the Franciscans were extremely prominent as insurgents in the Quito revolts of 1809–10,[216] so we may hypothesize the resurfacing of the San Francisco-San Roque axis of popular radicalism. The contribution of San Roque to the Quito revolts, with or without the influence of San Francisco, concludes a remarkable record of almost a century of barrio activism.

THE SECOND JUNTA

If the events of August 2 could be described as a loyalist victory this was very much a Pyrrhic one. The violence of the troops had reached unimaginable extremes: the Bishop, in a later letter dated August 21, 1810, reports the soldiers finishing off the wounded in the streets, riding over them with horses, knifing corpses.[217] Incidents caused by the troops were to continue for over two weeks after August 2, even though their departure had already been ordered. On August 4, the Spanish authorities sought to avoid a conflagration by reaching a modus vivendi with surviving Creole leaders, agreeing to the departure of the Lima troops and a pardon for the insurgents in order to cool the atmosphere.

214 "Estado general," fol. 259, entries 313, 319, 322.
215 "Estado general," fol. 248, entry 76.
216 Alexandra Kennedy Troya and Alfonso Ortiz Crespo, *Convento de San Diego de Quito*, (Quito, 1982), 138.
217 AHN/M Consejos 21677, Letter of José, Obispo de Quito, August 21, 1810.

Although as in 1809, the agreement of August 4 was ultimately contingent on external reaction, it was strengthened in the short-term by the arrival on September 12th, of don Carlos Montúfar. Son of the Marquis of Selva Alegre, Montúfar arrived as envoy of the Central Junta, with a now outdated conciliatory brief to authorize the earlier compromise agreement of October 1809; he had demonstrable sympathies for local autonomy[218] which were to be confirmed by his leading role in the second revolt. Montúfar helped consolidate the agreement of August 4 with the constitution on September 22 of a second junta, which recognized the authority of the Central Junta in Spain. Nevertheless, the marriage of circumstance which had Selva Alegre serving as Vice-President under Ruiz de Castilla underlined that this was a makeshift compromise unlikely to provide stability.

During the latter part of 1810 the Quito movement radicalized and split, partly under its own momentum and partly in reaction to the growing threat from outside. The Viceroy of Peru, Abascal, helped the Royalist bastions of Guayaquil and Cuenca to organize action against the ever suspect Quito. Joaquín de Molina, named President by the viceroy, arrived in Guayaquil on November 7, 1810,[219] and subsequently moved inland to establish his base in Cuenca. The August–September compromise was clearly no longer viable: Quito either had to bow to outside pressures, or risk full independence and face the military consequences. In fact, almost immediately after the installation of the second junta, the second alternative was chosen, with the drafting of a monarchical constitution which recognized Ferdinand VII, but not Spanish authority over the region. This approach reflected more closely the views of the monarchist followers of Selva Alegre than the "Sanchista" followers of Sánchez de Orellana, the Marquis of Villa Orellana, who favored a republican solution. The split between the two wings of the Independence movement sapped the foundations of the Quito revolt, a disunity sealed by the move by Villa Orellana and his supporters to Latacunga in February 1811. The failure of the attack on Cuenca has been attributed to military disunity, while the successful attack on Pasto owed much to the simultaneous military threat from the newly created military junta in Bogotá.[220]

If the first junta in 1809 had been purely aristocratic, the plebe of Quito remained on the stage during the second revolt after the massacre of August 2, 1810 had inflamed popular sentiments. Before hostilities had broken out with Loyalist forces, "the people insulted " and nearly killed Molina's envoy to Quito. This action was apparently not orchestrated by Creole leaders, one of whom claimed that they had on the contrary saved him.[221]

---

[218] Ponce Ribadaneira, *Quito 1809–1812*, 71.
[219] Ibid., 79.
[220] Washburn, *The Bourbon Reforms*, 236; Ponce Ribadaneira, *Quito 1809–1812*, 85–86, 89–91.
[221] Ponce Ribadaneira, *Quito 1809–1812*, 80.

Other acts of popular violence were to follow with more bloody consequences as the social climate deteriorated in the face of external danger. Two loyalist officials, Fuertes y Amar and Vergara were killed and had their bodies dragged through the streets.[222] In October 1812, in the later stages of the Quito revolt when any pretense of peninsular-Creole cooperation had been definitively interred (President Ruiz de Castilla had been deposed a year earlier), a peninsular plot was uncovered, and the former President died in the rioting which followed. This proved to be the prelude to the arrival of Montes and the reestablishment of Spanish authority in Quito in November of 1812.

Independence from Spain was to come only a decade later, this time as part of the great Independence movement which terminated Spanish power on mainland Latin America. The price to be paid for outside assistance in 1822 was the incorporation of Ecuador's territory (as the "Southern District") into Gran Colombia from 1822 through to its break-up in 1830. What one Quiteño thought of this change-over was graphically put by a wag daubing his sentiments on one of Quito's walls shortly after General Sucre had routed the Spaniards on the slopes of Mount Pichincha on May 24, 1822: "Last day of despotism and first of the same"[223]

When the Viceroy Fernando de Abascal y Sousa looked back on the early Independence movement, there was surprise and regret that Quito should have played such an active role: "Quito which by the enlightenment and nobility of which it boasts, seemed the least ready to be corrupted was one of those which most precipitated itself to embrace the chimera."[224] We might reply that it was precisely the conservative character of the Quito aristocracy which provided the impetus, and the equivocal role of leaders like Montúfar, as well as the reinforcement of the symbolism of elite privilege (as in the appointment of upper-class "representatives" for the barrios), that point to the restricted scope of aristocratic ambitions in 1809. The creation of the first junta owed much to the conjunctural opportunity which had opened up for a closed elite which saw dominion as its natural inheritance; subsequent divisions underlined the absence of a deeper sense of direction. The revolts of 1809–10 did show, however, that there was a deep well of anti-peninsular feeling to be drawn on, even if little effort was made by the juntas to channel this into a broad Independence movement. In July and August 1810 we find Quito's elite and its people following parallel roads in their opposition to peninsular authority, rather than developing a shared dynamic.

---

222 *Ibid.*, 81.

223 Cited by Demetrio Ramos Pérez, *Entre el Plata y Bogotá*, 360; Demélas and Saint-Geours, *Jerusalén*, 39.

224 José Fernando de Abascal y Sousa, *Memoria de Gobierno*, vol. II, Sevilla, 1944, 82.

Conclusion

In this chapter, the major rebellions in eighteenth and early nineteenth-century Quito have been examined, as well as a number of revealing moments of tension. By investigating all forms of unrest, rather than focusing uniquely on those which were explicitly riots of the plebe, I hope to have called attention to a continuous tradition of popular action, with barrio roots, which never lay far beneath the surface, even when the nominal *casus belli* lay elsewhere. Thus the disputes of the 1740s, which had previously only found a place in the old-fashioned narratives of religious disputes, proved on closer inspection to involve the full-scale mobilization of the plebe of San Roque. The official investigation into the nature and causes of the 1765 rebellion, along with other data, firmly located its origins in the popular barrios, rather than among those sectors influenced by the elite. The revolution of 1809–10 was clearly instigated by the Quito aristocracy, but there was also deep popular opposition to peninsular authority, and to what was seen as an army of occupation, which the Creole leadership made little effort to harness to its cause.

The material assembled here allows us to seek patterns in the chronology of Quito disturbances, as well as transformations in their motivation and social composition. In his recent study, Andrien examines the economic background of the Quito insurrection of 1765, stressing both longer term disruption of traditional economic patterns, as well as a short term downturn: "In many provinces such long-term structural changes merged with unique local problems to produce economic dislocation, social tensions and political unrest, affecting the entire populace."[225] The link with economic, demographic and agricultural fluctuations is strengthened by my correlation of the abandonment of foundlings with Indian deaths which provides a crude, but I think plausible, "hardship" index (Figure 6.4).

This points to the mid-1740s, the second half of the 1760s, the early 1780s, and the late 1790s as exceptionally unfavorable conjunctures in the period 1741–1800. This is not quite a "perfect fit" with social unrest, but it is certainly not far from being so. The early 1780s produced no major outbreak in Quito, but this was at a period of intense measures of security. 1795 was also a year of tension in Quito. The mid-1740s and the mid-1760s were both highly unfavorable "conjunctures" which exploded into major unrest. The witnesses called to testify in 1768 described the rebellion of 1765 as an act of desperation in response to a threat to the popular means of livelihood. I believe that the contemporary interpretation of the first 1765 Quito rebellion as a defensive "hunger riot" is essentially correct, and would downgrade the role of the Creole elite to helping to generate the social climate which made it possible. If there were any "hidden hands," the evidence of the 1740s riots and their subsequent major role in the Independence movement make the Franciscans the most plausible

---

[225] Andrien, "Economic crisis," 130.

candidates. The influence of dearth and epidemics in the mid-1740s may have helped to give the Franciscan riots their near messianic hue.

On the face of it, we can find evidence in support of Basadre's contention that there was a transformation in the pattern of unrest in colonial Spanish America, with civil rebellions replacing religious disturbances in the course of the eighteenth century. We could link this apparent secularization of social unrest to the Bourbon reform program, which as in other regions of Spanish America, provoked intense local opposition.[226] A recent study, however, emphasizes the quasi-religious aspect and intense ecclesiastical participation in Quito's early Independence movement of 1809–12.[227] The National Archives in Bogotá include a private letter from Visente Paredes to Juan Mexia of 1809 which confirms this approach. As it happens, we know a little about Paredes: in Ramón Núñez del Arco's 1813 report on the Quito revolutionaries he is described as a Creole merchant who participated in both rebellions, and in the second was responsible for enlisting the "troop of merchants" (*tropa de comerciantes*). He was described as "ferocious and sanguinary," and was responsible for having a bell melted down to make cannons. He had escaped to Panama.[228] Paredes' letter was dated August 21, 1809, only a week and a half after the autonomous junta had been created and conveys his elation.

> "That in this capital on the triumphant day of the captivity of the Pharaohs, who held us enslaved in the name of God, mistreated and oppressed beyond comparison ... Divine Providence with invincible hand dethroned them from the summits whence they were shooting off lightening bolts against the unhappy inhabitants to destroy us: today they are sad victims of Divine vengeance ... [They should go back to the peninsula, those who] here preserved their life of ease (regalona existencia) lived at the cost of the blood of the poor ...."[229]

In view of the survival of this religious dimension, we should distinguish between the "triggers" of unrest, which were gradually politicized, and the nature and structure of Quito's preindustrial crowd which had more continuity.

With regard to popular motivation, I would emphasize a radical "leveling" strain from the 1740s onwards, not least since I disagree with McFarlane's depiction of the 1765 rebellion as the action of the entire Quito community. McFarlane found Fernando de Echandía's account of the offer of the Crown to the Count of Selva Florida improbable along with its depiction of subversion and the rule of the people. Andrien, on the other

---

226   For New Granada see A. McFarlane, "Civil Disorders and Popular Protests in Late Colonial New Granada," *HAHR*, 64 (1984) 17–54.

227   Demélas and Saint-Geours, *Jerusalén*, 39.

228   "Estado general," fol. 259, Entry 312.

229   ANC/B Anexo. Historia Tomo 6, fol. 668, Letter of Visente Paredes, Quito, August 21, 1809.

hand, emphasizes "growing lower-class radicalism" after the June uprising and attaches more credence to Echandía's version of events.[230] Writing in July 1765, Fernando de Echandía had written that the "people have made themselves magistrates, ordering gibbets to be built in various places, dealing with disputes."[231] In fact, on this point, the secret report of 1768 provides confirmation that events had taken on a radical hue insofar as the gallows were indeed installed in Santo Domingo and a dead mulato hung there. This may only have been a single symbolic act, but its symbolism was radical enough. The preindustrial crowd was ideologically eclectic, and it may be that some of the rioters in 1765 shouted the slogan "Long Live the King and Down with Bad Government." In the 1768 report, however, we find a different, more radical, version of events with rioters running down the streets shouting "Viva el barrio."[232] Once again we are back with the barrio roots of the Quito insurrection.

The predominant role of San Roque as the "engine of unrest" allows us to go beyond issues of class and community. "Class" has long been a difficult issue in preindustrial societies, with historians seeking alternative formulations, such as class as an inchoate "field of force," rather than the defined concept it became with nineteenth century industrialization. In the case of Quito, as in the early modern Naples studied by Peter Burke[233], it was a particular neighborhood of the city which united class and community: San Roque, the relatively homogeneous, "Mestizo" parish with an artisan population and some form of local leadership. This enabled it to build up lateral links with the other popular barrios, notably San Sebastián. While hanan/hurin, the ritual division of the city, may not have played a role in its full pre-Hispanic sense, its perpetuation by the colonial authorities may have helped to solidify these contacts, through ritual battles between barrios, or the election of officials. The order of participation in the festivities of 1789, celebrated with fireworks, masks and costumes was Santa Bárbara and San Blas, (both hurin) followed by San Sebastián and San Marcos and San Roque (all hanan) the last of which was "outstanding."[234] Less hypothetically, urban geography, with the elite El Sagrario forming a wedge between north and south, clearly played a role. In the eighteenth century, riots took the form of attacks on the center from the periphery with the symbolic locus of authority, the main plaza being, notably, the battleground during the second rebellion of 1765.[235] The unity

---

[230] McFarlane, "Civil Disorders," and Andrien, "Economic crisis," 128.
[231] McFarlane, "Civil Disorders," 315.
[232] ANC/B Historia Civil Tomo 4, fol. 979.
[233] Burke, "The Virgin of the Carmine," 3–21.
[234] AMQ, LCQ (1781–91), "Relación de las fiestas ... de Don Carlos Quinto ... el día 21 de Septiembre de 1789." fols. 156–57 for the participation of the barrios.
[235] This was emphasized in BL Egerton 1808 "Información y probanza de la fidelidad de los oficiales reales," (Quito, December 14, 1765), fol. 460, and the narrative accounts. I witnessed this myself in Quito in 1982 when rioters protesting against

and organizational strength of San Roque in 1765 was specifically commented on by Recio who described the people of that barrio, as marching in ranks, armed and with banners.[236]

If there was a sense in which a "class" was embodied in San Roque, there was similarly a sense in which the peninsular merchants also formed a social class. Jorge Juan and Antonio de Ulloa noted that trade was carried out by this group.[237] The attacks on peninsular Spaniards in 1765, and the anti-peninsular sentiments which reemerged in 1795 or in 1809–10, can therefore be considered to have a hidden class-bias; or more exactly, I would argue, the natural "leveling" instinct often present in the pre-industrial crowd. McFarlane in his study of the Quito insurrection of 1765 argues that it was the work "of a community rather than a class." In Quito, that community was an agglomeration of urban Whites, Mestizos, and Indians, who could unite briefly behind resistance to taxation, but found no lasting cohesion.[238] I would argue rather that the eighteenth-century riots and rebellions were the work of a community *and* a class and that both were embodied in San Roque and the other popular barrios. The most eloquent proof of this was cited above, when witnesses were asked in 1779 whether one of the accused had participated in previous civil disorders (specifically, 1765), and the altogether revealing reply came that "as he lives inside the city he was not a companion of the 'mozos' of the barrios." [239]

---

the increase in bus prices sealed off the narrow entrance to the old city from Iñaquito with burning tyres, and rained stones on cars before retreating up the hillside.

[236] Recio, *Compendiosa relación*, 526–527.
[237] Juan and Ulloa, *Relación Histórica*, 373, 402.
[238] McFarlane, "Civil Disorders," 326–327.
[239] ANH/Q Ind. 97, doc. 1779–IV–27, fol. 43.

Chapter 9

CONCLUSIONS

How far were structures and changes discussed in this book typical of the Spanish American urban experience? Clearly, a concatenation of factors, some of them with unusually developed, although not unique, local significance—such as the lack of dynamism of the regional economy, the predominant role of the Church or the city's distinctive urban morphology—helped to shape and define Quito society.[1] When, at the end of the period covered by this book, we find the Quito aristocracy expressing the conviction (or perhaps the hope) that events were occurring in a place "withdrawn in a corner of the earth"[2] (and therefore presumably need not provoke an imperial counter-reaction), we are not far from a local version of James Orton's later nineteenth century description of Quito as a non-commercial backwater.[3] If we wish to establish the broader resonance and comparability of the Quito data, it is appropriate to accept that beneath all the fanciful or stereotyped language, there was indeed a sense in which this was a conservative and inward-looking peripheral region of the Spanish Empire. In this concluding chapter, I wish to adduce some of the population figures for other urban Spanish American urban centers in order to establish what kind of place Quito may have occupied in the broader pattern.

If Quito can be characterized as a relatively modest, un-dynamic Spanish American city by the late-eighteenth and early-nineteenth centuries, that is a mark of its absolute and relative decline from its seventeenth century peak. Despite the uncertainties and lack of uniformity of mid-colonial population data, it is clear that Quito had formerly been a member

---

[1] In this section, I have concentrated on certain inter-related themes and have tried to avoid undue repetition; in particular, religious material which was discussed in the conclusion to Chapter 4 is not reviewed again here.

[2] Alfredo Ponce Ribadaneira, *Quito, 1809–1812, Según los Documentos del Archivo Nacional de Madrid,* (Madrid, 1960), 143.

[3] J. Orton, *The Andes and the Amazon, or Across the Continent of South America,* (London- New York, 1870), 57, 59, text cited in the Introduction.

of the relatively exclusive club of great Spanish American cities, alongside Mexico City, Lima or the major mining centers like Potosí at their cyclical peaks. Although Mexico City was certainly much larger than Quito, the mid-colonial population of Lima, for example, may have been under 40,000, while it was in the 50–60,000 range for much of the eighteenth century.[4] In the second half of the seventeenth century, Quito's population, at perhaps 40–50,000, was probably at least double that of Norwich—then England's second largest city—so the figures for Quito were notable not only in Spanish American terms, but in those of the early modern world.[5]

This was no longer true when the official censuses of the 1780s and 1790s provided population data on an imperial-wide basis. Three levels of urban settlement can be distinguished for that period, emerging with particular clarity if we take as models the viceroyalties of Mexico and Peru, where population density and substantial rural peasantries implied urban scales and functions comparable to those of the Audiencia of Quito. (Some frontier regions, including parts of New Granada to which Quito was by then attached, had an "incomplete" or ongoing colonization, while plantation cultures lie beyond the scope of the present study). In these viceroyalties, there was a continuing dominance of the capital cities which was broadly comparable to that of their counterparts in pre-industrial Europe.[6] Beneath them came the medium-sized cities which exercised economic and political control over a network of smaller settlements spread through their agricultural hinterlands.

It is striking to observe from the Mexican and Andean patterns how distinct were the three levels of urban settlement. Mexico City and Lima (at 112,929 and 52,627 respectively in 1790) were followed at some distance by the important medium-sized provincial cities in the 20–30,000 range (Guanajuato had 32,098 inhabitants and Oaxaca 19,077; while in Peru the figures were Cuzco, 31,982, Huamanga 25,821 and Arequipa 23,551). The third group of settlements (equivalent to the Ecuadorian examples of Guayaquil, Ibarra, Latacunga, Ambato, Riobamba, Cuenca and Loja) had much smaller populations of between 3,000 and 12,000. Peru's fifth and sixth largest urban centers, Piura and Cajamarca, for example, only had populations of about 12,000. By this period, Quito had less than half of Lima's population and belonged only in the ranks of the important medium-

---

[4] María Pilar Pérez Cantó, *Lima en el siglo XVIII, Estudio socioeconómico,* (Madrid, 1985); Alberto Flores-Galindo, *Aristocracia y Plebe. Lima, 1760–1830,* (Lima, 1984), 101, for a 1636 *padrón* listing 13,620 slaves, and 10,758 Spaniards and 61, for figures from 1746 to1820.

[5] P. Abrams and E. A. Wrigley, *Essays in Economic History and Historical Sociology,* (Cambridge Univ. Press, 1978), 247, gives British population figures in 1600 and 1750. The figure of 50,000 for seventeenth century Quito (derived from Phelan) is widely found in the secondary literature, and is high but not inherently impossible to judge from surviving parish records.

[6] Mexico City and Paris, for example, each accounted for two percent or so of their "national" populations.

sized cities (20–30,000), alongside Guatemala city or Caracas, as well as Huamanga or Arequipa.[7]

These figures do not imply that the urban hierarchy of Spanish America was a static one, and the changing place of Quito in that hierarchy is itself proof to the contrary. The settlements which conformed most closely to the three-tier typology—the capitals and the local centers with a political and commercial role in agricultural hinterlands—tended to retain a broadly comparable place in the demographic hierarchy and would continue to do so beyond Independence. Latacunga, Ambato and Riobamba, the three Ecuadorian examples studied by Bromley, for example, all remained, and continue to remain, modest provincial towns even if Ambato profited from local conditions to improve its relative position. Although Cuzco's population rose from 17,000 to 31,000 in the century after 1690, it was, as it still is, an important middle ranking provincial capital.

Where the typology fails to do justice to the diversity of Spanish American urbanization is with regard to ports and mining centers as well as settlements in frontier regions, some of which fell into the pattern indicated above only by the statistical accident of "freezing" an overview around 1790. In the redistribution of wealth within the Bourbon empire associated with the loosening of commercial restrictions in the late eighteenth century, the classic beneficiary was Buenos Aires, growing from 11,000 in the early mid-eighteenth century to 65,000 a century later. The city was still on the second level of Spanish American urban centers in the late eighteenth century, but its elevation to a viceregal capital was both recognition of, and a stimulus to, its changing status. Within Ecuador, the growth of Guayaquil as a port and the center of coastal cacao production represents an analogous process, in this case of a progression from a small to a medium-ranking city at the end of the colonial period.[8]

The major mining and textile centers were cyclically important cities drawing in labor from their wider hinterlands in their periods of maximum production. Quito, however, well before the incorporation of Spanish America into the world market from the end of the eighteenth century onwards, clearly no longer belonged in this category. The three-tier typology sketched above emphasizes Quito's transition from a major urban textile center to a middle-ranking provincial capital with political, religious and commercial, but reduced economic functions. What may be stressed

---

[7] The comparative data are from María Pilar Pérez Cantó, *Lima*, and Alberto Flores Galindo, *Aristocracia y Plebe*; I. Langenberg, *Urbanization und Bevölkerungsstruktur der Stadt Guatemala (1773–1824)*, (Köln-Wien, 1981); J. Kinsbruner, "The Pulperos of Caracas and San Juan during the first half of the nineteenth century," *Latin American Research Review*, 3, 1978, 65–85; and his more detailed comparative study, *Petty Capitalism in Spanish America*, 1987; D. Gibbs, *Cuzco, 1680–1710: An Andean city seen through its economic activities*, doctoral dissertation, University of Texas, 1979.

[8] M. T. Hamerly, *Historia social y económica de la antigua Provincia de Guayaquil, 1763–1842*, Guayaquil, 1973.

here is that although Quito's population situates it at mid-distance between the viceregal capitals and the small settlements, its changing position in the urban hierarchy suggests that it can contribute best to an understanding of the urban experience among the second and third ranks of Spanish American urban centers, specifically that of the more peripheral and less dynamic centers which had few direct commercial links with international trade or the major political *foci*.

The divergent destinies of Quito and ports like Guayaquil or Buenos Aires, suggest that, in eighteenth-century Spanish America, as in early modern England, successful towns looked outwards.[9] The examples of "structural" stability (in the case of the viceregal capitals) or expansion (in the case of ports tied to international commerce) throw Quito's long-term decline into sharp relief. The city's new place in the urban hierarchy of Spanish America reflects a genuine redefinition of its nature and functions and provides an object lesson in the role of monocultural dependence.[10] From capital-cum-textile center, mobilizing a substantial Indian population and supplying the mining regions of Potosí, Quito's role had contracted to that of a political, religious and commercial center exercising control over an agricultural hinterland. In its new guise, the city would enjoy relative (if not absolute) stability, undergoing some population loss and stagnation in the early nineteenth century, but only on a scale comparable to that of other cities in a period of urban recession.

Unlike coastal cities or viceregal capitals, Quito's lifeline was with the peasant economy surrounding it, while the urban geography discussed in the first chapter also reinforced the quasi-rural nature of the barrios. Quito's urban sectors interacted closely with the peasant economy; the evidence points to the complementarity of different forms of economic activity (artisanal occupation, small-scale commercial activity, urban plots), while the role of the imposition of a tax on urban plots in triggering the 1765 rebellion underlines their key importance in the household economy. The switches from chagro to pulpería and back again warn us to use occupational and tax categories with care. Licensed commercial activity emerged as a very poor guide to the level and character of small-scale economic activity.

Another distinctive feature, the virtual absence of Blacks, a reflection of the abundant Indian labor of the mid-colonial period, distinguished Quito from the larger cities, and again brings it closer to the second-ranking experience of extremely "ruralized" urban centers. Flores-Galindo's examination of the colonial plebe of Lima speaks of a distinctive "urban colonial culture," of which one of the principal elements would be precisely

---

9 Compare the essays in Abrams and Wrigley, *Towns in Societies*.

10 See, for example, Murdo J. Macleod, *Spanish Central America. A socioeconomic history, 1520–1720*, (Berkeley, 1973), 385 for another "classic case of monocultural dependence."

the Black element.[11] It was the absence of a racial frontier between urban plebeians and rural Indians, which a more significant urban Black presence would have helped to create, which led in Quito to the quasi-racial tensions between the established "Mestizos" and the new cholos, who indirectly threatened to have urban plebeians "tarred" as Indians by over-enthusiastic tribute collectors.

In the period covered by this book, Quito, the overwhelmingly Indian city of the mid-colonial period, had been transformed into the White and Mestizo urban center recorded in the late imperial censuses. If we follow the evidence of the censuses and parish registers, the period from 1690 onwards saw Quito's socio-demographic structure revert unambiguously to its prototypical role as "White" enclave. From constituting a large majority of Quito's population in the late seventeenth century the Indians had come to be a relatively marginal 25–30 percent by the 1780s: in absolute terms, they had fallen from at least 30,000–40,000 to around 6,000. The socio-demographic transformation of the city can be attributed to three factors: substantive demographic change, displacement across ethnic boundaries, and a redefinition of the urban space.

That "real" population changes were indeed at work is underlined by the importance of mortality rates, and specifically, the place of the 1690s epidemic as a watershed in the demographic transformation of the city. The notable impact of that epidemic was reinforced by the documentation of Chapter 6 which further suggested that death rates remained high until the 1720s. By the 1730s when the evidence indicates a stabilization, the demographic landscape had already been substantially altered with annual Indian baptisms (and therefore the presumed Indian population), at a much lower level than in the late seventeenth century. The steadier evolution which followed makes it more difficult to separate the demographic from the "ethnic" factors in the continuing socio-racial drift of the city. Nevertheless, later epidemics such as those of the mid 1760s and mid 1780s continued to have a substantial impact on the Indian population of the city.

There are some data pointing towards ethnic drift, but there was no abrupt and unilinear process of acculturation bringing to an end Quito's Indian population, which on a very much reduced scale was characterized rather by its longevity. Indeed as late as the 1930s there were still to be some populations within the city with their own caciques, and Indian traditions.[12] On the other hand, the differential demographic pressure on the Indian as against the White-Mestizo populations meant that the former was ultimately condemned to decline unless it constantly renewed itself. The speed with which Quito "shed" its Indians is a mark of their incomplete absorption into urban society; there was a symbiosis between city and rural

---

11   A. Flores-Galindo, "Los Rostros de la Plebe," *Revista Andina*, (Cuzco), 1 (1983), 315–352.

12   Personal communication from Dr. Fernando Rosero.

hinterland which was characterized by continuous small-scale demographic movement, as well as more marked mobility at certain periods of economic or demographic pressure such as the early eighteenth century.

Indeed, extreme adaptability and mobility was characteristic of much of the lower social strata in forms which were sometimes observable (migration, occupational adaptation or the pursuit of a temporary livelihood in Quito for the duration of a lawsuit), but must more often have escaped us. We occasionally come across the traces of more colorful variations on this theme such as the dancers and acrobats who made an appearance in the historical record of Ecuador (and Colombia) because of their habit of leaving a trail of bad debts behind them. Mariano Dias de Guevara, (alias "Floridano"), from New Spain, passing through Ibarra in 1781, had managed to build up a debt of 520 pesos which it was agreed he would pay off by dancing. He and his fellow debtor had been through Cali, Santafé de Bogotá, and other cities, and went missing despite a commitment to perform the following Easter, at the time of the festivals. I found it a welcome relief from the organized collective structures of the barrios to make the acquaintance of this short, fat, paunchy Negro, accompanied by Francisco Javier Cuello (alias "Costallón") with his squint and his carbuncle, as well as a "tall old man with the rudiments of the Maroma dance" and a "slim lad with dark brown hair, round-faced and hairless."[13] The existence of these mobile, "street-wise" characters, also encountered in the series of Declarations of Mestizo, provides us with an arresting example of the vitality of popular traditions sustained by individuals who were independent of, but clearly interacted with, the settled "structures" of urban society.

The corpus of Declarations of Mestizo provided material relating to internal definition and group identity. It pointed towards a continuously shifting socio-racial terrain, with an essentially "Spanish" identity at the lower popular levels, and one in which the fixed point was the Indian/non-Indian frontier; in Ecuador the category of Mestizo was omitted from the imperial censuses. Through concrete examples, such as the career of Eugenio Espejo or specific demographic sources, I have attempted to show the pitfalls into which historical interpretation has fallen when it has treated "Mestizo" and "White" as distinct and autonomous categories. I believe this Ecuadorian evidence, taken from a peripheral region in which the imperial state made less of an effort to overhaul its machinery and systematize socio-racial definition than in more economically crucial ones, may well convey a customary reality which escapes us elsewhere. This imposes caution in ongoing attempts to correlate ethnic status with class in Andean society, where it would be helpful to develop a much stronger emphasis on the Indian/non-Indian divide as opposed to putative sub-groupings in White-Mestizo society. Within this narrowly restricted perspective, there was a high correlation of ethnic and occupational status in Quito. The city had

---

[13] ANC/B Juicios Civiles del Ecuador, Tomo 2, fol. 769 ff, description at fol. 774–775.

been founded, and was to remain, a White colonial implantation in predominantly Indian countryside with a non-assimilated Indian labor force which supplied manual labor and some specific artisanal and service functions.

Caste was not a legally or ecclesiastically sanctioned system in colonial Ecuador, and socio-racial boundaries were extremely permeable prior to the late eighteenth century. In the late-colonial period, there was a trend towards social exclusivity with a White elite marking its distance from the rest of non-Indian society, a process which in the 1780s accompanied a renewed program of fiscal reform which attempted to introduce some order into a situation of lax customary practice. This process hardly amounted to the creation, or re-creation, of a full caste society, and was partial and incomplete: the nineteenth century saw the reemergence of a "Mestizo" category, but in an unconvincing form in which, as in colonial Ecuador, it had to be continually invented and reinvented.

The strength of barrio identity allows one to go beyond community/class interpretations of civil unrest by locating both community and class in the relatively homogeneous, artisan, popular district of San Roque with its tradition of autonomous action and lateral barrio alliances. The cohesion of shared collective structures, notably in festivities or riots, was altogether striking. Lima, too, had its river marking off the more or less fashionable areas, but the state of comparative research does not allow us to know whether other Spanish American colonial cities had the same level of "village" identity which I found in Quito. Almost certainly many did have, given the strength of identity of equivalent districts in early modern European cities, of which the Parisian Faubourg St-Antoine was only the most famous. If it seems a paradox that migrant forasteros should have played such a decisive role in rural rebellions, while in the cities, this role was that of the more settled urban communities, we might reply that these were often socially analogous, artisan groups, and frequently similarly threatened by Bourbon tax changes.[14] Religious influence must have played a role in reinforcing the identity of the popular barrios: we have one clue to this in the municipal registers, which recorded at the time of the 1785 epidemic that "El Señor de la Misericordia" was particularly venerated in the parish of San Roque.[15]

In urban and rural rebellions we find women playing a major role that was matched by their economic role in the underground economy and by their demographic preponderance in urban society. Witnesses testifying at the official investigation explicitly called attention to the role of women in the Quito rebellion of 1765, and this underlines once again the importance

---

[14] For the prominence of *forasteros*, threatened by tributary charges, in rural rebellions see the accounts in S. Moreno Yánez, *Sublevaciones indígenas*, 45, for details of "albañiles" and other occupations.

[15] AM/Q, LCQ, October 7, 1785, fols. 184–185.

of the threat to the domestic economy in provoking that uprising.[16] Other testimony in the investigation that crowds had shouted "Viva el barrio" provides yet one more indication of the decisive popular barrio role in the Quito insurrection of 1765.[17] Beneath the apparent variability of slogans or motivation in civil unrest and a secularization of riots and rebellions, which proved to be more apparent than real, lay the strength of the idea of community and collective action. For much of the eighteenth century this was synonymous with the men and women of the barrio of San Roque, whose independence of Creole (although not religious) authority, and traditions of riot and rebellion, sustained the autonomous aspirations of the people of Quito.

---

[16] ANC/B, Historia Civil Tomo 4, fol. 917 ff. for multiple testimonies; the women collected the stones for the rebels.

[17] ANC/B, Historia Civil, Tomo 4, fol. 979.

Glossary

Aduana	Customs house
Aguardiente	Brandy, spirit
Alcabala	Sales tax
Alcalde	Mayor
Alcalde mayor	Indian leaders designated annually by the municipality
Alférez	Ensign
Alguacil	Sergeant, also, an official in a confraternity
Arancel	List of tariffs
Arbitrista	Utopian reformist
Arrabal	Population contiguous and adjacent to cities and towns but outside its walls, see *barrio*
Arriero	Mule driver
Asiento	Population center with a statute inferior to *villa*
Audiencia	Major judicial and administrative entity legally subordinate to a Viceroyalty
Ayllu	Indian kinship group
Barbero	Barber (and minor surgeon)
Barrio	Popular district of the city, derived from the word for "field."
Bayeta	Loosely woven cloth
Bordador	Embroiderer
Botonero	Button-maker
Cabildo	Municipal council
Cabildo abierto	Extraordinary, "open" council meeting
Cacica	Indian leader (fem.)
Cacicazgo	Position held by *cacique*
Cacique	Indian leader
Capellanía	Chaplaincy
Cargador	Carrier (porter of heavy loads)
Carnicería	Municipally controlled slaughterhouse and meatmarket

Casta	Caste; the non-White, non-Indian population (In the Audiencia of Quito, this refers mainly to the Black or part-Black population)
Cédula	Decree
Censo	Financial obligations assumed on property (especially to the Church), in exchange for loans, or for religious reasons
Chácara	See Chagra
Chagra	(quich.) field
Chagro	(quich. deriv. of *chagra*). A shop in which different grains, bread and other foodstuffs are sold
Chichero	Maker of maize beer (*chicha*)
China	Indian girl, sometimes feminine of *cholo*
Cholo	Acculturated Indian in the process of becoming Mestizo
Chorrillo	Small urban textile workshop producing coarse cloth
Cofradía	Confraternity, religious lay brotherhood
Compadrazgo	Spiritual kinship established between parents and god-parents
Composición	Fee paid to legalize a title (to land and other property)
Corona Real	"Royal Crown," tribute category grouping together Indians detached from the *llacta*. (often therefore: *forasteros de la Corona Real*)
Corregidor	Official with administrative and judicial authority over a district
Corregimiento	District administered by a *corregidor*
Criollo	Creole, person of European descent born in the Indies
Cuadra	Urban block, smaller in Quito than elsewhere
Curaca	See *Cacique* (rare in the Audiencia of Quito)
Cura	Parish priest
Dansante	Dancer dressed up for religious festivals
Diezmo	Tithe
Doctrina	In Spanish America, the form of Indian evangelization
Don	Courtesy title reserved to the White élite and important Indians

Ejido	Common land
Encomendero	Holder of *encomienda*
Encomienda	System of "entrusting" Indian groups to *encomenderos* to whom tribute was paid
Faldellín	Underskirt
Fiesta	(Religious) festival
Fiscal	State Prosecutor
Forastero	Outsider or Indian migrant, formalized as a tax category; *forasteros* paid less than the *llactayos* (normally around 4 pesos a year, or a little over half the *llactayo* rate)
Gremio	Guild
Guasicama	(*Guasi*, [quich.]: house), Indian providing household labor
Hacendado	Major landowner
Hacienda	Large landed estate
Hato	Sheep or cattle pen
Hidalgo	Originally, a member of the Spanish gentry
Hijo Expósito	Foundling
Huerta	Fruit and vegetable garden
Jerga	Coarse dark cloth
Latonero	Tin-worker
Legua	League, variable unit of time-space; "the distance covered in an hour," 5.5 kilometers.
Llacta	See: *llactayo*
Llactayo	Indian belonging to the *llacta,* i.e. the settled land-holding Indian community. The *llacatayo* paid a higher rate of tribute than the *forastero* and was liable to *mita* service
Limpio	Pure, c.f. the Spanish concept "limpieza de sangre," "purity of blood"
Maiordomo	Majordomo, administrator
Mercader	Merchant
Mestizaje	Process of racial and cultural mixing
Mestizo	Person of mixed Indian and white extraction. see also *montañes*
Mita	System of forced rotating Indian labour
Mitayo	Indian liable to the *mita*
Molino	Mill
Montañés	Mestizo of good social standing

Morador	Resident with lower status than a *vecino*
Moreno	Person of part-Black origin
Mulato	Person of mixed Black and White extraction
Obraje	Textile workshop
Obrajero	Owner of an *obraje*
Padrón	Census, usually nominal
Paño azul	Fine quality woolen export cloth
Pardo	Person of part-Black descent
Patacón	See *peso*
Peinadillo	Term used to describe the mobile Indian population in the early Colonial period
Peninsular	White person born in Spain
Peso	Unit of Spanish currency, divided into 8 reales
Petaquero	Trunk-maker
Pintor	Painter
Platero	Silversmith
Plaza	Square; also often serving as market-place
Plebe	Plebeian social strata
Pregonero	Town crier
Prioste	Official in a confraternity
Procurador	Attorney
Propios	Public lands and rents
Protector de Naturales	Officially designated Protector of the Indians
Pueblo	Village
Pulpería	Licensed retail outlet for salt, cheese, alcohol, knives etc.
Pulpero	Person who owns or rents a *pulpería*
Quadra	See *cuadra*
Quebrada	Ravine, river-gulley
Quinta	Small farm
Quintos	Indians who were liable for the supply of 1/5 of their labor force for the *mita*, see also *llactayo*
Real	One-eighth of a *peso*
Reducción	Reorganization of the Indian communities into concentrated village settlement in the late sixteenth century
Regatona	(from *catu* [quich.], market). Marketwoman

Relación	Account
Residencia	Official inquiry at the end of a period of office
Sambo	See *Zambo*
Sapatero	See *Zapatero*
Sastre	Tailor
Sayal	Poor quality coarse cloth
Sierra	Highlands
Sillero	Saddlemaker
Síndico	Administrator of a confraternity
Solar	Urban plot for construction (in Quito 1/4 of a *cuadra*)
Texedor	Weaver
Tienda	Shop
Vara	33 inches (83.5 cm)
Vecino	Citizen, freeman of the city
Villa	Town
Visita	Official administrative or ecclesiastical inspection
Visitador	Official or ecclesiastic who carries out a *visita*
Zambo	Person of Indian and Black descent
Zapatero	Shoe maker

Bibliography

Manuscript Sources

Colombia
ARCHIVO NACIONAL DE COLOMBIA, SANTAFÉ DE BOGOTÁ
Cartas de Contrabandos, Tomo XI
Censos Varios departamentos, Tomo 8
Colonia Aguardientes del Ecuador, Tomo 2
Colonia Tributos, XVI
Hacienda Real, Varios no. 2893, vol. "Censos del Ecuador"
Historia Civil, Tomo 4
Miscelánea de la Colonia, vols. 2, 60
Miscelánea de la República, vol. 123 (i)

BIBLIOTECA NACIONAL, SANTAFÉ DE BOGOTÁ
Libros raros y curiosos, ms. 179, 223

Denmark
THE ROYAL LIBRARY OF COPENHAGEN
"Cuaderno de Guachucal en la Provincia de los Pastos hasta la ciudad de Cuenca y Quito," (1766), Ny kgl. Samling 568 (4) (consulted in the transcription of Juan Castro y Velázquez).

Ecuador
ARCHIVO ARZOBISPAL, CUENCA
Unclassified

ARCHIVO DE LA CURIA METROPOLITANA, QUITO

Unclassified. Particular use was made of the ecclesiastical *padrones* of the 1790s, contained in a box marked "Visita Pastoral—Ilmo. Pérez de Calama (1790)," for which my own readings were incorporated into calculations provided by Señor Jorge Moreno Egas. The Director of the archive placed later censuses of neighbouring villages in this box after I had consulted them in December 1982.

ARCHIVO HISTÓRICO DEL BANCO CENTRAL DEL ECUADOR, QUITO

Fondo Jijón y Caamaño, 0003; 00010; 00029, Libros Verdes 1; 1ª Colección, ms. Azules, Tomo 7.

ARCHIVO HISTÓRICO DEL BANCO CENTRAL, IBARRA

Unclassified

ARCHIVO MUNICIPAL, QUITO

Vol. 54, Cartas de cabildo; vol. 64, "Padrón de población ... de Quito y Latacunga y Ambato" (1830–1); vol. 37, Demandas y Juicios (1642–87). The *Libros de Cabildo* of Quito, housed in this archive, have been published up to 1657.

ARCHIVO NACIONAL DE HISTORIA, QUITO

The following sections were of particular relevance:

Carnicerías y Pulperías 1. doc. 7–VII–1642.

Empadronamientos. Census data: vol. 26 for a summary of San Blas, Quito, in 1826. This section includes nineteenth-century censuses of Quito, but for the eighteenth century, there are only data in summary form.

Gobierno. Mixed official documentation, similar to the Presidencia de Quito, below.

Hijos naturales y expósitos. This section includes some litigation on inheritance.

Indígenas. Litigation in which Indians were involved, and therefore a mixed body of documentation, but weighed towards land-litigation.

Mestizos. The litigation to establish non-Indian tributary status examined in Chapter 7.

Notaries. The volume numbers in the catalogue of the ANH/Q do not always correspond to those marked on the binding of the notarial records; the date of a transaction is therefore the essential reference. A relatively complete series from the 1580s onwards.

Pobreza. Not as important as its name suggests, this section consists of civil lawsuits brought by those claiming the "legal aid" permitted on establishing the status of *pobre de solemnidad.*

Presidencia de Quito. Official correspondence, sometimes duplicated in Sevilla and Bogotá.

Rebeliones. The first five boxes consist essentially of the documentation used by S. Moreno Yánez for his study *Sublevaciones Indígenas.* Docs. 1748–I–I and 24–v–1762.

Archivo Nacional de Historia, Azuay (Cuenca)

In process of being classified in 1981–83, this archive is catalogued for the Republican period, but only partially for the eighteenth century.

Parish Archives, Quito

Registers of baptisms and burials in the parishes of El Sagrario, Santa Bárbara, and San Blas (Quito). Some late-colonial and republican material on San Marcos (Quito) can now be consulted in AHBC/Q (Section: "Adquisiciones."). Parish registers were also consulted in Cayambe, El Quinche and Tabacundo.

England

British Library, Department of Manuscripts

Additional, 15,331, 17,588

Egerton, 1,808, 1,809

Kings, 219

France

Bibliothèque Nationale, Paris

Cartes et Plans C3593

Peru

Archivo Arzobispal, Lima

Apelaciones de Quito, Leg 15

ARCHIVO GENERAL DE LA NACIÓN, LIMA
Superior Gobierno, Leg 15. Cuad 400
Tributos, Informes, Leg 3. Cuad 63

BIBLIOTECA NACIONAL DEL PERÚ, LIMA
"Estado actual ...," April 30, 1747, c. 881
"Juan de Dios Chubirayco ...," 1797, c. 931

Spain
ARCHIVO GENERAL DE INDIAS, SEVILLA
Audiencia de Quito 8, 17, 28, 32, 69, 72, 132, 138, 181, 188, 203, 206, 207, 223, 242, 243, 254, 276, 289, 378A, 379, 381, 398–399, 416–424, 430, 432, 435, 436

Contaduría, 1539

Estado (Quito, 1792–1817)

Mapas y Planos, Panamá, 134

ARCHIVO HISTÓRICO NACIONAL, MADRID
Consejos 21677

BIBLIOTECA NACIONAL, MADRID
Manuscript 3198

BIBLIOGRAPHICAL AIDS AND GUIDES TO ARCHIVES

Freile-Granizo, Juan, *Guía del Archivo Nacional de Historia*, Guayaquil, 1974.

Gómez Canedo, Lino, O. F., *Los archivos de la historia de América, Período colonial español*, 2 vols., México D.F., 1961.

Griffin, C. C. (ed.) *Latin America. A Guide to the Historical Literature*, University of Texas Press for the Conference on Latin American History, 1971.

Guía del Archivo Nacional de Historia, Quito: Casa de la Cultura, 1981.

Hamerly, M. T., "La demografía histórica del Ecuador, Perú y Bolivia: Una bibliografía preliminar," *Revista del Archivo Histórico del Guayas*, (Guayaquil) 6 (1974), 24–63.

Handbook of Latin American Studies, Hispanic Foundation, Library of Congress, Washington D.C., 1936–1993.

Hanke, L. (and Celso Rodríguez), *Guía de las fuentes en el Archivo General de Indias para el estudio de la administración virreinal española en México y en el Perú. 1535–1700*, Köln-Wien, 3 vols., 1977.

Heredia Herrera, Antonia, "Organización y descripción de los fondos de la Audiencia de Quito del Archivo General de Indias," *Historiografía y bibliografía americanistas*, XXI, (1977), 139–165.

Kennedy Troya, Alexandra, *Catálogo del Archivo General de la Orden Franciscana del Ecuador*, Quito, 1980.

Larrea, Carlos Manuel, *Cartografía Ecuatoriana de los siglos XVI, XVII y XVIII*, Quito, 1977.

Maiguashca, Juan, "Breves apuntes sobre la situación de la historia económica en el Ecuador," *Revista Ciencias Sociales*, (Quito) 1 (2) (1977),93–105.

Morales y Eloy, J., *Ecuador. Atlas Histórico-geográfico*, Quito: Ministerio de Relaciones Exteriores, 1942.

Naylor, B., *Accounts of Nineteenth-Century South America. An Annotated Checklist of Works by British and United States Observers*, London: The Athlone Press, 1969.

Norris, R. E., *Guía bibliográfica para el Estudio de la Historia Ecuatoriana*, Austin: University of Texas Press, 1978.

Peña Cámara, José María de la, *Archivo General de Indias de Sevilla. Guía del visitante*, Madrid, 1958; Sevilla, 1959.

Rumazo González, José, "Los legajos de la Audiencia de Quito en el Archivo de Indias," *Gaceta Municipal,* (Quito), 19, (1934), 86–93.

Sánchez Alonso, B., *Fuentes de la historia española e hispano-americana*, 3rd. ed., 3 vols., Madrid, 1952.

Szászdi, A., "The Historiography of the Republic of Ecuador," *Hispanic American Historical Review*, 44 (1964), 503–550.

Tepaske, J. et al. (eds.) *Research Guide to Andean History. Bolivia, Chile, Ecuador, and Peru*, Duke University Press, 1981.

Vasco de Escudero, G., *Los archivos quiteños*, Quito, 1977.

Vogel, C., "Los Archivos Coloniales del Ecuador," *Instituto de Historia Eclesiástica Ecuatoriana,* (Quito) I (1974), 191–227.

Published Sources

Alcedo, Antonio de, *Diccionario geográfico-histórico de las Indias Occidentales o América,* 5 vols., Madrid, 1786–1789.

Alsedo Herrero, Dionisio de, *Descripción geográfica de la Real Audiencia de Quito* [1766], Madrid, 1915.

Amat y Junient, Manuel de (Virrey del Perú), *Memoria de Gobierno,* Sevilla, Escuela de Estudios Hispanoamericanos, 1947.

Anónimo, "La cibdad de Sant Francisco de Quito, 1573," in Jiménez de la Espada, Marcos, *Relaciones geográficas de Indias,* Madrid, 1965; vol. 2, 205–232.

Anónimo, "Descripción de Quito en 1577," *Museo Histórico,* (Quito), 56 (1978), 45–66.

Anónimo, "Relación de las Cibdades y Villas que hay en el Distrito de la Audiencia Real que reside en la Cibdad de San Francisco del Quito y de los oficios de Administración de Justicia dellas vendibles y no vendibles y del valor de cada uno dellos y de los que se podrian criar y acrecentar," in Jiménez de la Espada, Marcos, *Relaciones geográficas de Indias,* Madrid, 1965; vol. 2, 183–189.

Anónimo, "Relación del distrito del Cerro de Zaruma y distancias a la ciudad de Quito, Loja y Cuenca y indios de aquella provincia y repartimiento dellos y otras cosas de aquella provincia," [1592], in Jiménez de la Espada, Marcos, *Relaciones geográficas de Indias,* Madrid, 1965; vol. 2, 315– 320.

Atienza, Lope de, "Relación de la Ciudad y Obispado de Sant Francisco de Quito, 1583," in Jiménez de la Espada, Marcos, *Relaciones geográficas de Indias,* Madrid, 1965; vol. 2, 190–200.

Autoridades, *Diccionario de Autoridades* [1726], facsimile edn., Madrid: Gredos, 1976.

Bates, H. E. (compiler), *Central America, The West Indies and South America,* London, 1878.

Bond, John J., *Handy-book of Rules and Tables for Veryfing Dates* London, 1875.

Bustos Losada, C. (ed.), "Sublevación de Quito en protesta por la aduana y los estancos 1765," *Museo Histórico,* (Quito) 3:8 (1951), 16–31.

Caillavet, C., "Una 'relación geográfica' inédita de 1582 sobre Ecuador: Oyunbicho y Amaguaña del valle de los Chilos," *Revista Andina,* Año 6, no. 2, (Dic. 1988), 525-536.

Caldas, Francisco José de, "Viaje de Quito a Popayán," *Semanario de la Nueva Granada,* Paris, 1849.

Cieza de León, Pedro, *La Crónica del Perú* [1553], Madrid, 1965; abridged and ed. V. W. von Hagen, *The Incas of Pedro Cieza de León,* 4th. ed., 1976.

Colección de Cédulas Reales dirigidas a la Audiencia de Quito, Tomo I. (1538–1600), Tomo II. (1601–1660), Quito, Archivo Municipal, 1935, 1946.

Coleti, Giandomenico, *Dizionario storico-geografico dell'America Meridionale,* 2 vols., Venice, 1771.

Colombia: Relación Geográfica, Topográfica, Agrícola, Comercial y Política de este País, London, 1822; edn. Bogotá: Archivo de Economía Nacional, 34, 2 vols., 1974.

Cornejo, Mariano H. and Osma, Felipe de (eds.) "Descripción de las ciudades, villas y pueblos del Obispado de Quito (1755)," in *Documentos anexos a la memoria del Perú,* vol. 3, Madrid, 1905.

Ecuador Pintoresco. Acuarelas de Joaquín Pinto, Quito-Barcelona: Salvat, 1977.

Enríquez B., Eliecer, *Quito a través de los siglos,* Quito, 1938–1940.

Garcés, J. A. (ed.) *Colección de Cédulas, Colección de Documentos sobre el Obispado de Quito,* Tomo I. (1546–1583), Tomo II. (1583–1594), Quito, Archivo Municipal, 1946–47.

Garcilaso de la Vega, El Inca, *Los Comentarios Reales de los Incas* [1609]; trans. and ed. H. V. Livermore: *Royal Commentaries of the Incas,* 2 vols., Austin, 1966.

Hallo, Wilson, (ed.) *Imágenes del Ecuador del siglo XIX. Juan Agustín Guerrero,* Quito-Madrid, 1981.

Hassaurek, F., *Four Years among Spanish-Americans,* New York, 1868; reprinted as *Four Years among the Ecuadorians,* ed., and abridged by C. H. Gardner, Southern Illinois University Press, 1967.

Herrera, Pablo; *Apuntamientos de algunos sucesos que pueden servir para la Historia de Quito, sacados de las actas del Concejo Municipal,* Quito, 1851; repr. in E. Enríquez, B., *Quito a través de los siglos,* Quito, Tomo II [Segunda parte],1942).

_____. (and Enríquez, Alcides); *Apunte Cronológico de las Obras y Trabajos del Cabildo o Municipalidad de Quito, desde 1534 hasta 1714; Desde 1715 hasta 1733,* Quito, 1916. [Overlaps with Herrera (1851)].

Holinski, Alexandre, *L'Équateur: scènes de la vie sud-américaine,* Paris, 1861.

Jiménez de la Espada., Marcos, (ed.), *Viaje de Quito a Lima de Carlos Montúfar con el Barón de Humboldt y don Alexandro Bonpland,* [Voyage of 1802], Madrid (?), n.d.; also published in *Boletín de la Sociedad Geográfica de Madrid,* XXV, (1888), 371 ff.

_____. *Relaciones Geográficas de Indias: Perú,* 3 vols., Madrid, 1965.

Juan, Jorge and Ulloa, Antonio de, *Relación Histórica del Viage a la América Meridional,* Madrid 1748; facsimile edn., 2 vols., Madrid, 1978.

_____. *Noticias Secretas de América,* London, 1826; facsimile edn. Madrid, 1982.

Kolberg, Joseph, *Hacia el Ecuador. Relatos de viaje.* Quito, 1977

Konetzke, R., *Colección de Documentos para la Historia de la Formación Social de Hispanoamérica, 1493–1810,* Madrid: Consejo Superior de Investigaciones Científicas, 1953, vol. 1.

Landázuri Soto, Alberto, *El régimen laboral en la Real Audiencia de Quito,* Madrid, 1959.

Libro de cabildos de la ciudad de Quito, 1573–74, Quito: Archivo Municipal, 1934.

Libro de cabildos de la ciudad de Quito, 1575–76, Quito: Archivo Municipal, 1935.

Libro de cabildos de la ciudad de Quito, 1593–97, Quito: Archivo Municipal, 1941.

Libro de cabildos de la ciudad de Quito, 1597–1603, (1–2) Quito: Archivo Municipal, 1937–40.

Libro de cabildos de la ciudad de Quito, 1603–10, Quito: Archivo Municipal, 1944.

Libro de cabildos de la ciudad de Quito, 1610–1616, Quito: Archivo Municipal, 1955.

Libro de cabildos de la ciudad de Quito, 1638–46, Quito: Archivo Municipal, 1960.

Libro de cabildos de la ciudad de Quito, 1650–57, Quito: Archivo Municipal, 1969.

Libro de proveimientos de tierras, cuadras, aguas, etc., por los cabildos de la ciudad de Quito, 1583–1594. Quito: Archivo Municipal, 1941.

Libro primero de cabildos de Quito, (1534–43) (I–II) Quito: Archivo Municipal, 1934.

Libro segundo de cabildos de Quito,(1544–51), (I–II) Quito: Archivo Municipal, 1934.

Lisbôa, Manuel María, *Relação de uma viagem a Venezuela, Nova Granada e Equador* [1853], Bruxelles, 1866.

Merisalde y Santisteban, D. Joaquín, " Relación Histórica política y moral de la ciudad de Cuenca, 1765," in: *Colección de libros que tratan de América raros o curiosos,* Tomo 11, Madrid, 1894; *Relación histórica, política,* Quito: Casa de la Cultura, 1957.

Montúfar y Frasso, Joan Pío de, "Razón [acerca] del estado de la Real Audiencia de Quito," *Revista del Archivo Nacional de Historia, Sección del Azuay* (Cuenca, Ecuador), 3 (1981), 95–147.

Moreno Egas, J., "Resumen alfabético del segundo libro de matrimonios de españoles de la Parroquia de El Sagrario de Quito 1764–1805," *Revista del Centro Nacional de Investigaciones Genealógicas* (Sección Genealogía), (Quito), Año 1 (3) (1981), 195–281.

—————. *Vecinos de la Catedral de Quito Bautizados entre 1801 y 1831,* Quito, 1984.

Navarro, Juan Romualdo, "Idea del Reino de Quito," in Rumazo González, José (ed.) *Documentos para la historia de la Audiencia de Quito,* Madrid, 1948–50, Tomo VIII, 396–555.

Orbigny, Alcide d', *Voyage pittoresque dans les deux Amériques,* Paris, 1836

"Padrón de Santa Bárbara en 1768," *Museo Histórico* (Quito), 56 (1978), 93–122.

Recio, Bernardo, P., *Compendiosa relación de la cristiandad de Quito* [c. 1773], Madrid: Instituto Santo Toribio de Mogrovejo, 1947.

Relaciones de Mando de los Virreyes de la Nueva Granada (Memorias económicas), Gabriel Giraldo Jaramillo (ed.), Bogotá, 1954.

Relaciones Histórico-geográficas de la Audiencia de Quito (siglo XVI–XIX), P. Ponce Leiva (ed.), Madrid 1991.

Robinson, David J. (ed.) *Mil leguas por América, de Lima a Caracas, 1740–1741: Diario de don Miguel de Santisteban*, Santafé de Bogotá, 1992.

Rodríguez de Aguayo, Pedro, "Descripción de la ciudad de Quito y vecindad de ella" (n. d.) in Jiménez de la Espada, M., *Relaciones geográficas de Indias*, Madrid, 1965; vol. 2, 201–204.

Rodríguez Docampo, Diego, "Descripción y relación del estado eclesiástico del Obispado de San Francisco de Quito que se ha hecho por mandado del Rey Nuestro Señor en virtud de su Real Cédula dirigida al Illmo. Sr. D. Agustín de Ugarte Saravia, Obispo de Quito, del Consejo de S. M., por cuya orden la hizo Diego Rodríguez Docampo, clérigo presbítero secretario del venerable deán y cabildo de aquella catedral" [1650] in Jiménez de la Espada, Marcos, *Relaciones geográficas de Indias*, Madrid, 1965, vol. 3, 5–77.

Rumazo González, José, *Documentos para la historia de la Audiencia de Quito*, 8 vols., Madrid, 1948–50.

Salomon, F., "Seis comunidades indígenas en las cercanías de Quito, 1559: la visita de Gaspar de San Martín y Juan Mosquera," *Boletín de la Academia Nacional de Historia*, (Quito), vol. LIX, Nos. 127–128 (1977), 139–90.

Salazar de Villasante, Juan de, "Relación General de las Poblaciones Españoles del Perú,"(156?), in Jiménez de la Espada, Marcos, *Relaciones geográficas de Indias*, Madrid, 1965; vol. 1, 121–143.

Santa Cruz y Espejo, Francisco J. E, "Defensa de los Curas de Riobamba," in Jijón y Caamaño, J. and Viteri Lafronte, H. (eds.), *Escritos del doctor Francisco Javier Eugenio Santa Cruz y Espejo*, III, Quito, 1923.

Stevenson, William Bennet, *A historical and descriptive narrative of twenty years' residence in South America, in three volumes; containing travels in Arauco, Chile, Peru and Colombia*, 3 vols. London, 1825.

Uriarte y Herrera, Miguel de, "Representación hecha al Rey sobre los adelantamientos de aquellos vastos países," in: Valladares de Sotomayor, A. (ed.) *Semanario Erudito*, Tomo XXIV, (Madrid, 1789), 229–264.

Velasco, Juan de, *Historia del Reino de Quito en la América meridional*, (c. 1789), 3 vols., Quito: Casa de la Cultura, 1977–78.

Whymper, E., *Travels amongst the Great Andes of the Equator*, London: John Murray, 1892.

Wolf, Teodoro, *Geografía y geología del Ecuador* [1892] Quito: Casa de la Cultura, 1975.

Zelaya, Juan Antonio, "Estado de la Provincia de Guayaquil, Agosto 17, 1765," *Revista del Archivo Histórico del Guayas,* (1974), 97–106.

Secondary Works

Acosta-Solís, M., *Investigadores de la geografía y la naturaleza de América tropical: viajeros cronistas e investigadores con especial referencia al Ecuador,* 2 vols., Quito, 1976–77.

Alchon, S. A., "The Effects of Epidemic Disease in Colonial Ecuador: the Epidemics of 1692 to 1695," Paper presented at the 1982 Annual Meeting of the American Historical Association, Washington, D.C.

——. "Epidemics in the city of Quito: disease, population, and public health during the eighteenth century" Paper presented at the 46th International Congress of Americanists, Amsterdam, 1988.

——. *Native Society and Disease in Colonial Ecuador,* Cambridge, 1991.

——. "Disease, Population, and Public Health in Eighteenth-Century Quito, in N. D. Cook and W. G. Lovell (eds.) *"Secret Judgments of God": Old World Disease in Colonial Spanish America* (Norman and London, 1992), 159–182.

Anderson, R. D., "Race and Social Stratification: A Comparison of Working-Class Spaniards, Indians, and Castas in Guadalajara, Mexico in 1821," *HAHR,* 68 (1988), 209–243.

Andrade Marín, L., "Origen y significado de los barrios y lugares populares de Quito," in: E. Enríquez B. (ed.) *Quito a través de los siglos,* Quito, 1938, vol. 1, 238–245.

Andrien, K. J., "Economic Crisis, Taxes and the Quito Insurrection of 1765," *Past and Present,* 129 (1990), 104–131.

"Anthropologie Historique des Sociétés Andines," *Annales, Economies, Sociétés, Civilisations,* (Special number), 33 (5–6), 1978.

Arrom, S., *The Women of Mexico City,* Stanford, 1985.

Assadourian, C. S., *El Sistema de la economía colonial. Mercado interno, regiones, y espacio económico,* Lima, 1982.

Astuto, P., "Eugenio Espejo: A man of the Enlightenment in Ecuador," *Revista de Historia de América,* 44 (1957), 369–391.

Ayala, Enrique, *Lucha política y origen de los partidos en Ecuador,* Quito, 1978.

Barrera, I. J., *Quito Colonial. Siglo XVIII, comienzos del Siglo XIX,* Quito, 1922.

Bauer, A. J., " The Church in the Economy of Spanish America: *Censos* and *Depósitos* in the Eighteenth and Nineteenth Centuries," *HAHR,* 63 (1983), 707–733.

Beerman, E., "Eugenio Espejo y la sociedad económica de los amigos del país de Quito," in: A. G. Novales, (ed.) *Homenaje a Noël Salomon: Ilustración española e Independencia de América*, (Barcelona, 1979), 380–387.

Bonilla, Heraclio, "Estructura colonial y rebeliones andinas," *Revista Ciencias Sociales* (Quito), 1 (1977), 107–113.

Borchart de Moreno, C., "Composiciones de tierras en el valle de los Chillos a finales del siglo XVII: una contribución a la Historia Agraria de la Audiencia de Quito," *Cultura, Revista del Banco Central del Ecuador,* (Quito), 5 (1980), 139–178.

————. "La transferencia de la propiedad agraria indígena en el corregimiento de Quito, hasta finales del siglo XVII," *Caravelle: Cahiers du Monde Hispanique et Luso-Brésilien,* 34 (1980), 5–19.

Bowser, F., *The African Slave in Colonial Peru,* Stanford, 1974.

Bromley, R. D. F., "Urban-rural interrelationships in colonial Hispanic America: A case study of three andean towns," *Swansea Geographer*, 12 (1974), 15–22.

————. *Urban Growth and Decline in the Central Sierra of Ecuador,* 1698–1940, doctoral dissertation, University of Wales, 1977.

————. "The functions and development of 'colonial' towns: Urban change in the Central Highlands of Ecuador, 1698–1940," *Transactions of the Institute of British Geographers,* 4 (1979), 30–43.

————. "Urban-rural demographic contrasts in Highland Ecuador: Town recession in a period of catastrophe, 1778–1841," *Journal of Historical Geography,* 5(3), (1979) : 281–95.

————. "Disasters and Population Change in Central Highland Ecuador, 1778–1825," in: Robinson, David J. (ed.) *Social Fabric and Spatial Structure In Colonial Latin America,* Ann Arbor, 1979, 85–116.

————. "Change in the Ethnic Composition of the Population of Central Highland Ecuador, 1778–1841," in: Borah, W. Hardoy, J. Stelter, G. A., (eds.) *Urbanization in the Americas: The Background in Comparative Perspective*, Ottawa, 1980.

————. (and R. J. Bromley), "The Debate on Sunday Markets in Nineteenth-Century Ecuador," *Journal of Latin American Studies,* 7 (1975), 85–108.

Bromley, R. J., "Precolonial trade and the transition to a colonial market system in the Audiencia of Quito," *Nova Americana,* (Turin) 1 (1978), 269–283.

Bronner, F. "Urban Society in Colonial Spanish America: Research Trends," *Latin American Research Review,* 21 (1986).

Browning D. G., and David J. Robinson, "The Origins and Comparability of Peruvian Population Data: 1776–1815," *Jahrbuch für Geschichte von Staat, Wirtschaft und Gesellschaft Lateinamerikas,* 14 (1977), 199–222.

Burgos-Guevara, H., *El Guaman, El Puma y el Amaru: Formación Estructural del Gobierno Indígena en Ecuador,* doctoral dissertation, University of Illinois at Urbana-Champaign, 1975

Burke, P., *Popular Culture in Early Modern Europe,* London, 1978.

─────── · "The Virgin of the Carmine and the Revolt of Masaniello," *Past and Present,* 99 (1983), 3–21.

Bushnell, D., *The Santander regime in Gran Colombia,* Westport, 1970.

Caillavet, C, "Tribut textile et caciques dans le Nord de l'Audience de Quito," *Mélanges de la Casa de Velásquez,* (Paris–Madrid), vol. XVI (1980), 179–201.

─────── · "Les rouages économiques d'une société minière: échanges et crédit. Loja: 1550–1630," *Bulletin de l'Institut Français d'Etudes Andines,* (Paris-Lima), XIII (1984), 31–63.

─────── · "L'artisanat textile à l'époque colonial: le rôle de la production domestique dans le nord de l'Audience de Quito," in D. Delaunay and M. Portais (eds.) *Equateur 1986,* Paris: Editions de l'ORSTOM, 1989, 241–250.

─────── · "Ex-voto coloniaux et pensée andine: une iconographie du syncrétisme religieux," in *Religions des Andes et Langues indigènes. Equateur. Pérou. Bolivie. Actes du IIIe Colloque d'Etudes Andines,* Université de Provence, 1993, 263–279.

─────── · (and M. Minchom) "Le Métis Imaginaire: idéaux classificatoires et stratégies socio-raciales en Amérique Latine (XVIe-XXe siècle)," *L'Homme,* 122–124, XXXII (2–3–4), (avr.- déc. 1992), 115–132.

Campbell, L. G., "Recent Research on Andean Peasant Revolt, 1750–1820," *Latin American Research Review,* 14 (1979), 3–49.

─────── · "Social Structure of the Tupac Amaru Army in Cuzco, 1780–1781," *HAHR,* 61 (1981), 675–693.

Carrera Colín, Juan, "Apuntes para una investigación etnohistórica de los cacicazgos del Corregimiento de Latacunga. Siglos XVI y XVII,"

Cultura, Revista del Banco Central del Ecuador (Quito), 11 (1981), 129–179.

Celestino, Olinda and Meyers, A., *Las cofradías en el Perú: región central*, Frankfurt, 1981.

──────. "La economía pastoral de las cofradías y el rol de la Nobleza India: El Valle del Mantaro en el Siglo XVIII," *Arbeitspapiere*, (Bielefeld), 25 (1981).

Chance, J. K., *Race and Class in Colonial Oaxaca*, Stanford, 1978.

──────. (and W. B. Taylor) "Estate and Class in a Colonial City: Oaxaca in 1792," *Comparative Studies in Society and History,* 19 (1977), 454–487.

Chandler, D. L., "Slave over master in colonial Colombia and Ecuador," *The Americas*, 38 (1982), 315–326.

Chiriboga, M., "Las fuerzas del Poder en 1830," *Cultura, Revista del Banco Central del Ecuador,* (Quito), 6 (1980), 171–208.

Collier, G. A. *et al.* (eds.) *The Inca and Aztec States, 1400–1800. Anthropology and History,* New York, 1982.

Colmenares, G., *Historia económica y social de Colombia, 1537–1719,* Bogotá, 3rd. edn., 1978.

Conniff, M. L., "Guayaquil through Independence: Urban development in a Colonial system," *The Americas,* 33 (1977), 385–411.

Cook, N. D., *Demographic Collapse. Indian Perú, 1520–1620,* Cambridge, 1981.

Cornblitt, O., "Society and Mass Rebellion in Eighteenth-Century Peru and Bolivia," *St. Anthony's Papers,* 22, Oxford, 1970, 9–44.

Cushner, N. P., *Farm and Factory: The Jesuits and the Development of Agrarian Capitalism in Colonial Quito,* Albany, 1982.

Deler, J. P., *Genèse de l'espace équatorien: essai sur le territoire et la formation de l'Etat National,* Paris, 1981.

Demélas, M-D. and Saint-Geours, Y., *La vie quotidienne en Amérique du Sud au temps de Bolivar, 1809–30,* Paris, 1987.

──────. *Jerusalén y Babilonia: Religión y política en el Ecuador, 1780–1880,* Quito, 1988.

Domínguez Ortiz, Antonio, *Sociedad y Estado en el siglo XVIII español,* Barcelona-Caracas-México, 1981.

Duviols, P., *La lutte contre les religions autochtones dans le Pérou colonial,* Paris-Lima, 1971.

Efimov, A. V., *Ecuador,* Moscow, 1963.

Elliott, J. H., "Self-Perception and Decline in Early Seventeenth-Century Spain," *Past and Present*, 74 (1977), 41–61.

Enock, R., *Ecuador. Its Ancient and Modern History, Topography and Natural Resources, Industries and Social Development*, London, 1914.

Espinoza Soriano, W. "El Alcalde Mayor en el Virreinato del Perú," *Anuario de Estudios Americanos*, vol. XVII, (1960), 183–300.

──────. "La vida pública de un príncipe Inca residente en Quito. Siglos XV y XVI," *Bulletin de l'Institut Français d'Études Andines*, (Paris-Lima), VII (1978), 1–31.

Estrada Ycaza, J., *Regionalismo y Migración*, Guayaquil, 1977.

Fernández Martínez, M., *La Alcabala en la Audiencia de Quito, 1765–1810*, Cuenca, 1984.

Fisher J. R., *Government and Society in Colonial Peru. The Intendant System, 1784–1814*, London, 1970.

Flores-Galindo, Alberto, "Los Rostros de la Plebe," *Revista Andina*, (Cuzco), 1 (1983), 315–352.

Gangotena y Jijón, Cristóbal de, "Fiestas que se celebran en Quito a fines del siglo XVIII," *Boletín de la Academia Nacional de Historia*, (Quito) 7 (1923), 263–269.

Gibbs, D., *Cuzco, 1680–1710: An Andean city seen through its economic activities*, doctoral dissertation, University of Texas, Austin, 1979.

Gibson, C., *The Aztecs under Spanish Rule: A History of the Indians of the Valley of Mexico, 1519–1810*, Stanford, 1964.

Gilmore, R. L., "The imperial crisis, rebellion, and the viceroy: Nueva Granada in 1809," *HAHR*, 40 (1960), 1–24.

Gómez, Nelson E., *Quito y su desarrollo urbano*, Quito, Edit. Camino, n.d.

Góngora, M., *Studies in the Colonial History of Spanish America*, Cambridge, 1975.

──────. "Urban Social Stratification in Colonial Chile," *HAHR*, 55 (1975), 421–448.

González Suárez, F., *Historia General de la República del Ecuador* (1890), 3 vols., Quito, 1969–70.

Grieshaber, E., "Survival of Indian Communities in Nineteenth Century Bolivia: A Regional Comparison," *Journal of Latin American Studies*, 12: 2 (1980), 223–269.

Hamerly, M. T., "La Demografía Histórica del Distrito de Cuenca," *Boletín de la Academia Nacional de Historia,* (Quito), vol. LIII (1970), 203–229.

───────. *Historia social y económica de la antigua Provincia de Guayaquil, 1763–1842,* Guayaquil, 1973.

Hardoy, J. E. and Schaedel, R. P., (eds.) *Las ciudades de América Latina y sus áreas de influencia a través de la Historia,* Buenos Aires, 1975.

Hoberman, L. S. and Socolow, S. M., *Cities and Society in Colonial Latin America,* Albuquerque, 1986.

Iwasaki Cauti, Fernando, "Ambulantes y comercio colonial. Iniciativas mercantiles en el Virreinato Peruano," *Jahrbuch für Geschichte von Staat, Wirtschaft und Gesellschaft LateinAmerikas,* 24 (1987), 179–211.

Jaramillo Uribe, J.,"Mestizaje y diferenciación en el Nuevo Reino de Granada en la Segunda mitad del siglo XVIII," *Anuario Colombiano de Historia y de la Cultura,* 2: 3 (1965), 21–48.

Johnson, L. J., "The Silversmiths of Buenos Aires: A Case Study in the Failure of Corporate Social Organisation," *Journal of Latin American Studies,* 8 (1976), 181–213.

Keeding, E., *Das Zeitalter der Aufklärung in der Provinz Quito,* Köln-Wien: Böhlau, 1983.

───────. "La polémica del nuevo mundo en la literatura de Quito del siglo XVIII: Americanos y pardocracia," *Memorias del primer simposio Europeo sobre Antropología del Ecuador,* S. Moreno Yánez (ed.) Quito, 1985, 245–254.

Kennedy Troya, Alexandra, and Ortiz Crespo, Alfonso, *Convento de San Diego de Quito,* Quito, 1982.

Kicza, J. A. "Life Patterns and Social Differentiation among Common People in Late Colonial Mexico City," *Estudios de Historia Novohispana,* 11 (1991), 183–200.

Kinsbruner, J., "The Pulperos of Caracas and San Juan during the first half of the nineteenth century," *Latin American Research Review,* 3 (1978), 65–85.

───────. *Petty Capitalism in Spanish America: The Pulperos of Puebla, Mexico City, Caracas, and Buenos Aires.* Boulder, 1987.

Klein, H., "Hacienda and free community in eighteenth century Alto Peru: a demographic study of the Aymara population of the districts of Chulumani and Pacajes in 1786," *Journal of Latin American Studies,* 7 (1975), 193–220.

Kuethe, A. J., *Military Reform and Society in New Granada, 1773–1808*, Gainesville, 1978.

Kuznesof, E., "Household, Family and Community Studies 1976–1986: a Bibliographic Essay," *Latin American History Population Newsletter* (Fall 1988), 9–23.

Langenberg, I., *Urbanisation und Bevölkerungsstruktur der Stadt Guatemala in der Ausgehenden Kolonialzeit: Eine sozialhistorische Analyse der Stadtverlegung und ihrer Auswirkungen auf die demographische, berufliche und soziale Gliederung der Bevölkerung (1773–1824)*, Köln-Wien, 1981.

Lanning, J. T., "La oposición a la Ilustración en Quito," *Revista Bimestre Cubano*, 53 (3), 1944, 224–241.

Larson, B., "Caciques, Class Structure and the Colonial State in Bolivia," *Nova Americana* 2 (1979), 197–235.

————· *Colonialism and Agrarian Transformation in Bolivia. Cochabamba, 1550–1900*, Princeton, 1988.

Lavallé, B., *Recherches sur l'apparition de la conscience créole dans la vice-royauté du Pérou: l'antagonisme hispano-créole dans les ordres religieux (XVI–XVIIs.)*, Lille, 1978.

————· "La rebelión de las alcabalas (Quito, Julio de 1592–Abril de 1593). Ensayo de interpretación," *Revista de Indias*, vol. XLIV, 173, (1984), 141–201.

————· *Quito et la crise de l'Alcabala (1580–1600)*, Paris, 1992.

Laviana Cuetos, María Teresa, *Guayaquil en el siglo XVIII. Recursos naturales y desarrollo económico*, Sevilla, 1987.

Lavrín, A., (ed.) *Latin American Women: historical perspectives*, Westport, 1978.

Leach, E., *Aspects of Caste in South India, Ceylon and North-West Pakistan*, Cambridge, 1971.

Lehmann, D., (ed.) *Ecology and Exchange in the Andes*, Cambridge, 1981.

Lévi-Strauss, C., *Anthropologie Structurale*, Paris, 1974.

Linke, L., *Ecuador country of contrasts*. Oxford, 1960.

Lockhart, J., *Spanish Peru, 1532–1560: A Colonial Society*, Madison, 1968.

————· *The Men of Cajamarca: A Social and Biographical Study of the First Conquerors of Peru*, Austin, 1972.

López Sarrelangue, D. "Mestizaje y catolicismo en la Nueva España," *Historia Mexicana,* 1 vol. XXIII, (1973), 1–42.

Lynch, J., *Spain under the Habsburgs. Volume 2: Spain and America, 1598–1700,* Oxford, 1981.

_____. *Las Revoluciones hispanoamericanos, 1808–1826,* Barcelona, 3rd edn. 1983.

Macera, Pablo, *Pintores Populares Andinos,* Lima, 1979.

Malvido, Elsa, "El abandono de los hijos: una forma de control del tamaño de la familia y del trabajo indígena. Tula (1683–1730)," *Historia Mexicana,* 4, vol. XXIX, (1980), 521–561.

Mannheim, Bruce, *The language of the Inca since the European invasion,* Austin, 1991.

Marchán Romero, Carlos, "Economía y Sociedad durante el siglo XVIII," *Cultura, Revista del Banco Central del Ecuador,* 24, (Quito) (1986), 55–76.

Martín, Luis, *Daughters of the Conquistadores. Women of the Viceroyalty of Peru,* Dallas, 2nd. edn., 1989.

Marzahl, P., *Town in Empire: Government, Politics and Society in Seventeenth-Century Popayán,* Austin, 1978.

McFarlane, A., "Civil Disorders and Popular Protests in Late Colonial New Granada," *HAHR,* 64 (1984), 17–54.

_____. "The 'Rebellion of the Barrios': Urban Insurrection in Bourbon Quito," *HAHR,* 69 (1989), 283–330.

Mesa, J. de, and Gisbert, T., "The painter Mateo Mexía, and his works in the Convent of San Francisco de Quito," *The Americas,* 16 (1960), 385–396.

Millones. L., and Tomoeda, H., (eds.), *El Hombre y su Ambiente en los Andes Centrales,* Osaka: Senri Anthropological Studies, 1980.

Mills, N. D. and Ortiz, G., "Economía y sociedad en el Ecuador poscolonial, 1759–1859," *Cultura, Revista del Banco Central del Ecuador,* 9 (1980), 71–152.

Minchom, M., "The making of a white province: demographic movement and ethnic transformation in the south of the Audiencia de Quito," *Bulletin de l'Institut Français d'Études Andines,* (Paris-Lima), XII (1983), 23–39.

_____. "Historia demográfica de Loja y su Provincia: Desde 1700 hasta fines de la Colonia," *Cultura, Revista del Banco Central del Ecuador,* (Edición monográfica dedicada a la Provincia de Loja),15 (Quito) (1983), 149–169.

———. "Demographic change in eighteenth-century Ecuador," in D. Delaunay and M. Portais (eds.) *Equateur 1986,* Paris: Editions de l'ORSTOM, 1989, 179–196.

Mond, R.E., "Indian Rebellion and Bourbon Reform in New Granada: Riots in Pasto,1780–1800," *HAHR,* 73:1 (1993), 99–124.

Moore, J. P., *The Cabildo in Peru under the Hapsburgs; a study in the Origins and Powers of the Town Council in the Viceroyalty of Peru, 1530–1700,* Duke University Press, 1954.

———. *The Cabildo in Peru under the Bourbons,* Duke University Press, 1966.

Moreno Egas, Jorge,"Apuntes sobre la población de Quito en el Siglo XVI," *Museo Histórico,* (Quito), 56 (1978), 71–93.

Moreno Yánez, Segundo, *Sublevaciones indígenas en la Audiencia de Quito, desde comienzos del siglo XVIII hasta finales de la Colonia,* Bonn: Estudios Americanistas, 1976; 2nd. edn. Quito, 1978.

———. (ed.) *Pichincha: Monografía histórica de la Región Nuclear Ecuatoriana,* Quito, 1981.

———. (with U. Oberem) *Contribución a la etnohistoria ecuatoriana,* Otavalo, 1981.

Mörner, M., *Race Mixture in the History of Latin America,* Boston, 1967.

———. "Aspectos socioraciales del proceso de poblamiento en la Audiencia de Quito durante los siglos XVI y XVII," in *Homenaje a don José María de la Peña y Cámara,* Madrid, 1969, 265–287.

———. *La corona española y los foráneos en los pueblos de indios de América,* Stockholm, 1970.

———. (ed.) *Race and Class in Latin America,* New York, 2nd. edn., 1971.

———. "Economic Factors and Stratification in Colonial Spanish America with special Regard to Elites," *HAHR,* 63 (1983), 335–369.

Moscoso, M. C., "Indígenas y ciudades en el siglo XVI," in E. Kingman (ed.), *La Ciudad en la Historia, Quito,* 1989, 343–356.

Muñoz-Bernand, C., *Les Renaissants de Pindilig (Province de Cañar). Anthropologie de la déculturation d'une population indigène des Andes Equatoriennes,* thèse de doctorat d'État, University of Paris VII, 1981.

Murra, J. V., "The Historic Tribes of Ecuador," in Steward, J. (ed.) *Handbook of South American Indians,* (Washington, 1946), vol. 2, 785–821.

_____. *Formaciones económicas y políticas del Mundo Andino,* Lima, 1975.

Navarro, José Gabriel, *La Revolución de Quito del 10 de Agosto de 1809,* Quito, 1962.

Newson, L., "Old World epidemics in early colonial Ecuador" in N. D. Cook and W. G. Lovell (eds.), *Secret Judgements of God: Old World Disease in Colonial Spanish America,* Norman, OK, 1992, 84–112.

_____. "Highland/Lowland contrasts in the impact of Old World Diseases in early colonial Ecuador," *Social Science Medicine,* 36 (1993), 1187–1195.

Oberem, U., "El acceso a recursos naturales de diferentes ecologías en la sierra ecuatoriana. Siglo XVI," in *Actes du XLII Congrés International des Américanistes,* (Paris, 1976) vol. IV, 51–64.

_____. "Indianische Aufstände in der *Sierra* Ecuadors im 18. Jhdt. im Vergleich zu den bäuerlichen Rebellionen im peruanisch-bolivianischen Hochland," *Jahrbuch für Geschichte von Staat, Wirtschaft und Gesellschaft LateinAmerikas,* 15 (1978), 75–82.

_____. "Ein Beispiel für die Soziale Selbsteinschätzung des Indianischen Hochadels im Kolonialzeitlichen Quito," *Ibero-Amerikanisches Archiv,* 5 (1979), 215–225.

O'Phelan Godoy, S., *Rebellions and Revolts in Eighteenth-Century Peru and Upper Peru* (Cologne, 1985).

Ortiz de la Tabla Ducasse, Javier, "Panorama económico y social del Corregimiento de Quito," *Revista de Indias,* 145–146, (1976), 83–98.

_____. "El obraje ecuatoriano. Aproximación a su estudio," *Revista de Indias,* 149–50, (1977), 471–542.

_____. "Extranjeros en la Audiencia de Quito (1595–1603)," Separata del *Tomo II, de América y la España del Siglo XVI,* Madrid, 1983.

Ossio A., Juan M., "Relaciones interétnicas y verticalidad en los Andes," *Debates en Antropología,* (Lima) 1 (1978), 1–23.

Palmer, R. R., *The age of the democratic revolution: a political history of Europe and America,* Princeton, 1959–64.

Pareja Diezcanseco, A. *Las Instituciones y la Administración de la Real Audiencia de Quito,* Quito: Ministerio del Tesoro, 1975.

Parry, J. H., *The Spanish Seaborne Empire,* London, 2nd edn., 1973.

Peñaherrera de Costales, P. and A. Costales Samaniego, *Katekil o Historia Cultural del Campesinado del Chimborazo,* (Series: *Llacta),* Quito, Año II, vol. IV, 1957.

Pérez, Aquiles, *Las Mitas en la Real Audiencia de Quito,* Quito, 1947.

Pérez, J., *Los movimientos precursores de la emancipación en Hispanoamérica,* Madrid, 1977.

Phelan, J. L., *The Kingdom of Quito in the Seventeenth Century: Bureaucratic Politics in the Spanish Empire,* Madison, 1967.

Ponce Ribadeneira, Alfredo, *Quito, 1809–1812, Según los Documentos del Archivo Nacional de Madrid,* Madrid, 1960.

Powers, K., "Indian migrations in the Audiencia of Quito: Crown manipulation and local co-option," in David J. Robinson (ed.), *Migration in Colonial Spanish America.* Cambridge, 1991, 313–323.

Prawer, J., *The Latin Kingdom of Jerusalem. European Colonialism in the Middle Ages,* London, 1972.

Ramos Pérez, Demetrio, *Entre el Plata y Bogotá. Cuatro Claves de la Emancipación Ecuatoriana,* Madrid: Ediciones Cultura Hispánica del Centro Iberoamericano de Cooperación, 1978.

Rieu-Millán, M-L., *Los diputados americanos en las Cortes de Cádiz,* Madrid, 1990.

Roberts, B., *Cities of Peasants : The Political Economy of Urbanization in the Third World,* London, 1978.

Robinson, David J. (ed.) *Social Fabric and Spatial Structure in Colonial Latin America,* Ann Arbor, 1979.

————· (ed.) *Migration in Colonial Spanish America,* Cambridge, 1991.

————· "Liberty, Fragile Fraternity, and Inequality in Early Republican Spanish America: analyzing the impact of French revolutionary ideas," *Journal of Historical Geography,* vol. 16 (1990), 51–75.

Roche, D., *Le Peuple de Paris. Essai sur la culture populaire au XVIIIe.,* Paris, 1981.

Rostworowski de Diez Canseco, María, *Estructuras Andinas del Poder. Ideología religiosa y política,* Lima, 1983.

Rout, L. B. (Jr.), *The African Experience in Spanish America: 1502 to the Present Day,* Cambridge, 1976.

Saint-Geours, Y., "La Sierra du Nord et du Centre en Équateur: 1830–1875," *Bulletin de l'Institut Français d'Études Andines,* (Paris-Lima), XIII (1984), 1–15.

————· "L'évolution démographique de l'Equateur au XIXe siècle," in *Equateur 1986,* D. Delaunay and M. Portais (eds.) Paris, 1989, 197–207.

Salomon, F., "Don Pedro de Zámbiza, un Varayuj del Siglo XVI," *Cuadernos de Historia y Arqueología*, (Guayaquil), 42 (1975), 285–315.

―――――. *Ethnic Lords of Quito in the Age of the Incas : The Political Economy of North-Andean Chiefdoms*, doctoral dissertation, Cornell University, 1978.

―――――. *Native Lords of Quito in the Age of the Incas. The Political Economy of North Andean Chiefdoms,* Cambridge, 1986.

―――――. "Systèmes politiques verticaux aux marches de l'empire inca," *Annales. E.S.C.* 33 (1978), 967–989.

―――――. "Shamanism and politics in late-colonial Ecuador," *American Ethnologist,* 90–3, (1983), 413–428.

―――――. "Indian women of early Colonial Quito as seen through their testaments," *The Americas,* 40 (1988), 325–341.

Sánchez-Albornoz, N., *Indios y Tributos en el Alto Perú,* Lima, 1978.

Sánchez Bella, I., *Quito, audiencia subordinada,* Quito, 1980.

Scardaville, M. C., "Alcohol Abuse and Tavern Reform in Late Colonial Mexico City," *Hispanic American Historical Review,* 60 (1980), 643–671.

―――――. *Crime and the Urban Poor: Mexico City in the Late Colonial Period*, doctoral dissertation, University of Florida, 1977.

Schaedel, R. P.; Borah, B.; Browning, H. L., et. al. *Urbanización y proceso social en América,* Lima, 1972.

Schotellius, J. W., "Die Gründung Quitos," *Ibero-Amerikanisches Archiv,* IX, (1936–37), 276–294; X (1936–37), 55–77.

Shafer, R. J., *The Economic Societies in the Spanish World. (1763–1821),* Syracuse, 1958.

Socolow, S. M., "Women and Crime: Buenos Aires, 1757–97," *Journal of Latin American Studies,* 12 (1980), 39–54.

―――――. "Acceptable Partners. Marriage Choice in Colonial Argentina," Working Paper, Augsberg, 1987.

Spalding, K., *Indian Rural Society in Colonial Peru: The Example of Huarochirí,* doctoral dissertation, University of California, Berkeley, 1967.

―――――. *Huarochirí. An Andean Society under Inca and Spanish Rule.* Stanford University Press, 1984.

―――――. *De Indio a Campesino: Cambios en la estructura social del Perú colonial*, Lima, 1974.

Spindler, F. M. *Nineteenth Century Ecuador. An Historical Introduction.* Washington DC, 1987.

Stern, S. J., *Peru's Indian Peoples and the Challenge of Spanish Conquest: Huamanga to 1640,* Madison, 1982.

Stevenson, R., "Music in Quito: Four Centuries," *Hispanic American Historical Review,* 43 (1963), 247–267.

Stols, A. M., *Historia de la Imprenta en el Ecuador de 1755 a 1830,* Quito, 1953.

Stone, L., *The Causes of the English Revolution, 1529–1642,* London, 1972, repr. 1973.

Super, J. C., "Partnership and profit in the early andean trade: experiences of Quito merchants, 1580–1610," *Journal of Latin American Studies,* 11 (1979), 265–281.

Swann, M. M., *Tierra Adentro: Settlement and Society in Colonial Durango,* Boulder, 1982.

Sweet, D. G. and G. B. Nash (eds.), *Struggle and Survival in Colonial America,* Berkeley, 1981.

Szászdi, A., "The Economic History of the Diocese of Quito, 1616–1787," *Latin American Research Review,* vol. 21 (1986), 266–275.

Taylor, W. B., *Drinking, Homicide and Rebellion in Colonial Mexican Villages,* Stanford, 1979.

Thomas, K., *Religion and the Decline of Magic,* London, 1971, repr. 1973.

Thompson, E. P., *The Making of the English Working Class,* London, 1963,

——————. "The Moral Economy of the English Crowd in the Eighteenth Century," *Past and Present,* 50 (1971), 76–136.

Thompson, G., "Local History in the Colonial Era," *Latin American Research Review,* vol. 18 (1983), 263–270.

Torre Reyes, Carlos de la, *La Revolución de Quito del 10 de agosto de 1809,* Quito, 1961.

Tyrer, R. B., *The Demographic and Economic History of the Audiencia of Quito: Indian Population and the Textile industry,* doctoral dissertation, Berkeley, University of California, 1976.

Van Aken, M.,"The lingering death of Indian tribute in Ecuador," *HAHR,* 61 (1981), 429–459.

Van Young, E., "Urban Market and Hinterland: Guadalajara and its Region in the Eighteenth Century," *HAHR,* 59 (1979), 593–635.

Vargas, José María, O. P., *La Economía Política del Ecuador durante la Colonia,* Quito, 1957; 2nd edn. n.d., introd. by C. Marchán R.

_____. *Historia de la Cultura Ecuatoriana,* Quito, 1965.

Vollmer, G., *Bevölkerungspolitik und Bevölkerungsstructur im Vizekönigreich zu Ende der Kolonialzeit 1741–1821,* Berlin-Zürich, 1967.

Wachtel, N., *La vision des vaincus: Les Indiens du Pérou devant la Conquête espagnole,* Paris, 1971; English edn., Sussex, 1977.

_____. "L'acculturation," in Le Goff, J. and Nora, P. (eds.) *Faire l'histoire: Nouveaux problèmes,* Paris, 1974, 124–146.

Washburn, D. A., *The Bourbon Reforms: A Social and Economic History of the Audiencia of Quito, 1760–1810,* doctoral dissertation, University of Texas at Austin, 1984.

Whitten N. E. Jr. (ed.) *Cultural Transformations and Ethnicity in Modern Ecuador,* University of Illinois Press, 1981.

Zuidema, R. T., "Masks in the Incaic Solstice and Equinoctial Rituals," in N. Ross Cumrine and Marjorie Halpin (eds.) *The Power of Symbols: Masks and Masquerades in the Americas,* Vancouver, 1983.

_____. "Batallas rituales en el Cuzco colonial," *Cultures et Sociétés. Andes et Méso-Amériques. Mélanges en hommage à Pierre Duviols,* vol. 2 (Univ. de Provence, 1991), 811–834.

Index

Abascal y Sousa, José Fernando de, Viceroy of Peru, 251
Acarí, Peru, 134
agricultural shortages, 70–71, 127, 129–131
aguardiente monopoly, 223–224
alcabala, 61, 108, 115, 224
alcalde mayor, 24
Alcedo, *see* Alsedo
Alsedo y Herrera, Dionisio, 18, 21, 26, 28, 40, 41–42
Amaguaña, 35
Añaquito, 33, 35
artisans, 4, 52–54, 85–94, 168, 183–189, 213, 218–219, 234, 250

baptisms, 54–55, 56–57, 169
barbers, 86–90, 160–162, 194
barley, 34, 39
barrios, mock-battles of, 96
Black population, 8, 50–51, 54–56, 81, 84, 105, 106, 172
Braudel, Fernand, 3
bull-fights, 95–96
butchers, 228

cabildo, 34
caciques, 24–25, 160, 167, 168, 182–183
Caldas, Francisco José de 29, 118–119
Cañar, 175
capellanías, 70
Caracas, 114
carpentry, 39
carriers, 46, 158
cattle, 32, 34
Cayambe, 141
censos, 69–70
censuses, 120–125, 157
chagro, 50–51, 110–112
Chillogallo, 35
Chillos (Los), 39
Chimbacalle, San Juan Evangelista de, 34

cholo, 172–173
chorrillos, 65, 66
Cieza de León, Pedro, 59
clergy, secular, 76–78
clothing, 63, 190
cofradías, 82–94, 168
common lands *see ejidos*
commonwealth, 214–215
communications, 44–46
communion, 79–82
compadrazgo, 55
Condamine, Charles de la, 28
Conocotoc, San Pedro de, 90
Corpus Christi, festival, 91–94, 221, 224, 228
corregimiento, of Quito, 37–42, 137–144
cotton, 40, 41
creole-peninsular tensions, 61, 76, 206–207, 220, 226, 257
Cuenca, 59
Cuzco, 40

dancers, 90–94
debt, 88–89, 224
demography, 117–152
Don, 173–174
donkeys, 32
drink, 88, 96, 218, 217–219
droughts, 129

earthquakes, 20, 127
Economic Societies, 236
economy, informal, 101–115
ejidos, 33–37
elite, 53, 61, 62
encomenderos, 52
epidemics, 126–127, 129–133, 223–224
Espejo, Eugenio, 191–197, 235–237, 241–242
Espejo, Juan Pablo, 239–241
ethnicity, 10, 63, 108, 153–199

festivals, 88, 90–97, 218, 221, 227
foreigners, 52
foundlings, *see hijos expósitos*
Franciscan order, 81–82, 215–220, 251–252
fruit, tropical, 25, 40

Garcilaso de la Vega, El Inca, 175–176
gender, 63, 107–108, 145–150, 263–264
goats, 32
godparents, 54–55
grazing, 33
Guápulo, 61
Guayaquil, 2, 44–45, 147, 259
Guayllabamba, 40

haciendas, 34–40, 89, 141, 156, 169
Hanan, 24–6
Hassaurek, Frederick, 46
hijos expósitos, 129, 136–137, 150, 160, 170, 180–182
horses, 32, 34
households, 149
Hurin, 24–26

Ichimbía, 29, 114
illegitimacy, 149, 177–178
Incas, 24, 32, 40, 51, 58
Indian communities, 34–37, 41
Indian labour, 41–42, 66
Indian "offices", 159, 165, 170, 183–189; *see* barbers, market-women
Indian population, urban, 126–127, 143, 263
insults, 172, 175

Jerusalén, ravine, 26, 30
Jesuits, 195–6
Juan, Jorge and Ulloa, Antonio de, 17, 25, 26, 28, 40, 87, 94, 96, 119, 147–148, 188, 257

Kolberg, Joseph, 25

land occupation, 34
language, 170–182; *see* Quichua
Lima troops, 245–250
limestone, 39
literacy, 92
llapango, 172

Machachi, 39
Machángara, river, 30, 67
maize, 34, 39, 40
Manifestos, 244
markets, 103–105
market-women, 56, 105–108, 110
marriage, 149–150
masks, 96, 255, 227
Merced (La), bridge, 19, 41–42
merchants, 52–53
Mestizo, Declarations of,
Mestizos, 11, 59–64, 153–99, 203, 220–221
Mexico, 171, 260
migration, Indian, 57–58, 65–66
miscegenation, 59
mita, 25, 41, 56, 58
mobility, Indian, 39, 141
Molina, Joaquín de, 251–252
montañés, 175–176
Montúfar, Carlos, 252
Montúfar, Juan Pío *see* Selva Alegre, Marquis of
moradores, 52
mortality rates, 129–133
mules, 32, 34–35
municipality, 34
Munive (President of the Audiencia), 65, 66
musicians, 162–164, 169

Núñez del Arco, Ramón, 241–242

obrajes, 30, 64–68, 111, 211
Orton, James, 1

Panecillo (hill), 28
parish organization, 23–32
parish registers, 119–120
peinadillos, 58
Pérez de Calama, Bishop, 125, 235–237
Peru, 260
pigs, 105
Pomasque, 39
Portugese, 52
potatoes, 39
Presentación, Nuestra Señora de la, 92
prison, 218
prostitution, 173
pulperías, 105–115

quebradas, see ravines
Quichua, 24, 63
Quinche, (El), 141, 234
Quito, Audiencia, 42–46
Quito, city foundation, 17–18,
Quito, urban environment, 17–48

race mixture, 59–64, 153–199
ravines, 18–23, 26, 30
rebellion of Quito (1592–93), 60–61
rebellion of Quito (1765), 222–232
reducciones, 25, 39, 58
relaciones geográficas, 52
religious disputes, 204–205
residence, urban, 29–30
revolt (1809), 241–253
Riobamba, 150
riots, of 1747–48, 205, 210, 214–220
roads, *see* communications
Rodríguez Docampo, Diego, 23, 37, 66
Romero de Tejada, Antonio, 109
Ruiz de Castilla, President of the Audiencia, 241-242, 245, 251, 252

Sagrario (El), parish, 23, 26, 30, 31, 32, 54, 57–58, 119–120, 127, 131–132, 143, 147, 151–152, 197
San Blas, parish, 21, 23, 26, 27, 29, 31, 32, 80, 143, 147, 152, 211, 220, 224–225
Sánchez de Orellana, Joaquín, 249–250, 252
San Francisco, Order of, *see* Franciscans
San Francisco, square, 20–21, 23, 26, 80
San Luis, seminary of, 206
San Marcos, parish, 23, 31, 32, 80, 125, 147, 151–152
San Roque, parish, 21, 23, 26, 28, 31, 32, 80–82, 120, 147, 151–152, 175, 202, 208, 209, 210–221, 222, 224, 225, 226, 231, 246, 248, 250–251, 265
San Sebastián, parish, 23, 26, 27, 28, 29, 31, 67, 80, 124, 147, 151–152, 210-220
Santa Bárbara, parish, 21, 23, 26, 29, 31, 80, 120, 127, 143, 147, 151–152, 183–189, 210-218, 250

Santa Cruz y Espejo, Francisco Xavier Eugenio *see* Espejo, Eugenio
Santa María Magdalena, 35
Santa Prisca, parish, 29, 31
Santillán, Fernando de, 104
Selva Alegre, Marquis of, 237, 241–246, 251
Selva Florida, Count of, 227, 254
servants, 81, 131–132
sheep, 32, 34
shops, 110, 112–113
silversmiths, 85–86
slaughterhouse, 21, 113
slaves, 50, 55–56, 57, 105, 110, 124
square, main, 20
Stevenson, William Bennet, 95–96, 172, 188
sugar, 40
surgeons, 194
surnames, 164, 189–190, 193

Tabacundo, 141
tailors, 40
taxes *see alcabala,* tribute
textiles, 3, 64–68
tianguez, 103–104
tithe, 109
tribute, 155–157, 165–167, 179–180
Tunja, New Granada,133–134
Turubamba, 33, 35

urban centers, 9–10
urban recession, 137–144
urban-rural characteristics, 32
Uyumbicho, 39

Velasco, Juan de, 120, 127
Villalengua y Márfil, Juan Josef, 157, 179–180
Villaorellana, Marquis of 35–36

War of Independence, 147
weavers, 66–67, 90–94
wheat, 34, 39, 40
women *see* gender
wood, 39

Yaruquí, 35